WORDSWORTH CLASSICS
OF WORLD LITERATURE

General Editor: Tom Griffith

THE COMMUNIST MANIFESTO

*The Condition of the Working Class
in England in 1844*

Socialism: Utopian and Scientific

KARL MARX AND FRIEDRICH ENGELS

The Communist Manifesto

with

The Condition of the Working Class
in England in 1844
Socialism: Utopian and Scientific

BY FRIEDRICH ENGELS

with an introduction by
Laurence Marlow

WORDSWORTH CLASSICS
OF WORLD LITERATURE

For my husband
ANTHONY JOHN RANSON
with love from your wife, the publisher
Eternally grateful for your
unconditional love

Readers who are interested in other titles from
Wordsworth Editions are invited to visit our
website at www.wordsworth-editions.com

For our latest list and a full mail order service contact
Bibliophile Books, Unit 5 Datapoint,
South Crescent, London E16 4TL
Tel: +44 (0) 20 74 74 24 74
Fax: +44 (0) 20 74 74 85 89
orders@bibliophilebooks.com
www.bibliophilebooks.com

This edition published 2008 by Wordsworth Editions Limited
8B East Street, Ware, Hertfordshire SG12 9HJ

ISBN 978 1 84022 096 4

This edition © Wordsworth Editions Limited 2008
Introduction © Laurence Marlow 2008

Wordsworth® is a registered trademark of
Wordsworth Editions Limited

Wordsworth Editions is
the company founded in 1987 by
MICHAEL TRAYLER

Typeset in Great Britain by Roperford Editorial
Printed and bound by Clays Ltd, St Ives plc

CONTENTS

INTRODUCTION

The three texts reproduced here provide an introduction to some of the key themes of the work of Karl Marx (1818–1883) and Friedrich Engels (1820–1895). The texts include their best-known work, *The Communist Manifesto*, as well as two works authored by Engels. These texts are a very small collection from a substantial portfolio of writings which include philosophical and economic writings, journalistic pieces, political tracts, polemics, drafts of un-completed works and a considerable range of correspondence. In English, the recently completed *Collected Works* runs to 50 lengthy volumes. This is a considerable intellectual legacy produced by one of the most interesting and enduring of intellectual partnerships. Marx and Engels were clearly as productive as the emergent capitalist system which they anatomised in such detail. Their inquiries, like capitalism, acknowledged no national boundaries, and many of their writings would achieve a global impact in their lifetime despite their relative neglect in the country which provided their home for most of their lives. The scope of their various writings remains impressive. In addition to the writings reproduced here the core writings would include Marx's work *Capital*, (3 volumes), the early writings including the *Economic and Philosophical Manuscripts of 1844*, *The German Ideology* (written jointly with Engels), and *The Grundrisse*, the incomplete manuscript sketching of the framework of Marx's overall approach to social development, economics and history of which *Capital* was the only substantial element Marx completed.

Two texts, *The Communist Manifesto*, jointly authored by Marx and Engels, and *The Condition of the Working Class in England*, written by Engels alone, continue to have, even on the most superficial reading, relevance for an understanding of our times. Both were written in the 1840s and while some specific references have lost their force or appear obscure to the modern reader, there is still a power in the writing that engages, that holds attention and invites response. The other text, popularly known as *Socialism: Utopian and Scientific*, might seem to have less immediate relevance but it does provide, reservations aside, a succinct commentary on some key terms underpinning the work of Marx and Engels, as well as opening up debate about the nature of 'scientific socialism' and its legacy today. This text was written by Engels as a specific contribution to debates in the late-nineteenth-century German Social Democratic Party.

The Communist Manifesto

The Communist Manifesto is without doubt the best-known creation of their joint endeavours. Written in the context of the troubled 1840s in a Europe which would see abortive revolutions take place in some states, and the first social movement demanding political rights for the masses, the British Chartist campaign, reach its zenith, the *Communist Manifesto* was both the product of, and the most telling commentary on, those social, economic and political forces which had brought such turbulence and discontent in their wake. The 1840s for much of Europe were marked by economic distress and political divisions. In some parts of Europe those who campaigned for political reform took heart from the victories of popular and liberal forces in 1848. But the sense of a new dawn breaking, a repeat of the hopes bound up with July 1789, was soon dissipated as the forces of the established order re-established themselves. The 'springtime of the peoples' was short-lived, political reaction the new order of the day, and the famine in Ireland, itself the product of the structure of British rule, tragically exemplified the theme of the 'hungry 'forties'. *The Communist Manifesto* reflected the immediacy of the events which marked its creation, but it also offered an account of the present which placed its specific interventions in a much wider historical, philosophical and economic context. It was more than simply an appeal or a statement of a particular political position. It offered a highly compressed, densely argued and distilled version of an understanding of social development and political change that Marx and Engels had already begun to set down and, subsequent to the heady enthusiasm of 1848, would go on to develop in their writings, individually and together, over the next four decades.

Published in Paris in 1848 *The Communist Manifesto*, whatever the slight political compromises struck with other members of the Communist League to ensure its production, can be seen as a hybrid document. It is a manifesto, a declaration of beliefs and aims, designed to set out the communist position, strengthen the resolve of those committed to the communist cause, and attract others to its banner. It is a foundational document of the era of manifestos. Besides the sense of immediacy which derives from the political context in which it was initially circulated, *The Communist Manifesto* by offering an account of the nature of the present discontents in terms of emergent patterns of social and economic change, opened up a new way of interpreting present events. It acted as a primer, in 1848 and beyond, for some of the ideas that Marx and Engels had already developed in the 1840s and would elaborate, reconsider, and document in their various writings after 1850.[1] So while some sections of *The Manifesto* which touch on some of the finer points of difference between radical thinkers and groups appear obscure to modern readers, sections on the rise of modern industry, the nature of the bourgeoisie, or the formation and destiny of the proletariat, do not require detailed textual exegesis. They still have a relevance and clarity, even if the reader does not always accept the logic of the argument made by Marx and Engels. *The Communist Manifesto* is a document central to understanding modern times, and we continue to live in modern times despite the illusory claims of various schools of post-modernism. Some of the content of the *Manifesto* had already been set out in *The Principles of Communism* composed by Engels in late 1847. But the format of the final version of the *Manifesto* differed markedly from how Engels had framed *The Principles*.

The *Manifesto* is strikingly written. From the arresting imagery of its opening sentence – 'A spectre is haunting Europe – the spectre of Communism' – to the ringing tones of its conclusion – 'Working Men of all countries, unite!' – the reader's attention is engaged by a complex yet well-focused set of arguments which explain the current crisis as well as account for the particular role that communism will play in resolving that crisis. Part of the task of the *Manifesto* is to explain communism to the world, an explanation free of the charges made against it by its enemies, but also to locate the communist movement in the wider forces shaping the epoch. The *Manifesto* is an appeal, a guide, an exercise in political demystification, a short history of the modern world, and a wager on the future. For subsequent generations it has been a source of inspiration, a text which has truly opened the eyes of its readers to the real nature of the world, thus inspiring many to sacrifice everything to follow its call to political action in the service of the proletariat. Rarely has any secular text been marked by such significance in the making of history.

In terms of its structure the *Manifesto* can be divided into four main sections. The rise of the bourgeoisie and the formation of modern industry constitutes the first main theme taking up a substantial part of text. This section also introduces material on the formation of the proletariat and its relations with the bourgeoisie. This is followed by a discussion of communists and their relation to the proletariat, providing Marx and Engels with an opportunity to challenge bourgeois critiques of communist ideas and assumptions. The final section reviews the emergence and ideas of communism in relation to earlier and current ideas of socialism. Here Marx and Engels provided a sharp critique of some of the ideas current on the European left. This appetite and ability for polemic, an intellectual legacy from popular struggles in the French Revolution as well as the experience of the two revolutionaries in the socialist philosophical and political circles of early nineteenth-century Germany, would be characteristic of much internal debate in progressive and left circles in the course of the nineteenth century. The final short section returns to the role of communists in the current struggles. It is useful to make a few observations in relation to the four sections.

The section 'Bourgeois and Proletarians' opens with one of the most quoted statements made by Marx and Engels – 'The history of all hitherto existing societies is the history of class struggles.'[2] While there has been much discussion about the meaning of that statement, this Marx and Engels took to be one of their great discoveries and a foundation of the idea of historical materialism. In terms of the refinement of that statement within the *Manifesto*, it is followed shortly after by the assertion that the distinguishing feature of the present epoch is that the division has been simplified – society is now constituted by two powerful contending classes:

Bourgeoisie and Proletariat. Marx and Engels then devote considerable space in this section to clarifying these two terms and explaining the structured nature of their antagonistic relationship. The *Manifesto* offers a compressed history of the rise of the bourgeoisie, taking in a number of significant causal factors – such as the discovery and colonisation of the Americas and the growth of long-distance trade which provided the foundations of the world market as created by modern industry. Socially the roots of the bourgeoisie lay in urban merchant groups of the feudal period who, as their economic power grew, challenged the dominance of the feudal order until revolutionary struggles replaced it with the bourgeois one. In the account offered by Marx and Engels less attention is given to the politics of bourgeois struggle against feudalism, the focus of their interest is on the link between the bourgeoisie and what they continually refer to as modern industry.

To many modern readers with particular expectations of what Marx and Engels have to say about the bourgeoisie, some of the discussion in the *Manifesto* seems at variance with those expectations. The authors dwell on the revolutionary and transformative role played by the bourgeoisie in creating the modern era. Its rational, calculative and materialist outlook had dissolved and destroyed without sentiment the social and economic bonds of the older order. The bourgeoisie 'has drowned the most heavenly ecstasies of religious fervour . . . of philistine sentimentalism, in the icy water of egotistical calculation.'[3] Echoing the critique of Thomas Carlyle (but for radically divergent political ends) Marx and Engels claimed the bourgeoisie had created a world in which nothing linked people together other than the bonds of the cash nexus and 'naked self-interest'. But these kinds of critiques only seemed to echo the kinds of charges laid against modern capitalism by various kinds of reactionary thinkers who feared the social, economic and intellectual disorder that seemed to accompany the rise of market societies. What distinguished the line of reasoning developed in the *Manifesto* was the way that the moral critique of capitalist civilisation was accompanied by a positive recognition of the many material achievements of the bourgeoisie, a material transformation that communism/socialism would use to provide a productive, secure and fulfilling life for all. Parts of this section of the text seem like a paean of praise to the achievements and vision of the bourgeoisie. Two quotations will be sufficient to illustrate this point. First, Marx and Engels argued that the bourgeoisie, using the conditions of modern industry (such as steam, the factory system, the mechanisation of production), has been the first to show 'what man's activity can bring about. It has accomplished wonders far surpassing Egyptian pyramids, Roman aqueducts, and Gothic cathedrals . . . ' [4] Second, Marx and Engels stressed the connection between the restless, turbulent, unfixed nature of the modern era and the advance of the bourgeoisie:

> Constant revolutionising of production, uninterrupted disturbance of all social conditions . . . distinguish the bourgeois epoch from all earlier ones. All fixed, fast-frozen relations . . . are swept away, all new-formed ones become antiquated before they can ossify. All that is solid melts into air, all that is holy is profaned, and man [sic] is at last compelled to face with sober sense, his real conditions of life, and his relations with his kind. [5]

Here, as elsewhere in the *Manifesto*, Marx and Engels made a profound and highly influential statement of the nature and experience of modernity. Much of the remaining part of this section continued this theme of the *revolutionary* character of the role of the bourgeoisie in their rise to power. Such themes include the dissolution of national boundaries, the advance of cosmopolitanism as industries are linked to world markets and nations become more interdependent, the rise of the modern city (freeing so many of the populace from 'the idiocy of rural life'), and the advance of political and economic centralisation. So in a short period of time the bourgeoisie has 'created more massive, more colossal productive forces than have all preceding generations together.' [6] It is the productive potential that modern industry has set free that defines the nature of the evolving political and social struggle as well as providing the material basis for the new classless society to come.

Having set out the rise and achievements of the bourgeoisie, the *Manifesto* moved on to consider the formation and role of the proletariat. While expanding the productive capacity of society, the nature of bourgeois property relations places a constraint on how far that capacity can be developed. The contradiction between the forces and relations of production – to use a familiar

Marxist theme – can be seen in part by the periodic economic crises which have been characteristic of the capitalist epoch. More than that, the social and economic transformations which brought the bourgeoisie power and wealth have been accompanied by the rise of a new social class – the proletarians, workers divorced from the means of subsistence who must sell their labour power to survive. In the intensively competitive world of modern industry workers must compete with each other for work, which often drives down wages, and in the nature of the work offered with the modern factory system the worker is little more than an appendage to the machine. Its rhythms set the pace of work, while in the hands of the factory-owner the social conditions of production often serve to intensify demands on the labourer, e.g. through lengthening the working day.

Marx and Engels offered a resumé of the rise of the modern proletariat, stressing how the conditions of modern industry, such as its centralisation and displacement of workers by machines, help to underpin the formation of a common identity among different groups of workers combined with a sense of the growing need for struggle against the bourgeoisie in order to improve their conditions. Continued industrial expansion speeds up the process of proletarianisation so that the numbers of the working class grow. Besides numbers, what also distinguishes the proletariat in modern times is that it is the revolutionary class. In terms of the advance of the class struggle, Marx and Engels suggested that initially the proletariat will engage in that conflict at the national level but the advance of working class organisation and the cosmopolitan character of modern industry mean that in time the struggle between bourgeois and proletarian is transformed into a revolutionary moment where 'the violent overthrow of the bourgeoisie lays the foundation for the sway of the proletariat.' [7] So in the process of developing modern industry the bourgeoisie produces 'its own grave-diggers. Its fall and the victory of the proletariat are equally *inevitable*.' [emphasis added]

Commentary on the other sections can be briefer, as these were tied more closely to the conditions in which the *Manifesto* was published. Marx and Engels used sections of the text to explicate the role of the communists in the emerging class struggle, showing how the communists were linked to the proletarian struggle. They

stressed that communists were not outside the proletarian movement, but made a particular contribution to the advance of class
conflict, linked to their understanding of 'the conditions, the
ultimate general results of the proletarian movement'.[8] Clarifying
the objectives of the communists provided Marx and Engels with
an opportunity to refine their understanding of particular terms
such as property or bourgeoisie, as well as answer criticisms of
what communists stand for. One interesting observation to make
in the section on Proletarians and Communists is how Marx
and Engels changed style as the text progresses – in replying to
criticisms made of communism they assumed the text to have a
bourgeois reader whose objections they set out and rebut before
returning to the impersonal narrative which frames most of
the *Manifesto*. In this section Marx and Engels offered a quite short
list of measures that will follow the revolutionary break; these are
changes which will provide the realisation of a society in which
class distinction has been abolished and conditions established for
'the free development of all'. Linked to the operation of these
measures Marx and Engels introduced an early version of the idea
of the 'dictatorship of the proletariat', which would be elaborated
and made more explicit in later works. The final substantive
section before the concluding statement is a short critical review
of some existing socialist and communist literature together with
some very brief comments on other radical movements. The
criticisms of the political competition are helpful in seeing Marx
and Engels return once again to what is distinctive about the idea
of communism in general and their particular purchase on the
term. It is not surprising to find Marx and Engels dismissive of
much German and French socialist writing – they drew attention
to their theoretical deficiencies, their weak grasp of the nature of
the modern transformations in social structure then taking place
and the facile nature of the solutions offered to the deepening
social crisis.[9] Their evaluative survey concluded with some pointed
criticisms of the diagnoses and solutions proposed by the utopian
socialist thinkers Fourier, Saint-Simon and Owen. While aspects
of the utopians' critique of the current order were welcomed as
helpful to the education of the working class, Marx and Engels
were dismissive of the utopians' modelling and planning of ideal
communities built on principles of harmony and integration.

Once again the failure of such socialists and communists to locate their understanding in the context of material development condemned the efficacy of their vision of the sources and nature of the coming transformation.

A short final section repeated Marx and Engels's earlier comments on the role of communists in the present struggle, showing how their choice of allies to carry forward the message of emancipation was linked to national patterns of development. In particular attention was rightly focused on Germany – ripe for bourgeois revolution which in terms of Germany's level of advance 'will be but the prelude to an immediately following proletarian revolution.' Set against this optimistic prediction the two authors concluded: 'The proletarians have nothing to lose but their chains. They have a world to win.' [10]

But in 1848 the working class was not victorious, the movements for national freedom and popular rights were crushed. Revolutionary movements were defeated, counter-revolution was in the ascendant. For Great Britain, the new home of the Marx family, Chartism peaked in 1848, entering a slow period of decline in the 1850s; the sense of impending economic crisis fell away, signalled by the opening of the Crystal Palace in 1851 which marked the beginning of a twenty-year period of economic growth. The 'hungry 'forties' were displaced by the mid-Victorian years of stability and prosperity. Marx's political pamphlets on the advance of reactionary politics of the early 1850s were, in part, an attempt to explain, within the materialist analytical framework provided in The Manifesto, the failure of the revolutionary moment.[11]

The Condition of the Working Class in England in 1844

By the time Marx and Engels came to publish the Manifesto they had both served an extensive apprenticeship in revolutionary politics and, since 1844 when they first met, had jointly published a number of philosophical and political writings. Before the appearance of the Manifesto, Engels had published a substantial text, part documentary, part exemplar of his and Marx's conception of history, in his own right. The book was The Condition of the Working Class in England in 1844. Published in Germany in 1845, it offered to its readers not only a bleak account of the social and urban conditions of British workers but a review of the progressive and radical causes which sought to ameliorate if not overthrow the forces of capital which in his narrative were the root cause of the deteriorating social conditions he recorded. His time working in the family's textile firm in Manchester was put to good use in the service of the communist cause.

Engels's text drew heavily for some its material on a number of detailed government inquiries and reports published from the late 1830s through to mid 1840s which reported on such matters as child labour, factory conditions and the health of towns. These official reports – known as Blue Books from the bright blue covers in which they bound – were complemented by careful study of a number of books evaluating the emerging factory system of northern England and the Midlands. Some sought to defend the advance of new industry; others were repelled, if not by the rationale of the new industrial system, then certainly by its current consequences. Engels was not alone in using these sources. A number of novelists – Dickens and Disraeli to cite two of the better-known – also drew on this literature for raw material to frame a series of highly popular novels using the themes of industry and poverty as a framing for the narrative. In the context of a sense of growing economic and social dislocation and class estrangement which characterised Britain in the 1840s, this literature – factual and fictional – helped to shape and direct a debate on the 'condition of England question'. Chartism, industrial unrest and strikes, the progress of Poor Law reform, the impact of epidemic diseases, economic crises, and the parlous state of public health in the ever-expanding cities, formed the subject-matter of novels such as *Hard Times* by Dickens (1854), and Benjamin Disraeli's *Sybil* (1845), the latter being a tale of the 'Two Nations', the rich and the poor. *Condition* has to be set in this context, although the analysis of the crisis offered by Engels takes his work far beyond the diagnoses and palliatives offered by novelists and government officials.

Also of significance in framing this debate was the figure of Thomas Carlyle, that exemplar of the Victorian sage, prophetic, uncompromising, a voice preaching to the nation to address its social ills or face the inevitable consequences. Carlyle had produced two distinctive contributions to the 'condition of England debate' – his study *Chartism*, published in 1839, and *Past and Present*, which appeared in 1843. Engels expressed his debt to the impact Carlyle had on his thinking – the 'cash nexus' phrase that figures in the *Manifesto* was taken from Carlyle's work. But it was the disorder evident in contemporary times that so troubled Carlyle; he had little time or enthusiasm for the potential for productive and progressive development revealed by capitalist industrialisation. Engels did not share the moralising lamentations of Carlyle, nor did he share the reveries of authoritarianism that animated Carlyle's vision of future redemption. What made *Condition* such an interesting and original contribution to the literature on the social question was its fusion of empirical critique of the consequences of unplanned urbanisation and industrialisation with an explanatory framework that linked the various instances of distress, poverty, hunger, oppression and exploitation with emergent patterns of material change and social conflict. *Condition* was not simply a narrative of misery but an early working out of ideas about the linkages between capitalist development, the formation of proletarian identity, and the patterning of the new social movements brought into being by the new order.

In addition to the information taken from official inquiries and reports, part of the originality of the account offered by Engels derived from material gathered from his contacts among the working class and various popular organisations. Many of those contacts came to him through Mary Burns, an Irish servant with whom Engels established an intimate and longstanding relationship. He also attended Chartist meetings and other radical gatherings. He was not the first continental observer to use the analysis of the emerging industrial city as a means of offering a wider commentary on social change, but his text continues to have a force and passion that make it unique.[12]

Condition opens with a survey of the rise of modern industry in England chronicling the impact of various technical innovations as well as the new organisational and social model of production represented by the factory. Engels documented the rapid growth of cities from the late eighteenth century showing how so much of this growth was linked to the processes of industrialisation. As he stressed, the rise of mechanical power, the expansion of production and the advance of new industries had 'no counterpart in the annals of humanity . . . The industrial revolution is of

the same importance for England [sic] as the political revolution
for France . . . the mightiest result of this industrial transformation
is the English [sic] proletariat.'[13] These observations encapsulate
the master themes that organise the unfolding of *Condition* –
the revolutionary nature of economic change, the social consequences of such dramatic discontinuity, and the formation of
the new class society. For Engels the decisive social fact was the
rise of the proletariat, much of the text being therefore given over
to examining how the ceaseless development of industry was
accompanied by the growth of the proletariat and its role in
challenging and eventually overthrowing the bourgeois order. A
substantial portion of *Condition* was given over to a survey as well
as indictment of life in the towns, beginning with the example of
London. Engels rehearsed some familiar motifs in the critique of
life in the capital – its size, impersonality, the over-crowding that
marks out the districts of the labouring poor, and the insecurity
that characterised working-class life. Engels presented in his
account of London the first of several graphic vignettes of the
nature of slum life, expanded in his discussion of the industrial
districts. He detailed the life of the cellar-dwellers, notes the filth
and stench which mark the thoroughfares – 'foul liquids emptied
before the doors gather in stinking pools'[14] – as well as the casualties
of the new, impersonal order that characterised modern life.
Moving from London Engels produced a panorama of the problems of poverty exemplified by low wages (for those with work),
overcrowding, poor diet, unspeakably insanitary conditions, and
general neglect. He draws examples from across the nation –
Liverpool and Edinburgh, Nottingham and Derby, Birmingham
and Sheffield, Bradford and Leeds. But Engels devoted most of his
attention to an indictment of the conditions found in the cities that
made up the heart of the new industrial nation, especially Manchester and its environs. Manchester, 'Cottonopolis', Britain's
premier city of industrialisation, provided Engels with his most
substantial case study linking the rule of capital with the conditions
of proletarian existence. *Condition* provided its readers with a
detailed tour of everyday life in the workers' quarters where
workers have become 'mere material, a mere chattel' for the use
of the manufacturers. Housing was unplanned, sanitation and
ventilation almost unknown, rents high – everywhere there was

dirt and overcrowding. Engels summed up his indictment of Manchester thus:

> We must admit that 350,000 working-people of Manchester and its environs live, almost all of them, in wretched, damp, filthy cottages, that the streets which surround them are usually in the most miserable and filthy condition . . . in the working-man's dwellings of Manchester, no cleanliness, no convenience, and consequently no comfortable family life is possible; that in such dwellings only a physically degenerate race, robbed of all humanity, degraded, reduced morally and physically to bestiality, could feel comfortable and at home.[15]

Engels's critique of life in the slums is comprehensive and unsparing – the poor clothing of the people, the immorality that followed from many families sharing a single room, the link between environment and crime, the deficiencies of the working-class diet, the problems of adulteration; Engels had comments to make on all these issues and more. At several points he returned to the issue of starvation, contrasting the slim hold that many had on subsistence with the small minority who grew rich. Engels did not romanticise the conditions of life for many urban dwellers – he was troubled by the extent of drunkenness, for example – but saw such ills as the consequence of the life capitalism had created for the masses.

Yet Engels wanted to do more than chronicle the lives of the dispossessed or rebut those apologists of industrial Britain who paid no heed to the suffering, insecurities and brutalities that were so evidently a feature of working-class urban life. His text wanted to locate these issues of exploitation and dispossession as a consequence of the dynamics of capitalist accumulation and its structure of property and production relations. One theme he stressed was the significance of competition in working-class formation, in determining wage levels and in shaping the everyday existence and outlook of proletarian life. Competition was also identified as a major cause in the periodic crises which marked the development of modern industry. Yet, anticipating the idea of the working class as the 'grave-diggers' of capitalism, Engels also stressed how the processes of urban and industrial change quickened the pace of proletarian development. In cities and under the conditions of centralised production the 'workers begin to feel as a class . . . their separation from the bourgeoisie, the development of views peculiar to the workers and corresponding to their position in life, is fostered, the consciousness of oppression awakens and the workers attain social and political importance. The great cities are the birthplaces of labour movements . . . '[16]

In the final sections of the book Engels continued with his survey of working-class conditions, looking, for example, at the working conditions of the different trades and occupations. His documentary account returned repeatedly to the theme of mechanisation, chronicling its disruptive effects on employment prospects and working conditions. What brings wealth to the bourgeois brings misery to the working class, whether measured in wages, infant mortality rates, the long hours of work, the extent of industrial accidents and injuries, or the deadening effects of working under the unremitting imperatives set by the machine. No reader could miss the theme, woven throughout the text, of the violent *insecurities* that characterised working-class life, material and psychological insecurities that would only be ameliorated to a degree in the United Kingdom by the post-1945 reforms that established the modern welfare state.

Engels was unsparing in his condemnation of the bourgeoisie for creating and sustaining this regime of brutalisation. Towards the end of *Condition* he turned to a discussion of the emergence and significance of the labour movement, outlining the shift from the revolt of the workers of the early nineteenth century through the establishment of trade unions to the rise of Chartism. His account acknowledged the 'obstinate, unconquerable courage' of those who contributed to the advance of the working-class cause, and he provided a succinct, thoughtful evaluation of the Chartist movement, its origins, its character and its progress. For Engels Chartism was 'a class movement'.

In the final two pages Engels speculated about the likely consequences of the next capitalist crises. In 1846-47 he expected the repeal of the Corn Laws and Parliament to pass the People's Charter. But it was the crisis of the early 1850s that Engels anticipated as bringing about a revolution − a 'war of the poor against the rich', if the bourgeoisie did not change and address working-class grievances. Engels was persuaded that:

The revolution must come; it is already too late to bring about a
peaceful solution . . . the classes are divided more and more sharply,
the spirit of resistance penetrates the workers, the spirit of bitterness
intensifies, the guerrilla skirmishes become concentrated in more
important battles, and soon a slight impulse will suffice to set the
avalanche in motion. [17]

Yet intriguingly for Engels communist doctrine, if adopted by
the workers' movement, would serve to 'diminish in bloodshed,
revenge and savagery' the revolutionary struggle and its after-
math, for communism 'is a question of humanity and not of the
workers alone . . . Communism stands above the strife between
bourgeoisie and proletariat . . . '[18]

Given its subject-matter and the time of its production *Condition* has featured prominently in the debate over the standard of
living in the Industrial Revolution era. Pessimists who argue that
early industrialisation led to a decline in popular living standards,
have found a ready source of evidence in Engels's work. For
the optimists, who argue that despite the experience of some
groups, the overall impact of industrialisation was to improve the
workers' standard of living, the *Condition* is little more than a tale
of woe marked by selective quotation and political bias. Without
commenting directly on that debate this brief review of aspects of
Condition suggests that the dismissal of the text is incorrect and
misleading. It is an extraordinarily rich document synthesising a
wide range of contemporary evidence and debate on the social
consequences of urbanism to produce a powerful, original materialist critique of the juggernaut of capitalist industrialisation.
It does not provide a picaresque ethnography of lives of the
poor as found a few years later in the work of Mayhew, but
framed its account of the production of poverty within a system
that had unlocked the potential for expanding productive capacity but whose structure of property relations and political rule
allowed only a few to profit from such extraordinary expansion of
national wealth.[19]

Socialism: Utopian and Scientific

The last work to be considered, also written by Engels, is *Socialism: Utopian and Scientific*, first published in France in 1880 with an English edition appearing in 1892.[20] *Socialism* had originally made up three chapters of a much longer book, *Herr Eugen Dühring's Revolution in Science* (1878). Engels had written this at the request of some colleagues in the German Social Democratic Party to rebut some views about socialism propounded by Dühring which had found favour in sections of the Party. A few years later, at the suggestion of Marx's son-in-law Paul Lafargue, Engels published the three chapters. It proved to be a very popular and influential text. It was seen by a subsequent generation of Marxists as a primer in some key ideas developed by Marx and a succinct explication of the nature of scientific socialism. Its popularity eclipsed that of the *Manifesto* although in the early twentieth century interest in it faded. Despite its shifting status in the canon of Marx-Engels collected works it does provide an accessible survey of the sources of socialist and communist thought in the early nineteenth century linked in with a succinct summary of what was distinctive about Marx's approach to history and the understanding of socialism. The text revisits, amplifies and revises ideas about radical social and political thought that Marx and Engels had set out in the third part of the *Manifesto*.

An account of the history and development of modern materialist thought makes up the core of the general introduction and parts of the first section. For Engels the lineage of materialism runs from figures such as Bacon in seventeenth-century England, through Hobbes, to its adoption by a number of French writers in the eighteenth century. Engels also uses this section to offer a commentary on the significance of agnosticism, as well as outlining what he takes to be some core principles of materialism in understanding the natural and social world. This wordy preamble serves as a preface to the succinct definition of 'historical materialism' that he sets out. It is 'that view of the course of history which seeks the ultimate cause and the great moving power of all important historic events in the economic development of society, in the changes in the mode of production and exchange, in the consequent division of society into distinct classes, and in the struggles of these classes against one another.'[21]

Engels then continues with an account of the rise of the bourgeoisie in Europe, highlighting three significant moments in the advance of the new class against the feudal order – the Protestant Reformation in Germany, the English Revolution which dispatched the monarch to the scaffold, and the French Revolution, which was the first of these struggles to end with the 'complete triumph of the . . . bourgeoisie.' But the political advance of the bourgeoisie in France was overshadowed by the advent in Britain of the industrial revolution, a transformation which substantially increased the wealth of the manufacturing middle class, leading it to challenge a political order which still accorded primary political power to the aristocracy. The struggle between these classes, which focused on political reform, ended with the Reform Act of 1832 which, together with the advance of the cause of free trade, marked the victory of the bourgeoisie over the landed interest. However, industrialism also provided the conditions for the production of a new class – the proletariat, who also fought a campaign for social and political rights. The rise of Chartism was the most substantial example of the new class movements born of modern industry. Engels then surveyed political developments from the 1840s to the 1880s, offering a commentary on the progress of class forces in Britain interlaced with observations on events in France and Germany. While the antagonisms of the 1840s seemed to have abated in the 1850s and 1860s, Engels took heart that from the late 1870s the pace of working-class advance seemed to be quickening again. In England, he observed, if 'the sons of the old Chartists . . . were not quite up to the mark, the grandsons bid fair to be worthy of their forefathers',[22] while the German working class displayed 'discipline, courage, energy and perseverance'. Engels mused – with good reason giving the growing size and confidence of the German Social Democratic Party – whether Germany would be the scene of 'the first great victory of the European proletariat'?

From political history Engels then moved to the second substantive discussion – that of utopian socialism. In his account the intellectual roots of modern socialism were to be found in eighteenth-century France, although representations and accounts of an ideal social order had been evident in events such as the Peasants' War during the German reformation. Three figures were linked together as representative of the modern utopian movement – Saint-Simon, Charles Fourier, and Robert Owen. Their writings, as well as their various interventions into the politics of the day, were developed in the early nineteenth century, a time when only Britain had begun to experience the impact of modern industry. Engels stressed the importance of this conjuncture – utopians conjured up solutions to social ills rooted not in the realities and potentialities of capitalist development but in the form of complex fantasies and elaborate plans of reformed communities designed to transcend the social divisions that impeded order and harmony. For each of the utopian figures Engels provided a short review and evaluation. He noted some of their positive qualities: Fourier, for example, 'lays bare remorselessly the material and moral misery of the bourgeois world',[23] and he commented that 'every social movement, every real advance in England on behalf of the workers links itself on to the name of Robert Owen.'[24] So Engels was warm in his acknowledgement of the contribution of these thinkers to the cause of freedom, but dismisses what he regards as the eclecticism of their ideas which failed to comprehend the real message of the transformations which capitalist industrialism had unlocked. That task was unique to scientific socialism.

To undertake explication of the unique character of scientific socialism Engels first reviewed what he termed 'the science of dialectics'. Engels offered an account of the development of philosophy, reviewing the emergence of metaphysics and its displacement by the rise of modern science with its stress on dialectics as a way of obtaining true knowledge of natural and social processes. It was in eighteenth-century German philosophy, in Kant and more especially Hegel, that the systematisation of dialectical reasoning began. As Engels suggested, the originality of Hegel was to be found in his insistence that the natural and social world was to be understood as a process, 'in constant motion, change, transformation, development', linked with an attempt to explain 'the internal connection that makes a continuous whole of all this movement and development'.[25] Hegel's schema was not without its limitations, its internal contradictions, but modern materialism would provide the means to transcend those constraints. The rise of modern industry and the social transformations which inevitably accompanied it provided raw material for a new – dialectical and material – understanding of history. At the centre of that explanation would be the notion of class struggle. Classes were products of the mode of production, consequently 'the economic structure of society always furnishes the real basis, starting from which we can alone work out the ultimate explanation of the whole superstructure of juridical and political institutions as well as of the religious, philosophical ideas of a given historical period.' [26] This was a succinct, unqualified statement of the base/superstructure model. In terms of the logic of Engels's argument socialism became 'the necessary outcome of the struggle between two historically developed classes – the proletariat and the bourgeoisie . . . ' [27] The critical feature of capitalist accumulation and development was to be found in its extraction of surplus-value. On the basis of these discoveries socialism moved from utopian plans and moral critiques to scientific understanding that could inform and analyse the unfolding class struggle. With due modesty Engels credited both discoveries to Marx, saying nothing of his own contributions to the genesis of historical materialism.

In the final section Engels elaborated his argument on the character of historical materialism, linking it to the development of socialist ideas and practice. The capitalist mode of production defined the modern era, with Engels, once again, stressing the revolutionary political and productive changes that had accompanied it. Using material and ideas already found in the *Manifesto* and *Condition* Engels provided an overview of the processes of capitalist development from the middle ages, but unlike passages in the *Manifesto* which stressed some of the global factors underpinning the emergence of the new mode of production, *Socialism* – drawing on Marx's work in *Capital*, gave particular emphasis to the role of machinery in modern production relations. Engels stressed that machinery 'becomes the most powerful weapon in the war of capital against the working class.' [28] Throughout the section Engels returned to the theme that in modern times the core contradiction driving forward class conflict derives from the fact that 'the socialised organisation of production within the factory has developed so far that it has become incompatible with the anarchy of production in society.' [29] He reviewed the examples of capitalist crises since the early nineteenth century to stress how such events 'demonstrate the incapacity of the bourgeoisie for managing any longer modern productive forces...'[30] It followed that the solution to the contradictions of capitalism is socialism – that is, in one definition, 'by society openly and directly taking possession of the productive forces which have outgrown all control, except that of society as a whole'.[31] This can be accomplished when the proletariat 'seizes political power and turns the means of production into State property.'[32] Yet in that process the proletariat abolishes itself, 'abolishes all class distinction and class antagonisms, abolishes also the State as State . . . It *dies out.*'[33] [original emphasis] For Engels, in the final pages of *Socialism,* there was the confident conviction that the day of proletarian revolution was drawing closer. That moment will mark the 'ascent of man from the kingdom of necessity to the kingdom of freedom'.[34]

For those seeking enlightenment on some of the core ideas of Marx and Engels and/or reassurance about a future of humanity free from oppression, poverty and insecurity, then *Socialism* was a very attractive text, notwithstanding the obscurity of some of its philosophical sections and its poor organisation of material in some places. Its final pages with their assured analysis of capitalist collapse, proletarian triumph and vision of a new, truly human, era of development shortly to begin, crystallised Engels's lifetime commitment to the cause of emancipation. While it features less prominently in present-day analyses of the canon of writing produced by Marx and Engels, it does continue to offer important statements and elaborations of a number of the core ideas associated with their analysis and critique of capitalism.

This is not the place to provide a comprehensive critique of the texts reproduced here, although even a cursory glance of these works throws up issues for consideration and reflection. The assertion in the *Manifesto* that capitalist development was bringing about a polarisation of the stratification system has been subject to much debate. Engels's eager anticipation of revolution combined with a belief that the successful proletarian conquest of power would be followed by a simplification of social and political complexity may appear chillingly naïve to some modern readers. None of the writings presented here attaches much significance to the sentiment and power of nationalism, a lacuna which would have disastrous consequences for some subsequent Marxist parties. For all of Engels's criticism of the utopians that they accorded to much faith to the power of reason, Marx and Engels were heirs to the Enlightenment, sharing a faith in progress, the importance of science as a form of knowledge, and a commitment to the project of emancipation.

The fall of Soviet-style communism in the late 1980s has for some been taken to mean the irrelevance of the writing of Marx and Engels, their ideas perished in the rubble that marked the end of a style of rule that had brought misery to millions. For others, ideas of socialism associated with Marx and Engels could be approached afresh as their work no longer had to be yoked to the fortunes of particular regimes. It is not difficult to see the continuing relevance their writings have for our own times as economic and ecological crises intensify, security – whether of nations or individuals – becomes ever more difficult to secure, and poverty remains the lot of a substantial proportion of global humanity. The social conditions of slum life – its brutality and sense of exclusion – have shifted from Manchester but can be found in Rio, Mumbai or Lagos.[35] Those processes of capitalist development which Marx and Engels analysed have not stopped, so across the world the working class continues to grow although the conditions of proletarian formation and identity may be very different from those set down in the nineteenth century. For anyone to understand modern times, engagement with the writings of Marx and Engels remains essential. Their work continues to offer a unique perspective on the contradictory tendencies of the age of modernity. They were more than radical Victorian gentleman whose ideas and domestic arrangements were at odds with the conventions of bourgeois respectability – they are our contemporaries.

LAURENCE MARLOW
South Bank University

References

1 The first English translation of the work would appear in the Chartist journal, *The Red Republican*, in 1850. It was translated by Helen Macfarlane.

2 Page 3 in this edition.

3 Page 5 in this edition.

4 Page 6 in this edition.

5 Page 6 in this edition.

6 Page 8 in this edition.

7 Page 14 in this edition.

8 Page 15 in this edition.

9 Marx and Engels had already produced a much more thorough and detailed critique of many of these ideas in *The German Ideology*, while Marx had written *The Poverty of Philosophy* (1846), offering a critique of Proudhon.

10 Page 34 in this edition.

11 See K. Marx, *The Class Struggles in France* (1850) and *The Eighteenth Brumaire of Louis Bonaparte* (1852).

12 For a superb discussion of the construction of the text as well as the most detailed and scholarly evaluation of its form and content, see S. Marcus, *Engels, Manchester and the Working Class* (1974).

13 Page 64 in this edition.

14 Page 74 in this edition.

15 Page 106 in this edition.

16 Page 158 in this edition.

17 Page 315 in this edition.

18 Page 316 in this edition.

19 It is worth recalling that an English edition would finally become available in the 1880s when debates about the extent of poverty in London, the ailing imperial metropolis, the establishment of Britain's first avowedly Marxist political party, a successful dock strike in London, and the emergence of a new literature on poverty – both fictional and factual – led to a revival of the 'condition of England' question. But it was the poverty surveys of Charles Booth in London and B. Seebohm Rowntree in York which would dominate discourse on the nature and measurement of poverty.

20 For the French edition Marx wrote an introduction.

21 Pages 339–40 in this edition.
22 Page 352 in this edition.
23 Page 360 in this edition.
24 Page 364 in this edition.
25 Page 370 in this edition.
26 Page 372 in this edition.
27 Page 373 in this edition.
28 Page 382 in this edition.
29 Page 384 in this edition.
30 Page 386 in this edition.
31 Page 387 in this edition.
32 Page 388 in this edition.
33 Pages 388–9 in this edition.
34 Page 392 in this edition.
35 See Mike Davis, *Planet of Slums* (2007).

For anyone wishing to follow up on some of the issues covered in the Introduction the following list has been provided. It does not claim to be comprehensive or definitive, simply a short guide to the vast literature on Marx, Engels and their times.

Context

C. Bayly, *The Birth of the Modern World, 1780–1914* (2004)

G. Eley, *Forging Democracy: the History of the Left in Europe, 1850–2000* (2002)

E. Hobsbawm, *The Age of Capital, 1848–1875* (1975)

J. Rule, *Albion's People: English Society, 1714–1815* (1992)

A. Körner (Ed), *1848 – a European Revolution* (2000)

D. Sassoon, *One Hundred Years of Socialism* (1996)

J. Sperber, *The European Revolutions, 1848–1851* (2nd edition, 2005)

Marx and Engels

There are some useful biographical studies of Marx, but in English Engels has been less well served, apart from the work of Carver. A number of full social and intellectual biographies of Engels are promised but have yet to appear.

S. Barer, *Doctors of Revolution* (1999)

T. Carver, *Friedrich Engels: His Life and Thought* (1989)

T. Carver, *Engels* (1981)

T. Carver and M. Steger (Eds), *Engels after Marx* (1999)

H. Collins and C. Abramsky, *Karl Marx and the British Labour Movement: the Years of the First International* (1965)

D. Glaser and D. Walker (Eds), *Twentieth-century Marxism: a Global Introduction* (2007)

R. Harrison, *Before the Socialists: Studies in Labour and Politics* (1965)

G. Stedman Jones, 'Engels and the History of Marxism', in E. Hobsbawm (Ed), *The History of Marxism*, vol.1 (1982)

D. McLellan, *Karl Marx: a Biography* (4th edition, 2006)

D. McLellan, *Marx before Marxism* (1970)

S. Marcus, *Engels, Manchester and the Working Class* (1974)

L. Panitch and C. Leys (Eds), 'The Communist Manifesto Revisited', *The Socialist Register, 1998* (1998)

G. Steenson, *After Marx, Before Lenin: Marxism and socialist working class parties in Europe, 1884–1914* (1991)

G. Teeple, *Marx's Critique of Politics, 1842–1847* (1984)

F. Wheen, *Karl Marx: a Life* (1999)

Early socialism & Chartism

M. Chase, *Chartism: a New History* (2007)

M. Finn, *After Chartism: Class and Nation in English Radical Politics, 1848–1874* (1993)

G. Claeys, *Citizens and Saints: Politics and Anti-politics in Early British Socialism* (1989)

J. Harrison, *Robert Owen and the Owenites in Britain and America: the Quest for a New Moral Order* (1969)

B. Taylor, *Eve and the New Jerusalem: Socialism and Feminism in the Nineteenth Century* (1983)

D. Thompson, *The Chartists* (1984)

N. Thompson, *The People's Science: the Popular Political Economy of Exploitation and Crisis, 1816–1834* (1984)

The rise of the working class

J. Foster, *Class Struggle in the Industrial Revolution: the Experience of Three Industrial Towns* (1974)

N. Kirk, *Change, Continuity and Class: Labour in British Society, 1850–1920* (1998)

A. Reid, *United We Stand: a History of British Trade Unionism* (2004)

E. Thompson, *The Making of the English Working Class* (1963)

Urban and industrial change

A. Briggs, *Victorian Cities* (1963)

S. Gunn, *The Public Culture of the Victorian Middle Class* (2000)

M. Hewitt, *The Emergence of Stability in the Industrial City: Manchester 1832–1867* (1996)

T. Hunt, *Building Jerusalem: the Rise and Fall of the Victorian City* (2004)

A. Kidd, *Manchester: a History* (4th edition, 2006)

A. Kidd and K. Roberts (Eds), *City, Class and Culture: Studies of Social Policy and Cultural Production in Victorian Manchester* (1985)

A. and L. Lees, *Cities and the Making of Modern Europe, 1750–1914* (2007)

K. Morgan, *The Birth of Industrial Britain: Social Change, 1750–1850* (2004)

H. Platt, *Shock Cities: the Environmental Transformation and Reform of Manchester and Chicago* (2005)

S. Smith, *The Other Nation: the Poor in the English Novels of the 1840s and 1850s* (1980)

P. Stearns, *The Industrial Revolution in World History* (3rd edition, 2007)

NOTE ON THE TEXTS

The Communist Manifesto, by Karl Marx and Friedrich Engels, from the English edition of 1888, edited by Friedrich Engels.

The Condition of the Working-Class in England in 1844, with a Preface written in 1892, by Friedrich Engels, translated by Florence Kelley Wischnewetzky.

Socialism: Scientific and Utopian, by Friedrich Engels, translated from the French by Paul Lafargue in 1892 (translation authorised by Engels).

THE COMMUNIST
MANIFESTO

The Communist Manifesto

A spectre is haunting Europe – the spectre of Communism. All the Powers of old Europe have entered into a holy alliance to exorcise this spectre: Pope and Czar, Metternich and Guizot, French Radicals and German police-spies.

Where is the party in opposition that has not been decried as Communistic by its opponents in power? Where is the Opposition that has not hurled back the branding reproach of Communism, against the more advanced opposition parties, as well as against its reactionary adversaries?

Two things result from this fact.

1. Communism is already acknowledged by all European Powers to be itself a Power.
2. It is high time that Communists should openly, in the face of the whole world, publish their views, their aims, their tendencies, and meet this nursery tale of the Spectre of Communism with a Manifesto of the party itself.

To this end, Communists of various nationalities have assembled in London, and sketched the following Manifesto, to be published in the English, French, German, Italian, Flemish and Danish languages.

I. BOURGEOIS AND PROLETARIANS

The history of all hitherto existing societies is the history of class struggles.

Freeman and slave, patrician and plebeian, lord and serf, guild-master and journeyman, in a word, oppressor and oppressed, stood in constant opposition to one another, carried on an uninterrupted, now hidden, now open fight, a fight that each time ended, either in a revolutionary re-constitution of society at large, or in the common ruin of the contending classes.

In the earlier epochs of history, we find almost everywhere a complicated arrangement of society into various orders, a manifold gradation of social rank. In ancient Rome we have patricians, knights, plebeians, slaves; in the Middle Ages, feudal lords, vassals, guild-masters, journeymen, apprentices, serfs; in almost all of these classes, again, subordinate gradations.

The modern bourgeois society that has sprouted from the ruins of feudal society has not done away with class antagonisms. It has but established new classes, new conditions of oppression, new forms of struggle in place of the old ones. Our epoch, the epoch of the bourgeoisie, possesses, however, this distinctive feature: it has simplified the class antagonisms. Society as a whole is more and more splitting up into two great hostile camps, into two great classes, directly facing each other: Bourgeoisie and Proletariat.

From the serfs of the Middle Ages sprang the chartered burghers of the earliest towns. From these burgesses the first elements of the bourgeoisie were developed.

The discovery of America, the rounding of the Cape, opened up fresh ground for the rising bourgeoisie. The East-Indian and Chinese markets, the colonisation of America, trade with the colonies, the increase in the means of exchange and in commodities generally, gave to commerce, to navigation, to industry, an impulse never before known, and thereby, to the revolutionary element in the tottering feudal society, a rapid development.

The feudal system of industry, under which industrial production was monopolised by closed guilds, now no longer sufficed for the growing wants of the new markets. The manufacturing system took its place. The guild-masters were pushed on one side by the manufacturing middle class; division of labour between the different corporate guilds vanished in the face of division of labour in each single workshop.

Meantime the markets kept ever growing, the demand ever rising. Even manufacture no longer sufficed. Thereupon, steam and machinery revolutionised industrial production. The place of manufacture was taken by the giant, Modern Industry, the place of the industrial middle class, by industrial millionaires, the leaders of whole industrial armies, the modern bourgeois.

Modern industry has established the world-market, for which the discovery of America paved the way. This market has given an immense development to commerce, to navigation, to communication by land. This development has, in its time, reacted on the extension of industry; and in proportion as industry, commerce, navigation, railways extended, in the same proportion the bourgeoisie developed, increased its capital, and pushed into the background every class handed down from the Middle Ages.

We see, therefore, how the modern bourgeoisie is itself the product of a long course of development, of a series of revolutions in the modes of production and of exchange.

Each step in the development of the bourgeoisie was accompanied by a corresponding political advance of that class. An oppressed class under the sway of the feudal nobility, an armed and self-governing association in the medieval commune; here independent urban republic (as in Italy and Germany), there taxable 'third estate' of the monarchy (as in France), afterwards, in the period of manufacture proper, serving either the semi-feudal or the absolute monarchy as a counterpoise against the nobility, and, in fact, corner-stone of the great monarchies in general, the bourgeoisie has at last, since the establishment of Modern Industry and of the world-market, conquered for itself, in the modern representative State, exclusive political sway. The executive of the modern State is but a committee for managing the common affairs of the whole bourgeoisie.

The bourgeoisie, historically, has played a most revolutionary part.

The bourgeoisie, wherever it has got the upper hand, has put an end to all feudal, patriarchal, idyllic relations. It has pitilessly torn asunder the motley feudal ties that bound man to his 'natural superiors', and has left remaining no other nexus between man and man than naked self-interest, than callous 'cash payment'. It has drowned the most heavenly ecstasies of religious fervour, of chivalrous enthusiasm, of philistine sentimentalism, in the icy water of egotistical calculation. It has resolved personal worth into exchange value, and in place of the numberless and feasible chartered freedoms, has set up that single, unconscionable freedom – Free Trade. In one word, for exploitation, veiled by religious and political illusions, naked, shameless, direct, brutal exploitation.

The bourgeoisie has stripped of its halo every occupation hitherto honoured and looked up to with reverent awe. It has converted the physician, the lawyer, the priest, the poet, the man of science, into its paid wage labourers.

The bourgeoisie has torn away from the family its sentimental veil, and has reduced the family relation to a mere money relation.

The bourgeoisie has disclosed how it came to pass that the brutal display of vigour in the Middle Ages, which Reactionists so much admire, found its fitting complement in the most slothful indolence. It has been the first to show what man's activity can bring about. It has accomplished wonders far surpassing Egyptian pyramids, Roman aqueducts, and Gothic cathedrals; it has conducted expeditions that put in the shade all former Exoduses of nations and crusades.

The bourgeoisie cannot exist without constantly revolutionising the instruments of production, and thereby the relations of production, and with them the whole relations of society. Conservation of the old modes of production in unaltered form, was, on the contrary, the first condition of existence for all earlier industrial classes. Constant revolutionising of production, uninterrupted disturbance of all social conditions, everlasting uncertainty and agitation distinguish the bourgeois epoch from all earlier ones. All fixed, fast-frozen relations, with their train of ancient and venerable prejudices and opinions, are swept away, all new-formed ones become antiquated before they can ossify. All that is solid melts into air, all that is holy is profaned, and man is at last compelled to face with sober senses, his real conditions of life, and his relations with his kind.

The need of a constantly expanding market for its products chases the bourgeoisie over the whole surface of the globe. It must nestle everywhere, settle everywhere, establish connections everywhere.

The bourgeoisie has through its exploitation of the world-market given a cosmopolitan character to production and consumption in every country. To the great chagrin of Reactionists, it has drawn from under the feet of industry the national ground on which it stood. All old-established national industries have been destroyed or are daily being destroyed. They are dislodged by new industries, whose introduction becomes a life and death question for all civilised nations, by industries that no longer work up indigenous raw material, but raw material drawn from the remotest zones; industries whose products are consumed, not only at home, but in every quarter of the globe. In place of the old wants, satisfied by the productions of the country, we find new wants, requiring for their satisfaction the products of distant lands and climes. In place of the old local and national seclusion and self-sufficiency, we have intercourse in every direction, universal interdependence of nations. And as in material, so also in intellectual production. The intellectual creations of individual nations become common property. National one-sidedness and narrow-mindedness become more and more impossible, and from the numerous national and local literatures, there arises a world literature.

The bourgeoisie, by the rapid improvement of all instruments of production, by the immensely facilitated means of communication, draws all, even the most barbarian, nations into civilisation. The cheap prices of its commodities are the heavy artillery with which it batters down all Chinese walls, with which it forces the barbarians' intensely obstinate hatred of foreigners to capitulate. It compels all nations, on pain of extinction, to adopt the bourgeois mode of production; it compels them to introduce what it calls civilisation into their midst, i.e. to become bourgeois themselves. In one word, it creates a world after its own image.

The bourgeoisie has subjected the country to the rule of the towns. It has created enormous cities, has greatly increased the urban population as compared with the rural, and has thus rescued a considerable part of the population from the idiocy of rural life. Just as it has made the country dependent on the towns, so it has made barbarian and semi-barbarian countries dependent on the civilised ones, nations of peasants on nations of bourgeois, the East on the West.

The bourgeoisie keeps more and more doing away with the scattered state of the population, of the means of production, and of property. It has agglomerated production, and has concentrated property in a few hands. The necessary consequence of this was political centralisation. Independent, or but loosely connected provinces, with separate interests, laws, governments and systems of taxation, became lumped together into one nation, with one government, one code of laws, one national class-interest, one frontier and one customs-tariff. The bourgeoisie, during its rule of scarce one hundred years, has created more massive and more colossal productive forces than have all preceding generations together. Subjection of Nature's forces to man, machinery, application of chemistry to industry and agriculture, steam-navigation, railways, electric telegraphs, clearing of whole continents for cultivation, canalisation of rivers, whole populations conjured out of the ground – what earlier century had even a presentiment that such productive forces slumbered in the lap of social labour?

We see then: the means of production and of exchange, on whose foundation the bourgeoisie built itself up, were generated in feudal society. At a certain stage in the development of these means of production and of exchange, the conditions under which feudal society produced and exchanged, the feudal organisation of agriculture and manufacturing industry, in one word, the feudal relations of property became no longer compatible with the already developed productive forces; they became so many fetters. They had to be burst asunder; they were burst asunder.

Into their place stepped free competition, accompanied by a social and political constitution adapted to it, and by the economical and political sway of the bourgeois class.

A similar movement is going on before our own eyes. Modern bourgeois society with its relations of production, of exchange and of property, a society that has conjured up such gigantic means of production and of exchange, is like the sorcerer, who is no longer able to control the powers of the nether world whom he has called up by his spells. For many a decade past the history of industry and commerce is but the history of the revolt of modern productive forces against modern conditions of production, against the property relations that are the conditions for the existence of the bourgeoisie and of its rule. It is enough to mention the commercial crises that by their periodical return put on its trial, each time more threateningly, the existence of the entire bourgeois society. In these crises a great part not only of the existing products, but also of the previously created productive forces, are periodically destroyed. In these crises there breaks out an epidemic that, in all earlier epochs, would have seemed an absurdity – the epidemic of over-production. Society suddenly finds itself put back into a state of momentary barbarism; it appears as if a famine, a universal war of devastation had cut off the supply of every means of subsistence; industry and commerce seem to be destroyed; and why? Because there is too much civilisation, too much means of subsistence, too much industry, too much commerce. The productive forces at the disposal of society no longer tend to further the development of the conditions of bourgeois property; on the contrary, they have become too powerful for these conditions, by which they are fettered, and so soon as they overcome these fetters, they bring disorder into the whole of bourgeois society, endanger the existence of bourgeois property. The conditions of bourgeois society are too narrow to comprise the wealth created by them. And how does the bourgeoisie get over these crises? On the one hand enforced destruction of a mass of productive forces; on the other, by the conquest of new markets, and by the more thorough exploitation of the old ones. That is to say, by paving the way for more extensive and more destructive crises, and by diminishing the means whereby crises are prevented.

The weapons with which the bourgeoisie felled feudalism to the ground are now turned against the bourgeoisie itself.

But not only has the bourgeoisie forged the weapons that bring death to itself; it has also called into existence the men who are to wield those weapons – the modern working class – the proletarians.

In proportion as the bourgeoisie, i.e. capital, is developed, in the same proportion is the proletariat, the modern working class, developed – a class of labourers, who live only so long as they find work, and who find work only so long as their labour increases capital. These labourers, who must sell themselves piecemeal, are a commodity, like every other article of commerce, and are consequently exposed to all the vicissitudes of competition, to all the fluctuations of the market.

Owing to the extensive use of machinery and to division of labour, the work of the proletarians has lost all individual character, and consequently, all charm for the workman. He becomes an appendage of the machine, and it is only the most simple, most monotonous, and most easily acquired knack, that is required of him. Hence, the cost of production of a workman is restricted, almost entirely, to the means of subsistence that he requires for his maintenance, and for the propagation of his race. But the price of a commodity, and therefore also of labour, is equal to its cost of production. In proportion therefore, as the repulsiveness of the work increases, the wage decreases. Nay more, in proportion as the use of machinery and division of labour increases, in the same proportion the burden of toil also increases, whether by prolongation of the working hours, by increase of the work exacted in a given time or by increased speed of the machinery, etc.

Modern industry has converted the little workshop of the patriarchal master into the great factory of the industrial capitalist. Masses of labourers, crowded into the factory, are organised like soldiers. As privates of the industrial army they are placed under the command of a perfect hierarchy of officers and sergeants. Not only are they slaves of the bourgeois class, and of the bourgeois State; they are daily and hourly enslaved by the machine, by the over-looker, and, above all, by the individual bourgeois manufacturer himself. The more openly this despotism proclaims gain to be its end and aim, the more petty, the more hateful and the more embittering it is.

The less the skill and exertion of strength implied in manual labour, in other words, the more modern industry becomes developed, the more is the labour of men superseded by that of women. Differences of age and sex have no longer any distinctive social validity for the working class. All are instruments of labour, more or less expensive to use, according to their age and sex.

No sooner is the exploitation of the labourer by the manufacturer, so far at an end, that he receives his wages in cash, than he is set upon by the other portions of the bourgeoisie, the landlord, the shopkeeper, the pawnbroker, etc.

The lower strata of the middle class – the small tradespeople, shopkeepers, retired tradesmen generally, the handicraftsmen and peasants – all these sink gradually into the proletariat, partly because their diminutive capital does not suffice for the scale on which Modern Industry is carried on, and is swamped in the competition with the large capitalists, partly because their specialised skill is rendered worthless by the new methods of production. Thus the proletariat is recruited from all classes of the population.

The proletariat goes through various stages of development. With its birth begins its struggle with the bourgeoisie. At first the contest is carried on by individual labourers, then by the workpeople of a factory, then by the operatives of one trade, in one locality, against the individual bourgeois who directly exploits them. They direct their attacks not against the bourgeois conditions of production, but against the instruments of production themselves; they destroy imported wares that compete with their labour, they smash to pieces machinery, they set factories ablaze, they seek to restore by force the vanished status of the workman of the Middle Ages.

At this stage the labourers still form an incoherent mass scattered over the whole country, and broken up by their mutual competition. If anywhere they unite to form more compact bodies, this is not yet the consequence of their own active union, but of the union of the bourgeoisie, which class, in order to attain its own political ends, is compelled to set the whole proletariat in motion, and is moreover yet, for a time, able to do so. At this stage, therefore, the proletarians do not fight their enemies, but the enemies of their enemies, the remnants of absolute monarchy, the landowners, the non-industrial bourgeois, the petty bourgeoisie. Thus the whole historical movement is concentrated in the hands of the bourgeoisie; every victory so obtained is a victory for the bourgeoisie.

But with the development of industry the proletariat not only increases in number; it becomes concentrated in greater masses, its strength grows, and it feels that strength more. The various interests and conditions of life within the ranks of the proletariat are more and more equalised, in proportion as machinery obliterates all distinctions of labour, and nearly everywhere reduces wages to the same low level. The growing competition among the bourgeois, and the resulting commercial crises, make the wages of the workers ever more fluctuating. The unceasing improvement of machinery, ever more rapidly developing, makes their livelihood more and more precarious; the collisions between individual workmen and individual bourgeois take more and more the character of collisions between two classes. Thereupon the workers begin to form combinations (Trades Unions) against the bourgeois; they club together in order to keep up the rate of wages; they found permanent associations in order to make provision beforehand for these occasional revolts. Here and there the contest breaks out into riots.

Now and then the workers are victorious, but only for a time. The real fruit of their battles lies, not in the immediate result, but in the ever-expanding union of the workers. This union is helped on by the improved means of communication that are created by modern industry and that place the workers of different localities in contact with one another. It was just this contact that was needed to centralise the numerous local struggles, all of the same character, into one national struggle between classes. But every class struggle is a political struggle. And that union, to attain which the burghers of the Middle Ages, with their miserable highways, required centuries, the modern proletarians, thanks to railways, achieve in a few years.

This organisation of the proletarians into a class, and consequently into a political party, is continually being upset again by the competition between the workers themselves. But it ever rises up again, stronger, firmer, mightier. It compels legislative recognition of particular interests of the workers, by taking advantage of the divisions among the bourgeoisie itself. Thus the ten-hours' bill in England was carried.

Altogether collisions between the classes of the old society further, in many ways, the course of development of the proletariat. The bourgeoisie finds itself involved in a constant battle. At first with the aristocracy; later on, with those portions of the bourgeoisie itself, whose interests have become antagonistic to the progress of industry; at all times, with the bourgeoisie of foreign countries. In all these battles it sees itself compelled to appeal to the proletariat, to ask for its help, and thus, to drag it into the political arena. The bourgeoisie itself, therefore, supplies the proletariat with its own instruments of political and general education, in other words, it furnishes the proletariat with weapons for fighting the bourgeoisie.

Further, as we have already seen, entire sections of the ruling classes are, by the advance of industry, precipitated into the proletariat, or are at least threatened in their conditions of existence. These also supply the proletariat with fresh elements of enlightenment and progress.

Finally, in times when the class struggle nears the decisive hour, the process of dissolution going on within the ruling class, in fact within the whole range of society, assumes such a violent, glaring character, that a small section of the ruling class cuts itself adrift, and joins the revolutionary class, the class that holds the future in its hands. Just as, therefore, at an earlier period, a section of the nobility went over to the bourgeoisie, so now a portion of the bourgeoisie goes over to the proletariat, and in particular, a portion of the bourgeois ideologists, who have raised themselves to the level of comprehending theoretically the historical movement as a whole.

Of all the classes that stand face to face with the bourgeoisie today, the proletariat alone is a really revolutionary class. The other classes decay and finally disappear in the face of Modern Industry; the proletariat is its special and essential product. The lower middle class, the small manufacturer, the shopkeeper, the artisan, the peasant, all these fight against the bourgeoisie, to save from extinction their existence as fractions of the middle class. They are therefore not revolutionary, but conservative. Nay more, they are reactionary, for they try to roll back the wheel of history. If by chance they are revolutionary, they are so only in view of their impending transfer into the proletariat; they thus defend not their present, but their future interests, they desert their own standpoint to place themselves at that of the proletariat.

The 'dangerous class', the social scum, that passively rotting mass thrown off by the lowest layers of old society, may, here and there, be swept into the movement by a proletarian revolution; its conditions of life, however, prepare it far more for the part of a bribed tool of reactionary intrigue.

In the conditions of the proletariat, those of old society at large are already virtually swamped. The proletarian is without property; his relation to his wife and children has no longer anything in common with the bourgeois family-relations; modern industrial labour, modern subjection to capital, the same in England as in France, in America as in Germany, has stripped him of every trace of national character. Law, morality, religion, are to him so many bourgeois prejudices, behind which lurk in ambush just as many bourgeois interests.

All the preceding classes that got the upper hand, sought to fortify their already acquired status by subjecting society at large to their conditions of appropriation. The proletarians cannot become masters of the productive forces of society, except by abolishing their own previous mode of appropriation, and thereby also every other previous mode of appropriation. They have nothing of their own to secure and to fortify; their mission is to destroy all previous securities for, and insurances of, individual property.

All previous historical movements were movements of minorities, or in the interests of minorities. The proletarian movement is the self-conscious, independent movement of the immense majority, in the interests of the immense majority. The proletariat, the lowest stratum of our present society, cannot stir, cannot raise itself up, without the whole superincumbent strata of official society being sprung into the air.

Though not in substance, yet in form, the struggle of the proletariat with the bourgeoisie is at first a national struggle. The proletariat of each country must, of course, first of all settle matters with its own bourgeoisie.

In depicting the most general phases of the development of the proletariat, we traced the more or less veiled civil war, raging within existing society, up to the point where that war breaks out into open revolution, and where the violent overthrow of the bourgeoisie lays the foundation for the sway of the proletariat.

Hitherto, every form of society has been based, as we have already seen, on the antagonism of oppressing and oppressed classes. But in order to oppress a class, certain conditions must be assured to it under which it can, at least, continue its slavish existence. The serf, in the period of serfdom, raised himself to membership in the commune, just as the petty bourgeois, under the yoke of feudal absolutism, managed to develop into a bourgeois. The modern labourer, on the contrary, instead of rising with the progress of industry, sinks deeper and deeper below the conditions of existence of his own class. He becomes a pauper, and pauperism develops more rapidly than population and wealth. And here it becomes evident, that the bourgeoisie is unfit any longer to be the ruling class in society, and to impose its conditions of existence upon society as an over-riding law. It is unfit to rule because it is incompetent to assure an existence to its slave within his slavery, because it cannot help letting him sink into such a state, that it has to feed him, instead of being fed by him. Society can no longer live under this bourgeoisie, in other words, its existence is no longer compatible with society.

The essential condition for the existence, and for the sway of the bourgeois class, is the formation and augmentation of capital; the condition for capital is wage-labour. Wage-labour rests exclusively on competition between the labourers. The advance of industry, whose involuntary promoter is the bourgeoisie, replaces the isolation of the labourers, due to competition, by their revolutionary combination, due to association. The development of Modern Industry, therefore, cuts from under its feet the very foundation on which the bourgeoisie produces and appropriates products. What the bourgeoisie, therefore, produces, above all, is its own grave-diggers. Its fall and the victory of the proletariat are equally inevitable.

2. PROLETARIANS AND COMMUNISTS

In what relation do the Communists stand to the proletarians as a whole?

The Communists do not form a separate party opposed to other working-class parties.

They have no interests separate and apart from those of the proletariat as a whole.

They do not set up any sectarian principles of their own, by which to shape and mould the proletarian movement.

The Communists are distinguished from the other working-class parties by this only: (1) In the national struggles of the proletarians of the different countries, they point out and bring to the front the common interests of the entire proletariat, independently of all nationality. (2) In the various stages of development which the struggle of the working class against the bourgeoisie has to pass through, they always and everywhere represent the interests of the movement as a whole.

The Communists, therefore, are on the one hand, practically, the most advanced and resolute section of the working-class parties of every country, that section which pushes forward all others; on the other hand, theoretically, they have over the great mass of the proletariat the advantage of clearly understanding the line of march, the conditions, and the ultimate general results of the proletarian movement.

The immediate aim of the Communist is the same as that of all the other proletarian parties: formation of the proletariat into a class, overthrow of the bourgeois supremacy, conquest of political power by the proletariat.

The theoretical conclusions of the Communists are in no way based on ideas or principles that have been invented, or discovered, by this or that would-be universal reformer. They merely express, in general terms, actual relations springing from an existing class struggle, from a historical movement going on under our very eyes. The abolition of existing property relations is not at all a distinctive feature of Communism.

All property relations in the past have continually been subject to historical change consequent upon the change in historical conditions.

The French Revolution, for example, abolished feudal property in favour of bourgeois property.

The distinguishing feature of Communism is not the abolition of property generally, but the abolition of bourgeois property. But modern bourgeois private property is the final and most complete expression of the system of producing and appropriating products, that is based on class antagonisms, on the exploitation of the many by the few.

In this sense, the theory of the Communists may be summed up in the single sentence: Abolition of private property.

We Communists have been reproached with the desire of abolishing the right of personally acquiring property as the fruit of a man's own labour, which property is alleged to be the groundwork of all personal freedom, activity and independence.

Hard-won, self-acquired, self-earned property! Do you mean the property of the petty artisan and of the small peasant, a form of property that preceded the bourgeois form? There is no need to abolish that; the development of industry has to a great extent already destroyed it, and is still destroying it daily.

Or do you mean modern bourgeois private property?

But does wage-labour create any property for the labourer? Not a bit. It creates capital, i.e. that kind of property which exploits wage-labour, and which cannot increase except upon condition of begetting a new supply of wage-labour for fresh exploitation. Property, in its present form, is based on the antagonism of capital and wage-labour. Let us examine both sides of this antagonism.

To be a capitalist, is to have not only a purely personal, but a social status in production. Capital is a collective product, and only by the united action of many members, nay, in the last resort, only by the united action of all members of society, can it be set in motion.

Capital is, therefore, not a personal, it is a social power.

When, therefore, capital is converted into common property, into the property of all members of society, personal property is not thereby transformed into social property. It is only the social character of the property that is changed. It loses its class-character.

Let us now take wage-labour.

The average price of wage-labour is the minimum wage, i.e. that quantum of the means of subsistence, which is absolutely requisite in bare existence as a labourer. What, therefore, the wage-labourer appropriates by means of his labour, merely suffices to prolong and reproduce a bare existence. We by no means intend to abolish this personal appropriation of the products of labour, an appropriation that is made for the maintenance and reproduction of human life, and that leaves no surplus wherewith to command the labour of others. All that we want to do away with, is the miserable character of this appropriation, under which the labourer lives merely to increase capital, and is allowed to live only in so far as the interest of the ruling class requires it.

In bourgeois society, living labour is but a means to increase accumulated labour. In Communist society, accumulated labour is but a means to widen, to enrich, to promote the existence of the labourer.

In bourgeois society, therefore, the past dominates the present; in Communist society, the present dominates the past. In bourgeois society capital is independent and has individuality, while the living person is dependent and has no individuality.

And the abolition of this state of things is called by the bourgeois, abolition of individuality and freedom! And rightly so. The abolition of bourgeois individuality, bourgeois independence, and bourgeois freedom is undoubtedly aimed at.

By freedom is meant, under the present bourgeois conditions of production, free trade, free selling and buying.

But if selling and buying disappears, free selling and buying disappears also. This talk about free selling and buying, and all the other 'brave words' of our bourgeoisie about freedom in general, have a meaning, if any, only in contrast with restricted selling and buying, with the fettered traders of the Middle Ages, but have no meaning when opposed to the Communistic abolition of buying and selling, of the bourgeois conditions of production, and of the bourgeoisie itself.

You are horrified at our intending to do away with private property. But in your existing society, private property is already done away with for nine-tenths of the population; its existence for the few is solely due to its non-existence in the hands of those nine-tenths. You reproach us, therefore, with intending to do away with a form of property, the necessary condition for whose existence is the non-existence of any property for the immense majority of society.

In one word, you reproach us with intending to do away with your property. Precisely so; that is just what we intend.

From the moment when labour can no longer be converted into capital, money, or rent, into a social power capable of being monopolised, i.e. from the moment when individual property can no longer be transformed into bourgeois property, into capital, from that moment, you say individuality vanishes.

You must, therefore, confess that by 'individual' you mean no other person than the bourgeois, than the middle-class owner of property. This person must, indeed, be swept out of the way, and made impossible.

Communism deprives no man of the power to appropriate the products of society; all that it does is to deprive him of the power to subjugate the labour of others by means of such appropriation.

It has been objected that upon the abolition of private property all work will cease, and universal laziness will overtake us.

According to this, bourgeois society ought long ago to have gone to the dogs through sheer idleness; for those of its members who work, acquire nothing, and those who acquire anything, do not work. The whole of this objection is but another expression of the tautology: that there can no longer be any wage-labour when there is no longer any capital.

All objections urged against the Communistic mode of producing and appropriating material products, have, in the same way, been urged against the Communistic modes of producing and appropriating intellectual products. Just as, to the bourgeois, the disappearance of class property is the disappearance of production itself, so the disappearance of class culture is to him identical with the disappearance of all culture.

That culture, the loss of which he laments, is, for the enormous majority, a mere training to act as a machine.

But don't wrangle with us so long as you apply, to our intended abolition of bourgeois property, the standard of your bourgeois notions of freedom, culture, law, etc. Your very ideas are but the outgrowth of the conditions of your bourgeois production and bourgeois property, just as your jurisprudence is but the will of your class made into a law for all, a will, whose essential character and direction are determined by the economical conditions of existence of your class.

The selfish misconception that induces you to transform into eternal laws of nature and of reason, the social forms springing from your present mode of production and form of property – historical relations that rise and disappear in the progress of production – this misconception you share with every ruling class that has preceded you. What you see clearly in the case of ancient property, what you admit in the case of feudal property, you are of course forbidden to admit in the case of your own bourgeois form of property.

Abolition of the family! Even the most radical flare up at this infamous proposal of the Communists.

On what foundation is the present family, the bourgeois family, based? On capital, on private gain. In its completely developed form this family exists only among the bourgeoisie. But this state of things finds its complement in the practical absence of the family among the proletarians, and in public prostitution.

The bourgeois family will vanish as a matter of course when its complement vanishes, and both will vanish with the vanishing of capital.

Do you charge us with wanting to stop the exploitation of children by their parents? To this crime we plead guilty.

But, you will say, we destroy the most hallowed of relations, when we replace home education by social.

And your education! Is not that also social, and determined by the social conditions under which you educate, by the intervention, direct or indirect, of society, by means of schools, etc.? The Communists have not invented the intervention of society in education; they do but seek to alter the character of that intervention, and to rescue education from the influence of the ruling class.

The bourgeois claptrap about the family and education, about the hallowed co-relation of parent and child, becomes all the more disgusting, the more, by the action of Modern Industry, all family ties among the proletarians are torn asunder, and their children transformed into simple articles of commerce and instruments of labour.

But you Communists would introduce community of women, screams the whole bourgeoisie in chorus.

The bourgeois sees in his wife a mere instrument of production. He hears that the instruments of production are to be exploited in common, and, naturally, can come to no other conclusion than that the lot of being common to all will likewise fall to the women.

He has not even a suspicion that the real point is to do away with the status of women as mere instruments of production.

For the rest, nothing is more ridiculous than the virtuous indignation of our bourgeois at the community of women which, they pretend, is to be openly and officially established by the Communists. The Communists have no need to introduce community of women; it has existed almost from time immemorial.

Our bourgeois, not content with having the wives and daughters of their proletarians at their disposal, not to speak of common prostitutes, take the greatest pleasure in seducing each other's wives.

Bourgeois marriage is in reality a system of wives in common and thus, at the most, what the Communists might possibly be reproached with, is that they desire to introduce, in substitution for a hypocritically concealed, an openly legalised community of women. For the rest, it is self-evident that the abolition of the present system of production must bring with it the abolition of the community of women springing from that system, i.e. of prostitution both public and private.

The Communists are further reproached with desiring to abolish countries and nationality.

The working men have no country. We cannot take from them what they have not got. Since the proletariat must first of all acquire political supremacy, must rise to be the leading class of the nation, must constitute itself the nation, it is, so far, itself national, though not in the bourgeois sense of the word.

National differences and antagonisms between peoples are daily more and more vanishing, owing to the development of the bourgeoisie, to freedom of commerce, to the world-market, to uniformity in the mode of production and in the conditions of life corresponding thereto.

The supremacy of the proletariat will cause them to vanish still faster. United action, of the leading civilised countries at least, is one of the first conditions for the emancipation of the proletariat.

In proportion as the exploitation of one individual by another is put an end to, the exploitation of one nation by another will also be put an end to. In proportion as the antagonism between classes within the nation vanishes, the hostility of one nation to another will come to an end.

The charges against Communism made from a religious, a philosophical, and, generally, from an ideological standpoint, are not deserving of serious examination.

Does it require deep intuition to comprehend that man's ideas, views and conceptions, in one word, man's consciousness, changes with every change in the conditions of his material existence, in his social relations and in his social life?

What else does the history of ideas prove, than that intellectual production changes its character in proportion as material production is changed? The ruling ideas of each age have ever been the ideas of its ruling class.

When people speak of ideas that revolutionise society, they do but express the fact, that within the old society, the elements of a new one have been created, and that the dissolution of the old ideas keeps even pace with the dissolution of the old conditions of existence.

When the ancient world was in its last throes, the ancient religions were overcome by Christianity. When Christian ideas succumbed in the eighteenth century to rationalist ideas, feudal society fought its death battle with the then revolutionary bourgeoisie. The ideas of religious liberty and freedom of conscience merely gave expression to the sway of free competition within the domain of knowledge.

'Undoubtedly,' it will be said, 'religious, moral, philosophical and juridical ideas have been modified in the course of historical development. But religion, morality, philosophy, political science, and law, constantly survived this change.'

'There are, besides, eternal truths, such as Freedom, Justice, etc. that are common to all states of society. But Communism abolishes eternal truths, it abolishes all religion, and all morality, instead of constituting them on a new basis; it therefore acts in contradiction to all past historical experience.'

What does this accusation reduce itself to? The history of all past society has consisted in the development of class antagonisms, antagonisms that assumed different forms at different epochs.

But whatever form they may have taken, one fact is common to all past ages, viz., the exploitation of one part of society by the other. No wonder, then, that the social consciousness of past ages, despite all the multiplicity and variety it displays, moves within certain common forms, or general ideas, which cannot completely vanish except with the total disappearance of class antagonisms.

The Communist revolution is the most radical rupture with traditional property relations; no wonder that its development involves the most radical rupture with traditional ideas.

But let us have done with the bourgeois objections to Communism.

We have seen above, that the first step in the revolution by the working class, is to raise the proletariat to the position of ruling class, to win the battle of democracy.

The proletariat will use its political supremacy to wrest, by degrees, all capital from the bourgeoisie, to centralise all instruments of production in the hands of the State, i.e. of the proletariat organised as the ruling class; and to increase the total of productive forces as rapidly as possible.

Of course, in the beginning, this cannot be effected except by means of despotic inroads on the rights of property, and on the conditions of bourgeois production; by means of measures, therefore, which appear economically insufficient and untenable, but which, in the course of the movement, outstrip themselves, necessitate further inroads upon the old social order, and are unavoidable as a means of entirely revolutionising the mode of production.

These measures will of course be different in different countries.

Nevertheless in the most advanced countries, the following will be pretty generally applicable.

1. Abolition of property in land and application of all rents of land to public purposes.
2. A heavy progressive or graduated income tax.
3. Abolition of all right of inheritance.
4. Confiscation of the property of all emigrants and rebels.
5. Centralisation of credit in the hands of the State, by means of a national bank with State capital and an exclusive monopoly.
6. Centralisation of the means of communication and transport in the hands of the State.
7. Extension of factories and instruments of production owned by the State; the bringing into cultivation of waste-lands, and the improvement of the soil generally in accordance with a common plan.
8. Equal liability of all to labour. Establishment of industrial armies, especially for agriculture.
9. Combination of agriculture with manufacturing industries; gradual abolition of the distinction between town and country, by a more equable distribution of the population over the country.
10. Free education for all children in public schools. Abolition of children's factory labour in its present form. Combination of education with industrial production, &c., &c.

When, in the course of development, class distinctions have disappeared, and all production has been concentrated in the hands of a vast association of the whole nation, the public power will lose its political character. Political power, properly so called, is merely the organised power of one class for oppressing another. If the proletariat during its contest with the bourgeoisie is compelled, by the force of circumstances, to organise itself as a class, if, by means of a revolution, it makes itself the ruling class, and, as such, sweeps away by force the old conditions of production, then it will, along with these conditions, have swept away the conditions for the existence of class antagonisms and of classes generally, and will thereby have abolished its own supremacy as a class.

In place of the old bourgeois society, with its classes and class antagonisms, we shall have an association, in which the free development of each is the condition for the free development of all.

3. SOCIALIST AND COMMUNIST LITERATURE

i. Reactionary Socialism

A. *Feudal Socialism*

Owing to their historical position, it became the vocation of the aristocracies of France and England to write pamphlets against modern bourgeois society. In the French revolution of July 1830, and in the English reform agitation, these aristocracies again succumbed to the hateful upstart. Thenceforth, a serious political contest was altogether out of the question. A literary battle alone remained possible. But even in the domain of literature the old cries of the restoration period had become impossible.

In order to arouse sympathy, the aristocracy were obliged to lose sight, apparently, of their own interests, and to formulate their indictment against the bourgeoisie in the interest of the exploited working class alone. Thus the aristocracy took their revenge by singing lampoons on their new master, and whispering in his ears sinister prophecies of coming catastrophe.

In this way arose Feudal Socialism: half lamentation, half lampoon; half echo of the past, half menace of the future; at times, by its bitter, witty and incisive criticism, striking the bourgeoisie to the very heart's core; but always ludicrous in its effect, through total incapacity to comprehend the march of modern history.

The aristocracy, in order to rally the people to them, waved the proletarian alms-bag in front for a banner. But the people, so often as it joined them, saw on their hindquarters the old feudal coats of arms, and deserted with loud and irreverent laughter.

One section of the French Legitimists and 'Young England' exhibited this spectacle.

In pointing out that their mode of exploitation was different to that of the bourgeoisie, the feudalists forget that they exploited under circumstances and conditions that were quite different, and that are now antiquated. In showing that, under their rule, the modern proletariat never existed, they forget that the modern bourgeoisic is the necessary offspring of their own form of society.

For the rest, so little do they conceal the reactionary character of their criticism that their chief accusation against the bourgeoisie amounts to this, that under the bourgeois régime a class is being developed, which is destined to cut up root and branch the old order of society.

What they upbraid the bourgeoisie with is not so much that it creates a proletariat, as that it creates a *revolutionary* proletariat.

In political practice, therefore, they join in all coercive measures against the working class; and in ordinary life, despite their high-falutin phrases, they stoop to pick up the golden apples dropped from the tree of industry, and to barter truth, love, and honour for traffic in wool, beetroot-sugar, and potato spirits.

As the parson has ever gone hand in hand with the landlord, so has Clerical Socialism with Feudal Socialism.

Nothing is easier than to give Christian asceticism a Socialist tinge. Has not Christianity declaimed against private property, against marriage, against the State? Has it not preached in the place of these, charity and poverty, celibacy and mortification of the flesh, monastic life and Mother Church? Christian Socialism is but the holy water with which the priest consecrates the heart-burnings of the aristocrat.

B. *Petty-Bourgeois Socialism*

The feudal aristocracy was not the only class that was ruined by the bourgeoisie, not the only class whose conditions of existence pined and perished in the atmosphere of modern bourgeois society. The medieval burgesses and the small peasant proprietors were the precursors of the modern bourgeoisie. In those countries which are but little developed, industrially and commercially, these two classes still vegetate side by side with the rising bourgeoisie.

In countries where modern civilisation has become fully developed, a new class of petty bourgeois has been formed, fluctuating between proletariat and bourgeoisie and ever renewing itself as a supplementary part of bourgeois society. The individual members of this class, however, are being constantly hurled down into the proletariat by the action of competition, and, as modern industry develops, they even see the moment approaching when they will completely disappear as an independent section of modern society, to be replaced, in manufactures, agriculture and commerce, by overlookers, bailiffs and shopmen.

In countries like France, where the peasants constitute far more than half of the population, it was natural that writers who sided with the proletariat against the bourgeoisie, should use, in their criticism of the bourgeois regime, the standard of the peasant and petty bourgeois, and from the standpoint of these intermediate classes should take up the cudgels for the working class. Thus arose petty-bourgeois Socialism. Sismondi was the head of this school, not only in France but also in England.

This school of Socialism dissected with great acuteness the contradictions in the conditions of modern production. It laid bare the hypocritical apologies of economists. It proved, incontrovertibly, the disastrous effects of machinery and division of labour; the concentration of capital and land in a few hands; overproduction and crises; it pointed out the inevitable ruin of the petty bourgeois and peasant, the misery of the proletariat, the anarchy in production, the crying inequalities in the distribution of wealth, the industrial war of extermination between nations, the dissolution of old moral bonds, of the old family relations, of the old nationalities.

In its positive aims, however, this form of Socialism aspires either to restoring the old means of production and of exchange, and with them the old property relations, and the old society, or to cramping the modern means of production and of exchange, within the framework of the old property relations that have been, and were bound to be, exploded by those means. In either case, it is both reactionary and Utopian.

Its last words are: corporate guilds for manufacture, patriarchal relations in agriculture.

Ultimately, when stubborn historical facts had dispersed all intoxicating effects of self-deception, this form of Socialism ended in a miserable fit of the blues.

C. German, or 'True', Socialism

The Socialist and Communist literature of France, a literature that originated under the pressure of a bourgeoisie in power, and that was the expression of the struggle against this power, was introduced into Germany at a time when the bourgeoisie, in that country, had just begun its contest with feudal absolutism.

German philosophers, would-be philosophers, and *beaux esprits*, eagerly seized on this literature, only forgetting, that when these writings immigrated from France into Germany, French social conditions had not immigrated along with them. In contact with German social conditions, this French literature lost all its immediate practical significance, and assumed a purely literary aspect. Thus, to the German philosophers of the eighteenth century, the demands of the first French Revolution were nothing more than the demands of 'Practical Reason' in general, and the utterance of the will of the revolutionary French bourgeoisie signified in their eyes the law of pure Will, of Will as it was bound to be, of true human Will generally.

The world of the German *literati* consisted solely in bringing the new French ideas into harmony with their ancient philosophical conscience, or rather, in annexing the French ideas without deserting their own philosophic point of view.

This annexation took place in the same way in which a foreign language is appropriated, namely, by translation.

It is well known how the monks wrote silly lives of Catholic Saints over the manuscripts on which the classical works of ancient heathendom had been written. The German *literati* reversed this process with the profane French literature. They wrote their philosophical nonsense beneath the French original. For instance, beneath the French criticism of the economic functions of money, they wrote 'Alienation of Humanity', and beneath the French criticism of the bourgeois State they wrote 'Dethronement of the Category of the General', and so forth.

The introduction of these philosophical phrases at the back of the French historical criticisms they dubbed 'Philosophy of Action',

'True Socialism', 'German Science of Socialism', 'Philosophical Foundation of Socialism', and so on.

The French Socialist and Communist literature was thus completely emasculated. And, since it ceased in the hands of the German to express the struggle of one class with the other, he felt conscious of having overcome 'French one-sidedness' and of representing, not true requirements, but the requirements of truth; not the interests of the proletariat, but the interests of Human Nature, of Man in general, who belongs to no class, has no reality, who exists only in the misty realm of philosophical fantasy.

This German Socialism, which took its schoolboy task so seriously and solemnly, and extolled its poor stock-in-trade in such mountebank fashion, meanwhile gradually lost its pedantic innocence.

The fight of the German, and especially, of the Prussian bourgeoisie, against feudal aristocracy and absolute monarchy, in other words, the liberal movement, became more earnest.

By this, the long wished-for opportunity was offered to 'True' Socialism of confronting the political movement with the Socialist demands, of hurling the traditional anathemas against liberalism, against representative government, against bourgeois competition, bourgeois freedom of the press, bourgeois legislation, bourgeois liberty and equality, and of preaching to the masses that they had nothing to gain, and everything to lose, by this bourgeois movement. German Socialism forgot, in the nick of time, that the French criticism, whose silly echo it was, presupposed the existence of modern bourgeois society, with its corresponding economic conditions of existence, and the political constitution adapted thereto, the very things whose attainment was the object of the pending struggle in Germany.

To the absolute governments, with their following of parsons, professors, country squires and officials, it served as a welcome scarecrow against the threatening bourgeoisie.

It was a sweet finish after the bitter pills of floggings and bullets with which these same governments, just at that time, dosed the German working-class risings.

While this 'True' Socialism thus served the governments as a weapon for fighting the German bourgeoisie, it, at the same time, directly represented a reactionary interest, the interest of the

German Philistines. In Germany the *petty-bourgeois* class, a relic of the sixteenth century, and since then constantly cropping up again under various forms, is the real social basis of the existing state of things.

To preserve this class is to preserve the existing state of things in Germany. The industrial and political supremacy of the bourgeoisie threatens it with certain destruction; on the one hand, from the concentration of capital; on the other, from the rise of a revolutionary proletariat. 'True' Socialism appeared to kill these two birds with one stone. It spread like an epidemic.

The robe of speculative cobwebs, embroidered with flowers of rhetoric, steeped in the dew of sickly sentiment, this transcendental robe in which the German Socialists wrapped their sorry 'eternal truths', all skin and bone, served to wonderfully increase the sale of their goods amongst such a public. And on its part, German Socialism recognised, more and more, its own calling as the bombastic representative of the petty-bourgeois Philistine.

It proclaimed the German nation to be the model nation, and the German petty Philistine to be the typical man. To every villainous meanness of this model man it gave a hidden, higher, Socialistic interpretation, the exact contrary of its real character. It went to the extreme length of directly opposing the 'brutally destructive' tendency of Communism, and of proclaiming its supreme and impartial contempt of all class struggles. With very few exceptions, all the so-called Socialist and Communist publications that now [1847] circulate in Germany belong to the domain of this foul and enervating literature.

ii. Conservative, or Bourgeois, Socialism

A part of the bourgeoisie is desirous of redressing social grievances, in order to secure the continued existence of bourgeois society.

To this section belong economists, philanthropists, humanitarians, improvers of the condition of the working class, organisers of charity, members of societies for the prevention of cruelty to animals, temperance fanatics, hole-and-corner reformers of every imaginable kind. This form of Socialism has, moreover, been worked out into complete systems.

We may cite Proudhon's *Philosophie de la Misère* as an example of this form.

The Socialistic bourgeois want all the advantages of modern social conditions without the struggles and dangers necessarily resulting therefrom. They desire the existing state of society minus its revolutionary and disintegrating elements. They wish for a bourgeoisie without a proletariat. The bourgeoisie naturally conceives the world in which it is supreme to be the best; and bourgeois Socialism develops this comfortable conception into various more or less complete systems. In requiring the proletariat to carry out such a system, and thereby to march straightway into the social New Jerusalem, it but requires in reality, that the proletariat should remain within the bounds of existing society, but should cast away all its hateful ideas concerning the bourgeoisie.

A second and more practical, but less systematic, form of this Socialism sought to depreciate every revolutionary movement in the eyes of the working class, by showing that no mere political reform, but only a change in the material conditions of existence, in economic relations, could be of any advantage to them. By changes in the material conditions of existence, this form of Socialism, however, by no means understands abolition of the bourgeois relations of production, an abolition that can be effected only by a revolution, but administrative reforms, based on the continued existence of these relations; reforms, therefore, that in no respect affect the relations between capital and labour, but, at the best, lessen the cost, and simplify the administrative work, of bourgeois government.

Bourgeois Socialism attains adequate expression, when, and only when, it becomes a mere figure of speech.

Free trade: for the benefit of the working class. Protective duties: for the benefit of the working class. Prison Reform: for the benefit of the working class. This is the last word and the only seriously meant word of bourgeois Socialism.

It is summed up in the phrase: the bourgeois is a bourgeois – for the benefit of the working class.

iii. Critical-Utopian Socialism and Communism

We do not here refer to that literature which, in every great modern revolution, has always given voice to the demands of the proletariat, such as the writings of Babeuf and others.

The first direct attempts of the proletariat to attain its own ends, made in times of universal excitement, when feudal society was being overthrown, these attempts necessarily failed, owing to the then undeveloped state of the proletariat, as well as to the absence of the economic conditions for its emancipation, conditions that had yet to be produced, and could be produced by the impending bourgeois epoch alone. The revolutionary literature that accompanied these first movements of the proletariat had necessarily a reactionary character. It inculcated universal asceticism and social levelling in its crudest form.

The Socialist and Communist systems properly so called, those of Saint-Simon, Fourier, Owen and others, spring into existence in the early undeveloped period, described above, of the struggle between proletariat and bourgeoisie (see Section 1. Bourgeois and Proletarians).

The founders of these systems see, indeed, the class antagonisms, as well as the action of the decomposing elements, in the prevailing form of society. But the proletariat, as yet in its infancy, offers to them the spectacle of a class without any historical initiative or any independent political movement.

Since the development of class antagonism keeps even pace with the development of industry, the economic situation, as they find it, does not as yet offer to them the material conditions for the emancipation of the proletariat. They therefore search after a new social science, after new social laws, that are to create these conditions.

Historical action is to yield to their personal inventive action, historically created conditions of emancipation to fantastic ones, and the gradual, spontaneous class-organisation of the proletariat to the organisation of society specially contrived by these inventors. Future history resolves itself, in their eyes, into the propaganda and the practical carrying out of their social plans.

In the formation of their plans they are conscious of caring chiefly for the interests of the working class, as being the most suffering class. Only from the point of view of being the most suffering class does the proletariat exist for them.

The undeveloped state of the class struggle, as well as their own surroundings, causes Socialists of this kind to consider themselves far superior to all class antagonisms. They want to improve the condition of every member of society, even that of the most favoured. Hence, they habitually appeal to society at large, without distinction of class; nay, by preference, to the ruling class. For how can people, when once they understand their system, fail to see in it the best possible plan of the best possible state of society?

Hence, they reject all political, and especially all revolutionary, action; they wish to attain their ends by peaceful means, and endeavour, by small experiments, necessarily doomed to failure, and by the force of example, to pave the way for the new social Gospel.

Such fantastic pictures of future society, painted at a time when the proletariat is still in a very undeveloped state and has but a fantastic conception of its own position, correspond with the first instinctive yearnings of that class for a general reconstruction of society.

But these Socialist and Communist publications contain also a critical element. They attack every principle of existing society. Hence they are full of the most valuable materials for the enlightenment of the working class. The practical measures proposed in them – such as the abolition of the distinction between town and country, of the family, of the carrying on of industries for the account of private individuals, and of the wage system, the proclamation of social harmony, the conversion of the functions of the State into a mere superintendence of production, all these proposals point solely to the disappearance of class antagonisms which were, at that time, only just cropping up, and which, in these publications, are recognised in their earliest, indistinct and undefined forms only. These proposals, therefore, are of a purely Utopian character.

The significance of Critical-Utopian Socialism and Communism bears an inverse relation to historical development. In proportion as the modern class struggle develops and takes definite shape, this fantastic standing apart from the contest, these fantastic attacks on it, lose all practical value and all theoretical justification. Therefore, although the originators of these systems were, in many respects, revolutionary, their disciples have, in every case, formed mere reactionary sects. They hold fast by the original views of their masters, in opposition to the progressive historical development of the proletariat. They, therefore, endeavour, and that consistently, to deaden the class struggle and to reconcile the class antagonisms. They still dream of experimental realisation of their social Utopias, of founding isolated '*phalanstères*', of establishing 'Home Colonies', of setting up a 'Little Icaria' – duodecimo editions of the New Jerusalem – and to realise all these castles in the air, they are compelled to appeal to the feelings and purses of the bourgeois. By degrees they sink into the category of the reactionary conservative Socialists depicted above, differing from these only by more systematic pedantry, and by their fanatical and superstitious belief in the miraculous effects of their social science.

They, therefore, violently oppose all political action on the part of the working class; such action, according to them, can only result from blind unbelief in the new Gospel.

The Owenites in England, and the Fourierists in France, respectively, oppose the Chartists and the *Réformistes*.

4. POSITION OF THE COMMUNISTS IN RELATION TO THE VARIOUS EXISTING OPPOSITION PARTIES

Section 2 has made clear the relations of the Communists to the existing working-class parties, such as the Chartists in England and the Agrarian Reformers in America.

The Communists fight for the attainment of the immediate aims, for the enforcement of the momentary interests of the working class; but in the movement of the present, they also represent and take care of the future of that movement. In France the Communists ally themselves with the Social-Democrats, against the conservative and radical bourgeoisie, reserving, however, the right to take up a critical position in regard to phrases and illusions traditionally handed down from the great Revolution.

In Switzerland they support the Radicals, without losing sight of the fact that this party consists of antagonistic elements, partly of Democratic Socialists, in the French sense, partly of radical bourgeois.

In Poland they support the party that insists on an agrarian revolution as the prime condition for national emancipation, that party which fomented the insurrection of Cracow in 1846.

In Germany they fight with the bourgeoisie whenever it acts in a revolutionary way, against the absolute monarchy, the feudal squirearchy, and the petty bourgeoisie.

But they never cease, for a single instant, to instil into the working class the clearest possible recognition of the hostile antagonism between bourgeoisie and proletariat, in order that the German workers may straightway use, as so many weapons against the bourgeoisie, the social and political conditions that the bourgeoisie must necessarily introduce along with its supremacy, and in order that, after the fall of the reactionary classes in Germany, the fight against the bourgeoisie itself may immediately begin.

The Communists turn their attention chiefly to Germany, because that country is on the eve of a bourgeois revolution that is bound to be carried out under more advanced conditions of European civilisation, and with a much more developed proletariat, than that of England was in the seventeenth, and of France in the eighteenth century, and because the bourgeois revolution in Germany will be but the prelude to an immediately following proletarian revolution.

In short, the Communists everywhere support every revolutionary movement against the existing social and political order of things.

In all these movements they bring to the front, as the leading question in each, the property question, no matter what its degree of development at the time.

Finally, they labour everywhere for the union and agreement of the democratic parties of all countries.

The Communists disdain to conceal their views and aims. They openly declare that their ends can be attained only by the forcible overthrow of all existing social conditions. Let the ruling classes tremble at a Communistic revolution. The proletarians have nothing to lose but their chains. They have a world to win.

WORKING MEN OF ALL COUNTRIES, UNITE!

THE CONDITION OF THE WORKING
CLASS IN ENGLAND IN 1844

with a Preface written in 1892

PREFACE
[to the 1892 English edition]

The book, an English translation of which is here republished, was first issued in Germany in 1845. The author, at that time, was young, twenty-four years of age, and his production bears the stamp of his youth with its good and its faulty features, of neither of which he feels ashamed. It was translated into English, in 1885, by an American lady, Mrs F. Kelley Wischnewetzky, and published in the following year in New York. The American edition being as good as exhausted, and having never been extensively circulated on this side of the Atlantic, the present English copyright edition is brought out with the full consent of all parties interested.

For the American edition, a new Preface and an Appendix were written in English by the author. The first had little to do with the book itself; it discussed the American Working-Class Movement of the day, and is, therefore, here omitted as irrelevant, the second – the original preface – is largely made use of in the present introductory remarks.

The state of things described in this book belongs today, in many respects, to the past, as far as England is concerned. Though not expressly stated in our recognised treatises, it is still a law of modern Political Economy that the larger the scale on which Capitalistic Production is carried on, the less can it support the petty devices of swindling and pilfering which characterise its early stages. The pettifogging business tricks of the Polish Jew, the representative in Europe of commerce in its lowest stage, those tricks that serve him so well in his own country, and are generally practised there, he finds to be out of date and out of place when he comes to Hamburg or Berlin; and, again, the commission agent, who hails from Berlin or Hamburg, Jew or Christian, after frequenting the Manchester Exchange for a few months, finds out that, in order to buy cotton yarn or cloth cheap, he, too, had better drop those slightly more refined but still miserable wiles and subterfuges which are considered the acme of cleverness in his native country. The fact is, those tricks do not pay any longer in a large market, where time is money, and where a certain standard of commercial morality is unavoidably developed, purely as a means of saving time and trouble. And it is the same with the relation between the manufacturer and his 'hands'.

The revival of trade, after the crisis of 1847, was the dawn of a new industrial epoch. The repeal of the Corn Laws and the financial reforms consequent thereon gave to English industry and commerce all the elbow-room they had asked for. The discovery of the Californian and Australian gold-fields followed in rapid succession. The colonial markets developed at an increasing rate their capacity for absorbing English manufactured goods. In India millions of hand-weavers were finally crushed out by the Lancashire power-loom. China was more and more being opened up. Above all, the United States – then, commercially speaking, a mere colonial market, but by far the biggest of them all – underwent an economic development astounding even for that rapidly progressive country. And, finally, the new means of communication introduced at the close of the preceding period – railways and ocean steamers – were now worked out on an international scale; they realised actually, what had hitherto existed only potentially, a world-market. This world-market, at first, was composed of a number of chiefly or entirely agricultural countries grouped around one manufacturing centre – England – which consumed the greater part of their surplus raw produce, and supplied them in return with the greater part of their requirements in manufactured articles. No wonder England's industrial progress was colossal and unparalleled, and such that the status of 1844 now appears to us as comparatively primitive and insignificant. And in proportion as this increase took place, in the same proportion did manufacturing industry become apparently moralised. The competition of manufacturer against manufacturer by means of petty thefts upon the workpeople did no longer pay. Trade had outgrown such low means of making money; they were not worth while practising for the manufacturing millionaire, and served merely to keep alive the competition of smaller traders, thankful to pick up a penny wherever they could. Thus the truck system was suppressed, the

Ten Hours' Bill was enacted, and a number of other secondary reforms introduced – much against the spirit of Free Trade and unbridled competition, but quite as much in favour of the giant-capitalist in his competition with his less favoured brother. Moreover, the larger the concern, and with it the number of hands, the greater the loss and inconvenience caused by every conflict between master and men; and thus a new spirit came over the masters, especially the large ones, which taught them to avoid unnecessary squabbles, to acquiesce in the existence and power of Trades' Unions, and finally even to discover in strikes – at opportune times – a powerful means to serve their own ends. The largest manufacturers, formerly the leaders of the war against the working class, were now the foremost to preach peace and harmony. And for a very good reason. The fact is, that all these concessions to justice and philanthropy were nothing else but means to accelerate the concentration of capital in the hands of the few, for whom the niggardly extra extortions of former years had lost all importance and had become actual nuisances; and to crush all the quicker and all the safer their smaller competitors, who could not make both ends meet without such perquisites. Thus the development of production on the basis of the capitalistic system has of itself sufficed – at least in the leading industries, for in the more unimportant branches this is far from being the case – to do away with all those minor grievances which aggravated the workman's fate during its earlier stages. And thus it renders more and more evident the great central fact, that the cause of the miserable condition of the working class is to be sought, not in these minor grievances, but *in the Capitalistic System itself*. The wage-worker sells to the capitalist his labour-power for a certain daily sum. After a few hours' work he has reproduced the value of that sum; but the substance of his contract is, that he has to work another series of hours to complete his working day; and the value he produces during these additional hours of surplus labour is surplus value, which costs the capitalist nothing, but yet goes into his pocket. That is the basis of the system which tends more and more to split up civilised society into a few Rothschilds and Vanderbilts, the owners of all the means of production and sub-sistence, on the one hand, and an immense number of wage-workers, the owners of nothing but their labour-power, on the other. And that this result is caused, not by this or that secondary grievance, but by the system itself – this fact has been brought out in bold relief by the development of Capitalism in England since 1847.

Again, the repeated visitations of cholera, typhus, smallpox, and other epidemics have shown the British bourgeois the urgent necessity of sanitation in his towns and cities, if he wishes to save himself and his family from falling victims to such diseases. Accordingly, the most crying abuses described in this book have either disappeared or have been made less conspicuous. Drainage has been introduced or improved, wide avenues have been opened out athwart many of the worst 'slums' I had to describe. 'Little Ireland' has disappeared, and the 'Seven Dials' are next on the list for sweeping away. But what of that? Whole districts which in 1844 I could describe as almost idyllic, have now, with the growth of the towns, fallen into the same state of dilapidation, discomfort, and misery. Only the pigs and the heaps of refuse are no longer tolerated. The bourgeoisie have made further progress in the art of hiding the distress of the working class. But that, in regard to their dwellings, no substantial improvement has taken place, is amply proved by the Report of the Royal Commission 'on the Housing of the Poor', 1885. And this is the case, too, in other respects. Police regulations have been plentiful as blackberries; but they can only hedge in the distress of the workers, they cannot remove it.

But while England has thus outgrown the juvenile state of capitalist exploitation described by me, other countries have only just attained it. France, Germany, and especially America, are the formidable competitors who, at this moment – as foreseen by me in 1844 – are more and more breaking up England's industrial monopoly. Their manufactures are young as compared with those of England, but increasing at a far more rapid rate than the latter; and, curious enough, they have at this moment arrived at about the same phase of development as English manufacture in 1844. With regard to America, the parallel is indeed most striking. True, the external surroundings in which the working class is placed in America are very different, but the same economical laws are at work, and the results, if not identical in every respect, must still be of the same order. Hence we find in America the same struggles for a shorter working day, for a legal limitation of the working-time, especially of women and children in factories; we find the truck-system in full blossom, and the cottage-system, in rural districts, made use of by the 'bosses' as a means of domination over the workers. When I received, in 1886, the American papers with accounts of the great strike of 12,000 Pennsylvanian coal-miners in the Connellsville district, I seemed but to read my own description of the North of England colliers' strike of 1844. The same cheating of the workpeople by false measure; the same truck-system; the same attempt to break the miners' resistance by the capitalists' last, but crushing, resource – the eviction of the men out of their dwellings, the cottages owned by the companies.

I have not attempted, in this translation, to bring the book up to date, or to point out in detail all the changes that have taken place since 1844. And for two reasons: Firstly, to do this properly, the size of the book must be about doubled; and, secondly, the first volume of *Das Kapital*, by Karl Marx, an English translation of which is before the public, contains a very ample description of the state of the British working class, as it was about 1865, that is to say, at the time when British industrial prosperity reached its culminating point. I should, then, have been obliged again to go over the ground already covered by Marx's celebrated work.

It will be hardly necessary to point out that the general theoretical standpoint of this book – philosophical, economical, political – does not exactly coincide with my standpoint of today. Modern international Socialism, since fully developed as a science, chiefly and almost exclusively through the efforts of Marx, did not as yet exist in 1844. My book represents one of the phases of its embryonic development; and as the human embryo, in its early stages, still reproduces the gill-arches of our fish-ancestors, so this book exhibits everywhere the traces of the descent of modern Socialism from one of its ancestors – German philosophy. Thus great stress is laid on the dictum that Communism is not a mere party doctrine of the working class, but a theory compassing the emancipation of society at large, including the capitalist class, from its present narrow conditions. This is true enough in the abstract, but absolutely useless, and sometimes worse, in practice. So long as the wealthy classes not only do not feel the want of any emancipation, but strenuously oppose the self-emancipation of the working class, so long the social revolution will have to be prepared and fought out by the working class alone. The French bourgeois of 1789, too, declared the emancipation of the bourgeoisie to be the emancipation of the whole human race; but the nobility and clergy would not see it; the proposition – though for the time being, with respect to feudalism, an abstract historical truth – soon became a mere sentimentalism, and disappeared from view altogether in the fire of the revolutionary struggle. And today, the very people who, from the 'impartiality' of their superior standpoint, preach to the workers a Socialism soaring high above their class interests and class struggles, and tending to reconcile in a higher humanity the interests of both the contending classes – these people are either neophytes, who have still to learn a great deal, or they are the worst enemies of the workers – wolves in sheeps' clothing.

The recurring period of the great industrial crisis is stated in the text as five years. This was the period apparently indicated by the course of events from 1825 to 1842. But the industrial history from 1842 to 1868 has shown that the real period is one of ten years; that the intermediate revulsions were secondary, and tended more and more to disappear. Since 1868 the state of things has changed again, of which more anon.

I have taken care not to strike out of the text the many prophecies, amongst others that of an imminent social revolution in England, which my youthful ardour induced me to venture upon. The wonder is, not that a good many of them proved wrong, but that so many of them have proved right, and that the critical state of English trade, to be brought on by Continental and especially American competition, which I then foresaw – though in too short a period – has now actually come to pass. In this respect I can, and am bound to, bring the book up to date, by placing here an article which I published in the *London Commonweal* of March 1, 1885, under the heading: 'England in 1845 and in 1885'. It gives at the same time a short outline of the history of the English working class during these forty years, and is as follows:

Forty years ago England stood face to face with a crisis, solvable to all appearances by force only. The immense and rapid development of manufactures had outstripped the extension of foreign markets and the increase of demand. Every ten years the march of industry was violently interrupted by a general commercial crash, followed, after a long period of chronic depression, by a few short years of prosperity, and always ending in feverish over-production and consequent renewed collapse. The capitalist class clamoured for Free Trade in corn, and threatened to enforce it by sending the starving population of the towns back to the country districts whence they came, to invade them, as John Bright said, not as paupers begging for bread, but as an army quartered upon the enemy. The working masses of the towns demanded their share of political power – the People's Charter; they were supported by the majority of the small trading class, and the only difference between the two was whether the Charter should be carried by physical or by moral force. Then came the commercial crash of 1847 and the Irish famine, and with both the prospect of revolution.

The French Revolution of 1848 saved the English middle class. The Socialistic pronunciamentos of the victorious French work-men frightened the small middle class of England and disorgan-ised the narrower, but more matter-of-fact movement of the English working class. At the very moment when Chartism was bound to assert itself in its full strength, it collapsed internally, before even it collapsed externally on the 10th of April, 1848. The action of the working class was thrust into the background. The capitalist class triumphed along the whole line.

The Reform Bill of 1831 had been the victory of the whole capitalist class over the landed aristocracy. The repeal of the Corn Laws was the victory of the manufacturing capitalist not only over the landed aristocracy, but over those sections of capitalists, too, whose interests were more or less bound up with the landed interest – bankers, stock-jobbers, fund-holders, etc. Free Trade meant the re-adjustment of the whole home and foreign, com-mercial and financial policy of England in accordance with the interests of the manufacturing capitalists – the class which now represented the nation. And they set about this task with a will. Every obstacle to industrial production was mercilessly removed. The tariff and the whole system of taxation were revolutionised. Everything was made subordinate to one end, but that end of the utmost importance to the manufacturing capitalist: the cheapening of all raw produce, and especially of the means of living of the working class; the reduction of the cost of raw material, and the keeping down – if not as yet the *bringing down* – of wages. England was to become the 'workshop of the world'; all other countries were to become for England what Ireland already was – markets for her manufactured goods, supplying her in return with raw materials and food. England the great manufacturing centre of an agricultural world, with an ever-increasing number of corn- and cotton-growing Irelands revolving around her, the industrial sun. What a glorious prospect!

The manufacturing capitalists set about the realisation of this their great object with that strong common sense and that contempt for traditional principles which has ever distinguished them from their more narrow-minded compeers on the Continent. Chartism was dying out. The revival of commercial prosperity, natural after the revulsion of 1847 had spent itself, was put down altogether to the credit of Free Trade. Both these circumstances had turned the English working class, politically, into the tail of the 'great Liberal party', the party led by the manufacturers. This advantage, once gained, had to be perpetuated. And the manufacturing capitalists, from the Chartist opposition, not to Free Trade, but to the transformation of Free Trade into the one vital national question, had learnt, and were learning more and more, that the middle class can never obtain full social and political power over the nation except by the help of the working class. Thus a gradual change came over the relations between both classes. The Factory Acts, once the bugbear of all manufacturers, were not only willingly submitted to, but their expansion into acts regulating almost all trades, was tolerated. Trades' Unions, hitherto considered inventions of the devil himself, were now petted and patronised as perfectly legitimate institutions, and as useful means of spreading sound economical doctrines amongst the workers. Even strikes, than which nothing had been more nefarious up to 1848, were now gradually found out to be occasionally very useful, especially when provoked by the masters themselves, at their own time. Of the legal enactments, placing the workman at a lower level or at a disadvantage with regard to the master, at least the most revolting were repealed. And, practically, that horrid 'People's Charter' actually became the political programme of the very manufacturers who had opposed it to the last.

'The Abolition of the Property Qualification' and 'Vote by Ballot' are now the law of the land. The Reform Acts of 1867 and 1884 make a near approach to 'universal suffrage', at least such as it now exists in Germany; the Redistribution Bill now before Parliament creates 'equal electoral districts' – on the whole not more unequal than those of Germany; 'payment of members', and shorter, if not actually 'annual Parliaments', are visibly looming in the distance – and yet there are people who say that Chartism is dead.

The Revolution of 1848, not less than many of its predecessors, has had strange bedfellows and successors. The very people who put it down have become, as Karl Marx used to say, its testamentary executors. Louis Napoleon had to create an independent and united Italy, Bismarck had to revolutionise Germany and to restore Hungarian independence, and the English manufacturers had to enact the People's Charter.

For England, the effects of this domination of the manufacturing capitalists were at first startling. Trade revived and extended to a degree unheard of even in this cradle of modern industry; the previous astounding creations of steam and machinery dwindled into nothing compared with the immense mass of productions of the twenty years from 1850 to 1870, with the overwhelming figures of exports and imports, of wealth accumulated in the hands of capitalists and of human working power concentrated in the large towns. The progress was indeed interrupted, as before, by a crisis every ten years, in 1857 as well as in 1866; but these revulsions were now considered as natural, inevitable events, which must be fatalistically submitted to, and which always set themselves right in the end.

And the condition of the working class during this period? There was temporary improvement even for the great mass. But this improvement always was reduced to the old level by the influx of the great body of the unemployed reserve, by the constant superseding of bands by new machinery, by the immigration of the agricultural population, now, too, more and more superseded by machines.

A permanent improvement can be recognised for two 'protected' sections only of the working class. Firstly, the factory hands. The fixing by Act of Parliament of their working day within relatively rational limits has restored their physical constitution and endowed them with a moral superiority, enhanced by their local concentration. They are undoubtedly better off than before 1848. The best proof is that, out of ten strikes they make, nine are provoked by the manufacturers in their own interests, as the only means of securing a reduced production. You can never get the masters to agree to work 'short time', let manufactured goods be ever so unsaleable; but get the workpeople to strike, and the masters shut their factories to a man.

Secondly, the great Trades' Unions. They are the organisations of those trades in which the labour of *grown-up men* predominates, or is alone applicable. Here the competition neither of women and children nor of machinery has so far weakened their organised strength. The engineers, the carpenters and joiners, the brick-layers, are each of them a power, to that extent that, as in the case of the bricklayers and bricklayers' labourers, they can even success-fully resist the introduction of machinery. That their condition has remarkably improved since 1848 there can be no doubt, and the best proof of this is in the fact, that for more than fifteen years not only have their employers been with them, but they with their employers, upon exceedingly good terms. They form an aristo-cracy among the working class; they have succeeded in enforcing for themselves a relatively comfortable position, and they accept it as final. They are the model working-men of Messrs Leone, Levi & Giffen, and they are very nice people indeed nowadays to deal with, for any sensible capitalist in particular and for the whole capitalist class in general.

But as to the great mass of working-people, the state of misery and insecurity in which they live now is as low as ever, if not lower. The East End of London is an ever-spreading pool of stag-nant misery and desolation, of starvation when out of work, and degradation, physical and moral, when in work. And so in all other large towns − abstraction made of the privileged minority of the workers; and so in the smaller towns and in the agricultural districts. The law which reduces the *value* of labour-power to the value of the necessary means of subsistence, and the other law which reduces its *average price*, as a rule, to the minimum of those means of subsistence, these laws act upon them with the irresistible force of an automatic engine, which crushes them between its wheels.

This, then, was the position created by the Free Trade policy of 1847, and by twenty years of the rule of the manufacturing capitalists. But then, a change came. The crash of 1866 was, indeed, followed by a slight and short revival about 1873; but that did not last. We did not, indeed, pass through the full crisis at the time it was due, in 1877 or 1878; but we have had, ever since 1876, a chronic state of stagnation in all dominant branches of industry. Neither will the full crash come; nor will the period of longed-for prosperity to which we used to be entitled before and after it. A dull depression, a chronic glut of all markets for all trades, that is what we have been living in for nearly ten years. How is this?

The Free Trade theory was based upon one assumption: that England was to be the one great manufacturing centre of an agricultural world. And the actual fact is that this assumption has turned out to be a pure delusion. The conditions of modern industry, steam-power and machinery, can be established wherever there is fuel, especially coals. And other countries beside England – France, Belgium, Germany, America, even Russia – have coals. And the people over there did not see the advantage of being turned into Irish pauper farmers merely for the greater wealth and glory of English capitalists. They set resolutely about manufacturing, not only for themselves, but for the rest of the world; and the consequence is, that the manufacturing monopoly enjoyed by England for nearly a century is irretrievably broken up.

But the manufacturing monopoly of England is the pivot of the present social system of England. Even while that monopoly lasted, the markets could not keep pace with the increasing productivity of English manufacturers; the decennial crises were the consequence. And new markets are getting scarcer every day, so much so that even the negroes of the Congo are now to be forced into the civilisation attendant upon Manchester calicos, Staffordshire pottery, and Birmingham hardware. How will it be when Continental, and especially American, goods flow in in ever-increasing quantities – when the predominating share, still held by British manufacturers, will become reduced from year to year? Answer, Free Trade, thou universal panacea.

I am not the first to point this out. Already in 1883, at the Southport meeting of the British Association, Mr Inglis Palgrave, the President of the Economic section, stated plainly that 'the days of great trade profits in England were over, and there was a pause in the progress of several great branches of industrial labour. *The country might almost be said to be entering the non-progressive state.*'

But what is to be the consequence? Capitalist production *cannot* stop. It must go on increasing and expanding, or it must die. Even now, the mere reduction of England's lion's share in the supply of the world's markets means stagnation, distress, excess of capital here, excess of unemployed workpeople there. What will it be when the increase of yearly production is brought to a complete stop?

Here is the vulnerable place, the heel of Achilles, for capitalistic production. Its very basis is the necessity of constant expansion, and this constant expansion now becomes impossible. It ends in a deadlock. Every year England is brought nearer face to face with the question: either the country must go to pieces, or capitalist production must. Which is it to be?

And the working class? If even under the unparalleled commercial and industrial expansion, from 1848 to 1866, they have had to undergo such misery; if even then the great bulk of them experienced at best but a temporary improvement of their condition, while only a small, privileged, 'protected' minority was permanently benefited, what will it be when this dazzling period is brought finally to a close; when the present dreary stagnation shall not only become intensified, but this, its intensified condition, shall become the permanent and normal state of English trade?

The truth is this: during the period of England's industrial monopoly the English working class have, to a certain extent, shared in the benefits of the monopoly. These benefits were very unequally parcelled out amongst them; the privileged minority pocketed most, but even the great mass had, at least, a temporary share now and then. And that is the reason why, since the dying-out of Owenism, there has been no Socialism in England. With the breakdown of that monopoly, the English working class will lose that privileged position; it will find itself generally – the privileged and leading minority not excepted – on a level with its fellow-workers abroad. And that is the reason why there will be Socialism again in England.

To this statement of the case, as that case appeared to me in 1885, I have but little to add. Needless to say that today there is indeed 'Socialism again in England', and plenty of it – Socialism of all shades: Socialism conscious and unconscious, Socialism prosaic and poetic, Socialism of the working class and of the middle class, for, verily, that abomination of abominations, Socialism, has not only become respectable, but has actually donned evening dress and lounges lazily on drawing-room *causeuses*. That shows the incurable fickleness of that terrible despot of 'society', middle class public opinion, and once more justifies the contempt in which we Socialists of a past generation always held that public opinion. At the same time, we have no reason to grumble at the symptom itself.

What I consider far more important than this momentary fashion among bourgeois circles of affecting a mild dilution of Socialism, and even more than the actual progress Socialism has made in England generally – that is the revival of the East End of London. That immense haunt of misery is no longer the stagnant pool it was six years ago. It has shaken off its torpid despair, has returned to life, and has become the home of what is called the 'New Unionism'; that is to say, of the organisation of the great mass of 'unskilled' workers. This organisation may to a great extent adopt the form of the old Unions of 'skilled' workers, but it is essentially different in character. The old Unions preserve the traditions of the time when they were founded, and look upon the wages system as a once for all established, final fact, which they at best can modify in the interest of their members. The new Unions were founded at a time when the faith in the eternity of the wages system was severely shaken; their founders and promoters were Socialists either consciously or by feeling; the masses, whose adhesion gave them strength, were rough, neglected, looked down upon by the working-class aristocracy; but they had this immense advantage, that *their minds were virgin soil*, entirely free from the inherited 'respectable' bourgeois prejudices which hampered the brains of the better situated 'old' Unionists. And thus we see now these new Unions taking the lead of the working-class movement generally, and more and more taking in tow the rich and proud 'old' Unions.

Undoubtedly, the East Enders have committed colossal blunders; so have their predecessors, and so do the doctrinaire Socialists who pooh-pooh them. A large class, like a great nation, never learns better or quicker than by undergoing the consequences of its own mistakes. And for all the faults committed in past, present, and future, the revival of the East End of London remains one of the greatest and most fruitful facts of this *fin de siècle*, and glad and proud I am to have lived to see it.

F. ENGELS
January 11th, 1892

Introduction

The history of the proletariat in England begins with the second half of the last century, with the invention of the steam-engine and of machinery for working cotton. These inventions gave rise, as is well known, to an industrial revolution, a revolution which altered the whole civil society; one, the historical importance of which is only now beginning to be recognised. England is the classic soil of this transformation, which was all the mightier, the more silently it proceeded; and England is, therefore, the classic land of its chief product also, the proletariat. Only in England can the proletariat be studied in all its relations and from all sides.

We have not, here and now, to deal with the history of this revolution, nor with its vast importance for the present and the future. Such a delineation must be reserved for a future, more comprehensive work. For the moment, we must limit ourselves to the little that is necessary for understanding the facts that follow, for comprehending the present state of the English proletariat.

Before the introduction of machinery, the spinning and weaving of raw materials was carried on in the working-man's home. Wife and daughter spun the yarn that the father wove or that they sold, if he did not work it up himself. These weaver families lived in the country in the neighbourhood of the towns, and could get on fairly well with their wages, because the home market was almost the only one, and the crushing power of competition that came later, with the conquest of foreign markets and the extension of trade, did not yet press upon wages. There was, further, a constant increase in the demand for the home market, keeping pace with the slow increase in population and employing all the workers; and there was also the impossibility of vigorous competition of the workers among themselves, consequent upon the rural dispersion of their homes. So it was that the weaver was usually in a position to lay by something, and rent a little piece of land, that he cultivated in his leisure hours, of which he had as many as he chose to take, since he could weave whenever and as long as he pleased. True, he was a bad farmer and managed his land inefficiently, often obtaining but poor crops; nevertheless, he was no proletarian, he had a stake in the country, he was permanently settled, and stood one step higher in society than the English workman of today.

So the workers vegetated throughout a passably comfortable existence, leading a righteous and peaceful life in all piety and probity; and their material position was far better than that of their successors. They did not need to overwork; they did no more than they chose to do, and yet earned what they needed. They had leisure for healthful work in garden or field, work which, in itself, was recreation for them, and they could take part besides in the recreations and games of their neighbours, and all these games – bowling, cricket, football, etc., contributed to their physical health and vigour. They were, for the most part, strong, well-built people, in whose physique little or no difference from that of their peasant neighbours was discoverable. Their children grew up in the fresh country air, and, if they could help their parents at work, it was only occasionally; while of eight or twelve hours work for them there was no question.

What the moral and intellectual character of this class was may be guessed. Shut off from the towns, which they never entered, their yarn and woven stuff being delivered to travelling agents for payment of wages – so shut off that old people who lived quite in the neighbourhood of the town never went thither until they were robbed of their trade by the introduction of machinery and obliged to look about them in the towns for work – the weavers stood upon the moral and intellectual plane of the yeomen with whom they were usually immediately connected through their little holdings. They regarded their squire, the greatest landholder of the region, as their natural superior; they asked advice of him, laid their small disputes before him for settlement, and gave him all honour, as this patriarchal relation involved. They were 'respectable' people, good husbands and fathers, led moral lives because they had no temptation to be immoral, there being no groggeries or low houses in their vicinity, and because the host, at whose inn they now and then quenched their thirst, was also a respectable man, usually a large tenant farmer who took pride in his good order, good beer, and early hours. They had their children the whole day at home, and brought them up in obedience and the fear of God; the patriarchal relationship remained undisturbed so long as the children were unmarried. The young people grew up in idyllic simplicity and intimacy with their playmates until they married; and even though sexual intercourse before marriage almost unfailingly took place, this happened only when the moral obligation of marriage was recognised on both sides, and a subsequent wedding made everything good. In short, the English industrial workers of those days lived and thought after the fashion still to be found here and there in Germany, in retirement and seclusion, without mental activity and without violent fluctuations in their position in life. They could rarely read and far more rarely write; went regularly to church, never talked politics, never conspired, never thought, delighted in physical exercise, listened with inherited reverence when the Bible was read, and were, in their unquestioning humility, exceedingly well-disposed towards the 'superior' classes. But intellectually, they were dead; lived only for their petty, private interest, for their looms and gardens, and knew nothing of the mighty movement which, beyond their horizon, was sweeping through mankind. They were comfortable in their silent vegetation, and but for the industrial revolution they would never have emerged from this existence, which, cosily romantic as it was, was nevertheless not worthy of human beings. In truth, they were not human beings; they were merely toiling machines in the service of the few aristocrats who had guided history down to that time. The industrial revolution has simply carried this out to its logical end by making the workers machines pure and simple, taking from them the last trace of independent activity, and so forcing them to think and demand a position worthy of men. As in France politics, so in England manufacture, and the movement of civil society in general, drew into the whirl of history the last classes which had remained sunk in apathetic indifference to the universal interests of mankind.

The first invention which gave rise to a radical change in the state of the English workers was the jenny, invented in the year 1764 by a weaver, James Hargreaves, of Standhill, near Blackburn, in North Lancashire. This machine was the rough beginning of the later invented mule, and was moved by hand. Instead of one spindle like the ordinary spinning-wheel, it carried sixteen or eighteen manipulated by a single workman. This invention made it possible to deliver more yarn than heretofore. Whereas, though one weaver had employed three spinners, there had never been enough yarn, and the weaver had often been obliged to wait for it, there was now more yarn to be had than could be woven by the available workers. The demand for woven goods, already increasing, rose yet more in consequence of the cheapness of these goods, which cheapness, in turn, was the outcome of the diminished cost of producing the yarn. More weavers were needed, and weavers' wages rose. Now that the weaver could earn more at his loom, he gradually abandoned his farming, and gave his whole time to weaving. At that time a family of four grown persons and two children (who were set to spooling) could earn, with eight hours' daily work, four pounds sterling in a week, and often more if trade was good and work pressed. It happened often enough that a single weaver earned two pounds a week at his loom. By degrees the class of farming weavers wholly disappeared, and was merged in the newly arising class of weavers who lived wholly upon wages, had no property whatever, not even the pretended property of a holding, and so became working-men, proletarians. Moreover, the old relation between spinner and weaver was destroyed. Hitherto, so far as this had been possible, yarn had been spun and woven under one roof. Now that the jenny as well as the loom required a strong hand, men began to spin, and whole families lived by spinning, while others laid the antiquated, superseded spinning-wheel aside; and, if they had not means of purchasing a jenny, were forced to live upon the wages of the father alone. Thus began with spinning and weaving that division of labour which has since been so infinitely perfected.

While the industrial proletariat was thus developing with the first still very imperfect machine, the same machine gave rise to the agricultural proletariat. There had, hitherto, been a vast number of small landowners, yeomen, who had vegetated in the same unthinking quiet as their neighbours, the farming weavers. They cultivated their scraps of land quite after the ancient and inefficient fashion of their ancestors, and opposed every change with the obstinacy peculiar to such creatures of habit, after remaining stationary from generation to generation. Among them were many smallholders also, not tenants in the present sense of the word, but people who had their land handed down from their fathers, either by hereditary lease, or by force of ancient custom, and had hitherto held it as securely as if it had actually been their own property. When the industrial workers withdrew from agriculture, a great number of smallholdings fell idle, and upon these the new class of large tenants established themselves, tenants-at-will, holding fifty, one hundred, two hundred or more acres, liable to be turned out at the end of the year, but able by improved tillage and larger farming to increase the yield of the land. They could sell their produce more cheaply than the yeomen, for whom nothing remained when his farm no longer supported him but to sell it, procure a jenny or a loom, or take service as an agricultural labourer in the employ of a large farmer. His inherited slowness and the inefficient methods of cultivation bequeathed by his ancestors, and above which he could not rise, left him no alternative when forced to compete with men who managed their holdings on sounder principles and with all the advantages bestowed by farming on a large scale and the investment of capital for the improvement of the soil.

Meanwhile, the industrial movement did not stop here. Single capitalists began to set up spinning jennies in great buildings and to use water-power for driving them, so placing themselves in a position to diminish the number of workers, and sell their yarn more cheaply than single spinners could do who moved their own machines by hand. There were constant improvements in the jenny, so that machines continually became antiquated, and must be altered or even laid aside; and though the capitalists could hold out by the application of water-power even with the old machinery, for the single spinner this was impossible. And the factory system, the beginning of which was thus made, received a fresh extension in 1767, through the spinning throstle invented by Richard Arkwright, a barber, in Preston, in North Lancashire. After the steam-engine, this is the most important mechanical invention of the eighteenth century. It was calculated from the beginning for mechanical motive power, and was based upon wholly new principles. By the combination of the peculiarities of the jenny and throstle, Samuel Crompton, of Firwood, Lancashire, contrived the mule in 1785, and as Arkwright invented the carding engine, and preparatory ('slubbing and roving') frames about the same time, the factory system became the prevailing one for the spinning of cotton. By means of trifling modifications these machines were gradually adapted to the spinning of flax, and so to the superseding of hand-work here, too. But even then, the end was not yet. In the closing years of the last century, Dr Cartwright, a country parson, had invented the power-loom, and about 1804 had so far perfected it, that it could successfully compete with the hand-weaver; and all this machinery was made doubly important by James Watt's steam-engine, invented in 1764, and used for supplying motive power for spinning since 1785.

With these inventions, since improved from year to year, the victory of machine-work over hand-work in the chief branches of English industry was won; and the history of the latter from that time forward simply relates how the hand-workers have been driven by machinery from one position after another. The consequences of this were, on the one hand, a rapid fall in price of all manufactured commodities, prosperity of commerce and manufacture, the conquest of nearly all the unprotected foreign markets, the sudden multiplication of capital and national wealth; on the other hand, a still more rapid multiplication of the proletariat, the destruction of all property-holding and of all security of employment for the working class, demoralisation, political excitement, and all those facts so highly repugnant to Englishmen in comfortable circumstances, which we shall have to consider in the following pages. Having already seen what a transformation in the social condition of the lower classes a single such clumsy machine as the jenny had wrought, there is no cause for surprise as to that which a complete and interdependent system of finely adjusted machinery has brought about, machinery which receives raw material and turns out woven goods.

Meanwhile, let us trace the development of English manufacture[1] somewhat more minutely, beginning with the cotton industry. In the years 1771–1775, there were annually imported into England rather less than 5,000,000 pounds of raw cotton; in the year 1841 there were imported 528,000,000 pounds, and the import for 1844 will reach at least 600,000,000 pounds. In 1834 England exported 556,000,000 yards of woven cotton goods, 76,500,000 pounds of cotton yarn, and cotton hosiery of the value of £1,200,000. In the same year over 8,000,000 mule spindles were at work, 110,000 power- and 250,000 hand-looms, throstle spindles not included, in the service of the cotton industry; and, according to MacCulloch's reckoning, nearly a million and a half human beings were supported by this branch, of whom but 220,000 worked in the mills; the power used in these mills was steam, equivalent to 33,000 horse-power, and water, equivalent to 11,000 horse-power. At present these figures are far from adequate, and it may be safely assumed that, in the year 1845, the power and number of the machines and the number of the workers is greater by one-half than it was in 1834. The chief centre of this industry is Lancashire, where it originated; it has thoroughly revolutionised this county, converting it from an obscure, ill-cultivated swamp into a busy, lively region, multiplying its population tenfold in eighty years, and causing giant cities such as Liverpool and Manchester, containing together 700,000 inhabitants, and their neighbouring towns, Bolton with 60,000, Rochdale with 75,000, Oldham with 50,000, Preston with 60,000, Ashton and Stalybridge with 40,000, and a whole list of other manufacturing towns, to spring up as if by a magic touch. The history of South Lancashire contains some of the greatest marvels of modern times, yet no one ever mentions them, and all these miracles are the product of the cotton industry. Glasgow, too, the centre for the cotton district of Scotland, for Lanarkshire and Renfrewshire, has increased in population from 30,000 to 300,000 since the introduction of the industry. The hosiery manufacture of Nottingham and Derby also received one fresh impulse from the lower price of yarn, and a second one from an improvement of the stocking loom, by means of which two stockings could be woven at once. The manufacture of lace, too, became an important branch of industry after the invention of the lace machine in 1777; soon after that date Lindley invented the point-net machine, and in 1809 Heathcote invented the bobbin-net machine, in consequence of which the production of lace was greatly simplified, and the demand increased proportionately in consequence of the diminished cost, so that now, at least 200,000 persons are supported by this industry. Its chief centres are Nottingham, Leicester, and the West of England, Wiltshire, Devonshire, etc. A corresponding extension has taken place in the branches dependent upon the cotton industry, in dyeing, bleaching, and printing. Bleaching by the application of chlorine in place of the oxygen of the atmosphere; dyeing and printing by the rapid development of chemistry, and printing by a series of most brilliant mechanical inventions, a yet greater advance which, with the extension of those branches caused by the growth of the cotton industry, raised them to a previously unknown degree of prosperity.

The same activity manifested itself in the manufacture of wool. This had hitherto been the leading department of English industry, but the quantities formerly produced are as nothing in comparison with that which is now manufactured. In 1782 the whole wool crop of the preceding three years lay unused for want of workers, and would have continued so to lie if the newly invented machinery had not come to its assistance and spun it. The adaptation of this machinery to the spinning of wool was most successfully accomplished. Then began the same sudden development in the wool district, which we have already seen in the cotton districts. In 1738 there were 75,000 pieces of woollen cloth produced in the West Riding of Yorkshire; in 1817 there were 490,000 pieces, and so rapid was the extension of the industry that in 1834, 450,000 more pieces were produced than in 1825. In 1801, 101,000,000 pounds of wool (7,000,000 pounds of it imported) were worked up; in 1835, 180,000,000 pounds were worked up, of which 42,000,000 pounds were imported. The principal centre of this industry is the West Riding of Yorkshire, where, especially at Bradford, long English wool is converted into worsted yarns, etc.; while in the other cities, Leeds, Halifax, Huddersfield, etc., short wool is converted into hard-spun yarn and cloth. Then come the adjacent part of Lancashire, the region of Rochdale, where in addition to the cotton industry much flannel is produced, and the West of England, which supplies the finest cloths. Here also the growth of population is worthy of observation:

	1801	1831
Bradford	29,000	77,000
Halifax	68,000	110,000
Huddersfield	15,000	34,000
Leeds	53,000	123,000
The whole West Riding	564,000	980,000

A population which, since 1831, must have increased at least 20 to 25 per cent. further. In 1835 the spinning of wool employed in the United Kingdom 1,313 mills, with 71,300 workers, these last being but a small portion of the multitude who are supported directly or indirectly by the manufacture of wool, and excluding nearly all weavers.

Progress in the linen trade developed later, because the nature of the raw material made the application of spinning machinery very difficult. Attempts had been made in the last years of the last century in Scotland, but the Frenchman, Girard, who introduced flax spinning in 1810, was the first who succeeded practically, and even Girard's machines first attained on British soil the importance they deserved by means of improvements which they underwent in England, and of their universal application in Leeds, Dundee, and Belfast. From this time the British linen trade rapidly extended. In 1814, 3,000 tons of flax were imported; in 1833, nearly 19,000 tons of flax and 3,400 tons of hemp. The export of Irish linen to Great Britain rose from 32,000,000 yards in 1800 to 53,000,000 in 1825, of which a large part was re-exported. The export of English and Scotch woven linen goods rose from 24,000,000 yards in 1820 to 51,000,000 yards in 1833. The number of flax-spinning establishments in 1835 was 347, employing 33,000 workers, of which one-half were in the South of Scotland, more than 60 in the West Riding of Yorkshire, Leeds, and its environs, 25 in Belfast, Ireland, and the rest in Dorset and Lancashire. Weaving is carried on in the South of Scotland, here and there in England, but principally in Ireland.

With like success did the English turn their attention to the manufacture of silk. Raw material was imported from Southern Europe and Asia ready spun, and the chief labour lay in the twisting of fine threads. Until 1824 the heavy import duty, four shillings per pound on raw material, greatly retarded the development of the English silk industry, while only the markets of England and the colonies were protected for it. In that year the duty was reduced to one penny, and the number of mills at once largely increased. In a single year the number of throwing spindles rose from 780,000 to 1,180,000; and, although the commercial crisis of 1825 crippled this branch of industry for the moment, yet in 1827 more was produced than ever, the mechanical skill and experience of the English having secured their twisting machinery the supremacy over the awkward devices of their competitors. In 1835 the British Empire possessed 263 twisting mills, employing 30,000 workers, located chiefly in Cheshire, in Macclesfield,

Congleton, and the surrounding districts, and in Manchester and Somersetshire. Besides these, there are numerous mills for working up waste, from which a peculiar article known as spun silk is manufactured, with which the English supply even the Paris and Lyons weavers. The weaving of the silk so twisted and spun is carried on in Paisley and elsewhere in Scotland, and in Spitalfields, London, but also in Manchester and elsewhere. Nor is the gigantic advance achieved in English manufacture since 1760 restricted to the production of clothing materials. The impulse, once given, was communicated to all branches of industrial activity, and a multitude of inventions wholly unrelated to those here cited, received double importance from the fact that they were made in the midst of the universal movement. But as soon as the immeasurable importance of mechanical power was practically demonstrated, every energy was concentrated in the effort to exploit this power in all directions, and to exploit it in the interest of individual inventors and manufacturers; and the demand for machinery, fuel, and materials called a mass of workers and a number of trades into redoubled activity. The steam-engine first gave importance to the broad coal-fields of England; the production of machinery began now for the first time, and with it arose a new interest in the iron mines which supplied raw material for it. The increased consumption of wool stimulated English sheep breeding, and the growing importation of wool, flax, and silk called forth an extension of the British ocean carrying trade. Greatest of all was the growth of production of iron. The rich iron deposits of the English hills had hitherto been little developed; iron had always been smelted by means of charcoal, which became gradually more expensive as agriculture improved and forests were cut away. The beginning of the use of coke in iron smelting had been made in the last century, and in 1780 a new method was invented of converting into available wrought-iron coke-smelted iron, which up to that time had been convertible into cast-iron only. This process, known as 'puddling', consists in withdrawing the carbon which had mixed with the iron during the process of smelting, and opened a wholly new field for the production of English iron. Smelting furnaces were built fifty times larger than before, the process of smelting was simplified by the introduction of hot blasts, and iron could thus be produced so cheaply that a multitude of objects which had before been made of stone or wood were now made of iron.

In 1788, Thomas Paine, the famous democrat, built in Yorkshire the first iron bridge, which was followed by a great number of others, so that now nearly all bridges, especially for railroad traffic, are built of cast-iron, while in London itself a bridge across the Thames, the Southwark bridge, has been built of this material. Iron pillars, supports for machinery, etc., are universally used, and since the introduction of gas-lighting and railroads, new outlets for English iron products are opened. Nails and screws gradually came to be made by machinery. Huntsman, a Sheffielder, discovered in 1790 a method for casting steel, by which much labour was saved, and the production of wholly new cheap goods rendered practicable; and through the greater purity of the material placed at its disposal, and the more perfect tools, new machinery and minute division of labour, the metal trade of England now first attained importance. The population of Birmingham grew from 73,000 in 1801 to 200,000 in 1844; that of Sheffield from 46,000 in 1801 to 110,000 in 1844, and the consumption of coal in the latter city alone reached in 1836, 515,000 tons. In 1805 there were exported 4,300 tons of iron products and 4,600 tons of pig-iron; in 1834, 16,200 tons of iron products and 107,000 tons of pig-iron, while the whole iron product reaching in 1740 but 17,000 tons, had risen in 1834 to nearly 700,000 tons. The smelting of pig-iron alone consumes yearly more than 3,000,000 tons of coal, and the importance which coal mining has attained in the course of the last 60 years can scarcely be conceived. All the English and Scotch deposits are now worked, and the mines of Northumberland and Durham alone yield annually more than 5,000,000 tons for shipping, and employ from 40 to 50,000 men. According to the *Durham Chronicle*, there were worked in these two counties: in 1753, 14 mines; in 1800, 40 mines; in 1836, 76 mines; in 1843, 130 mines. Moreover, all mines are now much more energetically worked than formerly. A similarly increased activity was applied to the working of tin, copper, and lead, and alongside of the extension of glass manufacture arose a new branch of industry in the production of pottery, rendered important by the efforts of Josiah Wedgewood, about 1763. This inventor placed the whole manufacture of stoneware on a scientific basis, introduced better taste, and founded the potteries of North Staffordshire, a district of eight English miles square, which, formerly a desert waste, is now sown with works and dwellings, and supports more than 60,000 people.

Into this universal whirl of activity everything was drawn. Agriculture made a corresponding advance. Not only did landed property pass, as we have already seen, into the hands of new owners and cultivators, agriculture was affected in still another way. The great holders applied capital to the improvement of the soil, tore down needless fences, drained, manured, employed better tools, and applied a rotation of crops. The progress of science came to their assistance also; Sir Humphrey Davy applied chemistry to agriculture with success, and the development of mechanical science bestowed a multitude of advantages upon the large farmer. Further, in consequence of the increase of population, the demand for agricultural products increased in such measure that from 1760 to 1834, 6,840,540 acres of waste land were reclaimed; and, in spite of this, England was transformed from a grain exporting to a grain importing country.

The same activity was developed in the establishment of communication. From 1818 to 1829, there were built in England and Wales, 1,000 English miles of roadway of the width prescribed by law, 60 feet, and nearly all the old roads were reconstructed on the new system of McAdam. In Scotland, the Department of Public Works built since 1803 nearly 900 miles of roadway and more than 1,000 bridges, by which the population of the Highlands was suddenly placed within reach of civilisation. The Highlanders had hitherto been chiefly poachers and smugglers; they now became farmers and hand-workers. And, though Gaelic schools were organised for the purpose of maintaining the Gaelic language, yet Gaelic-Celtic customs and speech are rapidly vanishing before the approach of English civilisation. So, too, in Ireland; between the counties of Cork, Limerick, and Kerry, lay hitherto a wilderness wholly without passable roads, and serving, by reason of its inaccessibility, as the refuge of all criminals and the chief protection of the Celtic Irish nationality in the South of Ireland. It has now been cut through by public roads, and civilisation has thus gained admission even to this savage region. The whole British Empire, and especially England, which, sixty years ago, had as bad roads as

Germany or France then had, is now covered by a network of the finest roadways; and these, too, like almost everything else in England, are the work of private enterprise, the State having done very little in this direction.

Before 1755 England possessed almost no canals. In that year a canal was built in Lancashire from Sankey Brook to St Helen's; and in 1759, James Brindley built the first important one, the Duke of Bridgewater's canal from Manchester, and the coal mines of the district to the mouth of the Mersey passing, near Barton, by aqueduct, over the river Irwell. From this achievement dates the canal building of England, to which Brindley first gave importance. Canals were now built, and rivers made navigable in all directions. In England alone, there are 2,200 miles of canals and 1,800 miles of navigable river. In Scotland, the Caledonian Canal was cut directly across the country, and in Ireland several canals were built. These improvements, too, like the railroads and roadways, are nearly all the work of private individuals and companies.

The railroads have been only recently built. The first great one was opened from Liverpool to Manchester in 1830, since which all the great cities have been connected by rail. London with Southampton, Brighton, Dover, Colchester, Exeter, and Birmingham; Birmingham with Gloucester, Liverpool, Lancaster (via Newton and Wigan, and via Manchester and Bolton); also with Leeds (via Manchester and Halifax, and via Leicester, Derby, and Sheffield); Leeds with Hull and Newcastle (via York). There are also many minor lines building or projected, which will soon make it possible to travel from Edinburgh to London in one day.

As it had transformed the means of communication by land, so did the introduction of steam revolutionise travel by sea. The first steamboat was launched in 1807, on the Hudson, in North America; the first in the British empire, in 1811, on the Clyde. Since then, more than 600 have been built in England; and in 1836 more than 500 were plying to and from British ports.

Such, in brief, is the history of English industrial development in the past sixty years, a history which has no counterpart in the annals of humanity. Sixty, eighty years ago, England was a country like every other, with small towns, few and simple industries, and a thin but *proportionally* large agricultural population. Today it is a country like *no* other, with a capital of two and a half million inhabitants; with vast manufacturing cities; with an industry that supplies the world, and produces almost everything by means of the most complex machinery; with an industrious, intelligent, dense population, of which two-thirds are employed in trade and commerce, and composed of classes wholly different; forming, in fact, with other customs and other needs, a different nation from the England of those days. The industrial revolution is of the same importance for England as the political revolution for France, and the philosophical revolution for Germany; and the difference between England in 1760 and in 1844 is at least as great as that between France under the *ancien régime* and during the revolution of July. But the mightiest result of this industrial transformation is the English proletariat.

We have already seen how the proletariat was called into existence by the introduction of machinery. The rapid extension of manufacture demanded hands, wages rose, and troops of workmen migrated from the agricultural districts to the towns. Population multiplied enormously, and nearly all the increase took place in the proletariat. Further, Ireland had entered upon an orderly development only since the beginning of the eighteenth century. There, too, the population, more than decimated by English cruelty in earlier disturbances, now rapidly multiplied, especially after the advance in manufacture began to draw masses of Irishmen towards England. Thus arose the great manufacturing and commercial cities of the British Empire, in which at least three-fourths of the population belong to the working class, while the lower middle class consists only of small shopkeepers, and very very few handicraftsmen. For, though the rising manufacture first attained importance by transforming tools into machines, workrooms into factories, and consequently, the toiling lower middle class into the toiling proletariat, and the former large merchants into manufacturers, though the lower middle class was thus early crushed out, and the population reduced to the two opposing elements, workers and capitalists, this happened outside of the domain of manufacture proper, in the province of handicraft and retail trade as well. In the place of the former masters and apprentices, came great capitalists and working-men who had no prospect of rising above their class. Hand-work was carried on after the fashion of factory work, the division of labour was strictly applied, and small employers who could not compete with great establishments were forced down into the proletariat. At the same time the destruction of the former organisation of hand-work, and the disappearance of the lower middle class deprived the working-man of all possibility of rising into the middle class himself. Hitherto he had always had the prospect of establishing himself somewhere as master artificer, perhaps employing journeymen and apprentices; but now, when master artificers were crowded out by manufacturers, when large capital had become necessary for carrying on work independently, the working class became, for the first time, an integral, permanent class of the population, whereas it had formerly often been merely a transition leading to the bourgeoisie. Now, he who was born to toil had no other prospect than that of remaining a toiler all his life. Now, for the first time, therefore, the proletariat was in a position to undertake an independent movement.

In this way were brought together those vast masses of working-men who now fill the whole British Empire, whose social condition forces itself every day more and more upon the attention of the civilised world. The condition of the working class is the condition of the vast majority of the English people. The question: what is to become of those destitute millions, who consume today what they earned yesterday; who have created the greatness of England by their inventions and their toil; who become with every passing day more conscious of their might, and demand, with daily increasing urgency, their share of the advantages of society? – This, since the Reform Bill, has become the national question. All Parliamentary debates, of any importance, may be reduced to this; and, though the English middle class will not as yet admit it, though they try to evade this great question, and to represent their own particular interests as the truly national ones, their action is utterly useless. With every session of Parliament the working class gains ground, the interests of the middle class diminish in importance; and, in spite of the fact that the middle class is the chief, in fact, the only power in Parliament, the last session of 1844 was a continuous debate upon subjects affecting the working class, the Poor Relief Bill, the Factory Act, the Masters' and Servants' Act; and Thomas Duncombe, the representative of the working-men in the House of Commons, was the great man of the session; while the Liberal middle class with its

motion for repealing the Corn Laws, and the Radical middle class
with its resolution for refusing the taxes, played pitiable roles.
Even the debates about Ireland were at bottom debates about the
Irish proletariat, and the means of coming to its assistance. It is
high time, too, for the English middle class to make some concessions to the working-men who no longer plead but threaten;
for in a short time it may be too late.

In spite of all this, the English middle class, especially the manufacturing class, which is enriched directly by means of the poverty
of the workers, persists in ignoring this poverty. This class, feeling
itself the mighty representative class of the nation, is ashamed to
lay the sore spot of England bare before the eyes of the world; will
not confess, even to itself, that the workers are in distress, because
it, the property-holding, manufacturing class, must bear the moral
responsibility for this distress. Hence the scornful smile which
intelligent Englishmen (and they, the middle class, alone are known
on the Continent) assume when anyone begins to speak of the
condition of the working class; hence the utter ignorance on the
part of the whole middle class of everything which concerns the
workers; hence the ridiculous blunders which men of this class, in
and out of Parliament, make when the position of the proletariat
comes under discussion; hence the absurd freedom from anxiety,
with which the middle class dwells upon a soil that is honey-
combed, and may any day collapse, the speedy collapse of which is
as certain as a mathematical or mechanical demonstration; hence
the miracle that the English have as yet no single book upon the
condition of their workers, although they have been examining
and mending the old state of things no one knows how many
years. Hence also the deep wrath of the whole working class, from
Glasgow to London, against the rich, by whom they are systematically plundered and mercilessly left to their fate, a wrath which
before too long a time goes by, a time almost within the power of
man to predict, must break out into a revolution in comparison
with which the French Revolution, and the year 1794, will prove
to have been child's play.

The Industrial Proletariat

The order of our investigation of the different sections of the proletariat follows naturally from the foregoing history of its rise. The first proletarians were connected with manufacture, were engendered by it, and accordingly, those employed in manufacture, in the working up of raw materials, will first claim our attention. The production of raw materials and of fuel for manufacture attained importance only in consequence of the industrial change, and engendered a new proletariat, the coal and metal miners. Then, in the third place, manufacture influenced agriculture, and in the fourth, the condition of Ireland; and the fractions of the proletariat belonging to each, will find their place accordingly. We shall find, too, that with the possible exception of the Irish, the degree of intelligence of the various workers is in direct proportion to their relation to manufacture; and that the factory hands are most enlightened as to their own interests, the miners somewhat less so, the agricultural labourers scarcely at all. We shall find the same order again among the industrial workers, and shall see how the factory hands, eldest children of the industrial revolution, have from the beginning to the present day formed the nucleus of the Labour Movement, and how the others have joined this movement just in proportion as their handicraft has been invaded by the progress of machinery. We shall thus learn from the example which England offers, from the equal pace which the Labour Movement has kept with the movement of industrial development, the historical significance of manufacture.

Since, however, at the present moment, pretty much the whole industrial proletariat is involved in the movement, and the condition of the separate sections has much in common, because they all are industrial, we shall have first to examine the condition of the industrial proletariat as a whole, in order later to notice more particularly each separate division with its own peculiarities.

It has been already suggested that manufacture centralises property in the hands of the few. It requires large capital with which to erect the colossal establishments that ruin the petty trading bourgeoisie and with which to press into its service the forces of Nature, so driving the hand labour of the independent workman out of the market. The division of labour, the application of water and especially steam, and the application of machinery, are the three great levers with which manufacture, since the middle of the last century, has been busy putting the world out of joint. Manufacture, on a small scale, created the middle class; on a large scale, it created the working class, and raised the elect of the middle class to the throne, but only to overthrow them the more surely when the time comes. Meanwhile, it is an undenied and easily explained fact that the numerous, petty middle class of the 'good old times' has been annihilated by manufacture, and resolved into rich capitalists on the one hand and poor workers on the other.[2]

The centralising tendency of manufacture does not, however, stop here. Population becomes centralised just as capital does; and, very naturally, since the human being, the worker, is regarded in manufacture simply as a piece of capital for the use of which the manufacturer pays interest under the name of wages. A manufacturing establishment requires many workers employed together in a single building, living near each other and forming a village of themselves in the case of a good-sized factory. They have needs for satisfying which other people are necessary; handicraftsmen, shoemakers, tailors, bakers, carpenters, stonemasons, settle at hand. The inhabitants of the village, especially the younger generation, accustom themselves to factory work, grow skilful in it, and when the first mill can no longer employ them all, wages fall, and the immigration of fresh manufacturers is the consequence. So the village grows into a small town, and the small town into a large one. The greater the town, the greater its advantages. It offers roads, railroads, canals; the choice of skilled labour increases constantly, new establishments can be built more cheaply because of the competition among builders and machinists who are at hand, than in remote country districts, whither timber, machinery, builders, and operatives must be brought; it offers a market to which buyers crowd, and direct communication with the markets supplying raw material or demanding finished goods. Hence the marvellously rapid growth of the great manufacturing towns. The country, on the other hand, has the advantage that wages are usually lower than in town, and so town and country are in constant competition; and, if the advantage is on the side of the town today, wages sink so low in the country tomorrow, that new investments are most profitably made there. But the centralising tendency of manufacture continues in full force, and every new factory built in the country bears in it the germ of a manufacturing town. If it were possible for this mad rush of manufacture to go on at this rate for another century, every manufacturing district of England would be one great manufacturing town, and Manchester and Liverpool would meet at Warrington or Newton; for in commerce, too, this centralisation of the population works in precisely the same way, and hence it is that one or two great harbours, such as Hull and Liverpool, Bristol, and London, monopolise almost the whole maritime commerce of Great Britain.

Since commerce and manufacture attain their most complete development in these great towns, their influence upon the proletariat is also most clearly observable here. Here the centralisation of property has reached the highest point; here the morals and customs of the good old times are most completely obliterated; here it has gone so far that the name Merry Old England conveys no meaning, for Old England itself is unknown save to memory and to the tales of our grandfathers. Hence, too, there exist here only a rich and a poor class, for the lower middle class vanishes more completely with every passing day. Thus the class formerly most stable has become the most restless one. It consists today of a few remnants of a past time, and a number of people eager to make fortunes, industrial Micawbers and speculators of whom one may amass a fortune, while ninety-nine become insolvent, and more than half of the ninety-nine live by perpetually repeated failure.

But in these towns the proletarians are the infinite majority, and how they fare, what influence the great town exercises upon them, we have now to investigate.

The Great Towns

A town such as London, where a man may wander for hours together without reaching the beginning of the end, without meeting the slightest hint which could lead to the inference that there is open country within reach, is a strange thing. This colossal centralisation, this heaping together of two and a half millions of human beings at one point, has multiplied the power of this two and a half millions a hundredfold; has raised London to the commercial capital of the world, created the giant docks and assembled the thousand vessels that continually cover the Thames. I know nothing more imposing than the view which the Thames offers during the ascent from the sea to London Bridge. The masses of buildings, the wharves on both sides, especially from Woolwich upwards, the countless ships along both shores, crowding ever closer and closer together, until, at last, only a narrow passage remains in the middle of the river, a passage through which hundreds of steamers shoot by one another; all this is so vast, so impressive, that a man cannot collect himself, but is lost in the marvel of England's greatness before he sets foot upon English soil.[3]

But the sacrifices which all this has cost become apparent later. After roaming the streets of the capital a day or two, making headway with difficulty through the human turmoil and the endless lines of vehicles, after visiting the slums of the metropolis, one realises for the first time that these Londoners have been forced to sacrifice the best qualities of their human nature, to bring to pass all the marvels of civilisation which crowd their city; that a hundred powers which slumbered within them have remained inactive, have been suppressed in order that a few might be developed more fully and multiply through union with those of others. The very turmoil of the streets has something repulsive, something against which human nature rebels. The hundreds of thousands of all classes and ranks crowding past each other, are they not all human beings with the same qualities and powers, and with the same interest in being happy? And have they not, in the

end, to seek happiness in the same way, by the same means? And
still they crowd by one another as though they had nothing in
common, nothing to do with one another, and their only agreement is the tacit one, that each keep to his own side of the
pavement, so as not to delay the opposing streams of the crowd,
while it occurs to no man to honour another with so much as a
glance. The brutal indifference, the unfeeling isolation of each in
his private interest becomes the more repellent and offensive, the
more these individuals are crowded together, within a limited
space. And, however much one may be aware that this isolation
of the individual, this narrow self-seeking is the fundamental
principle of our society everywhere, it is nowhere so shamelessly
barefaced, so self-conscious as just here in the crowding of the
great city. The dissolution of mankind into monads, of which each
one has a separate principle, the world of atoms, is here carried out
to its utmost extreme.

Hence it comes, too, that the social war, the war of each against
all, is here openly declared. Just as in Stirner's recent book, people
regard each other only as useful objects; each exploits the other,
and the end of it all is, that the stronger treads the weaker under
foot, and that the powerful few, the capitalists, seize everything for
themselves, while to the weak many, the poor, scarcely a bare
existence remains.

What is true of London, is true of Manchester, Birmingham,
Leeds, is true of all great towns. Everywhere barbarous indifference, hard egotism on one hand, and nameless misery on the
other, everywhere social warfare, every man's house in a state of
siege, everywhere reciprocal plundering under the protection of
the law, and all so shameless, so openly avowed that one shrinks
before the consequences of our social state as they manifest themselves here undisguised, and can only wonder that the whole crazy
fabric still hangs together.

Since capital, the direct or indirect control of the means of
subsistence and production, is the weapon with which this social
warfare is carried on, it is clear that all the disadvantages of such a
state must fall upon the poor. For him no man has the slightest
concern. Cast into the whirlpool, he must struggle through as well
as he can. If he is so happy as to find work, i.e. if the bourgeoisie
does him the favour to enrich itself by means of him, wages await

him which scarcely suffice to keep body and soul together; if he can get no work he may steal, if he is not afraid of the police, or starve, in which case the police will take care that he does so in a quiet and inoffensive manner. During my residence in England, at least twenty or thirty persons have died of simple starvation under the most revolting circumstances, and a jury has rarely been found possessed of the courage to speak the plain truth in the matter. Let the testimony of the witnesses be never so clear and unequivocal, the bourgeoisie, from which the jury is selected, always finds some back door through which to escape the frightful verdict, death from starvation. The bourgeoisie dare not speak the truth in these cases, for it would speak its own condemnation. But indirectly, far more than directly, many have died of starvation, where long continued want of proper nourishment has called forth fatal illness, when it has produced such debility that causes which might otherwise have remained inoperative, brought on severe illness and death. The English working-men call this 'social murder', and accuse our whole society of perpetrating this crime perpetually. Are they wrong?

True, it is only individuals who starve, but what security has the working-man that it may not be his turn tomorrow? Who assures him employment, who vouches for it that, if for any reason or no reason his lord and master discharges him tomorrow, he can struggle along with those dependent upon him, until he may find someone else 'to give him bread'? Who guarantees that willingness to work shall suffice to obtain work, that uprightness, industry, thrift, and the rest of the virtues recommended by the bour-geoisie, are really his road to happiness? No one. He knows that he has something today, and that it does not depend upon himself whether he shall have something tomorrow. He knows that every breeze that blows, every whim of his employer, every bad turn of trade may hurl him back into the fierce whirlpool from which he has temporarily saved himself, and in which it is hard and often impossible to keep his head above water. He knows that, though he may have the means of living today, it is very uncertain whether he shall tomorrow.

Meanwhile, let us proceed to a more detailed investigation of the position in which the social war has placed the non-possessing class. Let us see what pay for his work society does give the working-man in the form of dwelling, clothing, food, what sort of subsistence it grants those who contribute most to the maintenance of society; and, first, let us consider the dwellings.

Every great city has one or more slums, where the working class is crowded together. True, poverty often dwells in hidden alleys close to the palaces of the rich; but, in general, a separate territory has been assigned to it, where, removed from the sight of the happier classes, it may struggle along as it can. These slums are pretty equally arranged in all the great towns of England, the worst houses in the worst quarters of the towns; usually one- or two-storeyed cottages in long rows, perhaps with cellars used as dwellings, almost always irregularly built. These houses of three or four rooms and a kitchen form, throughout England, some parts of London excepted, the general dwellings of the working class. The streets are generally unpaved, rough, dirty, filled with vegetable and animal refuse, without sewers or gutters, but supplied with foul, stagnant pools instead. Moreover, ventilation is impeded by the bad, confused method of building of the whole quarter, and since many human beings here live crowded into a small space, the atmosphere that prevails in these working-men's quarters may readily be imagined. Further, the streets serve as drying grounds in fine weather; lines are stretched across from house to house, and hung with wet clothing.

Let us investigate some of the slums in their order. London comes first, and in London the famous rookery of St Giles which is now, at last, about to be penetrated by a couple of broad streets. St Giles is in the midst of the most populous part of the town, surrounded by broad, splendid avenues in which the gay world of London idles about, in the immediate neighbourhood of Oxford Street, Regent Street, of Trafalgar Square and the Strand. It is a disorderly collection of tall, three- or four-storeyed houses, with narrow, crooked, filthy streets, in which there is quite as much life as in the great thoroughfares of the town, except that, here, people of the working class only are to be seen. A vegetable market is held in the street, baskets with vegetables and fruits, naturally all bad and hardly fit to use, obstruct the sidewalk still further, and from these, as well as from the fish-dealers' stalls, arises a horrible smell. The houses are occupied from cellar to garret, filthy within and without, and their appearance is such that no human being could possibly wish to live in them. But all this is nothing in comparison with the dwellings in the narrow courts and alleys between the streets, entered by covered passages between the houses, in which the filth and tottering ruin surpass all description. Scarcely a whole window-pane can be found, the walls are crumbling, door-posts and window-frames loose and broken, doors of old boards nailed together, or altogether wanting in this thieves' quarter, where no doors are needed, there being nothing to steal. Heaps of garbage and ashes lie in all directions, and the foul liquids emptied before the doors gather in stinking pools. Here live the poorest of the poor, the worst paid workers with thieves and the victims of prostitution indiscriminately huddled together, the majority Irish, or of Irish extraction, and those who have not yet sunk in the whirlpool of moral ruin which surrounds them, sinking daily deeper, losing daily more and more of their power to resist the demoralising influence of want, filth, and evil surroundings.

Nor is St Giles the only London slum. In the immense tangle of streets, there are hundreds and thousands of alleys and courts lined with houses too bad for anyone to live in, who can still spend anything whatsoever upon a dwelling fit for human beings. Close to the splendid houses of the rich such a lurking-place of the bitterest poverty may often be found. So, a short time ago, on the occasion of a coroner's inquest, a region close to Portman Square, one of the very respectable squares, was characterised as an abode 'of a multitude of Irish demoralised by poverty and filth'. So, too, may be found in streets such as Long Acre and others, which, though not fashionable, are yet 'respectable', a great number of cellar dwellings out of which puny children and half-starved, ragged women emerge into the light of day. In the immediate neighbourhood of Drury Lane Theatre, the second in London, are some of the worst streets of the whole metropolis, Charles, King, and Park Streets, in which the houses are inhabited from cellar to garret exclusively by poor families. In the parishes of St John and St Margaret there lived in 1840, according to the *Journal of the Statistical Society*, 5,366 working-men's families in 5,294 'dwellings' (if they deserve the name!), men, women, and children thrown together without distinction of age or sex, 26,830 persons all told; and of these families three-fourths possessed but one room. In the aristocratic parish of St George, Hanover Square, there lived, according to the same authority, 1,465 working-men's families, nearly 6,000 persons, under similar conditions, and here, too, more than two-thirds of the whole number crowded together at the rate of one family in one room. And how the poverty of these unfortunates, among whom even thieves find nothing to steal, is exploited by the property-holding class in lawful ways! The abominable dwellings in Drury Lane, just mentioned, bring in the following rents: two cellar dwellings, 3s.; one room, ground-floor, 4s.; second-storey, 4s. 6d.; third-floor, 4s.; garret-room, 3s. weekly, so that the starving occupants of Charles Street alone, pay the house-owners a yearly tribute of 2,000 pounds, and the 5,336 families above mentioned in Westminster, a yearly rent of 40,000 pounds.

The most extensive working-people's district lies east of the Tower in Whitechapel and Bethnal Green, where the greatest masses of London working-people live. Let us hear Mr G. Alston, preacher of St Philip's, Bethnal Green, on the condition of his parish. He says:

It contains 1,400 houses, inhabited by 2,795 families, or about 12,000 persons. The space upon which this large population dwells, is less than 400 yards (1,200 feet) square, and in this overcrowding it is nothing unusual to find a man, his wife, four or five children, and, sometimes, both grandparents, all in one single room, where they eat, sleep, and work. I believe that before the Bishop of London called attention to this most poverty-stricken parish, people at the West End knew as little of it as of the savages of Australia or the South Sea Isles. And if we make ourselves acquainted with these unfortunates, through personal observation, if we watch them at their scanty meal and see them bowed by illness and want of work, we shall find such a mass of helplessness and misery, that a nation like ours must blush that these things can be possible. I was rector near Huddersfield during the three years in which the mills were at their worst, but I have never seen such complete helplessness of the poor as since then in Bethnal Green. Not one father of a family in ten in the whole neighbourhood has other clothing than his working suit, and that is as bad and tattered as possible; many, indeed, have no other covering for the night than these rags, and no bed, save a sack of straw and shavings.

The foregoing description furnishes an idea of the aspect of the interior of the dwellings. But let us follow the English officials, who occasionally stray thither, into one or two of these working-men's homes.

On the occasion of an inquest held November 14th, 1843, by Mr Carter, coroner for Surrey, upon the body of Ann Galway, aged 45 years, the newspapers related the following particulars concerning the deceased: she had lived at No. 3 White Lion Court, Bermondsey Street, London, with her husband and a nineteen-year-old son in a little room, in which neither a bedstead nor any other furniture was to be seen. She lay dead beside her son upon a heap of feathers which were scattered over her almost naked body, there being neither sheet nor coverlet. The feathers stuck so fast over the whole body that the physician could not examine the corpse until it was cleansed, and then found it starved and scarred from the bites of vermin. Part of the floor of the room was torn up, and the hole used by the family as a privy.

On Monday, January 15th, 1844, two boys were brought before the police magistrate because, being in a starving condition, they had stolen and immediately devoured a half-cooked calf's foot from a shop. The magistrate felt called upon to investigate the case further, and received the following details from the police-man: the mother of the two boys was the widow of an ex-soldier, afterwards policeman, and had had a very hard time since the death of her husband, to provide for her nine children. She lived at No. 2 Pool's Place, Quaker Court, Spitalfields, in the utmost poverty. When the policeman came to her, he found her with six of her children literally huddled together in a little back room, with no furniture but two old rush-bottomed chairs with the seats gone, a small table with two legs broken, a broken cup, and a small dish. On the hearth was scarcely a spark of fire, and in one corner lay as many old rags as would fill a woman's apron, which served the whole family as a bed. For bed clothing they had only their scanty day clothing. The poor woman told him that she had been forced to sell her bedstead the year before to buy food. Her bedding she had pawned with the victualler for food. In short, everything had gone for food. The magistrate ordered the woman a considerable provision from the poor-box.

In February, 1844, Theresa Bishop, a widow 60 years old, was recommended, with her sick daughter, aged 26, to the compassion of the police magistrate in Marlborough Street. She lived at No. 5 Brown Street, Grosvenor Square, in a small back room no larger than a closet, in which there was not one single piece of furniture. In one corner lay some rags upon which both slept; a chest served as table and chair. The mother earned a little by charring. The owner of the house said that they had lived in this way since May, 1843, had gradually sold or pawned everything that they had, and had still never paid any rent. The magistrate assigned them £1 from the poor-box.

I am far from asserting that *all* London working-people live in such want as the foregoing three families. I know very well that ten are somewhat better off, where one is so totally trodden under foot by society; but I assert that thousands of industrious and worthy people – far worthier and more to be respected than all the rich of London – do find themselves in a condition unworthy of human beings; and that every proletarian, every one, without exception, is exposed to a similar fate without any fault of his own and in spite of every possible effort.

But in spite of all this, they who have some kind of a shelter are fortunate, fortunate in comparison with the utterly homeless. In London fifty thousand human beings get up every morning, not knowing where they are to lay their heads at night. The luckiest of this multitude, those who succeed in keeping a penny or two until evening, enter a lodging-house, such as abound in every great city, where they find a bed. But what a bed! These houses are filled with beds from cellar to garret, four, five, six beds in a room; as many as can be crowded in. Into every bed four, five, or six human beings are piled, as many as can be packed in, sick and well, young and old, drunk and sober, men and women, just as they come, indiscriminately. Then come strife, blows, wounds, or, if these bedfellows agree, so much the worse; thefts are arranged and things done which our language, grown more humane than our deeds, refuses to record. And those who cannot pay for such a refuge? They sleep where they find a place, in passages, arcades, in corners where the police and the owners leave them undisturbed. A few individuals find their way to the refuges which are managed, here and there, by private charity, others sleep on the benches in

the parks close under the windows of Queen Victoria. Let us hear
the London *Times*:

It appears from the report of the proceedings at Marlborough
Street Police Court in our columns of yesterday, that there is
an average number of 50 human beings of all ages, who huddle
together in the parks every night, having no other shelter than
what is supplied by the trees and a few hollows of the embank-
ment. Of these, the majority are young girls who have been
seduced from the country by the soldiers and turned loose on
the world in all the destitution of friendless penury, and all the
recklessness of early vice.

This is truly horrible! Poor there must be everywhere. Indig-
ence will find its way and set up its hideous state in the heart of
a great and luxurious city. Amid the thousand narrow lanes and
by-streets of a populous metropolis there must always, we fear,
be much suffering – much that offends the eye – much that
lurks unseen.

But that within the precincts of wealth, gaiety, and fashion, nigh
the regal grandeur of St James, close on the palatial splendour
of Bayswater, on the confines of the old and new aristocratic
quarters, in a district where the cautious refinement of modern
design has refrained from creating one single tenement for
poverty; which seems, as it were, dedicated to the exclusive
enjoyment of wealth, that *there* want, and famine, and disease, and
vice should stalk in all their kindred horrors, consuming body by
body, soul, by soul!

It is indeed a monstrous state of things! Enjoyment the most
absolute, that bodily ease, intellectual excitement, or the more
innocent pleasures of sense can supply to man's craving, brought
in close contact with the most unmitigated misery! Wealth, from
its bright saloons, laughing – an insolently heedless laugh – at the
unknown wounds of want! Pleasure, cruelly but unconsciously
mocking the pain that moans below! All contrary things mocking
one another – all contrary, save the vice which tempts and the
vice which is tempted!

But let all men remember this – that within the most courtly
precincts of the richest city of God's earth, there may be found,
night after night, winter after winter, women – young in years –

old in sin and suffering – outcasts from society – ROTTING
FROM FAMINE, FILTH, AND DISEASE. Let them remember
this, and learn not to theorise but to act. God knows, there is
much room for action nowadays.[4]

I have referred to the refuges for the homeless. How greatly
overcrowded these are, two examples may show. A newly erected
Refuge for the Houseless in Upper Ogle Street, that can shelter
three hundred persons every night, has received since its opening,
January 27th to March 17th, 1844, 2,740 persons for one or more
nights; and, although the season was growing more favourable, the
number of applicants in this, as well as in the asylums of White-
cross Street and Wapping, was strongly on the increase, and a
crowd of the homeless had to be sent away every night for want of
room. In another refuge, the Central Asylum in Playhouse Yard,
there were supplied on an average 460 beds nightly, during the
first three months of the year 1844, 6,681 persons being sheltered,
and 96,141 portions of bread were distributed. Yet the committee
of directors declare this institution began to meet the pressure of
the needy to a limited extent only when the Eastern Asylum also
was opened.

Let us leave London and examine the other great cities of the
three kingdoms in their order. Let us take Dublin first, a city the
approach to which from the sea is as charming as that of London is
imposing. The Bay of Dublin is the most beautiful of the whole
British Island Kingdom, and is even compared by the Irish with
the Bay of Naples. The city, too, possesses great attractions, and its
aristocratic districts are better and more tastefully laid out than
those of any other British city. By way of compensation, however,
the poorer districts of Dublin are among the most hideous and
repulsive to be seen in the world. True, the Irish character, which,
under some circumstances, is comfortable only in the dirt, has
some share in this; but as we find thousands of Irish in every great
city in England and Scotland, and as every poor population must
gradually sink into the same uncleanliness, the wretchedness of
Dublin is nothing specific, nothing peculiar to Dublin, but something common to all great towns. The poor quarters of Dublin are
extremely extensive, and the filth, the uninhabitableness of the
houses and the neglect of the streets, surpass all description. Some

idea of the manner in which the poor are here crowded together may be formed from the fact that, in 1817, according to the report of the Inspector of Workhouses,[5] 1,318 persons lived in 52 houses with 390 rooms in Barral Street, and 1,997 persons in 71 houses with 393 rooms in and near Church Street; that:

> In this and the adjoining district there exists a multitude of foul courts and alleys; many cellars receive all their light through the door, while in not a few the inhabitants sleep upon the bare floor, though most of them possess bedsteads at least; Nicholson's Court, for example, contains twenty-eight wretched little rooms with 151 human beings in the greatest want, there being but two bedsteads and two blankets to be found in the whole court.

The poverty is so great in Dublin, that a single benevolent institution, the Mendicity Association, gives relief to 2,500 persons or one per cent. of the population daily, receiving and feeding them for the day and dismissing them at night.

Dr Alison describes a similar state of things in Edinburgh, whose superb situation, which has won it the title of the Modern Athens, and whose brilliant aristocratic quarter in the New Town, contrast strongly with the foul wretchedness of the poor in the Old Town. Alison asserts that this extensive quarter is as filthy and horrible as the worst district of Dublin, while the Mendicity Association would have as great a proportion of needy persons to assist in Edinburgh as in the Irish capital. He asserts, indeed, that the poor in Scotland, especially in Edinburgh and Glasgow, are worse off than in any other region of the three kingdoms, and that the poorest are not Irish, but Scotch. The preacher of the Old Church of Edinburgh, Dr Lee, testified in 1836, before the Commission of Religious Instruction, that:

> He had never before seen such misery as in his parish, where the people were without furniture, without everything, two married couples often sharing one room. In a single day he had visited seven houses in which there was not a bed, in some of them not even a heap of straw. Old people of eighty years sleep on the board floor, nearly all slept in their day-clothes. In one cellar room he found two families from a Scotch country district; soon after their removal to the city two of the children had died, and a

third was dying at the time of his visit. Each family had a filthy pile of straw lying in a corner; the cellar sheltered besides the two families a donkey, and was, moreover, so dark that it was impossible to distinguish one person from another by day. Dr Lee declared that it was enough to make a heart of adamant bleed to see such misery in a country like Scotland.

In the Edinburgh *Medical and Surgical Journal*, Dr Hennan reports a similar state of things. From a Parliamentary Report,[6] it is evident that in the dwellings of the poor of Edinburgh a want of cleanliness reigns, such as must be expected under these conditions. On the bed-posts chickens roost at night, dogs and horses share the dwellings of human beings, and the natural consequence is a shocking stench, with filth and swarms of vermin. The prevailing construction of Edinburgh favours these atrocious conditions as far as possible. The Old Town is built upon both slopes of a hill, along the crest of which runs the High Street. Out of the High Street there open downwards multitudes of narrow, crooked alleys, called wynds from their many turnings, and these wynds form the proletarian district of the city. The houses of the Scotch cities, in general, are five or six-storeyed buildings, like those of Paris, and in contrast with England where, so far as possible, each family has a separate house. The crowding of human beings upon a limited area is thus intensified.

These streets [says an English journal[7] in an article upon the sanitary condition of the working-people in cities] are often so narrow that a person can step from the window of one house into that of its opposite neighbour, while the houses are piled so high, storey upon storey, that the light can scarcely penetrate into the court or alley that lies between. In this part of the city there are neither sewers nor other drains, nor even privies belonging to the houses. In consequence, all refuse, garbage, and excrements of at least 50,000 persons are thrown into the gutters every night, so that, in spite of all street sweeping, a mass of dried filth and foul vapours are created, which not only offend the sight and smell, but endanger the health of the inhabitants in the highest degree. Is it to be wondered at, that in such localities all considerations of health, morals, and even the most ordinary decency are utterly neglected? On the contrary, all who are more intimately acquainted with the condition of the inhabitants will testify to the high degree which disease, wretchedness, and demoralisation have here reached. Society in such districts has sunk to a level indescribably low and hopeless. The houses of the poor are generally filthy, and are evidently never cleansed. They consist in most cases of a single room which, while subject to the worst ventilation, is yet usually kept cold by the broken and badly fitting windows, and is sometimes damp and partly below ground level, always badly furnished and thoroughly uncomfortable, a straw-heap often serving the whole family for a bed, upon which men and women, young and old, sleep in revolting confusion. Water can be had only from the public pumps, and the difficulty of obtaining it naturally fosters all possible filth.

In the other great seaport towns the prospect is no better. Liverpool, with all its commerce, wealth, and grandeur yet treats its workers with the same barbarity. A full fifth of the population, more than 45,000 human beings, live in narrow, dark, damp, badly-ventilated cellar dwellings, of which there are 7,862 in the city. Besides these cellar dwellings there are 2,270 courts, small spaces built up on all four sides and having but one entrance, a narrow, covered passage-way, the whole ordinarily very dirty and inhabited exclusively by proletarians. Of such courts we shall have more to say when we come to Manchester. In Bristol, on one occasion, 2,800 families were visited, of whom 46 per cent. occupied but one room each.

Precisely the same state of things prevails in the factory towns. In Nottingham there are in all 11,000 houses, of which between 7,000 and 8,000 are built back to back with a rear party-wall so that no through ventilation is possible, while a single privy usually serves for several houses. During an investigation made a short time since, many rows of houses were found to have been built over shallow drains covered only by the boards of the ground floor. In Leicester, Derby, and Sheffield, it is no better. Of Birmingham, the article above cited from the *Artisan* states:

In the older quarters of the city there are many bad districts, filthy and neglected, full of stagnant pools and heaps of refuse. Courts are very numerous in Birmingham, reaching two thousand, and containing the greater number of the working-people of the city.

These courts are usually narrow, muddy, badly ventilated, ill-drained, and lined with eight to twenty houses, which, by reason of having their rear walls in common, can usually be ventilated from one side only. In the background, within the court, there is usually an ash heap or something of the kind, the filth of which cannot be described. It must, however, be observed that the newer courts are more sensibly built and more decently kept, and that even in the old ones, the cottages are much less crowded than in Manchester and Liverpool, wherefore Birmingham shows even during the reign of an epidemic a far smaller mortality than, for instance, Wolverhampton, Dudley, and Bilston, only a few miles distant. Cellar dwellings are unknown, too, in Birmingham, though a few cellars are misused as workrooms. The lodging-houses for proletarians are rather numerous (over four hundred), chiefly in courts in the heart of the town. They are nearly all disgustingly filthy and ill-smelling, the refuge of beggars, thieves, tramps, and prostitutes, who eat, drink, smoke, and sleep here without the slightest regard to comfort or decency in an atmosphere endurable to these degraded beings only.

Glasgow is in many respects similar to Edinburgh, possessing the same wynds, the same tall houses. Of this city the *Artisan* observes:

The working class forms here some 78% of the whole population (about 300,000), and lives in parts of the city which exceed in wretchedness and squalor the lowest nooks of St Giles and Whitechapel, the Liberties of Dublin, the Wynds of Edinburgh. There are numbers of such localities in the heart of the city, south of the Trongate, westward from the Saltmarket, in Calton and off the High Street, endless labyrinths of lanes or wynds into which open at almost every step, courts or blind alleys, formed by ill-ventilated, high-piled, waterless, and dilapidated houses. These are literally swarming with inhabitants. They contain three or four families upon each floor, perhaps twenty persons. In some cases each storey is let out in sleeping places, so that fifteen to twenty persons are packed, one on top of the other, I cannot say accommodated, in a single room. These districts shelter the poorest, most depraved, and worthless members of the community, and may be regarded as the sources of those frightful epidemics which, beginning here, spread desolation over Glasgow.

Let us hear how J. C. Symonds, Government Commissioner for the investigation of the condition of the hand-weavers, describes these portions of the city: [8]

I have seen wretchedness in some of its worse phases both here and upon the Continent, but until I visited the wynds of Glasgow I did not believe that so much crime, misery, and disease could exist in any civilised country. In the lower lodging-houses ten, twelve, sometimes twenty persons of both sexes, all ages and various degrees of nakedness, sleep indiscriminately huddled together upon the floor. These dwellings are usually so damp, filthy, and ruinous, that no one could wish to keep his horse in one of them.

And in another place:

The wynds of Glasgow contain a fluctuating population of fifteen to thirty thousand human beings. This quarter consists wholly of narrow alleys and square courts, in the middle of every one of which there lies a dung heap. Revolting as was the outward appearance of these courts, I was yet not prepared for the filth and wretchedness within. In some of the sleeping-places which we visited at night [the Superintendent of Police, Captain Miller, and Symonds] we found a complete layer of human beings stretched upon the floor, often fifteen to twenty, some clad, others naked, men and women indiscriminately. Their bed was a litter of mouldy straw, mixed with rags. There was little or no furniture, and the only thing which gave these dens any shimmer of habitableness was a fire upon the hearth. Theft and prostitution form the chief means of subsistence of this population. No one seemed to take the trouble to cleanse this Augean stable, this Pandemonium, this tangle of crime, filth, and pestilence in the centre of the second city of the kingdom. An extended examination of the lowest districts of other cities never revealed anything half so bad, either in intensity of moral and physical infection, nor in comparative density of population. In this quarter most of the houses have been declared by the Court of Guild ruinous and unfit for habitation, but precisely these are the most densely populated, because, according to the law, no rent can be demanded for them.

The great manufacturing district in the centre of the British Islands, the thickly peopled stretch of West Yorkshire and South Lancashire, with its numerous factory towns, yields nothing to the other great manufacturing centres. The woollen district of the West Riding of Yorkshire is a charming region, a beautiful green hill-country, whose elevations grow more rugged towards the West until they reach their highest point in the bold ridge of Blackstone Edge, the watershed between the Irish Sea and the German Ocean. The valleys of the Aire, along which stretches Leeds, and of the Calder, through which the Manchester-Leeds railway runs, are among the most attractive in England, and are strewn in all directions with the factories, villages, and towns. The houses of rough grey stone look so neat and clean in comparison with the blackened brick buildings of Lancashire, that it is a pleasure to look at them. But on coming into the towns themselves, one finds little to rejoice over. Leeds lies as the *Artisan* describes it, and as I found confirmed upon examination:

. . . on a gentle slope that descends into the valley of the Aire. This stream flows through the city for about a mile-and-a-half and is exposed to violent floods during thaws or heavy rain. The higher western portions of the city are clean, for such a large town. But the low-lying districts along the river and its tributary becks are narrow, dirty, and enough in themselves to shorten the lives of the inhabitants, especially of little children. Added to this, the disgusting state of the working-men's districts about Kirkgate, Marsh Lane, Cross Street and Richmond Road, which is chiefly attributable to their unpaved, drainless streets, irregular architecture, numerous courts and alleys, and total lack of the most ordinary means of cleanliness, all this taken together is explanation enough of the excessive mortality in these unhappy abodes of filthy misery. In consequence of the overflows of the Aire, [which, it must be added, like all other rivers in the service of manufacture, flows into the city at one end clear and transparent, and flows out at the other end thick, black, and foul, smelling of all possible refuse] the houses and cellars are often so full of water that they have to be pumped out. And at such times the water rises, even where there are sewers, out of them into cellars,[9] engenders miasmatic vapours strongly impregnated with sulphuretted hydrogen, and leaves a disgusting residuum highly injurious to health. During the spring-floods of 1839 the action of such a choking of the sewers was so injurious, that, according to the report of the Registrar of Births and Deaths for this part of the town, there were three deaths to two births, whereas in the same three months, in every other part of the town, there were three births to two deaths. Other thickly populated districts are without any sewers whatsoever, or so badly provided as to derive no benefit from them. In some rows of houses the cellars are seldom dry; in certain districts there are several streets covered with soft mud a foot deep. The inhabitants have made vain attempts from time to time to repair these streets with shovelfuls of cinders, but in spite of all such attempts, dung-heaps, and pools of dirty water emptied from the houses, fill all the holes until wind and sun dry them up.[10] An ordinary cottage in Leeds occupies not more than five yards square of land, and usually consists of a cellar, a living room, and one sleeping-room. These contracted dwellings, filled day and night with human beings, are another point dangerous alike to the morals and the health of the inhabitants.

And how greatly these cottages are crowded, the Report on the Health of the Working-Classes, quoted above, bears testimony: 'In Leeds we found brothers and sisters, and lodgers of both sexes, sharing the parents' sleeping-room, whence arise consequences at the contemplation of which human feeling shudders.'

So, too, Bradford, which, but seven miles from Leeds at the junction of several valleys, lies upon the banks of a small, coal-black, foul-smelling stream. On weekdays the town is enveloped in a grey cloud of coal smoke, but on a fine Sunday it offers a superb picture, when viewed from the surrounding heights. Yet within reigns the same filth and discomfort as in Leeds. The older portions of the town are built upon steep hillsides, and are narrow and irregular. In the lanes, alleys, and courts lie filth and *débris* in heaps; the houses are ruinous, dirty, and miserable, and in the immediate vicinity of the river and the valley bottom I found many a one, whose ground-floor, half-buried in the hillside, was totally abandoned. In general, the portions of the valley bottom in which working-men's cottages have crowded between the tall factories, are among the worst built and dirtiest districts of the whole town. In the newer portions of this, as of every other factory town, the cottages are more regular, being built in rows, but they share here, too, all the evils incident to the customary method of providing working-men's dwellings, evils of which we shall have occasions to speak more particularly in discussing Manchester. The same is true of the remaining towns of the West Riding, especially of Barnsley, Halifax and Huddersfield. The last named, the handsomest by far of all the factory towns of Yorkshire and Lancashire, by reason of its charming situation and modern architecture, has yet its bad quarter; for a committee appointed by a meeting of citizens to survey the town, reported August 5th, 1844:

It is notorious that in Huddersfield whole streets and many lanes and courts are neither paved nor supplied with sewers nor other drains; that in them refuse, *débris*, and filth of every sort lies accumulating, festers and rots, and that, nearly everywhere, stagnant water accumulates in pools, in consequence of which the adjoining dwellings must inevitably be bad and filthy, so that in such places diseases arise and threaten the health of the whole town.

If we cross Blackstone Edge or penetrate it with the railroad, we enter upon that classic soil on which English manufacture has achieved its masterwork and from which all labour movements emanate, namely, South Lancashire with its central city Manchester. Again we have beautiful hill-country, sloping gently from the watershed westwards towards the Irish Sea, with the charming green valleys of the Ribble, the Irwell, the Mersey, and their tributaries, a country which, a hundred years ago chiefly swamp land, thinly populated, is now sown with towns and villages, and is the most densely populated strip of country in England. In Lancashire, and especially in Manchester, English manufacture finds at once its starting point and its centre. The Manchester Exchange is the thermometer for all the fluctuations of trade. The modern art of manufacture has reached its perfection in Manchester. In the cotton industry of South Lancashire, the application of the forces of Nature, the superseding of hand labour by machinery (especially by the power-loom and the self-acting mule), and the division of labour, are seen at the highest point; and, if we recognise in these three elements that which is characteristic of modern manufacture, we must confess that the cotton industry has remained in advance of all other branches of industry from the beginning down to the present day. The effects of modern manufacture upon the working class must necessarily develop here most freely and perfectly, and the manufacturing proletariat present itself in its fullest classic perfection. The degradation to which the application of steam-power, machinery and the division of labour reduce the working-man, and the attempts of the proletariat to rise above this abasement, must likewise be carried to the highest point and with the fullest consciousness. Hence because Manchester is the classic type of a modern manufacturing town, and because I know it as intimately as my own native town, more intimately than most of its residents know it, we shall make a longer stay here.

The towns surrounding Manchester vary little from the central city, so far as the working-people's quarters are concerned, except that the working class forms, if possible, a larger proportion of their population. These towns are purely industrial and conduct all their business through Manchester, upon which they are in every respect dependent, whence they are inhabited only by working-men and petty tradesmen, while Manchester has a very considerable commercial population, especially of commission and 'respectable' retail dealers. Hence Bolton, Preston, Wigan, Bury, Rochdale, Middleton, Heywood, Oldham, Ashton, Stalybridge, Stockport, etc., though nearly all towns of thirty, fifty, seventy to ninety thousand inhabitants, are almost wholly working-people's districts, interspersed only with factories, a few thoroughfares lined with shops, and a few lanes along which the gardens and houses of the manufacturers are scattered like villas. The towns themselves are badly and irregularly built, with foul courts, lanes, and back alleys, reeking of coal smoke, and especially dingy from the originally bright red brick, turned black with time, which is here the universal building material. Cellar dwellings are general here; wherever it is in any way possible, these subterranean dens are constructed, and a very considerable portion of the population dwells in them.

Among the worst of these towns after Preston and Oldham is Bolton, eleven miles north-west of Manchester. It has, so far as I have been able to observe in my repeated visits, but one main street, a very dirty one, Deansgate, which serves as a market, and is even in the finest weather a dark, unattractive hole in spite of the fact that, except for the factories, its sides are formed by low one and two-storeyed houses. Here, as everywhere, the older part of the town is especially ruinous and miserable. A dark-coloured body of water, which leaves the beholder in doubt whether it is a brook or a long string of stagnant puddles, flows through the town and contributes its share to the total pollution of the air, by no means pure without it.

There is Stockport, too, which lies on the Cheshire side of the Mersey, but belongs nevertheless to the manufacturing district of Manchester. It lies in a narrow valley along the Mersey, so that the streets slope down a steep hill on one side and up an equally steep one on the other, while the railway from Manchester to Birmingham passes over a high viaduct above the city and the whole valley. Stockport is renowned throughout the entire district as one of the duskiest, smokiest holes, and looks, indeed, especially when viewed from the viaduct, excessively repellent. But far more repulsive are the cottages and cellar dwellings of the working class, which stretch in long rows through all parts of the town from the valley bottom to the crest of the hill. I do not remember to have seen so many cellars used as dwellings in any other town of this district.

A few miles north-east of Stockport is Ashton-under-Lyne, one of the newest factory towns of this region. It stands on the slope of a hill at the foot of which are the canal and the river Tame, and is, in general, built on the newer, more regular plan. Five or six parallel streets stretch along the hill intersected at right angles by others leading down into the valley. By this method, the factories would be excluded from the town proper, even if the proximity of the river and the canal-way did not draw them all into the valley where they stand thickly crowded, belching forth black smoke from their chimneys. To this arrangement Ashton owes a much more attractive appearance than that of most factory towns; the streets are broad and cleaner, the cottages look new, bright red, and comfortable. But the modern system of building cottages for working-men has its own disadvantages; every street has its concealed back lane to which a narrow paved path leads, and which is all the dirtier. And, although I saw no buildings, except a few on entering, which could have been more than fifty years old, there are even in Ashton streets in which the cottages are getting bad, where the bricks in the house-corners are no longer firm but shift about, in which the walls have cracks and will not hold the chalk whitewash inside; streets, whose dirty, smoke-begrimed aspect is nowise different from that of the other towns of the district, except that in Ashton, this is the exception, not the rule.

A mile eastward lies Stalybridge, also on the Tame. In coming over the hill from Ashton, the traveller has, at the top, both right and left, fine large gardens with superb villa-like houses in their midst, built usually in the Elizabethan style, which is to the Gothic precisely what the Anglican Church is to the Apostolic Roman Catholic. A hundred paces farther and Stalybridge shows itself in the valley, in sharp contrast with the beautiful country seats, in sharp contrast even with the modest cottages of Ashton! Stalybridge lies in a narrow, crooked ravine, much narrower even than the valley at Stockport, and both sides of this ravine are occupied by an irregular group of cottages, houses, and mills. On entering, the very first cottages are narrow, smoke-begrimed, old and ruinous; and as the first houses, so the whole town. A few streets lie in the narrow valley bottom, most of them run criss-cross, pell-mell, up hill and down, and in nearly all the houses, by reason of this sloping situation, the ground floor is half-buried in the earth; and what multitudes of courts, back lanes, and remote nooks arise out of this confused way of building may be seen from the hills, whence one has the town, here and there, in a bird's-eye view almost at one's feet. Add to this the shocking filth, and the repulsive effect of Stalybridge, in spite of its pretty surroundings, may be readily imagined.

But enough of these little towns. Each has its own peculiarities, but in general, the working-people live in them just as in Manchester. Hence I have especially sketched only their peculiar construction, and would observe, that all more general observations as to the condition of the labouring population in Manchester are fully applicable to these surrounding towns as well.

Manchester lies at the foot of the southern slope of a range of hills, which stretch hither from Oldham, their last peak, Kersallmoor, being at once the racecourse and the *Mons Sacer* of Manchester. Manchester proper lies on the left bank of the Irwell, between that stream and the two smaller ones, the Irk and the

Medlock, which here empty into the Irwell. On the left bank of the Irwell, bounded by a sharp curve of the river, lies Salford, and farther westward Pendleton; northward from the Irwell lie Upper and Lower Broughton; northward of the Irk, Cheetham Hill; south of the Medlock lies Hulme; farther east Chorlton on Medlock; still farther, pretty well to the east of Manchester, Ardwick. The whole assemblage of buildings is commonly called Manchester, and contains about four hundred thousand inhabitants, rather more than less. The town itself is peculiarly built, so that a person may live in it for years, and go in and out daily without coming into contact with a working-people's quarter or even with workers, that is, so long as he confines himself to his business or to pleasure walks. This arises chiefly from the fact, that by unconscious tacit agreement, as well as with outspoken conscious determination, the working-people's quarters are sharply separated from the sections of the city reserved for the middle class; or, if this does not succeed, they are concealed with the cloak of charity. Manchester contains, at its heart, a rather extended commercial district, perhaps half a mile long and about as broad, and consisting almost wholly of offices and warehouses. Nearly the whole district is abandoned by dwellers, and is lonely and deserted at night; only watchmen and policemen traverse its narrow lanes with their dark lanterns. This district is cut through by certain main thoroughfares upon which the vast traffic concentrates, and in which the ground level is lined with brilliant shops. In these streets the upper floors are occupied, here and there, and there is a good deal of life upon them until late at night. With the exception of this commercial district, all Manchester proper, all Salford and Hulme, a great part of Pendleton and Chorlton, two-thirds of Ardwick, and single stretches of Cheetham Hill and Broughton are all unmixed working-people's quarters, stretching like a girdle, averaging a mile and a half in breadth, around the commercial district. Outside, beyond this girdle, lives the upper and middle bourgeoisie, the middle bourgeoisie in regularly laid out streets in the vicinity of the working quarters, especially in Chorlton and the lower lying portions of Cheetham Hill; the upper bourgeoisie in remoter villas with gardens in Chorlton and Ardwick, or on the breezy heights of Cheetham Hill, Broughton, and Pendleton, in free, wholesome country air, in fine, comfortable homes, passed once every half or quarter hour by omnibuses going into the city. And the finest part of the arrangement is this, that the members of this money aristocracy can take the shortest road through the middle of all the labouring districts to their places of business, without ever seeing that they are in the midst of the grimy misery that lurks to the right and the left. For the thoroughfares leading from the Exchange in all directions out of the city are lined, on both sides, with an almost unbroken series of shops, and are so kept in the hands of the middle and lower bourgeoisie, which, out of self-interest, cares for a decent and cleanly external appearance and *can* care for it. True, these shops bear some relation to the districts which lie behind them, and are more elegant in the commercial and residential quarters than when they hide grimy working-men's dwellings; but they suffice to conceal from the eyes of the wealthy men and women of strong stomachs and weak nerves the misery and grime which form the complement of their wealth. So, for instance, Deansgate, which leads from the Old Church directly southward, is lined first with mills and warehouses, then with second-rate shops and alehouses; farther south, when it leaves the commercial district, with less inviting shops, which grow dirtier and more interrupted by beerhouses and gin palaces the farther one goes, until at the southern end the appearance of the shops leaves no doubt that workers and workers only are their customers. So Market Street running south-east from the Exchange; at first brilliant shops of the best sort, with counting-houses or ware-houses above; in the continuation, Piccadilly, immense hotels and warehouses; in the farther continuation, London Road; in the neighbourhood of the Medlock, factories, beerhouses, shops for the humbler bourgeoisie and the working population; and from this point onward, large gardens and villas of the wealthier merchants and manufacturers. In this way anyone who knows Manchester can infer the adjoining districts, from the appearance of the thoroughfare, but one is seldom in a position to catch from the street a glimpse of the real labouring districts. I know very well that this hypocritical plan is more or less common to all great cities; I know, too, that the retail dealers are forced by the nature of their business to take possession of the great highways; I know that there are more good buildings than bad ones upon such streets everywhere, and that the value of land is greater near them than in remoter districts; but at the same time I have never seen so systematic a shutting out of the working class from the thoroughfares, so tender a concealment of everything which might affront the eye and the nerves of the bourgeoisie, as in Manchester. And yet, in other respects, Manchester is less built according to a plan, after official regulations, is more an outgrowth of accident, than any other city; and when I consider in this connection the eager assurances of the middle class, that the working class is doing famously, I cannot help feeling that the liberal manufacturers, the 'Big Wigs' of Manchester, are not so innocent after all, in the matter of this sensitive method of construction.

I may mention just here that the mills almost all adjoin the rivers or the different canals that ramify throughout the city, before I proceed at once to describe the labouring quarters. First of all, there is the old town of Manchester, which lies between the northern boundary of the commercial district and the Irk. Here the streets, even the better ones, are narrow and winding, as Todd Street, Long Millgate, Withy Grove, and Shude Hill, the houses dirty, old, and tumble-down, and the construction of the side streets utterly horrible. Going from the Old Church to Long Millgate, the stroller has at once a row of old-fashioned houses at the right, of which not one has kept its original level; these are remnants of the old pre-manufacturing Manchester, whose former inhabitants have removed with their descendants into better-built districts, and have left the houses, which were not good enough for them, to a population strongly mixed with Irish blood. Here one is in an almost undisguised working-men's quarter, for even the shops and beerhouses hardly take the trouble to exhibit a trifling degree of cleanliness. But all this is nothing in comparison with the courts and lanes which lie behind, to which access can be gained only through covered passages, in which no two human beings can pass at the same time. Of the irregular cramming together of dwellings in ways which defy all rational plan, of the tangle in which they are crowded literally one upon the other, it is impossible to convey an idea. And it is not the buildings surviving from the old times of Manchester which are to blame for this; the confusion has only recently reached its height when every scrap of space left by the old way of building has been filled up and patched over until not a foot of land is left to be further occupied.

The south bank of the Irk is here very steep and between fifteen and thirty feet high. On this declivitous hillside there are planted three rows of houses, of which the lowest rise directly out of the river, while the front walls of the highest stand on the crest of the hill in Long Millgate. Among them are mills on the river, in short, the method of construction is as crowded and disorderly here as in the lower part of Long Millgate. Right and left a multitude of covered passages lead from the main street into numerous courts, and he who turns in thither gets into a filth and disgusting grime, the equal of which is not to be found — especially in the courts which lead down to the Irk, and which contain unqualifiedly the most horrible dwellings which I have yet beheld. In one of these courts there stands directly at the entrance, at the end of the covered passage, a privy without a door, so dirty that the inhabitants can pass into and out of the court only by passing through foul pools of stagnant urine and excrement. This is the first court on the Irk above Ducie Bridge — in case anyone should care to look into it. Below it on the river there are several tanneries which fill the whole neighbourhood with the stench of animal putrefaction. Below Ducie Bridge the only entrance to most of the houses is by means of narrow, dirty stairs and over heaps of refuse and filth. The first court below Ducie Bridge, known as Allen's Court, was in such a state at the time of the cholera that the sanitary police ordered it evacuated, swept, and disinfected with chloride of lime. Dr Kay gives a terrible description of the state of this court at that time.[11] Since then, it seems to have been partially torn away and rebuilt; at least looking down from Ducie Bridge, the passer-by sees several ruined walls and heaps of débris with some newer houses. The view from this bridge, mercifully concealed from mortals of small stature by a parapet as high as a man, is characteristic for the whole district. At the bottom flows, or rather stagnates, the Irk, a narrow, coal-black, foul-smelling stream, full of débris and refuse, which it deposits on the shallower right bank. In dry weather, a long string of the most disgusting, blackish-green, slime pools are left standing on this bank, from the depths of which bubbles of miasmatic gas constantly arise and give forth a stench unendurable even on the bridge forty or fifty feet above the surface of the stream. But besides this, the stream itself is checked every few paces by high weirs, behind which slime and refuse accumulate and rot in thick masses. Above the bridge are tanneries, bonemills, and gasworks, from which all drains and refuse find their way into the Irk, which receives further the contents of all the neighbouring sewers and privies. It may be easily imagined, therefore, what sort of residue the stream deposits. Below the bridge you look upon the piles of débris, the refuse, filth, and offal from the courts on the steep left bank; here each house is packed close behind its neighbour and a piece of each is visible, all black, smoky, crumbling, ancient, with broken panes and window frames. The background is furnished by old barrack-like factory buildings. On the lower right bank stands a long row of houses and mills; the second house being a ruin without a roof, piled with débris; the third stands so low that the lowest floor is uninhabitable, and therefore without windows or doors. Here the background embraces the pauper burial-ground, the station of the Liverpool and Leeds railway, and, in the rear of this, the Workhouse, the 'Poor-Law Bastille' of Manchester, which, like a citadel, looks threateningly down from behind its high walls and parapets on the hilltop, upon the working-people's quarter below.

Above Ducie Bridge, the left bank grows more flat and the right bank steeper, but the condition of the dwellings on both banks grows worse rather than better. He who turns to the left here from the main street, Long Millgate, is lost; he wanders from one court to another, turns countless corners, passes nothing but narrow, filthy nooks and alleys, until after a few minutes he has lost all clue, and knows not whither to turn. Everywhere half or wholly ruined buildings, some of them actually uninhabited, which means a great deal here; rarely a wooden or stone floor to be seen in the houses, almost uniformly broken, ill-fitting windows and doors, and a state of filth! Everywhere heaps of débris, refuse, and offal; standing pools for gutters, and a stench which alone would make it impossible for a human being in any degree civilised to live in such a district. The newly-built extension of the Leeds railway, which crosses the Irk here, has swept away some of these courts and lanes, laying others completely open to view. Immediately under the railway bridge there stands a court, the filth and horrors of which surpass all the others by far, just because it was hitherto so shut off, so secluded that the way to it could not be found without a good deal of trouble. I should never have discovered it myself, without the breaks made by the railway, though I thought I knew this whole region thoroughly. Passing along a rough bank, among stakes and washing-lines, one penetrates into this chaos of small one-storeyed, one-roomed huts, in most of which there is no artificial floor; kitchen, living and sleeping-room all in one. In such a hole, scarcely five feet long by six broad, I found two beds – and such bedsteads and beds! – which, with a staircase and chimney-place, exactly filled the room. In several others I found absolutely nothing, while the door stood open, and the inhabitants leaned against it. Everywhere before the doors refuse and offal; that any sort of pavement lay underneath could not be seen but only felt, here and there, with the feet. This whole collection of cattle-sheds for human beings was surrounded on two sides by houses and a factory, and on the third by the river, and besides the narrow stair up the bank, a narrow doorway alone led out into another almost equally ill-built, ill-kept labyrinth of dwellings.

Enough! The whole side of the Irk is built in this way, a planless, knotted chaos of houses, more or less on the verge of uninhabitableness, whose unclean interiors fully correspond with their filthy external surroundings. And how could the people be clean with no proper opportunity for satisfying the most natural and ordinary wants? Privies are so rare here that they are either filled up every day, or are too remote for most of the inhabitants to use. How can people wash when they have only the dirty Irk water at hand, while pumps and water pipes can be found in decent parts of the city alone? In truth, it cannot be charged to the account of these helots of modern society if their dwellings are not more cleanly than the pig-sties which are here and there to be seen among them. The landlords are not ashamed to let dwellings like the six or seven cellars on the quay directly below Scotland Bridge, the floors of which stand at least two feet below the low-water level of the Irk that flows not six feet away from them; or like the upper floor of the corner-house on the opposite shore directly above the bridge, where the ground floor, utterly uninhabitable, stands deprived of all fittings for doors and windows, a case by no means rare in this region, when this open ground floor is used as a privy by the whole neighbourhood for want of other facilities!

If we leave the Irk and penetrate once more on the opposite side from Long Millgate into the midst of the working-men's dwellings, we shall come into a somewhat newer quarter, which stretches from St Michael's Church to Withy Grove and Shude Hill. Here there is somewhat better order. In place of the chaos of buildings, we find at least long straight lanes and alleys or courts, built according to a plan and usually square. But if, in the former case, every house was built according to caprice, here each lane and court is so built, without reference to the situation of the adjoining ones. The lanes run now in this direction, now in that, while every two minutes the wanderer gets into a blind alley, or, on turning a corner, finds himself back where he started from; certainly no one who has not lived a considerable time in this labyrinth can find his way through it.

If I may use the word at all in speaking of this district, the ventilation of these streets and courts is, in consequence of this confusion, quite as imperfect as in the Irk region; and if this quarter may, nevertheless, be said to have some advantage over that of the Irk, the houses being newer and the streets occasionally having gutters, nearly every house has, on the other hand, a cellar dwelling, which is rarely found in the Irk district, by reason of the greater age and more careless construction of the houses. As for the rest, the filth, débris, and offal heaps, and the pools in the streets are common to both quarters, and in the district now under discussion, another feature most injurious to the cleanliness of the inhabitants, is the multitude of pigs walking about in all the alleys, rooting into the offal heaps, or kept imprisoned in small pens. Here, as in most of the working-men's quarters of Manchester, the pork-raisers rent the courts and build pig-pens in them. In almost every court one or even several such pens may be found, into which the inhabitants of the court throw all refuse and offal, whence the swine grow fat; and the atmosphere, confined on all four sides, is utterly corrupted by putrefying animal and vegetable substances. Through this quarter, a broad and measurably decent street has been cut, Millers Street, and the background has been pretty successfully concealed. But if anyone should be led by curiosity to pass through one of the numerous passages which lead into the courts, he will find this piggery repeated at every twenty paces.

Such is the Old Town of Manchester, and on re-reading my description, I am forced to admit that instead of being exaggerated, it is far from black enough to convey a true impression of the filth, ruin, and uninhabitableness, the defiance of all considerations of cleanliness, ventilation, and health which characterise the construction of this single district, containing at least twenty to thirty thousand inhabitants. And such a district exists in the heart of the second city of England, the first manufacturing city of the world. If anyone wishes to see in how little space a human being can move, how little air – and *such* air! – he can breathe, how little of civilisation he may share and yet live, it is only necessary to travel hither. True, this is the *Old* Town, and the people of Manchester emphasise the fact whenever anyone mentions to them the frightful condition of this Hell upon Earth; but what does that prove? Everything which here arouses horror and indignation is of recent origin, belongs to the *industrial epoch*. The couple of hundred houses, which belong to old Manchester, have been long since abandoned by their original inhabitants; the industrial epoch alone has crammed into them the swarms of workers whom they now shelter; the industrial epoch alone has built up every spot between these old houses to win a covering for the masses whom it has conjured hither from the agricultural districts and from Ireland; the industrial epoch alone enables the owners of these cattle-sheds to rent them for high prices to human beings, to plunder the poverty of the workers, to undermine the health of thousands, in order that they *alone*, the owners, may grow rich. In the industrial epoch alone has it become possible that the worker scarcely freed from feudal servitude could be used as mere material, a mere chattel; that he must let himself be crowded into a dwelling too bad for every other, which he for his hard-earned wages buys the right to let go utterly to ruin. This manufacture has achieved, which, without these workers, this poverty, this slavery could not have lived. True, the original construction of this quarter was bad, little good could have been made out of it; but, have the land-owners, has the municipality done anything to improve it when rebuilding? On the contrary, wherever a nook or corner was free, a house has been run up; where a superfluous passage remained, it has been built up; the value of land rose with the blossoming out of manufacture, and the more it rose, the more madly was the work of building up carried on, without reference to the health or comfort of the inhabitants, with sole reference to the highest possible profit on the principle that *no hole is so bad but that some poor creature must take it who can pay for nothing better.* However, it is the Old Town, and with this reflection the bourgeoisie is comforted. Let us see, therefore, how much better it is in the New Town.

The New Town, known also as Irish Town, stretches up a hill of clay, beyond the Old Town, between the Irk and St George's Road. Here all the features of a city are lost. Single rows of houses or groups of streets stand, here and there, like little villages on the naked, not even grass-grown clay soil; the houses, or rather cottages, are in bad order, never repaired, filthy, with damp, un-clean, cellar dwellings; the lanes are neither paved nor supplied with sewers, but harbour numerous colonies of swine penned in small sties or yards, or wandering unrestrained through the neigh-bourhood. The mud in the streets is so deep that there is never a chance, except in the dryest weather, of walking without sinking into it ankle deep at every step. In the vicinity of St George's Road, the separate groups of buildings approach each other more closely, ending in a continuation of lanes, blind alleys, back lanes and courts, which grow more and more crowded and irregular the nearer they approach the heart of the town. True, they are here oftener paved or supplied with paved sidewalks and gutters; but the filth, the bad order of the houses, and especially of the cellars, remains the same.

It may not be out of place to make some general observations just here as to the customary construction of working-men's quarters in Manchester. We have seen how in the Old Town pure accident determined the grouping of the houses in general. Every house is built without reference to any other, and the scraps of space between them are called courts for want of another name. In the somewhat newer portions of the same quarter, and in other working-men's quarters, dating from the early days of industrial activity, a somewhat more orderly arrangement may be found. The space between two streets is divided into more regular, usually square courts.

These courts were built in this way from the beginning, and communicate with the streets by means of covered passages. If the totally planless construction is injurious to the health of the workers by preventing ventilation, this method of shutting them up in courts surrounded on all sides by buildings is far more so. The air simply cannot escape; the chimneys of the houses are the sole drains for the imprisoned atmosphere of the courts, and they serve the purpose only so long as fire is kept burning.[12] Moreover, the houses surrounding such courts are usually built back to back, having the rear wall in common; and this alone suffices to prevent any sufficient through ventilation. And, as the police charged with care of the streets, does not trouble itself about the condition of these courts, as everything quietly lies where it is thrown, there is no cause for wonder at the filth and heaps of ashes and offal to be found here. I have been in courts, in Millers Street, at least half a foot below the level of the thoroughfares, and without the slightest drainage for the water that accumulates in them in rainy weather! More recently another different method of building was adopted, and has now become general. Working-men's cottages are almost never built singly, but always by the dozen or score; a single contractor building up one or two streets at a time. These are then arranged as follows: one front is formed of cottages of the best class, so fortunate as to possess a back door and small court, and these command the highest rent. In the rear of these cottages runs a narrow alley, the back street, built up at both ends, into which either a narrow roadway or a covered passage leads from one side. The cottages which face this back street command least rent, and are most neglected. These have their rear walls in common with the third row of cottages which face a second street, and command less rent than the first row and more than the second.

By this method of construction, comparatively good ventilation can be obtained for the first row of cottages, and the third row is no worse off than in the former method. The middle row, on the other hand, is at least as badly ventilated as the houses in the courts, and the back street is always in the same filthy, disgusting condition as they. The contractors prefer this method because it saves them space, and furnishes the means of fleecing better-paid workers through the higher rents of the cottages in the first and third rows. These three different forms of cottage building are found all over Manchester and throughout Lancashire and Yorkshire, often mixed up together, but usually separate enough to indicate the relative age of parts of towns. The third system, that of the back alleys, prevails largely in the great working-men's district east of St George's Road and Ancoats Street, and is the one most often found in the other working-men's quarters of Manchester and its suburbs.

In the last-mentioned broad district included under the name Ancoats, stand the largest mills of Manchester lining the canals, colossal six- and seven-storeyed buildings towering with their slender chimneys far above the low cottages of the workers. The population of the district consists, therefore, chiefly of mill hands, and in the worst streets, of hand-weavers. The streets nearest the heart of the town are the oldest, and consequently the worst; they are, however, paved, and supplied with drains. Among them I include those nearest to and parallel with Oldham Road and Great Ancoats Street. Farther to the north-east lie many newly-built-up streets; here the cottages look neat and cleanly, doors and windows are new and freshly painted, the rooms within newly white-washed; the streets themselves are better aired, the vacant building lots between them larger and more numerous. But this can be said of a minority of the houses only, while cellar dwellings are to be found under almost every cottage; many streets are unpaved and without sewers; and, worse than all, this neat appearance is all pretence, a pretence which vanishes within the first ten years. For the construction of the cottages individually is no less to be condemned than the plan of the streets. All such cottages look neat and substantial at first; their massive brick walls deceive the eye, and, on passing through a *newly-built* working-men's street, with-out remembering the back alleys and the construction of the houses themselves, one is inclined to agree with the assertion of the Liberal manufacturers that the working population is nowhere so well housed as in England. But on closer examination, it becomes evident that the walls of these cottages are as thin as it is possible to make them. The outer walls, those of the cellar, which bear the weight of the ground floor and roof, are one whole brick thick at most, the bricks lying with their long sides touching; but I have seen many a cottage of the same height, some in process of building, whose outer walls were but one-half brick thick, the bricks lying not sidewise but lengthwise, their narrow ends touch-ing. The object of this is to spare material, but there is also another reason for it; namely, the fact that the contractors never own the land but lease it, according to the English custom, for twenty, thirty, forty, fifty, or ninety-nine years, at the expiration of which time it falls, with everything upon it, back into the possession of the original holder, who pays nothing in return for improvements upon it. The improvements are therefore so calculated by the lessee as to be worth as little as possible at the expiration of the stipulated term. And as such cottages are often built but twenty or thirty years before the expiration of the term, it may easily be imagined that the contractors make no unnecessary expenditures upon them. Moreover, these contractors, usually carpenters and builders, or manufacturers, spend little or nothing in repairs, partly to avoid diminishing their rent receipts, and partly in view of the approaching surrender of the improvement to the landowner; while in consequence of commercial crises and the loss of work that follows them, whole streets often stand empty, the cottages falling rapidly into ruin and uninhabitableness. It is calculated in general that working-men's cottages last only forty years on the average. This sounds strangely enough when one sees the beautiful, massive walls of newly-built ones, which seem to give promise of lasting a couple of centuries; but the fact remains that the niggardliness of the original expenditure, the neglect of all repairs, the frequent periods of emptiness, the constant change of inhabitants, and the destruction carried on by the dwellers during the final ten years, usually Irish families, who do not hesitate to use the wooden portions for fire-wood – all this, taken together, accomplishes the complete ruin of the cottages by the end of forty years. Hence it comes that Ancoats, built chiefly since the sudden growth of manufacture, chiefly indeed within the present century, contains a vast number of ruinous houses, most of them being, in fact, in the last stages of inhabitableness. I will not dwell upon the amount of capital thus wasted, the small additional expenditure upon the original improvement and upon repairs which would suffice to keep this whole district clean, decent, and inhabitable for years together. I have to deal here with the state of the houses and their inhabitants, and it must be admitted that no more injurious and demoralising method of housing the workers has yet been discovered than precisely this. The working-man is constrained to occupy such ruinous dwellings because he cannot pay for others, and because there are no others in the vicinity of his mill; perhaps, too, because they belong to the employer, who engages him only on condition of his taking such a cottage. The calculation with reference to the forty years' duration of the cottage is, of course, not always perfectly strict; for, if the dwellings are in a thickly-built-up portion of the town, and there is a good prospect of finding steady occupants for them, while the ground rent is high, the contractors do a little something to keep the cottages inhabitable after the expiration of the forty years. They never do anything more, however, than is absolutely unavoidable, and the dwellings so repaired are the worst of all. Occasionally when an epidemic threatens, the otherwise sleepy conscience of the sanitary police is a little stirred, raids are made into the working-men's districts, whole rows of cellars and cottages are closed, as happened in the case of several lanes near Oldham Road; but this does not last long: the condemned cottages soon find occupants again, the owners are much better off by letting them, and the sanitary police won't come again so soon. These east and north-east sides of Manchester are the only ones on which the bourgeoisie has not built, because ten or eleven months of the year the west and south-west wind drives the smoke of all the factories hither, and that the working-people alone may breathe.

Southward from Great Ancoats Street, lies a great, straggling, working-men's quarter, a hilly, barren stretch of land, occupied by detached, irregularly built rows of houses or squares; between these, empty building lots, uneven, clayey, without grass and scarcely passable in wet weather. The cottages are all filthy and old, and recall the New Town to mind. The stretch cut through by the Birmingham railway is the most thickly built-up and the worst. Here flows the Medlock with countless windings through a valley, which is, in places, on a level with the valley of the Irk. Along both sides of the stream, which is coal black, stagnant and foul, stretches a broad belt of factories and working-men's dwellings, the latter all in the worst condition. The bank is chiefly declivitous and is built over to the water's edge, just as we saw along the Irk; while the houses are equally bad, whether built on the Manchester side or in Ardwick, Chorlton, or Hulme. But the most horrible spot (if I should describe all the separate spots in detail I should never come to the end) lies on the Manchester side, immediately south-west of Oxford Road, and is known as Little Ireland. In a rather deep hole, in a curve of the Medlock and surrounded on all four sides by tall factories and high embankments, covered with buildings, stand two groups of about two hundred cottages, built chiefly back to back, in which live about four thousand human beings, most of them Irish. The cottages are old, dirty, and of the smallest sort, the streets uneven, fallen into ruts and in part without drains or pavement; masses of refuse, offal and sickening filth lie among standing pools in all directions; the atmosphere is poisoned by the effluvia from these, and laden and darkened by the smoke of a dozen tall factory chimneys. A horde of ragged women and children swarm about here, as filthy as the swine that thrive upon the garbage heaps and in the puddles. In short, the whole rookery furnishes such a hateful and repulsive spectacle as can hardly be equalled in the worst court on the Irk. The race that lives in these ruinous cottages, behind broken windows, mended with oilskin, sprung doors, and rotten door-posts, or in dark, wet cellars, in measureless filth and stench, in this atmosphere penned in as if with a purpose, this race must really have reached the lowest stage of humanity. This is the impression and the line of thought which the exterior of this district forces upon the beholder. But what must one think when he hears that in each of these pens, containing at most two rooms, a garret and perhaps a cellar, on the average twenty human beings live; that in the whole region, for each one hundred and twenty persons, one usually inaccessible privy is provided; and that in spite of all the preachings of the physicians, in spite of the excitement into which the cholera epidemic plunged the sanitary police by reason of the condition of Little Ireland, in spite of everything, in this year of grace 1844, it is in almost the same state as in 1831! Dr Kay asserts that not only the cellars but the first floors of all the houses in this district are damp; that a number of cellars once filled up with earth have now been emptied and are occupied once more by Irish people; that in one cellar the water constantly wells up through a hole stopped with clay, the cellar lying below the river level, so that its occupant, a hand-loom weaver, had to bale out the water from his dwelling every morning and pour it into the street!

Farther down, on the left side of the Medlock, lies Hulme, which, properly speaking, is one great working-people's district, the condition of which coincides almost exactly with that of Ancoats; the more thickly built-up regions chiefly bad and approaching ruin, the less populous of more modern structure, but generally sunk in filth. On the other side of the Medlock, in Manchester proper, lies a second great working-men's district which stretches on both sides of Deansgate as far as the business quarter, and in certain parts rivals the Old Town. Especially in the immediate vicinity of the business quarter, between Bridge and Quay Streets, Princess and Peter Streets, the crowded construction exceeds in places the narrowest courts of the Old Town. Here are long, narrow lanes between which run contracted, crooked courts and passages, the entrances to which are so irregular that the explorer is caught in a blind alley at every few steps, or comes out where he least expects to, unless he knows every court and every alley exactly and separately. According to Dr Kay, the most demoralised class of all Manchester lived in these ruinous and filthy districts, people whose occupations are thieving and prostitution; and, to all appearance, his assertion is still true at the present moment. When the sanitary police made its expedition hither in 1831, it found the uncleanness as great as in Little Ireland or along the Irk (that it is not much better today, I can testify); and among other items, they found in Parliament Street for three hundred and eighty persons, and in Parliament Passage for thirty thickly populated houses, but a single privy.

If we cross the Irwell to Salford, we find on a peninsula formed by the river, a town of eighty thousand inhabitants, which, properly speaking, is one large working-men's quarter, penetrated by a single wide avenue. Salford, once more important than Manchester, was then the leading town of the surrounding district to which it still gives its name, Salford Hundred. Hence it is that an old and therefore very unwholesome, dirty, and ruinous locality is to be found here, lying opposite the Old Church of Manchester, and in as bad a condition as the Old Town on the other side of the Irwell. Farther away from the river lies the newer portion, which is, however, already beyond the limit of its forty years of cottage life, and therefore ruinous enough. All Salford is built in courts or narrow lanes, so narrow, that they remind me of the narrowest I have ever seen, the little lanes of Genoa. The average construction of Salford is in this respect much worse than that of Manchester, and so, too, in respect to cleanliness. If, in Manchester, the police, from time to time, every six or ten years, makes a raid upon the working-people's districts, closes the worst dwellings, and causes the filthiest spots in these Augean stables to be cleansed, in Salford it seems to have done absolutely nothing. The narrow side lanes and courts of Chapel Street, Greengate, and Gravel Lane have certainly never been cleansed since they were built. Of late, the Liverpool railway has been carried through the middle of them, over a high viaduct, and has abolished many of the filthiest nooks; but what does that avail? Whoever passes over this viaduct and looks down, sees filth and wretchedness enough; and, if anyone takes the trouble to pass through these lanes, and glance through the open doors and windows into the houses and cellars, he can convince himself afresh with every step that the workers of Salford live in dwellings in which cleanliness and comfort are impossible. Exactly the same state of affairs is found in the more distant regions of Salford, in Islington, along Regent Road, and back of the Bolton railway. The working-men's dwellings between Oldfield Road and Cross Lane, where a mass of courts and alleys are to be found in the worst possible state, vie with the dwellings of the Old Town in filth and overcrowding. In this district I found a man, apparently about sixty years old, living in a cow stable. He had constructed a sort of chimney for his square pen, which had neither windows, floor, nor ceiling, had obtained a bedstead and lived there, though the rain dripped through his rotten roof. This man was too old and weak for regular work, and supported himself by removing manure with a hand-cart; the dung-heaps lay next door to his palace!

. Such are the various working-people's quarters of Manchester as I had occasion to observe them personally during twenty months. If we briefly formulate the result of our wanderings, we must admit that 350,000 working-people of Manchester and its environs live, almost all of them, in wretched, damp, filthy cottages, that the streets which surround them are usually in the most miserable and filthy condition, laid out without the slightest reference to ventilation, with reference solely to the profit secured by the contractor. In a word, we must confess that in the working-men's dwellings of Manchester, no cleanliness, no convenience, and consequently no comfortable family life is possible; that in such dwellings only a physically degenerate race, robbed of all humanity, degraded, reduced morally and physically to bestiality, could feel comfortable and at home. And I am not alone in making this assertion. We have seen that Dr Kay gives precisely the same description; and, though it is superfluous, I quote further the words of a Liberal,[13] recognised and highly valued as an authority by the manufacturers, and a fanatical opponent of all independent movements of the workers:

As I passed through the dwellings of the mill hands in Irish Town, Ancoats, and Little Ireland, I was only amazed that it is possible to maintain a reasonable state of health in such homes. These towns, for in extent and number of inhabitants they are towns, have been erected with the utmost disregard of everything except the immediate advantage of the speculating builder. A carpenter and builder unite to buy a series of building sites [i.e. they lease them for a number of years], and cover them with so-called houses. In one place we found a whole street following the course of a ditch, because in this way deeper cellars could be secured without the cost of digging, cellars not for storing wares or rubbish, but for dwellings for human beings. *Not one house of this street escaped the cholera*. In general, the streets of these suburbs are unpaved, with a dung-heap or ditch in the middle; the houses are built back to back, without ventilation or drainage, and whole families are limited to a corner of a cellar or a garret.

I have already referred to the unusual activity which the sanitary police manifested during the cholera visitation. When the epidemic was approaching, a universal terror seized the bourgeoisie of the city. People remembered the unwholesome dwellings of the poor, and trembled before the certainty that each of these slums would become a centre for the plague, whence it would spread desolation in all directions through the houses of the propertied class. A Health Commission was appointed at once to investigate these districts, and report upon their condition to the Town Council. Dr Kay, himself a member of this Commission, who visited in person every separate police district except one, the eleventh, quotes extracts from their reports: there were inspected, in all, 6,951 houses – naturally in Manchester proper alone, Salford and the other suburbs being excluded. Of these, 6,565 urgently needed whitewashing within; 960 were out of repair; 939 had insufficient drains; 1,435 were damp; 452 were badly ventilated; 2,221 were without privies. Of the 687 streets inspected, 248 were unpaved, 53 but partially paved, 112 ill-ventilated, 352 containing standing pools, heaps of débris, refuse, etc. To cleanse such an

Augean stable before the arrival of the cholera was, of course, out of the question. A few of the worst nooks were therefore cleansed, and everything else left as before. In the cleansed spots, as Little Ireland proves, the old filthy condition was naturally restored in a couple of months. As to the internal condition of these houses, the same Commission reports a state of things similar to that which we have already met with in London, Edinburgh, and other cities.[14]

It often happens that a whole Irish family is crowded into one bed; often a heap of filthy straw or quilts of old sacking cover all in an indiscriminate heap, where all alike are degraded by want, stolidity, and wretchedness. Often the inspectors found, in a single house, two families in two rooms. All slept in one, and used the other as a kitchen and dining-room in common. Often more than one family lived in a single damp cellar, in whose pestilent atmosphere twelve to sixteen persons were crowded together. To these and other sources of disease must be added that pigs were kept, and other disgusting things of the most revolting kind were found.

We must add that many families, who had but one room for themselves, receive boarders and lodgers in it, that such lodgers of both sexes by no means rarely sleep in the same bed with the married couple; and that the single case of a man and his wife and his adult sister-in-law sleeping in one bed was found, according to the 'Report concerning the sanitary condition of the working class', six times repeated in Manchester. Common lodging-houses, too, are very numerous; Dr Kay gives their number in 1831 at 267 in Manchester proper, and they must have increased greatly since then. Each of these receives from twenty to thirty guests, so that they shelter all told, nightly, from five to seven thousand human beings. The character of the houses and their guests is the same as in other cities. Five to seven beds in each room lie on the floor – without bedsteads, and on these sleep, mixed indiscriminately, as many persons as apply. What physical and moral atmosphere reigns in these holes I need not state. Each of these houses is a focus of crime, the scene of deeds against which human nature revolts, which would perhaps never have been executed but for this forced centralisation of vice.[15] Gaskell gives the number of persons living in cellars in Manchester proper as 20,000. The *Weekly Dispatch* gives the number, 'according to official reports', as twelve per cent. of the working class, which agrees with Gaskell's number; the workers being estimated at 175,000, 21,000 would form twelve per cent. of it. The cellar dwellings in the suburbs are at least as numerous, so that the number of persons living in cellars in Manchester – using its name in the broader sense – is not less than forty to fifty thousand. So much for the dwellings of the workers in the largest cities and towns. The manner in which the need of a shelter is satisfied furnishes a standard for the manner in which all other necessities are supplied. That in these filthy holes a ragged, ill-fed population alone can dwell is a safe conclusion, and such is the fact. The clothing of the working-people, in the majority of cases, is in a very bad condition. The material used for it is not of the best adapted. Wool and linen have almost vanished from the wardrobe of both sexes, and cotton has taken their place. Shirts are made of bleached or coloured cotton goods; the dresses of the women are chiefly of cotton print goods, and woollen petticoats are rarely to be seen on the washline. The men wear chiefly trousers of fustian or other heavy cotton goods, and jackets or coats of the same. Fustian has become the proverbial costume of the working-men, who are called 'fustian jackets', and call themselves so in contrast to the gentlemen who wear broadcloth, which latter words are used as characteristic for the middle class. When Feargus O'Connor, the Chartist leader, came to Manchester during the insurrection of 1842, he appeared, amidst the deafening applause of the working-men, in a fustian suit of clothing. Hats are the universal head-covering in England, even for working-men, hats of the most diverse forms, round, high, broad-brimmed, narrow-brimmed, or without brims – only the younger men in factory towns wearing caps. Anyone who does not own a hat folds himself a low, square paper cap.

The whole clothing of the working class, even assuming it to be in good condition, is little adapted to the climate. The damp air of England, with its sudden changes of temperature, more calculated than any other to give rise to colds, obliges almost the whole middle class to wear flannel next the skin, about the body, and flannel scarfs and shirts are in almost universal use. Not only is the working class deprived of this precaution, it is scarcely ever in a position to use a thread of woollen clothing; and the heavy cotton goods, though thicker, stiffer, and heavier than woollen clothes, afford much less protection against cold and wet, remain damp much longer because of their thickness and the nature of the stuff, and have nothing of the compact density of fulled woollen cloths. And, if a working-man once buys himself a woollen coat for Sunday, he must get it from one of the cheap shops where he finds bad, so-called 'Devil's-dust' cloth, manufactured for sale and not for use, and liable to tear or grow threadbare in a fortnight, or he must buy of an old clothes'-dealer a half-worn coat which has seen its best days, and lasts but a few weeks. Moreover, the working-man's clothing is, in most cases, in bad condition, and there is the oft-recurring necessity for placing the best pieces in the pawn-broker's shop. But among very large numbers, especially among the Irish, the prevailing clothing consists of perfect rags often beyond all mending, or so patched that the original colour can no longer be detected. Yet the English and Anglo-Irish go on patching, and have carried this art to a remarkable pitch, putting wool or bagging on fustian, or the reverse – it's all the same to them. But the true, transplanted Irish hardly ever patch except in the extremest necessity, when the garment would otherwise fall apart. Ordinarily the rags of the shirt protrude through the rents in the coat or trousers. They wear, as Thomas Carlyle says [16] – 'A suit of tatters, the getting on or off of which is said to be a difficult operation, transacted only in festivals and the high tides of the calendar.'

The Irish have introduced, too, the custom previously unknown in England, of going barefoot. In every manufacturing town there is now to be seen a multitude of people, especially women and children, going about barefoot, and their example is gradually being adopted by the poorer English.

As with clothing, so with food. The workers get what is too bad for the property-holding class. In the great towns of England everything may be had of the best, but it costs money; and the workman, who must keep house on a couple of pence, cannot afford much expense. Moreover, he usually receives his wages on Saturday evening, for, although a beginning has been made in the payment of wages on Friday, this excellent arrangement is by no means universal; and so he comes to market at five or even seven o'clock, while the buyers of the middle class have had the first choice during the morning, when the market teems with the best of everything. But when the workers reach it, the best has vanished, and, if it was still there, they would probably not be able to buy it. The potatoes which the workers buy are usually poor, the vegetables wilted, the cheese old and of poor quality, the bacon rancid, the meat lean, tough, taken from old, often diseased, cattle, or such as have died a natural death, and not fresh even then, often half decayed. The sellers are usually small hucksters who buy up inferior goods, and can sell them cheaply by reason of their badness. The poorest workers are forced to use still another device to get together the things they need with their few pence. As nothing can be sold on Sunday, and all shops must be closed at twelve o'clock on Saturday night, such things as would not keep until Monday are sold at any price between ten o'clock and midnight. But nine-tenths of what is sold at ten o'clock is past using by Sunday morning, yet these are precisely the provisions which make up the Sunday dinner of the poorest class. The meat which the workers buy is very often past using; but having bought it, they must eat it. On the 6th of January, 1844 (if I am not greatly mistaken), a court leet was held in Manchester, when eleven meat-sellers were fined for having sold tainted meat. Each of them had a whole ox or pig, or several sheep, or from fifty to sixty pounds of meat, which were all confiscated in a tainted condition. In one case, sixty-four stuffed Christmas geese were seized which had proved unsaleable in Liverpool, and had been forwarded to Manchester, where they were brought to market foul and rotten. All the particulars, with names and fines, were published at the time in the *Manchester Guardian*. In the six weeks, from July 1st to August 14th, the same sheet reported three similar cases. According to the *Guardian* for August 3rd, a pig, weighing 200 pounds, which had been found dead and decayed, was cut up and exposed for sale by a butcher at Heywood, and was then seized. According to the number for July 31st, two butchers at Wigan, of whom one had previously been convicted of the same offence, were fined £2 and £4 respectively, for exposing tainted meat for sale; and, according to the number for August 10th, twenty-six tainted hams seized at a dealer's in Bolton, were publicly burnt, and the dealer fined twenty shillings. But these are by no means all the cases; they do not even form a fair average for a period of six weeks, according to which to form an average for the year. There are often seasons in which every number of the semi-weekly *Guardian* mentions a

similar case found in Manchester or its vicinity. And when one
reflects upon the many cases which must escape detection in the
extensive markets that stretch along the front of every main street,
under the slender supervision of the market inspectors – and how
else can one explain the boldness with which whole animals are
exposed for sale? – when one considers how great the temptation
must be, in view of the incomprehensibly small fines mentioned
in the foregoing cases; when one reflects what condition a piece
of meat must have reached to be seized by the inspectors, it is
impossible to believe that the workers obtain good and nourishing
meat as a usual thing. But they are victimised in yet another way
by the money-greed of the middle class. Dealers and manufacturers adulterate all kinds of provisions in an atrocious manner,
and without the slightest regard to the health of the consumers.
We have heard the *Manchester Guardian* upon this subject; let us
hear another organ of the middle class – I delight in the testimony
of my opponents – let us hear the *Liverpool Mercury*: 'Salted butter
is sold for fresh, the lumps being covered with a coating of fresh
butter, or a pound of fresh being laid on top to taste, while the
salted article is sold after this test, or the whole mass is washed and
then sold as fresh. With sugar, pounded rice and other cheap
adulterating materials are mixed, and the whole sold at full price.
The refuse of soap-boiling establishments also is mixed with other
things and sold as sugar. Chicory and other cheap stuff is mixed
with ground coffee, and artificial coffee beans with the unground
article. Cocoa is often adulterated with fine brown earth, treated
with fat to render it more easily mistakable for real cocoa. Tea is
mixed with the leaves of the sloe and with other refuse, or dry tea-
leaves are roasted on hot copper plates, so returning to the proper
colour and being sold as fresh. Pepper is mixed with pounded
nutshells; port wine is manufactured outright (out of alcohol, dye-
stuffs, etc.), while it is notorious that more of it is consumed in
England alone than is grown in Portugal; and tobacco is mixed
with disgusting substances of all sorts and in all possible forms in
which the article is produced.' I can add that several of the most
respected tobacco dealers in Manchester announced publicly last
summer, that, by reason of the universal adulteration of tobacco,
no firm could carry on business without adulteration, and that no
cigar costing less than threepence is made wholly from tobacco.

These frauds are naturally not restricted to articles of food, though I could mention a dozen more, the villainy of mixing gypsum or chalk with flour among them. Fraud is practised in the sale of articles of every sort: flannel, stockings, etc., are stretched, and shrink after the first washing; narrow cloth is sold as being from one and a half to three inches broader than it actually is; stoneware is so thinly glazed that the glazing is good for nothing, and cracks at once, and a hundred other rascalities, *tout comme chez nous*. But the lion's share of the evil results of these frauds falls to the workers. The rich are less deceived, because they can pay the high prices of the large shops which have a reputation to lose, and would injure themselves more than their customers if they kept poor or adulterated wares; the rich are spoiled, too, by habitual good eating, and detect adulteration more easily with their sensitive palates. But the poor, the working-people, to whom a couple of farthings are important, who must buy many things with little money, who cannot afford to inquire too closely into the quality of their purchases, and cannot do so in any case because they have had no opportunity of cultivating their taste – to their share fall all the adulterated, poisoned provisions. They must deal with the small retailers, must buy perhaps on credit, and these small retail dealers who cannot sell even the same quality of goods so cheaply as the largest retailers, because of their small capital and the large proportional expenses of their business, must knowingly or unknowingly buy adulterated goods in order to sell at the lower prices required, and to meet the competition of the others. Further, a large retail dealer who has extensive capital invested in his business is ruined with his ruined credit if detected in a fraudulent practice; but what harm does it do a small grocer, who has customers in a single street only, if frauds are proved against him? If no one trusts him in Ancoats, he moves to Chorlton or Hulme, where no one knows him, and where he continues to defraud as before; while legal penalties attach to very few adulterations unless they involve revenue frauds. Not in the quality alone, but in the quantity of his goods as well, is the English working-man defrauded. The small dealers usually have false weights and measures, and an incredible number of convictions for such offences may be read in the police reports. How universal this form of fraud is in the manufacturing districts, a couple of extracts from the *Manchester Guardian* may serve to show. They cover only a short period, and, even here, I have not all the numbers at hand:

Guardian, June 16, 1844, Rochdale Sessions. – Four dealers fined five to ten shillings for using light weights. Stockport Sessions. – Two dealers fined one shilling, one of them having seven light weights and a false scale, and both having been warned.

Guardian, June 19, Rochdale Sessions. – One dealer fined five, and two farmers ten shillings.

Guardian, June 22, Manchester Justices of the Peace. – Nineteen dealers fined two shillings and sixpence to two pounds.

Guardian, June 26, Ashton Sessions. – Fourteen dealers and farmers fined two shillings and sixpence to one pound. Hyde Petty Sessions. – Nine farmers and dealers condemned to pay costs and five shillings fines.

Guardian, July 9, Manchester – Sixteen dealers condemned to pay costs and fines not exceeding ten shillings.

Guardian, July 13, Manchester. – Nine dealers fined from two shillings and sixpence to twenty shillings.

Guardian, July 24, Rochdale. – Four dealers fined ten to twenty shillings.

Guardian, July 27, Bolton. – Twelve dealers and innkeepers condemned to pay costs.

Guardian, August 3, Bolton. – Three dealers fined two shillings and sixpence, and five shillings.

Guardian, August 10, Bolton. – One dealer fined five shillings.

And the same causes which make the working class the chief sufferers from frauds in the quality of goods make them the usual victims of frauds in the question of quantity too.

The habitual food of the individual working-man naturally varies according to his wages. The better-paid workers, especially those in whose families every member is able to earn something, have good food as long as this state of things lasts; meat daily, and bacon and cheese for supper. Where wages are less, meat is used only two or three times a week, and the proportion of bread and potatoes increases. Descending gradually, we find the animal food reduced to a small piece of bacon cut up with the potatoes; lower still, even this disappears, and there remain only bread, cheese, porridge, and potatoes, until on the lowest round of the ladder,

among the Irish, potatoes form the sole food. As an accompani-
ment, weak tea, with perhaps a little sugar, milk, or spirits, is
universally drunk. Tea is regarded in England, and even in Ireland,
as quite as indispensable as coffee in Germany, and where no tea is
used, the bitterest poverty reigns. But all this presupposes that the
workman has work. When he has none, he is wholly at the mercy
of accident, and eats what is given him, what he can beg or steal.
And, if he gets nothing, he simply starves, as we have seen. The
quantity of food varies, of course, like its quality, according to the
rate of wages, so that among ill-paid workers, even if they have no
large families, hunger prevails in spite of full and regular work; and
the number of the ill-paid is very large. Especially in London,
where the competition of the workers rises with the increase of
population, this class is very numerous, but it is to be found in
other towns as well. In these cases all sorts of devices are used;
potato parings, vegetable refuse, and rotten vegetables are eaten for
want of other food, and everything greedily gathered up which
may possibly contain an atom of nourishment. And, if the week's
wages are used up before the end of the week, it often enough
happens that in the closing days the family gets only as much food,
if any, as is barely sufficient to keep off starvation. Of course such
a way of living unavoidably engenders a multitude of diseases, and
when these appear, when the father from whose work the family is
chiefly supported, whose physical exertion most demands nourishment, and who therefore first succumbs – when the father is
utterly disabled, then misery reaches its height, and then the
brutality with which society abandons its members, just when
their need is greatest, comes out fully into the light of day.

To sum up briefly the facts thus far cited. The great towns are
chiefly inhabited by working-people, since in the best case there
is one bourgeois for two workers, often for three, here and there
for four; these workers have no property whatsoever of their
own, and live wholly upon wages, which usually go from hand to
mouth. Society, composed wholly of atoms, does not trouble itself
about them; leaves them to care for themselves and their families,
yet supplies them no means of doing this in an efficient and permanent manner. Every working-man, even the best, is therefore
constantly exposed to loss of work and food, that is to death by
starvation, and many perish in this way. The dwellings of the

workers are everywhere badly planned, badly built, and kept in the worst condition, badly ventilated, damp, and unwholesome. The inhabitants are confined to the smallest possible space, and at least one family usually sleeps in each room. The interior arrangement of the dwellings is poverty-stricken in various degrees, down to the utter absence of even the most necessary furniture. The clothing of the workers, too, is generally scanty, and that of great multitudes is in rags. The food is, in general, bad; often almost unfit for use, and in many cases, at least at times, insufficient in quantity, so that, in extreme cases, death by starvation results. Thus the working class of the great cities offers a graduated scale of conditions in life, in the best cases a temporarily endurable existence for hard work and good wages, good and endurable, that is, from the worker's standpoint; in the worst cases, bitter want, reaching even homelessness and death by starvation. The average is much nearer the worst case than the best. And this series does not fall into fixed classes, so that one can say, this fraction of the working class is well off, has always been so, and remains so. If that is the case here and there, if single branches of work have in general an advantage over others, yet the condition of the workers in each branch is subject to such great fluctuations that a single working-man may be so placed as to pass through the whole range from comparative comfort to the extremest need, even to death by starvation, while almost every English working-man can tell a tale of marked changes of fortune. Let us examine the causes of this somewhat more closely.

Competition

We have seen in the introduction how competition created the proletariat at the very beginning of the industrial movement, by increasing the wages of weavers in consequence of the increased demand for woven goods, so inducing the weaving peasants to abandon their farms and earn more money by devoting themselves to their looms. We have seen how it crowded out the small farmers by means of the large farm system, reduced them to the rank of proletarians, and attracted them in part into the towns; how it further ruined the small bourgeoisie in great measure and reduced its members also to the ranks of the proletariat; how it centralised capital in the hands of the few, and population in the great towns. Such are the various ways and means by which competition, as it reached its full manifestation and free development in modern industry, created and extended the proletariat. We shall now have to observe its influence on the working class already created. And here we must begin by tracing the results of competition of single workers with one another.

Competition is the completest expression of the battle of all against all which rules in modern civil society. This battle, a battle for life, for existence, for everything, in case of need a battle of life and death, is fought not between the different classes of society only, but also between the individual members of these classes. Each is in the way of the other, and each seeks to crowd out all who are in his way, and to put himself in their place. The workers are in constant competition among themselves, as the members of the bourgeoisie among themselves. The power-loom weaver is in competition with the hand-loom weaver, the unemployed or ill-paid hand-loom weaver with him who has work or is better paid, each trying to supplant the other. But this competition of the workers among themselves is the worst side of the present state of things in its effect upon the worker, the sharpest weapon against the proletariat in the hands of the bourgeoisie. Hence the effort of the workers to nullify this competition by associations, hence the hatred of the bourgeoisie towards these associations, and its triumph in every defeat which befalls them.

The proletarian is helpless; left to himself, he cannot live a single day. The bourgeoisie has gained a monopoly of all means of existence in the broadest sense of the word. What the proletarian needs, he can obtain only from this bourgeoisie, which is protected in its monopoly by the power of the State. The proletarian is, therefore, in law and in fact, the slave of the bourgeoisie, which can decree his life or death. It offers him the means of living, but only for an 'equivalent' for his work. It even lets him have the appearance of acting from a free choice, of making a contract with free, unconstrained consent, as a responsible agent who has attained his majority.

Fine freedom, where the proletarian has no other choice than that of either accepting the conditions which the bourgeoisie offers him, or of starving, of freezing to death, of sleeping naked among the beasts of the forests! A fine 'equivalent' valued at pleasure by the bourgeoisie! And if one proletarian is such a fool as to starve rather than agree to the equitable propositions of the bourgeoisie, his 'natural superiors', another is easily found in his place; there are proletarians enough in the world, and not all so insane as to prefer dying to living.

Here we have the competition of the workers among themselves. If *all* the proletarians announced their determination to starve rather than work for the bourgeoisie, the latter would have to surrender its monopoly. But this is not the case – is, indeed, a rather impossible case – so that the bourgeoisie still thrives. To this competition of the worker there is but one limit; no worker will work for less than he needs to subsist. If he must starve, he will prefer to starve in idleness rather than in toil. True, this limit is relative; one needs more than another, one is accustomed to more comfort than another; the Englishman who is still somewhat civilised, needs more than the Irishman who goes in rags, eats potatoes, and sleeps in a pig-sty. But that does not hinder the Irishman's competing with the Englishman, and gradually forcing the rate of wages, and with it the Englishman's level of civilisation, down to the Irishman's level. Certain kinds of work require a certain grade of civilisation, and to these belong almost all forms of industrial occupation; hence the interest of the bourgeoisie requires in this case that wages should be high enough to enable the workman to keep himself upon the required plane.

The newly immigrated Irishman, encamped in the first stable that offers, or turned out in the street after a week because he spends everything upon drink and cannot pay rent, would be a poor mill-hand. The mill-hand must, therefore, have wages enough to enable him to bring up his children to regular work; but no more, lest he should be able to get on without the wages of his children, and so make something else of them than mere working-men. Here, too, the limit, the minimum wage, is relative. When every member of the family works, the individual worker can get on with proportionately less, and the bourgeoisie has made the most of the opportunity of employing and making profitable the labour of women and children afforded by machine-work. Of course it is not in every family that every member can be set to work, and those in which the case is otherwise would be in a bad way if obliged to exist upon the minimum wage possible to a wholly employed family. Hence the usual wages form an average according to which a fully employed family gets on pretty well, and one which embraces few members able to work, pretty badly. But in the worst case, every working-man prefers surrendering the trifling luxury to which he was accustomed to not living at all; prefers a pig-pen to no roof, wears rags in preference to going naked, confines himself to a potato diet in preference to starvation. He contents himself with half-pay and the hope of better times rather than be driven into the street to perish before the eyes of the world, as so many have done who had no work whatever. This trifle, therefore, this something more than nothing, is the min-imum of wages. And if there are more workers at hand than the bourgeoisie thinks well to employ – if at the end of the battle of competition there yet remain workers who find nothing to do, they must simply starve; for the bourgeois will hardly give them work if he cannot sell the produce of their labour at a profit.

From this it is evident what the minimum of wages is. The maximum is determined by the competition of the bourgeoisie among themselves; for we have seen how they, too, must compete with each other. The bourgeois can increase his capital only in commerce and manufacture, and in both cases he needs workers.

Even if he invests his capital at interest, he needs them indirectly; for without commerce and manufacture, no one would pay him interest upon his capital, no one could use it. So the bourgeois certainly needs workers, not indeed for his immediate living, for at need he could consume his capital, but as we need an article of trade or a beast of burden – as a means of profit. The proletarian produces the goods which the bourgeois sells with advantage. When, therefore, the demand for these goods increases so that all the competing working-men are employed, and a few more might perhaps be useful, the competition among the workers falls away, and the bourgeoisie begin to compete among themselves. The capitalist in search of workmen knows very well that his profits increase as prices rise in consequence of the increased demand for his goods, and pays a trifle higher wages rather than let the whole profit escape him. He sends the butter to fetch the cheese, and getting the latter, leaves the butter ungrudgingly to the workers. So one capitalist after another goes in chase of workers, and wages rise; but only as high as the increasing demand permits. If the capitalist, who willingly sacrificed a part of his extraordinary profit, runs into danger of sacrificing any part of his ordinary average profit, he takes very good care not to pay more than average wages.

From this we can determine the average rate of wages. Under average circumstances, when neither workers nor capitalists have reason to compete, especially among themselves, when there are just as many workers at hand as can be employed in producing precisely the goods that are demanded, wages stand a little above the minimum. How far they rise above the minimum will depend upon the average needs and the grade of civilisation of the workers. If the workers are accustomed to eat meat several times in the week, the capitalists must reconcile themselves to paying wages enough to make this food attainable, not less, because the workers are not competing among themselves and have no occasion to content themselves with less; not more, because the capitalists, in the absence of competition among themselves, have no occasion to attract working-men by extraordinary favours. This standard of the average needs and the average civilisation of the workers has become very complicated by reason of the complications of English industry, and is different for different sorts of workers, as has been pointed out. Most industrial occupations demand a certain skill and regularity, and for these qualities which involve a certain grade of civilisation, the rate of wages must be such as to induce the worker to acquire such skill and subject himself to such regularity. Hence it is that the average wages of industrial workers are higher than those of mere porters, day-labourers, etc., higher especially than those of agricultural labourers, a fact to which the additional cost of the necessities of life in cities contributes somewhat. In other words, the worker is, in law and in fact, the slave of the property-holding class, so effectually a slave that he is sold like a piece of goods, rises and falls in value like a commodity. If the demand for workers increases, the price of workers rises; if it falls, their price falls. If it falls so greatly that a number of them become unsaleable, if they are left in stock, they are simply left idle; and as they cannot live upon that, they die of starvation. For, to speak in the words of the economists, the expense incurred in maintaining them would not be reproduced, would be money thrown away, and to this end no man advances capital; and, so far, Malthus was perfectly right in his theory of population. The only difference as compared with the old, outspoken slavery is this, that the worker of today seems to be free because he is not sold once for all, but piecemeal by the day, the week, the year, and because no one owner sells him to another, but he is forced to sell himself in this way instead, being the slave of no particular person, but of the whole property holding class. For him the matter is unchanged at bottom, and if this semblance of liberty necessarily gives him some real freedom on the one hand, it entails on the other the disadvantage that no one guarantees him a subsistence, he is in danger of being repudiated at any moment by his master, the bourgeoisie, and left to die of starvation, if the bourgeoisie ceases to have an interest in his employment, his existence. The bourgeoisie, on the other hand, is far better off under the present arrangement than under the old slave system; it can dismiss its employees at discretion without sacrificing invested capital, and gets its work done much more cheaply than is possible with slave labour, as Adam Smith comfortingly pointed out.[17]

Hence it follows, too, that Adam Smith was perfectly right in making the assertion: 'That the demand for men, like that for any other commodity, necessarily regulates the production of men, quickens it when it goes on too slowly, and stops it when it advances too fast.' *Just as in the case of any other commodity*! If there are too few labourers at hand, prices, i.e. wages, rise, the workers are more prosperous, marriages multiply, more children are born and more live to grow up, until a sufficient number of labourers has been secured. If there are too many on hand, prices fall, want of work, poverty and starvation, and consequent diseases arise, and the 'surplus population' is put out of the way. And Malthus, who carried the foregoing proposition of Smith farther, was also right, in his way, in asserting that there are always more people on hand than can be maintained from the available means of subsistence. Surplus population is engendered rather by the competition of the workers among themselves, which forces each separate worker to labour as much each day as his strength can possibly admit. If a manufacturer can employ ten hands nine hours daily, he can employ nine if each works ten hours, and the tenth goes hungry. And if a manufacturer can force the nine hands to work an extra hour daily for the same wages by threatening to discharge them at a time when the demand for hands is not very great, he discharges the tenth and saves so much wages. This is the process on a small scale, which goes on in a nation on a large one. The productiveness of each hand raised to the highest pitch by the competition of the workers among themselves, the division of labour, the introduction of machinery, the subjugation of the forces of nature, deprive a multitude of workers of bread. These starving workers are then removed from the market, they can buy nothing, and the quantity of articles of consumption previously required by them is no longer in demand, need no longer be produced; the workers previously employed in producing them are therefore driven out of work, and are also removed from the market, and so it goes on, always the same old round, or rather, so it would go if other circumstances did not intervene. The introduction of the industrial forces already referred to for increasing production leads, in the course of time, to a reduction of prices of the articles produced and to consequent increased consumption, so that a large part of the displaced workers finally, after long suffering, find work again. If, in addition to this, the conquest of foreign markets constantly and rapidly increases the demand for manufactured goods, as has been the case in England during the past sixty years, the demand for hands increases, and, in proportion to it, the population. Thus, instead of diminishing, the population of the British Empire has increased with extraordinary rapidity, and is still increasing. Yet, in spite of the extension of industry, in spite of the demand for working-men which, in general, has increased, there is, according to the confession of all the official political parties (Tory, Whig, and Radical), permanent surplus, superfluous population; the competition among the workers is constantly greater than the competition to secure workers.

Whence comes this incongruity? It lies in the nature of industrial competition and the commercial crises which arise from them. In the present unregulated production and distribution of the means of subsistence, which is carried on not directly for the sake of supplying needs, but for profit, in the system under which every-one works for himself to enrich himself, disturbances inevitably arise at every moment. For example, England supplies a number of countries with most diverse goods. Now, although the manu-facturer may know how much of each article is consumed in each country annually, he cannot know how much is on hand at every given moment, much less can he know how much his competitors export thither. He can only draw most uncertain inferences from the perpetual fluctuations in prices, as to the quantities on hand and the needs of the moment. He must trust to luck in exporting his goods. Everything is done blindly, as guesswork, more or less at the mercy of accident. Upon the slightest favourable report, each one exports what he can, and before long such a market is glutted, sales stop, capital remains inactive, prices fall, and English manufacture has no further employment for its hands. In the beginning of the development of manufacture, these checks were limited to single branches and single markets; but the centralising tendency of competition which drives the hands thrown out of one branch into such other branches as are most easily accessible, and transfers the goods which cannot be disposed of in one market to other markets, has gradually brought the single minor crises nearer together and united them into one periodically recurring crisis. Such a crisis usually recurs once in five years after a brief period of activity and general prosperity; the home market, like all foreign ones, is glutted with English goods, which it can only slowly absorb, the industrial movement comes to a standstill in almost every branch, the small manufacturers and merchants who cannot survive a prolonged inactivity of their invested capital fail, the larger ones suspend business during the worst season, close their mills or work short time, perhaps half the day; wages fall by reason of the competition of the unemployed, the diminution of working-time and the lack of profitable sales; want becomes universal among the workers, the small savings, which individuals may have made, are rapidly consumed, the philanthropic institutions are overburdened, the poor-rates are doubled, trebled, and still insufficient, the number of the starving increases, and the whole multitude of 'surplus' population presses in terrific numbers into the foreground. This continues for a time; the 'surplus' exist as best they may, or perish; philanthropy and the Poor Law help many of them to a painful prolongation of their existence. Others find scant means of subsistence here and there in such kinds of work as have been least open to competition, are most remote from manufacture. And with how little can a human being keep body and soul together for a time! Gradually the state of things improves; the accumulations of goods are consumed, the general depression among the men of commerce and manufacture prevents a too hasty replenishing of the markets, and at last rising prices and favourable reports from all directions restore activity. Most of the markets are distant ones; demand increases and prices rise constantly while the first exports are arriving; people struggle for the first goods, the first sales enliven trade still more, the prospective ones promise still higher prices; expecting a further rise, merchants begin to buy upon speculation, and so to withdraw from consumption the articles intended for it, just when they are most needed. Speculation forces prices still higher, by inspiring others to purchase, and appropriating new importations at once. All this is reported to England, manufacturers begin to produce with a will, new mills are built, every means is employed to make the most of the favourable moment. Speculation arises here, too, exerting the same influence as upon foreign markets, raising prices, withdrawing goods from consumption, spurring manufacture in both ways to the highest pitch of effort. Then come the daring speculators working with fictitious capital, living upon credit, ruined if they cannot speedily sell; they hurl themselves into this universal, disorderly race for profits, multiply the disorder and

haste by their unbridled passion, which drives prices and production to madness. It is a frantic struggle, which carries away even
the most experienced and phlegmatic; goods are spun, woven,
hammered, as if all mankind were to be newly equipped, as though
two thousand million new consumers had been discovered in the
moon. All at once the shaky speculators abroad, who must have
money, begin to sell, below market price, of course, for their need
is urgent; one sale is followed by others, prices fluctuate, speculators throw their goods upon the market in terror, the market is
disordered, credit shaken, one house after another stops payments,
bankruptcy follows bankruptcy, and the discovery is made that
three times more goods are on hand or under way than can be
consumed. The news reaches England, where production has been
going on at full speed meanwhile, panic seizes all hands, failures
abroad cause others in England, the panic crushes a number of firms,
all reserves are thrown upon the market here, too, in the moment
of anxiety, and the alarm is still further exaggerated. This is the
beginning of the crisis, which then takes precisely the same course as
its predecessor, and gives place in turn to a season of prosperity. So
it goes on perpetually – prosperity, crisis, prosperity, crisis, and this
perennial round in which English industry moves is, as has been
before observed, usually completed once in five or six years.

From this it is clear that English manufacture must have, at all
times save the brief periods of highest prosperity, an unemployed
reserve army of workers, in order to be able to produce the masses
of goods required by the market in the liveliest months. This
reserve army is larger or smaller, according as the state of the
market occasions the employment of a larger or smaller proportion
of its members. And if at the moment of highest activity of the
market the agricultural districts and the branches least affected
by the general prosperity temporarily supply to manufacture a
number of workers, these are a mere minority, and these too
belong to the reserve army, with the single difference that the
prosperity of the moment was required to reveal their connection
with it. When they enter upon the more active branches of work,
their former employers draw in somewhat, in order to feel the loss
less, work longer hours, employ women and younger workers,
and when the wanderers discharged at the beginning of the crisis
return, they find their places filled and themselves superfluous – at

least in the majority of cases. This reserve army, which embraces an immense multitude during the crisis and a large number during the period which may be regarded as the average between the highest prosperity and the crisis, is the 'surplus population' of England, which keeps body and soul together by begging, stealing, street-sweeping, collecting manure, pushing handcarts, driving donkeys, peddling, or performing occasional small jobs. In every great town a multitude of such people may be found. It is astonishing in what devices this 'surplus population' takes refuge. The London crossing-sweepers are known all over the world; but hitherto the principal streets in all the great cities, as well as the crossings, have been swept by people out of other work, and employed by the Poor Law guardians or the municipal authorities for the purpose. Now, however, a machine has been invented which rattles through the streets daily, and has spoiled this source of income for the unemployed. Along the great highways leading into the cities, on which there is a great deal of waggon traffic, a large number of people may be seen with small carts, gathering fresh horse-dung at the risk of their lives among the passing coaches and omnibuses, often paying a couple of shillings a week to the authorities for the privilege. But this occupation is forbidden in many places, because the ordinary street-sweepings thus impoverished cannot be sold as manure. Happy are such of the 'surplus' as can obtain a push-cart and go about with it. Happier still those to whom it is vouchsafed to possess an ass in addition to the cart. The ass must get his own food or is given a little gathered refuse, and can yet bring in a trifle of money. Most of the 'surplus' betake themselves to huckstering. On Saturday afternoons, especially, when the whole working population is on the streets, the crowd who live from huckstering and peddling may be seen. Shoe and corset laces, braces, twine, cakes, oranges, every kind of small articles are offered by men, women, and children; and at other times also, such peddlers are always to be seen standing at the street corners, or going about with cakes and ginger-beer or nettle-beer. Matches and such things, sealing-wax, and patent mixtures for lighting fires are further resources of such venders. Others, so-called jobbers, go about the streets seeking small jobs. Many of these succeed in getting a day's work, many are not so fortunate.

'At the gates of all the London docks', says the Rev. W. Champney, preacher of the East End, 'hundreds of the poor appear every morning in winter before daybreak, in the hope of getting a day's work. They await the opening of the gates; and, when the youngest and strongest and best known have been engaged, hundreds cast down by disappointed hope, go back to their wretched homes.'

When these people find no work and will not rebel against society, what remains for them but to beg? And surely no one can wonder at the great army of beggars, most of them able-bodied men, with whom the police carries on perpetual war. But the beggary of these men has a peculiar character. Such a man usually goes about with his family singing a pleading song in the streets or appealing, in a speech, to the benevolence of the passers-by. And it is a striking fact that these beggars are seen almost exclusively in the working-people's districts, that it is almost exclusively the gifts of the poor from which they live. Or the family takes up its position in a busy street, and without uttering a word, lets the mere sight of its helplessness plead for it. In this case, too, they reckon upon the sympathy of the workers alone, who know from experience how it feels to be hungry, and are liable to find themselves in the same situation at any moment; for this dumb, yet most moving appeal, is met with almost solely in such streets as are frequented by working-men, and at such hours as working-men pass by; but especially on summer evenings, when the 'secrets' of the working-people's quarters are generally revealed, and the middle class withdraws as far as possible from the district thus polluted. And he among the 'surplus' who has courage and passion enough openly to resist society, to reply with declared war upon the bourgeoisie to the disguised war which the bourgeoisie wages upon him, goes forth to rob, plunder, murder, and burn!

Of this surplus population there are, according to the reports of the Poor Law commissioners, on an average, a million and a half in England and Wales; in Scotland the number cannot be ascertained for want of Poor Law regulations, and with Ireland we shall deal separately. Moreover, this million and a half includes only those who actually apply to the parish for relief; the great multitude who struggle on without recourse to this most hated expedient, it does not embrace. On the other hand, a good part of the number belongs to the agricultural districts, and does not enter into the present discussion. During a crisis this number naturally increases markedly, and want reaches its highest pitch. Take, for instance, the crisis of 1842, which, being the latest, was the most violent; for the intensity of the crisis increases with each repetition, and the next, which may be expected not later than 1847,[18] will probably be still more violent and lasting. During this crisis the poor-rates rose in every town to a hitherto unknown height. In Stockport, among other towns, for every pound paid in house-rent, eight shillings of poor-rate had to be paid, so that the rate alone formed forty per cent. of the house-rent. Moreover, whole streets stood vacant, so that there were at least twenty thousand fewer inhabitants than usual, and on the doors of the empty houses might be read: 'Stockport to let'. In Bolton, where, in ordinary years, the rents from which rates are paid average £86,000, they sank to £36,000. The number of the poor to be supported rose, on the other hand, to 14,000, or more than twenty per cent. of the whole number of inhabitants. In Leeds, the Poor Law guardians had a reserve fund of £10,000. This, with a contribution of £7,000, was wholly exhausted before the crisis reached its height. So it was everywhere. A report drawn up in January, 1843, by a committee of the Anti-Corn Law League, on the condition of the industrial districts in 1842, which was based upon detailed statements of the manufacturers, asserts that the poor-rate was, taking the average, twice as high as in 1839, and that the number of persons requiring relief has trebled, even quintupled, since that time; that a multitude of applicants belong to a class which had never before solicited relief; that the working class commands more than two-thirds less of the means of subsistence than from 1834–1836; that the consumption of meat had been decidedly less, in some places twenty per cent., in others reaching sixty per cent. less; that even handicraftsmen, smiths, bricklayers, and others, who usually have full employment in the most depressed periods, now suffered greatly from want of work and reduction of wages; and that, even now, in January, 1843, wages are still steadily falling. And these are the reports of manufacturers! The starving workmen, whose mills were idle, whose employers could give them no work, stood in the streets in all directions, begged singly or in crowds, besieged the sidewalks in armies, and appealed to the passers-by for help; they begged, not cringing like ordinary beggars, but threatening by their numbers, their gestures, and their words. Such was the state of things in all the industrial districts, from Leicester to Leeds, and from Manchester to Birmingham. Here and there disturbances arose, as in the Staffordshire potteries, in July. The most frightful excitement prevailed among the workers until the general insurrection broke out throughout the manufacturing districts in August. When I came to Manchester in November, 1842, there were crowds of unemployed working-men at every street corner, and many mills were still standing idle. In the following months these unwilling corner loafers gradually vanished, and the factories came into activity once more.

To what extent want and suffering prevail among these unemployed during such a crisis, I need not describe. The poor-rates are insufficient, vastly insufficient; the philanthropy of the rich is a rain-drop in the ocean, lost in the moment of falling; beggary can support but few among the crowds. If the small dealers did not sell to the working-people on credit at such times as long as possible – paying themselves liberally afterwards, it must be confessed – and if the working-people did not help each other, every crisis would remove a multitude of the surplus through death by starvation. Since, however, the most depressed period is brief, lasting, at worst, but one, two, or two and a half years, most of them emerge from it with their lives after dire privations. But indirectly by disease, etc., every crisis finds a multitude of victims, as we shall see. First, however, let us turn to another cause of abasement to which the English worker is exposed, a cause permanently active in forcing the whole class downwards.

Irish Immigration

We have already referred several times in passing to the Irish who have immigrated into England; and we shall now have to investigate more closely the causes and results of this immigration. The rapid extension of English industry could not have taken place if England had not possessed in the numerous and impoverished population of Ireland a reserve at command. The Irish had nothing to lose at home, and much to gain in England; and from the time when it became known in Ireland that the east side of St George's Channel offered steady work and good pay for strong arms, every year has brought armies of the Irish hither. It has been calculated that more than a million have already immigrated, and not far from fifty thousand still come every year, nearly all of whom enter the industrial districts, especially the great cities, and there form the lowest class of the population. Thus there are in London, 120,000; in Manchester, 40,000; in Liverpool, 34,000; Bristol, 24,000; Glasgow, 40,000; Edinburgh, 29,000, poor Irish people.[19] These people having grown up almost without civilisation, accustomed from youth to every sort of privation, rough, intemperate, and improvident, bring all their brutal habits with them among a class of the English population which has, in truth, little inducement to cultivate education and morality. Let us hear Thomas Carlyle upon this subject:[20]

> The wild Milesian features, looking false ingenuity, restlessness, unreason, misery, and mockery, salute you on all highways and byways. The English coachman, as he whirls past, lashes the Milesian with his whip, curses him with his tongue; the Milesian is holding out his hat to beg. He is the sorest evil this country has to strive with. In his rags and laughing savagery, he is there to undertake all work that can be done by mere strength of hand and back – for wages that will purchase him potatoes. He needs only salt for condiment, he lodges to his mind in any pig-hutch or

dog-hutch, roosts in outhouses, and wears a suit of tatters, the getting on and off of which is said to be a difficult operation, transacted only in festivals and the high tides of the calendar. The Saxon-man, if he cannot work on these terms, finds no work. The uncivilised Irishman, not by his strength, but by the opposite of strength, drives the Saxon native out, takes possession in his room. There abides he, in his squalor and unreason, in his falsity and drunken violence, as the ready-made nucleus of degradation and disorder. Whoever struggles, swimming with difficulty, may now find an example how the human being can exist not swimming, but sunk. That the condition of the lower multitude of English labourers approximates more and more to that of the Irish, competing with them in all the markets: that whatsoever labour, to which mere strength with little skill will suffice, is to be done, will be done not at the English price, but at an approximation to the Irish price; at a price superior as yet to the Irish, that is, superior to scarcity of potatoes for thirty weeks yearly; superior, yet hourly, with the arrival of every new steamboat, sinking nearer to an equality with that.

If we except his exaggerated and one-sided condemnation of the Irish national character, Carlyle is perfectly right. These Irishmen who migrate for fourpence to England, on the deck of a steamship on which they are often packed like cattle, insinuate themselves everywhere. The worst dwellings are good enough for them: their clothing causes them little trouble, so long as it holds together by a single thread; shoes they know not; their food consists of potatoes and potatoes only; whatever they earn beyond these needs they spend upon drink. What does such a race want with high wages? The worst quarters of all the large towns are inhabited by Irishmen. Whenever a district is distinguished for especial filth and especial ruinousness, the explorer may safely count upon meeting chiefly those Celtic faces which one recognises at the first glance as different from the Saxon physiognomy of the native, and the singing, aspirate brogue which the true Irishman never loses. I have occasionally heard the Irish-Celtic language spoken in the most thickly populated parts of Manchester. The majority of the families who live in cellars are almost everywhere of Irish origin. In short, the Irish have, as Dr Kay says, discovered the minimum of the necessities of life, and are now making the English workers acquainted with it. Filth and drunkenness, too, they have brought with them. The lack of cleanliness, which is not so injurious in the country, where population is scattered, and which is the Irishman's second nature, becomes terrifying and gravely dangerous through its concentration here in the great cities. The Milesian deposits all garbage and filth before his house door here, as he was accustomed to do at home, and so accumulates the pools and dirt-heaps which disfigure the working-people's quarters and poison the air. He builds a pig-sty against the house wall as he did at home, and if he is prevented from doing this, he lets the pig sleep in the room with himself. This new and unnatural method of cattle-raising in cities is wholly of Irish origin. The Irishman loves his pig as the Arab his horse, with the difference that he sells it when it is fat enough to kill. Otherwise, he eats and sleeps with it, his children play with it, ride upon it, roll in the dirt with it, as anyone may see a thousand times repeated in all the great towns of England. The filth and comfortlessness that prevail in the houses themselves it is imposs-ible to describe. The Irishman is unaccustomed to the presence of furniture; a heap of straw, a few rags, utterly beyond use as clothing, suffice for his nightly couch. A piece of wood, a broken chair, an old chest for a table, more he needs not; a tea-kettle, a few pots and dishes, equip his kitchen, which is also his sleeping and living room. When he is in want of fuel, everything combust-ible within his reach, chairs, door-posts, mouldings, flooring, finds its way up the chimney. Moreover, why should he need much room? At home in his mud-cabin there was only one room for all domestic purposes; more than one room his family does not need in England. So the custom of crowding many persons into a single room, now so universal, has been chiefly implanted by the Irish immigration. And since the poor devil must have one enjoyment, and society has shut him out of all others, he betakes himself to the drinking of spirits. Drink is the only thing which makes the Irishman's life worth having, drink and his cheery carefree temp-erament; so he revels in drink to the point of the most bestial drunkenness. The southern facile character of the Irishman, his crudity, which places him but little above the savage, his contempt for all humane enjoyments, in which his very crudeness makes him incapable of sharing, his filth and poverty, all favour drunkenness.

The temptation is great, he cannot resist it, and so when he has money he gets rid of it down his throat. What else should he do? How can society blame him when it places him in a position in which he almost of necessity becomes a drunkard; when it leaves him to himself, to his savagery?

With such a competitor the English working-man has to struggle with a competitor upon the lowest plane possible in a civilised country, who for this very reason requires less wages than any other. Nothing else is therefore possible than that, as Carlyle says, the wages of English working-men should be forced down further and further in every branch in which the Irish compete with him. And these branches are many. All such as demand little or no skill are open to the Irish. For work which requires long training or regular, pertinacious application, the dissolute, unsteady, drunken Irishman is on too low a plane. To become a mechanic, a mill-hand, he would have to adopt the English civilisation, the English customs, become, in the main, an Englishman. But for all simple, less exact work, wherever it is a question more of strength than skill, the Irishman is as good as the Englishman. Such occupations are therefore especially overcrowded with Irishmen: hand-weavers, brick-layers, porters, jobbers, and such workers, count hordes of Irishmen among their number, and the pressure of this race has done much to depress wages and lower the working class. And even if the Irish, who have forced their way into other occupations, should become more civilised, enough of the old habits would cling to them to have a strong degrading influence upon their English companions in toil, especially in view of the general effect of being surrounded by the Irish. For when, in almost every great city, a fifth or a quarter of the workers are Irish, or children of Irish parents, who have grown up among Irish filth, no one can wonder if the life, habits, intelligence, moral status – in short, the whole character of the working class assimilates a great part of the Irish characteristics. On the contrary, it is easy to understand how the degrading position of the English workers, engendered by our modern history, and its immediate consequences, has been still more degraded by the presence of Irish competition.

Results

Having now investigated, somewhat in detail, the conditions under which the English working class lives, it is time to draw some further inferences from the facts presented, and then to compare our inferences with the actual state of things. Let us see what the workers themselves have become under the given circumstances, what sort of people they are, what their physical, mental, and moral status.

When one individual inflicts bodily injury upon another, such injury that death results, we call the deed manslaughter; when the assailant knew in advance that the injury would be fatal, we call his deed murder. But when society[21] places hundreds of proletarians in such a position that they inevitably meet a too early and an unnatural death, one which is quite as much a death by violence as that by the sword or bullet; when it deprives thousands of the necessaries of life, places them under conditions in which they *cannot* live – forces them, through the strong arm of the law, to remain in such conditions until that death ensues which is the inevitable consequence – knows that these thousands of victims must perish, and yet permits these conditions to remain, its deed is murder just as surely as the deed of the single individual; disguised, malicious murder, murder against which none can defend himself, which does not seem what it is, because no man sees the murderer, because the death of the victim seems a natural one, since the offence is more one of omission than of commission. But murder it remains. I have now to prove that society in England daily and hourly commits what the working-men's organs, with perfect correctness, characterise as social murder, that it has placed the workers under conditions in which they can neither retain health nor live long; that it undermines the vital force of these workers gradually, little by little, and so hurries them to the grave before their time. I have further to prove that society knows how injurious such conditions are to the health and the life of the workers, and yet does nothing to improve these conditions. That it *knows* the consequences of its deeds; that its act is, therefore, not mere manslaughter, but murder, I shall have proved, when I cite official documents, reports of Parliament and of the Government, in substantiation of my charge.

That a class which lives under the conditions already sketched and is so ill-provided with the most necessary means of subsistence, cannot be healthy and can reach no advanced age, is self-evident. Let us review the circumstances once more with especial reference to the health of the workers. The centralisation of population in great cities exercises of itself an unfavourable influence; the atmosphere of London can never be so pure, so rich in oxygen, as the air of the country; two and a half million pairs of lungs, two hundred and fifty thousand fires, crowded upon an area three to four miles square, consume an enormous amount of oxygen, which is replaced with difficulty, because the method of building cities in itself impedes ventilation. The carbonic acid gas, engendered by respiration and fire, remains in the streets by reason of its specific gravity, and the chief air current passes over the roofs of the city. The lungs of the inhabitants fail to receive the due supply of oxygen, and the consequence is mental and physical lassitude and low vitality. For this reason, the dwellers in cities are far less exposed to acute, and especially to inflammatory, affections than rural populations, who live in a free, normal atmosphere; but they suffer the more from chronic affections. And if life in large cities is, in itself, injurious to health, how great must be the harmful influence of an abnormal atmosphere in the working-people's quarters, where, as we have seen, everything combines to poison the air. In the country, it may, perhaps, be comparatively innoxious to keep a dung-heap adjoining one's dwelling, because the air has free ingress from all sides; but in the midst of a large town, among closely built lanes and courts that shut out all movement of the atmosphere, the case is different. All putrefying vegetable and animal substances give off gases decidedly injurious to health, and if these gases have no free way of escape, they inevitably poison the atmosphere. The filth and stagnant pools of the working-people's quarters in the great cities have, therefore, the worst effect upon the public health, because they produce precisely those gases which engender disease; so, too, the exhalations from contaminated streams. But this is by no means all. The manner in which the great multitude of the poor is treated by society today is revolting. They are drawn into the large cities where they breathe a poorer atmosphere than in the country; they are relegated to districts which, by reason of the method of construction, are worse ventilated than any others; they are deprived of all means of cleanliness, of water itself, since pipes are laid only when paid for, and the rivers so polluted that they are useless for such purposes; they are obliged to throw all offal and garbage, all dirty water, often all disgusting drainage and excrement into the streets, being without other means of disposing of them; they are thus compelled to infect the region of their own dwellings. Nor is this enough. All conceivable evils are heaped upon the heads of the poor. If the population of great cities is too dense in general, it is they in particular who are packed into the least space. As though the vitiated atmosphere of the streets were not enough, they are penned in dozens into single rooms, so that the air which they breathe at night is enough in itself to stifle them. They are given damp dwellings, cellar dens that are not waterproof from below, or garrets that leak from above. Their houses are so built that the clammy air cannot escape. They are supplied bad, tattered, or rotten clothing, adulterated and indigestible food. They are exposed to the most exciting changes of mental condition, the most violent vibrations between hope and fear; they are hunted like game, and not permitted to attain peace of mind and quiet enjoyment of life. They are deprived of all enjoyments except that of sexual indulgence and drunkenness, are worked every day to the point of complete exhaustion of their mental and physical energies, and are thus constantly spurred on to the maddest excess in the only two enjoyments at their command. And if they surmount all this, they fall victims to want of work in a crisis when all the little is taken from them that had hitherto been vouchsafed them.

How is it possible, under such conditions, for the lower class to be healthy and long-lived? What else can be expected than an excessive mortality, an unbroken series of epidemics, a progressive deterioration in the physique of the working population? Let us see how the facts stand.

That the dwellings of the workers in the worst portions of the cities, together with the other conditions of life of this class, engender numerous diseases, is attested on all sides. The article already quoted from the *Artisan* asserts with perfect truth, that lung diseases must be the inevitable consequence of such conditions, and that, indeed, cases of this kind are disproportionately frequent in this class. That the bad air of London, and especially of the working-people's districts, is in the highest degree favourable to the development of consumption, the hectic appearance of great numbers of persons sufficiently indicates. If one roams the streets a little in the early morning, when the multitudes are on their way to their work, one is amazed at the number of persons who look wholly or half-consumptive. Even in Manchester the people have not the same appearance; these pale, lank, narrow-chested, hollow-eyed ghosts, whom one passes at every step, these languid, flabby faces, incapable of the slightest energetic expression, I have seen in such startling numbers only in London, though consumption carries off a horde of victims annually in the factory towns of the North. In competition with consumption stands typhus, to say nothing of scarlet fever, a disease which brings most frightful devastation into the ranks of the working class. Typhus, that universally diffused affliction, is attributed by the official report on the sanitary condition of the working class, directly to the bad state of the dwellings in the matters of ventilation, drainage, and cleanliness. This report, compiled, it must not be forgotten, by the leading physicians of England from the testimony of other physicians, asserts that a single ill-ventilated court, a single blind alley without drainage, is enough to engender fever, and usually does engender it, especially if the inhabitants are greatly crowded. This fever has the same character almost everywhere, and develops in nearly every case into specific typhus. It is to be found in the working-people's quarters of all great towns and cities, and in single ill-built, ill-kept streets of smaller places, though it naturally seeks out single victims in better districts also. In London it has now prevailed for a considerable time; its extraordinary violence in the year 1837 gave rise to the report already referred to. According to the annual report of Dr Southwood Smith on the London Fever Hospital, the number of patients in 1843 was 1,462, or 418 more than in any previous year. In the damp, dirty regions of the north, south, and east districts of London, this disease raged with extraordinary violence. Many of the patients were working-people from the country, who had endured the severest privation while migrating, and, after their arrival, had slept hungry and half-naked in the streets, and so fallen victims to the fever. These people were brought into the hospital in such a state of weakness, that unusual quantities of wine, cognac, and preparations of ammonia and other stimulants were required for their treatment; 16.5 per cent. of all patients died. This malignant fever is to be found in Manchester; in the worst quarters of the Old Town, Ancoats, Little Ireland, etc., it is rarely extinct; though here, as in the *English* towns generally, it prevails to a less extent than might be expected. In Scotland and Ireland, on the other hand, it rages with a violence that surpasses all conception. In Edinburgh and Glasgow it broke out in 1817, after the famine, and in 1826 and 1837 with especial violence, after the commercial crisis, subsiding somewhat each time after having raged about three years. In Edinburgh about 6,000 persons were attacked by the fever during the epidemic of 1817, and about 10,000 in that of 1837, and not only the number of persons attacked but the violence of the disease increased with each repetition.[22]

But the fury of the epidemic in all former periods seems to have been child's play in comparison with its ravages after the crisis of 1842. One-sixth of the whole indigent population of Scotland was seized by the fever, and the infection was carried by wandering beggars with fearful rapidity from one locality to another. It did not reach the middle and upper classes of the population, yet in two months there were more fever cases than in twelve years before. In Glasgow, twelve per cent. of the population were seized in the year 1843; 32,000 persons, of whom thirty-two per cent. perished, while this mortality in Manchester and Liverpool does not ordinarily exceed eight per cent. The illness reached a crisis on the seventh and fifteenth days; on the latter, the patient usually became yellow, which our authority[23] regards as an indication that the cause of the malady was to be sought in mental excitement and anxiety. In Ireland, too, these fever epidemics have become domesticated. During twenty-one months of the years 1817–18, 39,000 fever patients passed through the Dublin hospital; and in a more recent year, according to Sheriff Alison,[24] 60,000. In Cork the fever hospital received one-seventh of the population in 1817–18, in Limerick in the same time one-fourth, and in the bad quarter of Waterford, nineteen-twentieths of the whole population were ill of the fever at one time.

When one remembers under what conditions the working-people live, when one thinks how crowded their dwellings are, how every nook and corner swarms with human beings, how sick and well sleep in the same room, in the same bed, the only wonder is that a contagious disease like this fever does not spread yet farther. And when one reflects how little medical assistance the sick have at command, how many are without any medical advice whatsoever, and ignorant of the most ordinary precautionary measures, the mortality seems actually small. Dr Alison, who has made a careful study of this disease, attributes it directly to the want and the wretched condition of the poor, as in the report already quoted. He asserts that privations and the insufficient satisfaction of vital needs are what prepare the frame for contagion and make the epidemic widespread and terrible. He proves that a period of privation, a commercial crisis or a bad harvest, has each time produced the typhus epidemic in Ireland as in Scotland, and that the fury of the plague has fallen almost exclusively on the working class. It is a noteworthy fact, that according to his testimony, the majority of persons who perish by typhus are fathers of families, precisely the persons who can least be spared by those dependent upon them; and several Irish physicians whom he quotes bear the same testimony.

Another category of diseases arises directly from the food rather than the dwellings of the workers. The food of the labourer, indigestible enough in itself, is utterly unfit for young children, and he has neither means nor time to get his children more suitable food. Moreover, the custom of giving children spirits, and even opium, is very general; and these two influences, with the rest of the conditions of life prejudicial to bodily development, give rise to the most diverse affections of the digestive organs, leaving life-long traces behind them. Nearly all workers have stomachs more or less weak, and are yet forced to adhere to the diet which is the root of the evil. How should they know what is to blame for it? And if they knew, how could they obtain a more suitable regimen so long as they cannot adopt a different way of living and are not better educated? But new disease arises during childhood from impaired digestion. Scrofula is almost universal among the working class, and scrofulous parents have scrofulous children, especially when the original influences continue in full force to operate upon the inherited tendency of the children. A second consequence of this insufficient bodily nourishment, during the years of growth and development, is rachitis, which is extremely common among the children of the working class. The hardening of the bones is delayed, the development of the skeleton in general is restricted, and deformities of the legs and spinal column are frequent, in addition to the usual rachitic affections. How greatly all these evils are increased by the changes to which the workers are subject in consequence of fluctuations in trade, want of work, and the scanty wages in time of crisis, it is not necessary to dwell upon. Temporary want of sufficient food, to which almost every working-man is exposed at least once in the course of his life, only contributes to intensify the effects of his usual sufficient but bad diet. Children who are half-starved, just when they most need ample and nutritious food – and how many such there are during every crisis and even when trade is at its best – must inevitably become weak, scrofulous and rachitic in a high degree. And that they do become so, their appearance amply shows. The neglect to which the great mass of working-men's children are condemned leaves ineradicable traces and brings the enfeeblement of the whole race of workers with it. Add to this, the unsuitable clothing of this class, the impossibility of precautions against colds, the necessity of toiling so long as health permits, want made more dire when sickness appears, and the only too common lack of all medical assistance; and we have a rough idea of the sanitary condition of the English working class. The injurious effects peculiar to single employments as now conducted, I shall not deal with here.

Besides these, there are other influences which enfeeble the health of a great number of workers, intemperance most of all. All possible temptations, all allurements combine to bring the workers to drunkenness. Liquor is almost their only source of pleasure, and all things conspire to make it accessible to them. The working-man comes from his work tired, exhausted, finds his home comfortless, damp, dirty, repulsive; he has urgent need of recreation, he *must* have something to make work worth his trouble, to make the prospect of the next day endurable. His unnerved, uncomfortable, hypochondriac state of mind and body arising from his unhealthy condition, and especially from indigestion, is aggravated beyond endurance by the general conditions of his life, the uncertainty of his existence, his dependence upon all possible accidents and chances, and his inability to do anything towards gaining an assured position. His enfeebled frame, weakened by bad air and bad food, violently demands some external stimulus; his social need can be gratified only in the public-house, he has absolutely no other place where he can meet his friends. How can he be expected to resist the temptation? It is morally and physically inevitable that, under such circumstances, a very large number of working-men should fall into intemperance. And apart from the chiefly physical influences which drive the working-man into drunkenness, there is the example of the great mass, the neglected education, the impossibility of protecting the young from temptation, in many cases the direct influence of intemperate parents, who give their own children liquor, the certainty of forgetting for an hour or two the wretchedness and burden of life, and a hundred other circumstances so mighty that the workers can, in truth, hardly be blamed for yielding to such overwhelming pressure. Drunkenness has here ceased to be a vice, for which the vicious can be held responsible; it becomes a phenomenon, the necessary, inevitable effect of certain conditions upon an object possessed of no volition in relation to those conditions. They who have degraded the working-man to a mere object have the responsibility to bear. But as inevitably as a great number of working-men fall a prey to drink, just so inevitably does it manifest its ruinous influence upon the body and mind of its victims. All the tendencies to disease arising from the conditions of life of the workers are promoted by it, it stimulates in the highest degree the development of lung and digestive troubles, the rise and spread of typhus epidemics.

Another source of physical mischief to the working class lies in the impossibility of employing skilled physicians in cases of illness. It is true that a number of charitable institutions strive to supply this want, that the infirmary in Manchester, for instance, receives or gives advice and medicine to 2,200 patients annually. But what is that in a city in which, according to Gaskell's calculation,[25] three-fourths of the population need medical aid every year? English doctors charge high fees, and working-men are not in a position to pay them. They can therefore do nothing, or are compelled to call in cheap charlatans, and use quack remedies, which do more harm than good. An immense number of such quacks thrive in every English town, securing their *clientèle* among the poor by means of advertisements, posters, and other such devices. Besides these, vast quantities of patent medicines are sold, for all conceivable ailments: Morrison's Pills, Parr's Life Pills, Dr Mainwaring's Pills, and a thousand other pills, essences, and balsams, all of which have the property of curing all the ills that flesh is heir to. These medicines rarely contain actually injurious substances, but, when taken freely and often, they affect the system prejudicially; and as the unwary purchasers are always recommended to take as much as possible, it is not to be wondered at that they swallow them wholesale whether wanted or not.

It is by no means unusual for the manufacturer of Parr's Life Pills to sell twenty to twenty-five thousand boxes of these salutary pills in a week, and they are taken for constipation by this one, for diarrhoea by that one, for fever, weakness, and all possible ailments. As our German peasants are cupped or bled at certain seasons, so do the English working-people now consume patent medicines to their own injury and the great profit of the manufacturer. One of the most injurious of these patent medicines is a drink prepared with opiates, chiefly laudanum, under the name Godfrey's Cordial. Women who work at home, and have their own and other people's children to take care of, give them this drink to keep them quiet, and, as many believe, to strengthen them. They often begin to give this medicine to newly-born children, and continue, without knowing the effects of this 'heartsease', until the children die. The less susceptible the child's system to the action of the opium, the greater the quantities administered. When the cordial ceases to act, laudanum alone is given, often to the extent of fifteen to twenty drops at a dose. The Coroner of Nottingham testified before a Parliamentary Commission [26] that one apothecary had, according to his own statement, used thirteen hundredweight of laudanum in one year in the preparation of Godfrey's Cordial. The effects upon the children so treated may be readily imagined. They are pale, feeble, wilted, and usually die before completing the second year. The use of this cordial is very extensive in all great towns and industrial districts in the kingdom.

The result of all these influences is a general enfeeblement of the frame in the working class. There are few vigorous, well-built, healthy persons among the workers, i.e. among the factory operatives, who are employed in confined rooms, and we are here discussing these only. They are almost all weakly, of angular but not powerful build, lean, pale, and of relaxed fibre, with the exception of the muscles especially exercised in their work. Nearly all suffer from indigestion, and consequently from a more or less hypochondriac, melancholy, irritable, nervous condition. Their enfeebled constitutions are unable to resist disease, and are therefore seized by it on every occasion. Hence they age prematurely, and die early. On this point the mortality statistics supply unquestionable testimony.

According to the Report of Registrar-General Graham, the annual death-rate of all England and Wales is something less than 2.25 per cent. That is to say, out of forty-five persons, one dies every year.[27] This was the average for the year 1839 40. In 1840–41 the mortality diminished somewhat, and the death-rate was but one in forty-six. But in the great cities the proportion is wholly different. I have before me official tables of mortality (*Manchester Guardian*, July 31st, 1844), according to which the death-rate of several large towns is as follows: in Manchester, including Chorlton and Salford, one in 32.72; and excluding Chorlton and Salford, one in 30.75. In Liverpool, including West Derby (suburb), 31.90, and excluding West Derby, 29.90; while the average of all the districts of Cheshire, Lancashire, and Yorkshire cited, including a number of wholly or partially rural districts and many small towns, with a total population of 2,172,506 for the whole, is one death in 39.80 persons. How unfavourably the workers are placed in the great cities, the mortality for Prescott in Lancashire shows: a district inhabited by miners, and showing a lower sanitary condition than that of the agricultural districts, mining being by no means a healthful occupation. But these miners live in the country, and the death-rate among them is but one in 47.54, or nearly two-and-a-half per cent. better than that for all England. All these statements are based upon the mortality tables for 1843. Still higher is the death-rate in the Scotch cities; in Edinburgh, in 1838–39, one in 29; in 1831, in the Old Town alone, one in 22. In Glasgow, according to Dr Cowen,[28] the average has been, since 1830, one in 30; and in single years, one in 22 to 24. That this enormous shortening of life falls chiefly upon the working class, that the general average is improved by the smaller mortality of the upper and middle classes, is attested upon all sides. One of the most recent depositions is that of a physician, Dr P. H. Holland, in Manchester, who investigated Chorlton-on-Medlock, a suburb of Manchester, under official commission. He divided the houses and streets into three classes each, and ascertained the following variations in the death-rate:

First class of Streets.					Houses I. class.	Mortality one in			51
,,	,,	,,	,,	,,	II. ,,	,,	,,	,,	45
,,	,,	,,	,,	,,	III. ,,	,,	,,	,,	36
Second ,,	,,	,,	,,	I. ,,	,,	,,	,,		55
,,	,,	,,	,,	,,	II. ,,	,,	,,	,,	38
,,	,,	,,	,,	,,	III. ,,	,,	,,	,,	35
Third ,,	,,	,,	,,	I. ,,	Wanting				—
,,	,,	,,	,,	,,	II. ,,	Mortality one in			35
,,	,,	,,	,,	,,	III. ,,	,,	,,	,,	25

It is clear from other tables given by Holland that the mortality in the *streets* of the second class is 18 per cent. greater, and in the streets of the third class 68 per cent. greater than in those of the first class; that the mortality in the *houses* of the second class is 31 per cent greater, and in the third class 78 per cent. greater than in those of the first class; that the mortality is those bad streets which were improved, decreased 25 per cent. He closes with the remark, very frank for an English bourgeois:[29]

When we find the rate of mortality four times as high in some streets as in others, and twice as high in whole classes of streets as in other classes, and further find that it is all but invariably high in those streets which are in bad condition, and almost invariably low in those whose condition is good, we cannot resist the conclusion that multitudes of our fellow-creatures, *hundreds of our immediate neighbours*, are annually destroyed for want of the most evident precautions.

The Report on the Sanitary Condition of the Working-Class contains information which attests the same fact. In Liverpool, in 1840, the average longevity of the upper classes, gentry, professional men, etc., was thirty-five years; that of the business men and better-placed handicraftsmen, twenty-two years; and that of the operatives, day-labourers, and serviceable class in general, but fifteen years. The Parliamentary reports contain a mass of similar facts.

The death-rate is kept so high chiefly by the heavy mortality among young children in the working class. The tender frame of a child is least able to withstand the unfavourable influences of an inferior lot in life; the neglect to which they are often subjected, when both parents work or one is dead, avenges itself promptly, and no one need wonder that in Manchester, according to the report last quoted, more than fifty-seven per cent. of the children of the working class perish before the fifth year, while but twenty per cent. of the children of the higher classes, and not quite thirty-two per cent. of the children of all classes in the country die under five years of age.[30] The article of the *Artisan*, already several times referred to, furnishes exacter information on this point, by comparing the city death-rate in single diseases of children with the country death-rate, thus demonstrating that, in general, epidemics in Manchester and Liverpool are three times more fatal than in country districts; that affections of the nervous system are quintupled, and stomach troubles trebled, while deaths from affections of the lungs in cities are to those in the country as 2.5 to 1. Fatal cases of smallpox, measles, scarlet fever, and whooping cough, among small children, are four times more frequent; those of water on the brain are trebled, and convulsions ten times more frequent. To quote another acknowledged authority, I append the following table. Out of 10,000 persons, there die — [31]

	< 5yrs	5–19	20–39	40–59	60–69	70–79	80–89	90–99	100+
A	2,865	891	1,275	1,299	1,189	1,428	938	112	3
B	3,159	1,110	1,526	1,413	963	1,019	630	177	3
C	4,408	921	1,006	1,201	940	826	633	153	22
D	4,738	930	1,201	1,134	677	727	452	80	1
E	4,947	1,136	1,379	1,114	553	532	298	38	3
F	5,286	927	1,228	1,198	593	512	225	29	2

A   Rutlandshire, a healthy agricultural district
B   Essex, marshy agricultural district
C   Town of Carlisle, 1779–87, before introduction of mills
D   Town of Carlisle, after introduction of mills
E   Preston, factory town
F   Leeds, factory town

Apart from the divers diseases which are the necessary consequence of the present neglect and oppression of the poorer classes, there are other influences which contribute to increase the mortality among small children. In many families the wife, like the husband, has to work away from home, and the consequence is the total neglect of the children, who are either locked up or given out to be taken care of. It is, therefore, not to be wondered at if hundreds of them perish through all manner of accidents. Nowhere are so many children run over, nowhere are so many killed by falling, drowning, or burning, as in the great cities and towns of England. Deaths from burns and scalds are especially frequent, such a case occurring nearly every week during the winter months in Manchester, and very frequently in London, though little mention is made of them in the papers. I have at hand a copy of the *Weekly Despatch* of December 15th, 1844, according to which, in the week from December 1st to December 7th inclusive, *six* such cases occurred. These unhappy children, perishing in this terrible way, are victims of our social disorder, and of the property-holding classes' interest in maintaining and prolonging this disorder. Yet one is left in doubt whether even this terribly torturing death is not a blessing for the children in rescuing them from a long life of toil and wretchedness, rich in suffering and poor in enjoyment. So far has it gone in England; and the bourgeoisie reads these things every day in the newspapers and takes no further trouble in the matter. But it cannot complain if, after the official and non-official testimony here cited which must be known to it, I broadly accuse it of social murder. Let the ruling class see to it that these frightful conditions are ameliorated, or let it surrender the administration of the common interests to the labouring class. To the latter course it is by no means inclined; for the former task, so long as it remains the bourgeoisie crippled by bourgeois prejudice, it has not the needed power. For if, at last, after hundreds of thousands of victims have perished, it manifests some little anxiety for the future, passing a 'Metropolitan Buildings Act', under which the most unscrupulous overcrowding of dwellings is to be, at least in some slight degree, restricted; if it points with pride to measures which, far from attacking the root of the evil, do not by any means meet the demands of the commonest sanitary policy, it cannot thus vindicate itself from the accusation. The English bourgeoisie has but

one choice, either to continue its rule under the unanswerable
charge of murder and in spite of this charge, or to abdicate in favour
of the labouring class. Hitherto it has chosen the former course.

Let us turn from the physical to the mental state of the workers.
Since the bourgeoisie vouchsafes them only so much of life as is
absolutely necessary, we need not wonder that it bestows upon
them only so much education as lies in the interest of the bourgeoisie; and that, in truth, is not much. The means of education in
England are restricted out of all proportion to the population. The
few day schools at the command of the working class are available
only for the smallest minority, and are bad besides. The teachers,
worn-out workers, and other unsuitable persons who only turn to
teaching in order to live, are usually without the indispensable
elementary knowledge, without the moral discipline so needful for
the teacher, and relieved of all public supervision. Here, too, free
competition rules, and, as usual, the rich profit by it, and the poor,
for whom competition is *not* free, who have not the knowledge
needed to enable them to form a correct judgment, have the evil
consequences to bear. Compulsory school attendance does not
exist. In the mills it is, as we shall see, purely nominal; and when in
the session of 1843 the Ministry was disposed to make this nominal
compulsion effective, the manufacturing bourgeoisie opposed the
measure with all its might, though the working class was out-
spokenly in favour of compulsory school attendance. Moreover, a
mass of children work the whole week through in the mills or at
home, and therefore cannot attend school. The evening schools,
supposed to be attended by children who are employed during the
day, are almost abandoned or attended without benefit. It is asking
too much, that young workers who have been using themselves
up twelve hours in the day, should go to school from eight to
ten at night. And those who try it usually fall asleep, as is testified
by hundreds of witnesses in the Children's Employment Commission's Report. Sunday schools have been founded, it is true, but
they, too, are most scantily supplied with teachers, and can be of
use to those only who have already learnt something in the day
schools. The interval from one Sunday to the next is too long for
an ignorant child to remember in the second sitting what it learned
in the first, a week before. The Children's Employment Commission's Report furnishes a hundred proofs, and the Commission

itself most emphatically expresses the opinion, that neither the weekday nor the Sunday schools, in the least degree, meet the needs of the nation. This report gives evidence of ignorance in the working class of England, such as could hardly be expected in Spain or Italy. It cannot be otherwise; the bourgeoisie has little to hope, and much to fear, from the education of the working class. The Ministry, in its whole enormous budget of £55,000,000, has only the single trifling item of £40,000 for public education, and, but for the fanaticism of the religious sects which does at least as much harm as good, the means of education would be yet more scanty. As it is, the State Church manages its national schools and the various sects their sectarian schools for the sole purpose of keeping the children of the brethren of the faith within the congregation, and of winning away a poor childish soul here and there from some other sect. The consequence is that religion, and precisely the most unprofitable side of religion, polemical discussion, is made the principal subject of instruction, and the memory of the children overburdened with incomprehensible dogmas and theological distinctions; that sectarian hatred and bigotry are awakened as early as possible, and all rational mental and moral training shamefully neglected. The working class has repeatedly demanded of Parliament a system of strictly secular public education, leaving religion to the ministers of the sects; but, thus far, no Ministry has been induced to grant it. The Minister is the obedient servant of the bourgeoisie, and the bourgeoisie is divided into countless sects; but each would gladly grant the workers the otherwise dangerous education on the sole condition of their accepting, as an antidote, the dogmas peculiar to the especial sect in question. And as these sects are still quarrelling among themselves for supremacy, the workers remain for the present without education. It is true that the manufacturers boast of having enabled the majority to read, but the quality of the reading is appropriate to the source of the instruction, as the Children's Employment Commission proves. According to this report, he who knows his letters can read enough to satisfy the conscience of the manufacturers. And when one reflects upon the confused orthography of the English language which makes reading one of the arts, learned only under long instruction, this ignorance is readily understood. Very few working-people write readily; and writing orthographically is beyond the powers even of many 'educated' persons. The Sunday schools of the State Church, of the Quakers, and, I think, of several other sects, do not teach writing, 'because it is too worldly an employment for Sunday'. The quality of the instruction offered the workers in other directions may be judged from a specimen or two, taken from the Children's Employment Commission's Report, which unfortunately does not embrace mill-work proper:

'In Birmingham', says Commissioner Grainger, 'the children examined by me are, as a whole, utterly wanting in all that could be in the remotest degree called a useful education. Although in almost all the schools religious instruction alone is furnished, the profoundest ignorance even upon that subject prevailed.' – 'In Wolverhampton', says Commissioner Horne, 'I found, among others, the following example. A girl of eleven years had attended both day and Sunday school, "had never heard of another world, of Heaven, or another life". A boy, seventeen years old, did not know that twice two are four, nor how many farthings in two pence even when the money was placed in his hand. Several boys had never heard of London nor of Willenhall, though the latter was but an hour's walk from their homes, and in the closest relations with Wolverhampton. Several had never heard the name of the Queen nor other names, such as Nelson, Wellington, Bonaparte; but it was noteworthy that those who had never heard even of St Paul, Moses, or Solomon, were very well instructed as to the life, deeds, and character of Dick Turpin, and especially of Jack Sheppard. A youth of sixteen did not know how many twice two are, nor how much four farthings make. A youth of seventeen asserted that four farthings are four half pence; a third, seventeen years old, answered several very simple questions with the brief statement, that he "was ne jedge o' nothin' "'.[32] These children who are crammed with religious doctrines four or five years at a stretch, know as little at the end as at the beginning. One child 'went to Sunday school regularly for five years; does not know who Jesus Christ is, but had heard the name; had never heard of the twelve Apostles, Samson, Moses, Aaron, etc.'[33] Another 'attended Sunday school regularly six years; knows who Jesus Christ was; he died on the Cross to save our Saviour; had never heard of St Peter or St Paul.'[34] A third 'attended different Sunday schools seven years;

can read only the thin, easy books with simple words of one syllable; has heard of the Apostles, but does not know whether St Peter was one or St John; the latter must have been St John Wesley.'[35] To the question who Christ was, Horne received the following answers among others: 'He was Adam', 'He was an Apostle', 'He was the Saviour's Lord's Son', and from a youth of sixteen: 'He was a king of London long ago.' In Sheffield, Commissioner Symonds let the children from the Sunday school read aloud; they could not tell what they had read, or what sort of people the Apostles were, of whom they had just been reading. After he had asked them all one after the other about the Apostles without securing a single correct answer, one sly-looking little fellow, with great glee, called out: 'I know, mister; they were the lepers!'[36] From the pottery districts and from Lancashire the reports are similar.

This is what the bourgeoisie and the State are doing for the education and improvement of the working class. Fortunately the conditions under which this class lives are such as give it a sort of practical training, which not only replaces school cramming, but renders harmless the confused religious notions connected with it, and even places the workers in the vanguard of the national movement of England. Necessity is the mother of invention, and what is still more important, of thought and action. The English working-man who can scarcely read and still less write, nevertheless knows very well where his own interest and that of the nation lies. He knows, too, what the especial interest of the bourgeoisie is, and what he has to expect of that bourgeoisie. If he cannot write he can speak, and speak in public; if he has no arithmetic, he can, nevertheless, reckon with the Political Economists enough to see through a Corn-Law-repealing bourgeois, and to get the better of him in argument; if celestial matters remain very mixed for him in spite of all the effort of the preachers, he sees all the more clearly into terrestrial, political, and social questions. We shall have occasion to refer again to this point; and pass now to the moral characteristics of our workers.

It is sufficiently clear that the instruction in morals can have no better effect than the religious teaching, with which in all English schools it is mixed up. The simple principles which, for plain human beings, regulate the relations of man to man, brought into the direst confusion by our social state, our war of each against all, necessarily remain confused and foreign to the working-man when mixed with incomprehensible dogmas, and preached in the religious form of an arbitrary and dogmatic commandment. The schools contribute, according to the confession of all authorities, and especially of the Children's Employment Commission, almost nothing to the morality of the working class. So short-sighted, so stupidly narrow-minded is the English bourgeoisie in its egotism, that it does not even take the trouble to impress upon the workers the morality of the day, which the bourgeoisie has patched together in its own interest for its own protection! Even this precautionary measure is too great an effort for the enfeebled and sluggish bourgeoisie. A time must come when it will repent its neglect, too late. But it has no right to complain that the workers know nothing of its system of morals, and do not act in accordance with it.

Thus are the workers cast out and ignored by the class in power, morally as well as physically and mentally. The only provision made for them is the law, which fastens upon them when they become obnoxious to the bourgeoisie. Like the dullest of the brutes, they are treated to but one form of education, the whip, in the shape of force, not convincing but intimidating. There is, therefore, no cause for surprise if the workers, treated as brutes, actually become such; or if they can maintain their consciousness of manhood only by cherishing the most glowing hatred, the most unbroken inward rebellion against the bourgeoisie in power. They are men so long only as they burn with wrath against the reigning class. They become brutes the moment they bend in patience under the yoke, and merely strive to make life endurable while abandoning the effort to break the yoke.

This, then, is all that the bourgeoisie has done for the education of the proletariat — and when we take into consideration all the circumstances in which this class lives, we shall not think the worse of it for the resentment which it cherishes against the ruling class. The moral training which is not given to the worker in school is not supplied by the other conditions of his life; that moral training, at least, which alone has worth in the eyes of the bourgeoisie; his whole position and environment involves the strongest temptation to immorality. He is poor, life offers him no charm, almost every enjoyment is denied him, the penalties of the law have no further terrors for him; why should he restrain his desires, why leave to the rich the enjoyment of his birthright, why not seize a part of it for himself? What inducement has the proletarian not to steal! It is all very pretty and very agreeable to the ear of the bourgeois to hear the 'sacredness of property' asserted; but for him who has none, the sacredness of property dies out of itself. Money is the god of this world; the bourgeois takes the proletarian's money from him and so makes a practical atheist of him. No wonder, then, if the proletarian retains his atheism and no longer respects the sacredness and power of the earthly God. And when the poverty of the proletarian is intensified to the point of actual lack of the barest necessaries of life, to want and hunger, the temptation to disregard all social order does but gain power. This the bourgeoisie for the most part recognises. Symonds [37] observes that poverty exercises the same ruinous influence upon the mind which drunkenness exercises upon the body; and Dr Alison explains to property-holding readers, with the greatest exactness, what the consequences of social oppression must be for the working class.[38] Want leaves the working-man the choice between starving slowly, killing himself speedily, or taking what he needs where he finds it – in plain English, stealing. And there is no cause for surprise that most of them prefer stealing to starvation and suicide.

True, there are, within the working class, numbers too moral to steal even when reduced to the utmost extremity, and these starve or commit suicide. For suicide, formerly the enviable privilege of the upper classes, has become fashionable among the English workers, and numbers of the poor kill themselves to avoid the misery from which they see no other means of escape.

But far more demoralising than his poverty in its influence upon the English working-man is the insecurity of his position, the necessity of living upon wages from hand to mouth, that in short which makes a proletarian of him. The smaller peasants in Germany are usually poor, and often suffer want, but they are less at the mercy of accident, they have at least something secure. The proletarian, who has nothing but his two hands, who consumes today what he earned yesterday, who is subject to every possible chance, and has not the slightest guarantee for being able to earn the barest necessities of life, whom every crisis, every whim of his employer may deprive of bread, this proletarian is placed in the most revolting, inhuman position conceivable for a human being. The slave is assured of a bare livelihood by the self-interest of his master, the serf has at least a scrap of land on which to live; each has at worst a guarantee for life itself. But the proletarian must depend upon himself alone, and is yet prevented from so applying his abilities as to be able to rely upon them. Everything that the proletarian can do to improve his position is but a drop in the ocean compared with the floods of varying chances to which he is exposed, over which he has not the slightest control. He is the passive subject of all possible combinations of circumstances, and must count himself fortunate when he has saved his life even for a short time; and his character and way of living are naturally shaped by these conditions. Either he seeks to keep his head above water in this whirlpool, to rescue his manhood, and this he can do solely in rebellion [39] against the class which plunders him so mercilessly and then abandons him to his fate, which strives to hold him in this position so demoralising to a human being; or he gives up the struggle against his fate as hopeless, and strives to profit, so far as he can, by the most favourable moment. To save is unavailing, for at the utmost he cannot save more than suffices to sustain life for a short time, while if he falls out of work, it is for no brief period. To accumulate lasting property for himself is impossible; and if it were not, he would only cease to be a working-man and another would take his place. What better thing can he do, then, when he gets high wages, than live well upon them? The English bourgeoisie is violently scandalised at the extravagant living of the workers when wages are high; yet it is not only very natural but very sensible of them to enjoy life when they can, instead of laying up treasures which are of no lasting use to them, and which in the end moth and rust (i.e. the bourgeoisie) get possession of. Yet such a life is demoralising beyond all others. What Carlyle says of the cotton spinners is true of all English industrial workers. [40]

> Their trade, now in plethoric prosperity, anon extenuated into inanition and 'short time', is of the nature of gambling; they live by it like gamblers, now in luxurious superfluity, now in starvation. Black, mutinous discontent devours them; simply the miserablest feeling that can inhabit the heart of man. English

commerce, with its world-wide, convulsive fluctuations, with its immeasurable Proteus Steam demon, makes all paths uncertain for them, all life a bewilderment; society, steadfastness, peaceable continuance, the first blessings of man are not theirs. – This world is for them no home, but a dingy prison-house, of reckless unthrift, rebellion, rancour, indignation against themselves and against all men. Is it a green, flowery world, with azure ever-lasting sky stretched over it, the work and government of a God; or a murky, simmering Tophet, of copperas fumes, cotton fuz, gin riot, wrath and toil, created by a Demon, governed by a Demon?

And elsewhere: [41]

Injustice, infidelity to truth and fact and Nature's order, being properly the one evil under the sun, and the feeling of injustice the one intolerable pain under the sun, our grand question as to the condition of these working-men would be: is it just? And, first of all, what belief have they themselves formed about the justice of it? The words they promulgate are notable by way of answer; their actions are still more notable. Revolt, sullen, revengeful humour of revolt against the upper classes, decreasing respect for what their temporal superiors command, decreasing faith for what their spiritual superiors teach, is more and more the universal spirit of the lower classes. Such spirit may be blamed, may be vindicated, but all men must recognise it as extant there, all may know that it is mournful, that unless altered it will be fatal.

Carlyle is perfectly right as to the facts and wrong only in censuring the wild rage of the workers against the higher classes. This rage, this passion, is rather the proof that the workers feel the inhumanity of their position, that they refuse to be degraded to the level of brutes, and that they will one day free themselves from servitude to the bourgeoisie. This may be seen in the case of those who do not share this wrath; they either bow humbly before the fate that overtakes them, live a respectful private life as well as they can, do not concern themselves as to the course of public affairs, help the bourgeoisie to forge the chains of the workers yet more securely, and stand upon the plane of intellectual nullity that prevailed before the industrial period began; or they are tossed about by fate, lose their moral hold upon themselves as they have already lost their economic hold, live along from day to day, drink and fall into licentiousness; and in both cases they are brutes. The last-named class contributes chiefly to the 'rapid increase of vice', at which the bourgeoisie is so horrified after itself setting in motion the causes which give rise to it.

Another source of demoralisation among the workers is their being condemned to work. As voluntary, productive activity is the highest enjoyment known to us, so is compulsory toil the most cruel, degrading punishment. Nothing is more terrible than being constrained to do some one thing every day from morning until night against one's will. And the more a man the worker feels himself, the more hateful must his work be to him, because he feels the constraint, the aimlessness of it for himself. Why does he work? For love of work? From a natural impulse? Not at all! He works for money, for a thing which has nothing whatsoever to do with the work itself; and he works so long, moreover, and in such unbroken monotony, that this alone must make his work a torture in the first weeks if he has the least human feeling left. The division of labour has multiplied the brutalising influences of forced work. In most branches the worker's activity is reduced to some paltry, purely mechanical manipulation, repeated minute after minute, unchanged year after year.[42] How much human feeling, what abilities can a man retain in his thirtieth year, who has made needle points or filed toothed wheels twelve hours every day from his early childhood, living all the time under the conditions forced upon the English proletarian? It is still the same thing since the introduction of steam. The worker's activity is made easy, muscular effort is saved, but the work itself becomes unmeaning and monotonous to the last degree. It offers no field for mental activity, and claims just enough of his attention to keep him from thinking of anything else. And a sentence to such work, to work which takes his whole time for itself, leaving him scarcely time to eat and sleep, none for physical exercise in the open air, or the enjoyment of Nature, much less for mental activity, how can such a sentence help degrading a human being to the level of a brute? Once more the worker must choose, must either surrender himself to his fate, become a 'good' workman, heed 'faithfully' the interest of the bourgeoisie, in which case he most certainly becomes a brute, or else he must rebel, fight for his manhood to the last, and this he can only do in the fight against the bourgeoisie.

And when all these conditions have engendered vast demoralisation among the workers, a new influence is added to the old, to spread this degradation more widely and carry it to the extremest point. This influence is the centralisation of the population. The writers of the English bourgeoisie are crying murder at the demoralising tendency of the great cities; like perverted Jeremiahs, they sing dirges, not over the destruction, but the growth of the cities. Sheriff Alison attributes almost everything, and Dr Vaughan, author of *The Age of Great Cities*, still more to this influence. And this is natural, for the propertied class has too direct an interest in the other conditions which tend to destroy the worker body and soul. If they should admit that 'poverty, insecurity, overwork, forced work, are the chief ruinous influences', they would have to draw the conclusion, 'then let us give the poor property, guarantee their subsistence, make laws against overwork', and this the bourgeoisie dare not formulate. But the great cities have grown up so spontaneously, the population has moved into them so wholly of its own motion, and the inference that manufacture and the middle class which profits from it alone have created the cities is so remote, that it is extremely convenient for the ruling class to ascribe all the evil to this apparently unavoidable source; whereas the great cities really only secure a more rapid and certain development for evils already existing in the germ. Alison is humane enough to admit this; he is no thoroughbred Liberal manufacturer, but only a half developed Tory bourgeois, and he has, therefore, an open eye, now and then, where the full-fledged bourgeois is still stone blind. Let us hear him.[43]

It is in the great cities that vice has spread her temptations, and pleasure her seductions, and folly her allurements; that guilt is encouraged by the hope of impunity, and idleness fostered by the frequency of example. It is to these great marts of human corruption that the base and the profligate resort from the simplicity of country life; it is here that they find victims whereon to practise their iniquity, and gains to reward the dangers that attend them. Virtue is here depressed from the obscurity in which it is involved. Guilt is matured from the difficulty of its detection;

licentiousness is rewarded by the immediate enjoyment which it promises. If any person will walk through St Giles's, the crowded alleys of Dublin, or the poorer quarters of Glasgow by night, he will meet with ample proof of these observations; he will no longer wonder at the disorderly habits and profligate enjoyments of the lower orders; his astonishment will be, not that there is so much, but that there is so little crime in the world. The great cause of human corruption in these crowded situations is the contagious nature of bad example and the extreme difficulty of avoiding the seductions of vice when they are brought into close and daily proximity with the younger part of the people. Whatever we may think of the strength of virtue, experience proves that the higher orders are indebted for their exemption from atrocious crime or disorderly habits chiefly to their fortunate removal from the scene of temptation; and that where they are exposed to the seductions which assail their inferiors, they are noways behind them in yielding to their influence. It is the peculiar misfortune of the poor in great cities that they cannot fly from these irresistible temptations, but that, turn where they will, they are met by the alluring forms of vice, or the seductions of guilty enjoyment. It is the experienced impossibility of concealing the attractions of vice from the younger part of the poor in great cities which exposes them to so many causes of demoralisation. All this proceeds not from any unwonted or extraordinary depravity in the character of these victims of licentiousness, but from the almost irresistible nature of the temptations to which the poor are exposed. The rich, who censure their conduct, would in all probability yield as rapidly as they have done to the influence of similar causes. There is a certain degree of misery, a certain proximity to sin, which virtue is rarely able to withstand, and which the young, in particular, are generally unable to resist. The progress of vice in such circumstances is almost as certain and often nearly as rapid as that of physical contagion.

And elsewhere:

When the higher orders for their own profit have drawn the labouring classes in great numbers into a small space, the contagion of guilt becomes rapid and unavoidable. The lower orders, situated as they are in so far as regards moral or religious instruction, are frequently hardly more to be blamed for yielding to the temptations which surround them than for falling victims to the typhus fever.

Enough! The half-bourgeois Alison betrays to us, however narrow his manner of expressing himself, the evil effect of the great cities upon the moral development of the workers. Another, a bourgeois *pur sang*, a man after the heart of the Anti-Corn Law League, Dr Andrew Ure,[44] betrays the other side. He tells us that life in great cities facilitates cabals among the workers and confers power on the Plebs. If here the workers are not educated (i.e. to obedience to the bourgeoisie), they may view matters one-sidedly, from the standpoint of a sinister selfishness, and may readily permit themselves to be hoodwinked by sly demagogues; nay, they might even be capable of viewing their greatest benefactors, the frugal and enterprising capitalists, with a jealous and hostile eye. Here proper training alone can avail, or national bankruptcy and other horrors must follow, since a revolution of the workers could hardly fail to occur. And our bourgeois is perfectly justified in his fears. If the centralisation of population stimulates and develops the property-holding class, it forces the development of the workers yet more rapidly. The workers begin to feel as a class, as a whole; they begin to perceive that, though feeble as individuals, they form a power united; their separation from the bourgeoisie, the development of views peculiar to the workers and corresponding to their position in life, is fostered, the consciousness of oppression awakens, and the workers attain social and political importance. The great cities are the birthplaces of labour movements; in them the workers first began to reflect upon their own condition, and to struggle against it; in them the opposition between proletariat and bourgeoisie first made itself manifest; from them proceeded the Trades-Unions, Chartism, and Socialism. The great cities have transformed the disease of the social body, which appears in chronic form in the country, into an acute one, and so made manifest its real nature and the means of curing it. Without the great cities and their forcing influence upon the popular intelligence, the working class would be far less advanced than it is. Moreover, they have destroyed the last remnant of the patriarchal relation between working-men and employers, a result to which manufacture on a large scale has contributed by multiplying the employees dependent upon a single employer. The bourgeoisie deplores all this, it is true, and has good reason to do so; for, under the old conditions, the bourgeois was comparatively secure against a revolt on the part of his hands. He could tyrannise over them and plunder them to his heart's content, and yet receive obedience, gratitude, and assent from these stupid people by bestowing a trifle of patronising friendliness which cost him nothing, and perhaps some paltry present, all apparently out of pure, self-sacrificing, uncalled-for goodness of heart, but really not one-tenth part of his duty. As an individual bourgeois, placed under conditions which he had not himself created, he might do his duty at least in part; but, as a member of the ruling class, which, by the mere fact of its ruling, is responsible for the condition of the whole nation, he did nothing of what his position involved. On the contrary, he plundered the whole nation for his own individual advantage. In the patriarchal relation that hypocritically concealed the slavery of the worker, the latter must have remained an intellectual zero, totally ignorant of his own interest, a mere private individual. Only when estranged from his employer, when convinced that the sole bond between employer and employee is the bond of pecuniary profit, when the sentimental bond between them, which stood not the slightest test, had wholly fallen away, then only did the worker begin to recognise his own interests and develop independently; then only did he cease to be the slave of the bourgeoisie in his thoughts, feelings, and the expression of his will. And to this end manufacture on a grand scale and in great cities has most largely contributed.

Another influence of great moment in forming the character of the English workers is the Irish immigration already referred to. On the one hand it has, as we have seen, degraded the English workers, removed them from civilisation, and aggravated the hardship of their lot; but, on the other hand, it has thereby deepened the chasm between workers and bourgeoisie, and hastened the approaching crisis. For the course of the social disease from which England is suffering is the same as the course of a physical disease; it develops according to certain laws, has its own crisis, the last and most violent of which determines the fate of the patient. And as the English nation cannot succumb under the final crises, but must go forth from it, born again, rejuvenated, we can but rejoice over everything which accelerates the course of the disease. And to this the Irish immigration further contributes by reason of the passionate, mercurial Irish temperament, which it imports into England and into the English working class. The Irish and English are to each other much as the French and the Germans; and the mixing of the more facile, excitable, fiery Irish temperament with the stable, reasoning, persevering English must, in the long run, be productive only of good for both. The rough egotism of the English bourgeoisie would have kept its hold upon the working class much more firmly if the Irish nature, generous to a fault, and ruled primarily by sentiment, had not intervened, and softened the cold, rational English character in part by a mixture of the races, and in part by the ordinary contact of life.

In view of all this, it is not surprising that the working class has gradually become a race wholly apart from the English bourgeoisie. The bourgeoisie has more in common with every other nation of the earth than with the workers in whose midst it lives. The workers speak other dialects, have other thoughts and ideals, other customs and moral principles, a different religion and other politics than those of the bourgeoisie. Thus they are two radically dissimilar nations, as unlike as difference of race could make them, of whom we on the Continent have known but one, the bourgeoisie. Yet it is precisely the other, the people, the proletariat, which is by far the more important for the future of England.

Of the public character of the English working-man, as it finds expression in associations and political principles, we shall have occasion to speak later; let us here consider the results of the influences cited above, as they affect the private character of the worker. The workman is far more humane in ordinary life than the bourgeois. I have already mentioned the fact that the beggars are accustomed to turn almost exclusively to the workers, and that, in general, more is done by the workers than by the bourgeoisie for the maintenance of the poor. This fact, which anyone may prove for himself any day, is confirmed, among others, by Dr Parkinson, Canon of Manchester, who says: [45]

> The poor give one another more than the rich give the poor. I
> can confirm my statement by the testimony of one of our eldest,

most skilful, most observant, and humane physicians, Dr Bards-
ley, who has often declared that the total sum which the poor
yearly bestow upon one another, surpasses that which the rich
contribute in the same time.

In other ways, too, the humanity of the workers is constantly
manifesting itself pleasantly. They have experienced hard times
themselves, and can therefore feel for those in trouble, whence
they are more approachable, friendlier, and less greedy for money,
though they need it far more, than the property-holding class. For
them money is worth only what it will buy, whereas for the
bourgeois it has an especial inherent value, the value of a god, and
makes the bourgeois the mean, low money-grabber that he is. The
working-man who knows nothing of this feeling of reverence for
money is therefore less grasping than the bourgeois, whose whole
activity is for the purpose of gain, who sees in the accumulations of
his money-bags the end and aim of life. Hence the workman is
much less prejudiced, has a clearer eye for facts as they are than the
bourgeois, and does not look at everything through the spectacles
of personal selfishness. His faulty education saves him from religious prepossessions, he does not understand religious questions,
does not trouble himself about them, knows nothing of the
fanaticism that holds the bourgeoisie bound; and if he chances to
have any religion, he has it only in name, not even in theory.
Practically he lives for this world, and strives to make himself at
home in it. All the writers of the bourgeoisie are unanimous on
this point, that the workers are not religious, and do not attend
church. From the general statement are to be excepted the Irish,
a few elderly people, and the half-bourgeois, the overlookers,
foremen, and the like. But among the masses there prevails almost
universally a total indifference to religion, or at the utmost, some
trace of Deism too undeveloped to amount to more than mere
words, or a vague dread of the words infidel, atheist, etc. The
clergy of all sects is in very bad odour with the working-men,
though the loss of its influence is recent. At present, however,
the mere cry: 'He's a parson!' is often enough to drive one of
the clergy from the platform of a public meeting. And like the
rest of the conditions under which he lives, his want of religious
and other culture contributes to keep the working-man more

unconstrained, freer from inherited stable tenets and cut-and-dried opinions, than the bourgeois who is saturated with the class prejudices poured into him from his earliest youth. There is nothing to be done with the bourgeois; he is essentially conservative in however liberal a guise, his interest is bound up with that of the property-holding class, he is dead to all active movement; he is losing his position in the forefront of England's historical development. The workers are taking his place, in rightful claim first, then in fact.

All this, together with the correspondent public action of the workers, with which we shall deal later, forms the favourable side of the character of this class; the unfavourable one may be quite as briefly summed up, and follows quite as naturally out of the given causes. Drunkenness, sexual irregularities, brutality, and disregard for the rights of property are the chief points with which the bourgeois charges them. That they drink heavily is to be expected. Sheriff Alison asserts that in Glasgow some thirty thousand working-men get drunk every Saturday night, and the estimate is certainly not exaggerated; and that in that city in 1830, one house in twelve, and in 1840, one house in ten, was a public-house; that in Scotland, in 1823, excise was paid upon 2,300,000 gallons; in 1837, upon 6,620,000 gallons; in England, in 1823, upon 1,976,000 gallons, and in 1837, upon 7,875,000 gallons of spirits. The Beer Act of 1830, which facilitated the opening of beerhouses (jerry shops), whose keepers are licensed to sell beer to be drunk on the premises, facilitated the spread of intemperance by bringing a beerhouse, so to say, to everybody's door. In nearly every street there are several such beerhouses, and among two or three neighbouring houses in the country one is sure to be a jerry shop. Besides these, there are hush-shops in multitudes, i.e. secret drinking-places which are not licensed, and quite as many secret distilleries which produce great quantities of spirits in retired spots, rarely visited by the police, in the great cities. Gaskell estimates these secret distilleries in Manchester alone at more than a hundred, and their product at 156,000 gallons at the least. In Manchester there are, besides, more than a thousand public-houses selling all sorts of alcoholic drinks, or quite as many in proportion to the number of inhabitants as in Glasgow. In all other great towns, the state of things is the same. And when one considers, apart from the usual consequences of intemperance, that men and women, even children, often mothers with babies in their arms, come into contact in these places with the most degraded victims of the bourgeois regime, with thieves, swindlers, and prostitutes; when one reflects that many a mother gives the baby on her arm gin to drink, the demoralising effects of frequenting such places cannot be denied.

On Saturday evenings, especially when wages are paid and work stops somewhat earlier than usual, when the whole working class pours from its own poor quarters into the main thoroughfares, intemperance may be seen in all its brutality. I have rarely come out of Manchester on such an evening without meeting numbers of people staggering and seeing others lying in the gutter. On Sunday evening the same scene is usually repeated, only less noisily. And when their money is spent, the drunkards go to the nearest pawnshop, of which there are plenty in every city – over sixty in Manchester, and ten or twelve in a single street of Salford, Chapel Street – and pawn whatever they possess. Furniture, Sunday clothes where such exist, kitchen utensils in masses are fetched from the pawnbrokers on Saturday night only to wander back, almost without fail, before the next Wednesday, until at last some accident makes the final redemption impossible, and one article after another falls into the clutches of the usurer, or until he refuses to give a single farthing more upon the battered, used-up pledge. When one has seen the extent of intemperance among the workers in England, one readily believes Lord Ashley's statement that this class annually expends something like twenty-five million pounds sterling upon intoxicating liquor: and the deterioration in external conditions, the frightful shattering of mental and physical health, the ruin of all domestic relations which follow may readily be imagined. True, the temperance societies have done much, but what are a few thousand teetotallers among the millions of workers? When Father Matthew, the Irish apostle of temperance, passes through the English cities, from thirty to sixty thousand workers take the pledge; but most of them break it again within a month. If one counts up the immense numbers who have taken the pledge in the last three or four years in Manchester, the total is greater than the whole population of the town – and still it is by no means evident that intemperance is diminishing.

Next to intemperance in the enjoyment of intoxicating liquors, one of the principal faults of English working-men is sexual licence. But this, too, follows with relentless logic, with inevitable necessity out of the position of a class left to itself, with no means of making fitting use of its freedom. The bourgeoisie has left the working class only these two pleasures, while imposing upon it a multitude of labours and hardships, and the consequence is that the working-men, in order to get something from life, concentrate their whole energy upon these two enjoyments, carry them to excess, surrender to them in the most unbridled manner. When people are placed under conditions which appeal to the brute only, what remains to them but to rebel or to succumb to utter brutality? And when, moreover, the bourgeoisie does its full share in maintaining prostitution – and how many of the 40,000 prostitutes who fill the streets of London every evening live upon the virtuous bourgeoisie! How many of them owe it to the seduction of a bourgeois, that they must offer their bodies to the passers-by in order to live? – surely it has least of all a right to reproach the workers with their sexual brutality.

The failings of the workers in general may be traced to an unbridled thirst for pleasure, to want of providence, and of flexibility in fitting into the social order, to the general inability to sacrifice the pleasure of the moment to a remoter advantage. But is that to be wondered at? When a class can purchase few and only the most sensual pleasures by its wearying toil, must it not give itself over blindly and madly to those pleasures? A class about whose education no one troubles himself, which is a playball to a thousand chances, knows no security in life – what incentives has such a class to providence, to 'respectability', to sacrifice the pleasure of the moment for a remoter enjoyment, most uncertain precisely by reason of the perpetually varying, shifting conditions under which the proletariat lives? A class which bears all the disadvantages of the social order without enjoying its advantages, one to which the social system appears in purely hostile aspects – who can demand that such a class respect this social order? Verily that is asking much! But the working-man cannot escape the present arrangement of society so long as it exists, and when the individual worker resists it, the greatest injury falls upon himself.

Thus the social order makes family life almost impossible for the worker. In a comfortless, filthy house, hardly good enough for mere nightly shelter, ill-furnished, often neither rain-tight nor warm, a foul atmosphere filling rooms overcrowded with human beings, no domestic comfort is possible. The husband works the whole day through, perhaps the wife also and the elder children, all in different places; they meet night and morning only, all under perpetual temptation to drink; what family life is possible under such conditions? Yet the working-man cannot escape from the family, must live in the family, and the consequence is a perpetual succession of family troubles, domestic quarrels, most demoralising for parents and children alike. Neglect of all domestic duties, neglect of the children, especially, is only too common among the English working-people, and only too vigorously fostered by the existing institutions of society. And children growing up in this savage way, amidst these demoralising influences, are expected to turn out goody-goody and moral in the end! Verily the requirements are naïve, which the self-satisfied bourgeois makes upon the working-man!

The contempt for the existing social order is most conspicuous in its extreme form – that of offences against the law. If the influences demoralising to the working-man act more powerfully, more concentratedly than usual, he becomes an offender as certainly as water abandons the fluid for the vaporous state at 80 degrees, Reaumur. Under the brutal and brutalising treatment of the bourgeoisie, the working-man becomes precisely as much a thing without volition as water, and is subject to the laws of nature with precisely the same necessity; at a certain point all freedom ceases. Hence with the extension of the proletariat, crime has increased in England, and the British nation has become the most criminal in the world. From the annual criminal tables of the Home Secretary, it is evident that the increase of crime in England has proceeded with incomprehensible rapidity. The numbers of arrests for *criminal* offences reached in the years:

1805	4,605	1810	5,146	1815	7,898	1820	13,710
1825	14,437	1830	18,107	1835	20,731	1840	27,187
1841	27,760	1842	31,309					

in England and Wales alone.

That is to say, they increased sevenfold in thirty-seven years. Of these arrests, in 1842, 4,497 were made in Lancashire alone, or more than 14 per cent. of the whole; and 4,094 in Middlesex, including London, or more than 13 per cent. So that two districts which include great cities with large proletarian populations, produced one-fourth of the total amount of crime, though their population is far from forming one-fourth of the whole. Moreover, the criminal tables prove directly that nearly all crime arises within the proletariat; for, in 1842, taking the average, out of 100 criminals, 32.35 could neither read nor write; 58.32 read and wrote imperfectly; 6.77 could read and write well; 0.22 had enjoyed a higher education, while the degree of education of 2.34 could not be ascertained. In Scotland, crime has increased yet more rapidly. There were but 89 arrests for criminal offences in 1819, and as early as 1837 the number had risen to 3,176, and in 1842 to 4,189. In Lanarkshire, where Sheriff Alison himself made out the official report, population has doubled once in thirty years, and crime once in five and a half, or six times more rapidly than the population. The offences, as in all civilised countries, are, in the great majority of cases, against property, and have, therefore, arisen from want in some form; for what a man has, he does not steal. The proportion of offences against property to the population, which in the Netherlands is as 1:7,140, and in France, as 1:1,804, was in England, when Gaskell wrote, as 1:799. The proportion of offences against persons to the population is, in the Netherlands, 1:28,904; in France, 1:17,573; in England, 1:23,395; that of crimes in general to the population in the agricultural districts, as 1:1,043; in the manufacturing districts as 1:840.[46] In the whole of England today the proportion is 1:660;[47] though it is scarcely ten years since Gaskell's book appeared!

These facts are certainly more than sufficient to bring anyone, even a bourgeois, to pause and reflect upon the consequences of such a state of things. If demoralisation and crime multiply twenty years longer in this proportion (and if English manufacture in these twenty years should be less prosperous than heretofore, the progressive multiplication of crime can only continue the more rapidly), what will the result be? Society is already in a state of visible dissolution; it is impossible to pick up a newspaper without seeing the most striking evidence of the giving way of all social ties. I look at random into a heap of English journals lying before me; there is the *Manchester Guardian* for October 30, 1844, which reports for three days. It no longer takes the trouble to give exact details as to Manchester, and merely relates the most interesting cases: that the workers in a mill have struck for higher wages without giving notice, and been condemned by a Justice of the Peace to resume work; that in Salford a couple of boys had been caught stealing, and a bankrupt tradesman tried to cheat his creditors. From the neighbouring towns the reports are more detailed: in Ashton, two thefts, one burglary, one suicide; in Bury, one theft; in Bolton, two thefts, one revenue fraud; in Leigh, one theft; in Oldham, one strike for wages, one theft, one fight between Irish women, one non-Union hatter assaulted by Union men, one mother beaten by her son, one attack upon the police, one robbery of a church; in Stockport, discontent of working-men with wages, one theft, one fraud, one fight, one wife beaten by her husband; in Warrington, one theft, one fight; in Wigan, one theft, and one robbery of a church. The reports of the London papers are much worse; frauds, thefts, assaults, family quarrels crowd one another. A *Times* of September 12, 1844, falls into my hand, which gives a report of a single day, including a theft, an attack upon the police, a sentence upon a father requiring him to support his illegitimate son, the abandonment of a child by its parents, and the poisoning of a man by his wife. Similar reports are to be found in all the English papers. In this country, social war is under full headway, everyone stands for himself, and fights for himself against all comers, and whether or not he shall injure all the others who are his declared foes, depends upon a cynical calculation as to what is most advantageous for himself. It no longer occurs to anyone to come to a peaceful understanding with his fellow-man; all differences are settled by threats, violence, or in a law-court. In short, everyone sees in his neighbour an enemy to be got out of the way, or, at best, a tool to be used for his own advantage. And this war grows from year to year, as the criminal tables show, more violent, passionate, irreconcilable. The enemies are dividing gradually into two great camps – the bourgeoisie on the one hand, the workers on the other. This war of each against all, of the bourgeoisie against the proletariat, need cause us no surprise, for it is only the logical sequel of the principle involved in free competition. But it may very well surprise us that the bourgeoisie remains so quiet and composed in the face of the rapidly gathering storm-clouds, that it can read all these things daily in the papers without, we will not say indignation at such a social condition, but fear of its consequences, of a universal outburst of that which manifests itself symptomatically from day to day in the form of crime. But then it is the bourgeoisie, and from its standpoint cannot even see the facts, much less perceive their consequences. One thing only is astounding, that class prejudice and preconceived opinions can hold a whole class of human beings in such perfect, I might almost say, such mad blindness. Meanwhile, the development of the nation goes its way whether the bourgeoisie has eyes for it or not, and will surprise the property-holding class one day with things not dreamed of in its philosophy.

Single Branches of Industry. Factory Hands

In dealing now with the more important branches of the English manufacturing proletariat, we shall begin, according to the principle already laid down, with the factory-workers, i.e. those who are comprised under the Factory Act. This law regulates the length of the working day in mills in which wool, silk, cotton, and flax are spun or woven by means of water- or steam-power, and embraces, therefore, the more important branches of English manufacture. The class employed by them is the most intelligent and energetic of all the English workers, and, therefore, the most restless and most hated by the bourgeoisie. It stands as a whole, and the cotton workers pre-eminently stand, at the head of the labour movement, as their masters the manufacturers, especially those of Lancashire, take the lead of the bourgeois agitation.

We have already seen in the introduction how the population employed in working up the textile materials were first torn from their former way of life. It is, therefore, not surprising that the progress of mechanical invention in later years also affected precisely these workers most deeply and permanently. The history of cotton manufacture as related by Ure,[48] Baines,[49] and others is the story of improvements in every direction, most of which have become domesticated in the other branches of industry as well. Hand-work is superseded by machine-work almost universally, nearly all manipulations are conducted by the aid of steam or water, and every year is bringing further improvements.

In a well-ordered state of society, such improvements could only be a source of rejoicing; in a war of all against all, individuals seize the benefit for themselves, and so deprive the majority of the means of subsistence. Every improvement in machinery throws workers out of employment, and the greater the advance, the more numerous the unemployed; each great improvement produces, therefore, upon a number of workers the effect of a commercial crisis, creates want, wretchedness, and crime. Take a few examples. The very first invention, the jenny, worked by one man, produced at least sixfold what the spinning-wheel had yielded in the same time; thus every new jenny threw five spinners out of employment. The throstle, which, in turn, produced much more than the jenny, and like it, was worked by one man, threw still more people out of employment. The mule, which required yet fewer hands in proportion to the product, had the same effect, and every improvement in the mule, every multiplication of its spindles, diminished still further the number of workers employed. But this increase of the number of spindles in the mule is so great that whole armies of workers have been thrown out of employment by it. For, whereas one spinner, with a couple of children for piecers, formerly set six hundred spindles in motion, he could now manage fourteen hundred to two thousand spindles upon two mules, so that two adult spinners and a part of the piecers whom they employed were thrown out. And since self-acting mules have been introduced into a very large number of spinning-mills, the spinners' work is wholly performed by the machine. There lies before me a book from the pen of James Leach,[50] one of the recognised leaders of the Chartists in Manchester. The author has worked for years in various branches of industry, in mills and coal mines, and is known to me personally as an honest, trustworthy, and capable man. In consequence of his political position, he had at command extensive detailed information as to the different factories, collected by the workers themselves, and he publishes tables from which it is clear that in 1841, in 35 factories, 1,060 fewer mule spinners were employed than in 1829, though the number of spindles in these 35 factories had increased by 99,239. He cites five factories in which no spinners whatever are employed, self-actors only being used. While the number of spindles increased by 10 per cent., the number of spinners diminished more than 60 per cent. And Leach adds that since 1841, so many improvements have been introduced by double-decking and other means, that in some of the factories named, half the operatives have been discharged. In one factory alone, where eighty spinners were employed a short time ago, there are now but twenty left; the others having been discharged or set at children's work for children's wages. Of Stockport Leach tells a similar story, that in 1835, 800 spinners were employed, and in 1840 but 140, though the manufacture of Stockport has greatly increased during the last eight or nine years. Similar improvements have now been made in carding frames, by which one-half the operatives have been thrown out of employment. In one factory improved frames have been set up, which have thrown four hands out of eight out of work, besides which the employer reduced the wages of the four retained from eight shillings to seven. The same process has gone on in the weaving industry; the power-loom has taken possession of one branch of hand-weaving after another, and since it produces much more than the hand-loom, while one weaver can work two looms, it has superseded a multitude of working-people. And in all sorts of manufacture, in flax and wool-spinning, in silk-twisting, the case is the same. The power-loom, too, is beginning to appropriate one branch after another of wool- and linen-weaving; in Rochdale alone, there are more power than hand-looms in flannel- and other wool-weaving branches. The bourgeoisie usually replies to this, that improvements in machinery, by decreasing the cost of production, supply finished goods at lower prices, and that these reduced prices cause such an increase in consumption that the unemployed operatives soon find full employment in newly-founded factories.[51] The bourgeoisie is so far correct that under certain conditions favourable for the general development of manufacture, every reduction in price of goods *in which the raw material is cheap*, greatly increases consumption, and gives rise to the building of new factories; but every further word of the assertion is a lie. The bourgeoisie ignores the fact that it takes years for these results of the decrease in price to follow and for new factories to be built; it is silent upon the point that every improvement in machinery throws the real work, the expenditure of force, more and more upon the machine, and so transforms the work of full-grown men into mere supervision, which a feeble woman or even a child can do quite as well, and does for half or two-thirds wages; that, therefore, grown men are constantly more and more supplanted and *not re-employed* by the increase in manufacture; it conceals the fact that whole branches of industry fall away, or are so changed that they must be learned afresh; and it takes good care not to confess what it usually harps upon, whenever the question of forbidding the work of children is broached, that factory-work must be learned in earliest youth in order to be learned properly. It does not mention the fact that the process of improvement goes steadily on, and that as soon as the operative has succeeded in making himself at home in a new branch, if he actually does succeed in so doing, this, too, is taken from him, and with it the last remnant of security which remained to him for winning his bread. But the bourgeoisie gets the benefit of the improvements in machinery; it has a capital opportunity for piling up money during the first years while many old machines are still in use, and the improvement not yet universally introduced; and it would be too much to ask that it should have an open eye for the disadvantages inseparable from these improvements.

The fact that improved machinery reduces wages has also been as violently disputed by the bourgeoisie, as it is constantly reiterated by the working-men. The bourgeoisie insists that although the price of piece-work has been reduced, yet the total of wages for the week's work has rather risen than fallen, and the condition of the operatives rather improved than deteriorated. It is hard to get to the bottom of the matter, for the operatives usually dwell upon the price of piece-work. But it is certain that the weekly wage, also, has, in many branches of work, been reduced by the improvement of machinery. The so-called fine spinners (who spin fine mule yarn), for instance, do receive high wages, thirty to forty shillings a week, because they have a powerful association for keeping wages up, and their craft requires long training; but the coarse spinners who have to compete against self-actors (which are not as yet adapted for fine spinning), and whose association was broken down by the introduction of these machines, receive very low wages. A mule spinner told me that he does not earn more than fourteen shillings a week, and his statement agrees with that of Leach, that in various factories the coarse spinners earn less than sixteen shillings and sixpence a week, and that a spinner, who years ago earned thirty shillings, can now hardly scrape up twelve and a half, and had not earned more on an average in the past year. The wages of women and children may perhaps have fallen less, but only because they were not high from the beginning. I know several women, widows with children, who have trouble enough to earn eight to nine shillings a week; and that they and their families cannot live decently upon that sum, everyone must admit who knows the price of the barest necessaries of life in England. That wages in general have been reduced by the improvement of machinery is the unanimous testimony of the operatives. The bourgeois assertion that the condition of the working class has been improved by machinery is most vigorously proclaimed a falsehood in every meeting of working-men in the factory districts. And even if it were true that the relative wage, the price of piece-work only, has fallen, while the absolute wage, the sum to be earned in the week, remained unchanged, what would follow? That the operatives have had quietly to look on while the manufacturers filled their purses from every improvement without giving the hands the smallest share in the gain. The bourgeois forgets, in fighting the working-man, the most ordinary principles of his own Political Economy. He who at other times swears by Malthus, cries out in his anxiety before the workers: 'Where could the millions by which the population of England has increased find work, without the improvements in machinery?' [52] As though the bourgeois did not know well enough that without machinery and the expansion of industry which it produced, these 'millions' would never have been brought into the world and grown up! The service which machinery has rendered the workers is simply this: that it has brought home to their minds the necessity of a social reform by means of which machinery shall no longer work against but for them. Let the wise bourgeois ask the people who sweep the streets in Manchester and elsewhere (though even this is past now, since machines for the purpose have been invented and introduced), or sell salt, matches, oranges, and shoe-strings on the streets, or even beg, what they were formerly, and he will see how many will answer: 'Mill-hands thrown out of work by machinery.' The consequences of improvement in machinery under our present social conditions are, for the working-man, solely injurious, and often in the highest degree oppressive. Every new advance brings with it loss of employment, want, and suffering, and in a country like England where, without that, there is usually a 'surplus population', to be discharged from work is the worst that can befall the operative. And what a dispiriting, unnerving influence this uncertainty of his position in life, consequent upon the unceasing progress of machinery, must exercise upon the worker, whose lot is precarious enough without it! To escape despair, there are but two ways open to him; either inward and outward revolt against the bourgeoisie, or drunkenness and general demoralisation. And the English operatives are accustomed to take refuge in both. The history of the English proletariat relates hundreds of uprisings against machinery and the bourgeoisie; we have already spoken of the moral dissolution which, in itself, is only another form of despair.

The worst situation is that of those workers who have to compete against a machine that is making its way. The price of the goods which they produce adapts itself to the price of the kindred product of the machine, and as the latter works more cheaply, its human competitor has but the lowest wages. The same thing happens to every operative employed upon an old machine in competition with later improvements. And who else is there to bear the hardship? The manufacturer will not throw out his old apparatus, nor will he sustain the loss upon it; out of the dead mechanism he can make nothing, so he fastens upon the living worker, the universal scapegoat of society. Of all the workers in competition with machinery, the most ill-used are the hand-loom cotton weavers. They receive the most trifling wages, and, with full work, are not in a position to earn more than ten shillings a week. One class of woven goods after another is annexed by the power-loom, and hand-weaving is the last refuge of workers thrown out of employment in other branches, so that the trade is always overcrowded. Hence it comes that, in average seasons, the hand-weaver counts himself fortunate if he can earn six or seven shillings a week, while to reach this sum he must sit at his loom fourteen to eighteen hours a day. Most woven goods require moreover a damp weaving-room, to keep the weft from snapping, and in part for this reason, in part because of their poverty, which prevents them from paying for better dwellings, the workrooms of these weavers are usually without wooden or paved floors. I have been in many dwellings of such weavers, in remote, vile courts and alleys, usually in cellars. Often half-a-dozen of these hand-loom weavers, several of them married, live together in a cottage with one or two workrooms, and one large sleeping-room. Their food consists almost exclusively of potatoes, with perhaps oatmeal porridge, rarely milk, and scarcely ever meat. Great numbers of them are Irish or of Irish descent. And these poor hand-loom weavers, first to suffer from every crisis, and last to be relieved from it, must serve the bourgeoisie as a handle in meeting attacks upon the factory system. 'See', cries the bourgeois, triumphantly, 'see how these poor creatures must famish, while the mill operatives are thriving, and *then* judge the factory system!' [53] As though it were not precisely the factory system and the machinery belonging to it which had so shamefully crushed the hand-loom weavers, and as though the bourgeoisie did not know this quite as well as ourselves! But the bourgeoisie has interests at stake, and so a falsehood or two and a bit of hypocrisy won't matter much.

Let us examine somewhat more closely the fact that machinery more and more supersedes the work of men. The human labour, involved in both spinning and weaving, consists chiefly in piecing broken threads, as the machine does all the rest. This work requires no muscular strength, but only flexibility of finger. Men are, therefore, not only not needed for it, but actually, by reason of the greater muscular development of the hand, less fit for it than women and children, and are, therefore, naturally almost superseded by them. Hence, the more the use of the arms, the expenditure of strength, can be transferred to steam- or water-power, the fewer men need be employed; and as women and children work more cheaply, and in these branches better than men, they take their places. In the spinning-mills women and girls are to be found in almost exclusive possession of the throstles; among the mules one man, an adult spinner (with self-actors, he too becomes superfluous), and several piecers for tying the threads, usually children or women, sometimes young men of from eighteen to twenty years, here and there an old spinner [54] thrown out of other employment. At the power-looms women, from fifteen to twenty years, are chiefly employed, and a few men; these, however, rarely remain at this trade after their twenty-first year. Among the preparatory machinery, too, women alone are to be found, with here and there a man to clean and sharpen the carding-frames. Besides all these, the factories employ numbers of children – doffers – for mounting and taking down bobbins, and a few men as overlookers, a mechanic and an engineer for the steam-engines, carpenters, porters, etc.; but the actual work of the mills is done by women and children. This the manufacturers deny.

They published last year elaborate tables to prove that machinery does not supersede adult male operatives. According to these tables, rather more than half of all the factory-workers employed, viz., 52 per cent., were females and 48 per cent. males, and of those operatives more than half were over eighteen years old. So far, so good. But the manufacturers are very careful not to tell us, how many of the adults were men and how many women. And this is just the point. Besides this, they have evidently counted the mechanics, engineers, carpenters, all the men employed in any way in the factories, perhaps even the clerks, and still they have not the courage to tell the whole truth. These publications teem generally with falsehoods, perversions, crooked statements, with calculations of averages, that prove a great deal for the uninitiated reader and nothing for the initiated, and with suppressions of facts bearing on the most important points; and they prove only the selfish blindness and want of uprightness of the manufacturers concerned. Let us take some of the statements of a speech with which Lord Ashley introduced the Ten Hours' Bill, March 15th, 1844, into the House of Commons. Here he gives some data as to the relations of sex and age of the operatives, not yet refuted by the manufacturers, whose statements, as quoted above, cover more-over only a part of the manufacturing industry of England. Of 419,560 factory operatives of the British Empire in 1839, 192,887, or nearly half, were under eighteen years of age, and 242,296 of the female sex, of whom 112,192 were less than eighteen years old. There remain, therefore, 80,695 male operatives under eighteen years, and 96,569 adult male operatives, *or not one full quarter* of the whole number. In the cotton factories, 56.25 per cent.; in the woollen mills, 69.5 per cent.; in the silk mills, 70.5 per cent.; in the flax-spinning mills, 70.5 per cent. of all operatives are of the female sex. These numbers suffice to prove the crowding out of adult males. But you have only to go into the nearest mill to see the fact confirmed. Hence follows of necessity that inversion of the exist-ing social order which, being forced upon them, has the most ruinous consequences for the workers. The employment of women at once breaks up the family; for when the wife spends twelve or thirteen hours every day in the mill, and the husband works the same length of time there or elsewhere, what becomes of the children? They grow up like wild weeds; they are put out to nurse for a shilling or eighteenpence a week, and how they are treated may be imagined. Hence the accidents to which little children fall victims multiply in the factory districts to a terrible extent. The lists of the Coroner of Manchester[55] showed for nine months: 69 deaths from burning, 56 from drowning, 23 from falling, 77 from other causes, or a total of 225[56] deaths from accidents, while in non-manufacturing Liverpool during twelve months there were but 146 fatal accidents. The mining accidents are excluded in both cases; and since the Coroner of Manchester has no authority in Salford, the population of both places mentioned in the comparison is about the same. The *Manchester Guardian* reports one or more deaths by burning in almost every number. That the general mortality among young children must be increased by the employment of the mothers is self-evident, and is placed beyond all doubt by notorious facts. Women often return to the mill three or four days after confinement, leaving the baby, of course; in the dinner hour they must hurry home to feed the child and eat something, and what sort of suckling that can be is also evident. Lord Ashley repeats the testimony of several workwomen: 'M. H., twenty years old, has two children, the youngest a baby, that is tended by the other, a little older. The mother goes to the mill shortly after five o'clock in the morning, and comes home at eight at night; all day the milk pours from her breasts, so that her clothing drips with it.' 'H. W. has three children, goes away Monday morning at five o'clock, and comes back Saturday evening; has so much to do for the children then that she cannot get to bed before three o'clock in the morning; often wet through to the skin, and obliged to work in that state.' She said: 'My breasts have given me the most frightful pain, and I have been dripping wet with milk.' The use of narcotics to keep the children still is fostered by this infamous system, and has reached a great extent in the factory districts. Dr Johns, Registrar in Chief for Manchester, is of opinion that this custom is the chief source of the many deaths from convulsions. The employment of the wife dissolves the family utterly and of necessity, and this dissolution, in our present society, which is based upon the family, brings the most demoralising consequences for parents as well as children. A mother who has no time to trouble herself about her child, to perform the most ordinary loving services for it during its first year, who scarcely indeed sees it, can be no real mother to the child, must inevitably grow indifferent to it, treat it unlovingly like a stranger. The children who grow up under such conditions are utterly ruined for later family life, can never feel at home in the family which they themselves found, because they have always been accustomed to isolation, and they contribute therefore to the already general undermining of the family in the working class. A similar dissolution of the family is brought about by the employment of the children. When they get on far enough to earn more than they cost their parents from week to week, they begin to pay the parents a fixed sum for board and lodging, and keep the rest for themselves. This often happens from the fourteenth or fifteenth year.[57] In a word, the children emancipate themselves, and regard the paternal dwelling as a lodging-house, which they often exchange for another, as suits them.

In many cases the family is not wholly dissolved by the employment of the wife, but turned upside down. The wife supports the family, the husband sits at home, tends the children, sweeps the room and cooks. This case happens very frequently; in Manchester alone, many hundred such men could be cited, condemned to domestic occupations. It is easy to imagine the wrath aroused among the working-men by this reversal of all relations within the family, while the other social conditions remain unchanged. There lies before me a letter from an English working-man, Robert Pounder, Baron's Buildings, Woodhouse, Moorside, in Leeds (the bourgeoisie may hunt him up there; I give the exact address for the purpose), written by him to Oastler.[58]

He relates how another working-man, being on tramp, came to St Helens, in Lancashire, and there looked up an old friend. He found him in a miserable, damp cellar, scarcely furnished; and when my poor friend went in, there sat poor Jack near the fire, and what did he, think you? Why, he sat and mended his wife's stockings with the bodkin; and as soon as he saw his old friend at the door-post, he tried to hide them. But Joe, that is my friend's name, had seen it, and said: 'Jack, what the devil art thou doing? Where is the missus? Why, is that thy work?' and poor Jack was ashamed, and said: 'No, I know this is not my work, but my poor missus is i' th' factory; she has to leave at half-past five and works till eight at night, and then she is so knocked up that she cannot do aught when she gets home, so I have to do everything for her what I can, for I have no work, nor had any for more nor three years, and I shall never have any more work while I live;' and then he wept a big tear. Jack again said: 'There is work enough for women folks and childer hereabouts, but none for men; thou mayest sooner find a hundred pound on the road than work for men – but I should never have believed that either thou or anyone else would have seen me mending my wife's stockings, for, it is bad work. But she can hardly stand on her feet; I am afraid she will be laid up, and then I don't know what is to become of us, for it's a good bit that she has been the man in the house and I the woman; it is bad work, Joe;' and he cried bitterly, and said, 'It has not been always so.' 'No', said Joe; 'but when thou hadn't no work, how hast thou not shifted?' 'I'll tell thee, Joe, as well as I can, but it was bad enough; thou knowest when I got married I had work plenty, and thou knows I was not lazy.' 'No, that thou wert not.' 'And we had a good furnished house, and Mary need not go to work. I could work for the two of us; but now the world is upside down. Mary has to work and I have to stop at home, mind the childer sweep and wash, bake and mend; and, when the poor woman comes home at night, she is knocked up. Thou knows, Joe, it's hard for one that was used different.' 'Yes, boy, it is hard.' And then Jack began to cry again, and he wished he had never married, and that he had never been born; but he had never thought, when he wed Mary, that it would come to this. 'I have often cried over it', said Jack. Now when Joe heard this, he told me that he had cursed and damned the factories, and the masters, and the Government, with all the curses that he had learned while he was in the factory from a child.

Can anyone imagine a more insane state of things than that described in this letter? And yet this condition, which unsexes the man and takes from the woman all womanliness, without being able to bestow upon the man true womanliness, or the woman true manliness – this condition which degrades, in the most shameful way, both sexes, and, through them, Humanity, is the last result of our much-praised civilisation, the final achievement of all the efforts and struggles of hundreds of generations to improve their own situation and that of their posterity. We must either despair of mankind, and its aims and efforts, when we see all our labour and toil result in such a mockery, or we must admit that human society has hitherto sought salvation in a false direction; we must admit that so total a reversal of the position of the sexes can have come to pass only because the sexes have been placed in a false position from the beginning. If the reign of the wife over the husband, as inevitably brought about by the factory system, is inhuman, the pristine rule of the husband over the wife must have been inhuman too. If the wife can now base her supremacy upon the fact that she supplies the greater part, nay, the whole of the common possession, the necessary inference is that this community of possession is no true and rational one, since one member of the family boasts offensively of contributing the greater share. If the family of our present society is being thus dissolved, this dissolution merely shows that, at bottom, the binding tie of this family was not family affection, but private interest lurking under the cloak of a pretended community of possessions.[59] The same relation exists on the part of those children who support unemployed parents when they do not directly pay board as already referred to. Dr Hawkins testified in the Factories' Inquiry Commission's Report that this relation is common enough, and in Manchester it is notorious. In this case the children are the masters in the house, as the wife was in the former case, and Lord Ashley gives an example of this in his speech:[60] A man berated his two daughters for going to the public house, and they answered that they were tired of being ordered about, saying, 'Damn you, we have to keep you!' Determined to keep the proceeds of their work for themselves, they left the family dwelling, and abandoned their parents to their fate.

The unmarried women, who have grown up in mills, are no better off than the married ones. It is self-evident that a girl who has worked in a mill from her ninth year is in no position to understand domestic work, whence it follows that female operatives prove wholly inexperienced and unfit as housekeepers. They cannot knit or sew, cook or wash, are unacquainted with the most ordinary duties of a housekeeper, and when they have young children to take care of, have not the vaguest idea how to set about it. The Factories' Inquiry Commission's Report gives dozens of examples of this, and Dr Hawkins, Commissioner for Lancashire, expresses his opinion as follows:[61]

The girls marry early and recklessly; they have neither means, time, nor opportunity to learn the ordinary duties of household life; but if they had them all, they would find no time in married life for the performance of these duties. The mother is more than twelve hours away from her child daily; the baby is cared for by a young girl or an old woman, to whom it is given to nurse. Besides this, the dwelling of the mill-hands is too often no home but a cellar, which contains no cooking or washing utensils, no sewing or mending materials, nothing which makes life agreeable and civilised, or the domestic hearth attractive. For these and other reasons, and especially for the sake of the better chances of life for the little children, I can but wish and hope that a time may come in which married women will be shut out of the factories.[62]

But that is the least of the evil. The moral consequences of the employment of women in factories are even worse. The collecting of persons of both sexes and all ages in a single workroom, the inevitable contact, the crowding into a small space of people, to whom neither mental nor moral education has been given, is not calculated for the favourable development of the female character. The manufacturer, if he pays any attention to the matter, can interfere only when something scandalous actually happens; the permanent, less conspicuous influence of persons of dissolute character, upon the more moral, and especially upon the younger ones, he cannot ascertain, and consequently cannot prevent. But precisely this influence is the most injurious. The language used in the mills is characterised by many witnesses in the report of 1833, as 'indecent', 'bad', 'filthy', etc.[63] It is the same process upon a small scale which we have already witnessed upon a large one in the great cities. The centralisation of population has the same influence upon the same persons, whether it affects them in a great city or a small factory. The smaller the mill the closer the packing, and the more unavoidable the contact; and the consequences are not wanting. A witness in Leicester said that he would rather let his daughter beg than go into a factory; that they are perfect gates of hell; that most of the prostitutes of the town had their employment in the mills to thank for their present situation.[64] Another, in Manchester, 'did not hesitate to assert that three-fourths of the young factory employees, from fourteen to twenty years of age, were unchaste.'[65] Commissioner Cowell expresses it as his opinion, that the morality of the factory operatives is somewhat below the average of that of the working class in general.[66] And Dr Hawkins[67] says:

> An estimate of sexual morality cannot readily be reduced to figures; but if I may trust my own observations and the general opinion of those with whom I have spoken, as well as the whole tenor of the testimony furnished me, the aspect of the influence of factory life upon the morality of the youthful female population is most depressing.

It is, besides, a matter of course that factory servitude, like any other, and to an even higher degree, confers the *jus primae noctis* upon the master. In this respect also the employer is sovereign over the persons and charms of his employees. The threat of discharge suffices to overcome all resistance in nine cases out of ten, if not in ninety-nine out of a hundred, in girls who, in any case, have no strong inducements to chastity. If the master is mean enough, and the official report mentions several such cases, his mill is also his harem; and the fact that not all manufacturers use their power, does not in the least change the position of the girls. In the beginning of manufacturing industry, when most of the employers were upstarts without education or consideration for the hypocrisy of society, they let nothing interfere with the exercise of their vested rights.

To form a correct judgment of the influence of factory-work upon the health of the female sex, it is necessary first to consider the work of children, and then the nature of the work itself. From the beginning of manufacturing industry, children have been employed in mills, at first almost exclusively by reason of the smallness of the machines, which were later enlarged. Even children from the workhouses were employed in multitudes, being rented out for a number of years to the manufacturers as apprentices. They were lodged, fed, and clothed in common, and were, of course, completely the slaves of their masters, by whom they were treated with the utmost recklessness and barbarity. As early as 1796, the public objection to this revolting system found such vigorous expression through Dr Percival and Sir Robert Peel (father of the Cabinet Minister, and himself a cotton manufacturer), that in 1802 Parliament passed an Apprentices' Bill, by which the most crying evils were removed. Gradually the increasing competition of free workpeople crowded out the whole apprentice system; factories were built in cities, machinery was constructed on a larger scale, and workrooms were made more airy and wholesome; gradually, too, more work was found for adults and young persons. The number of children in the mills diminished somewhat, and the age at which they began to work rose a little; few children under eight or nine years were now employed. Later, as we shall see, the power of the State intervened several times to protect them from the money-greed of the bourgeoisie.

The great mortality among children of the working class, and especially among those of the factory operatives, is proof enough of the unwholesome conditions under which they pass their first year. These influences are at work, of course, among the children who survive, but not quite so powerfully as upon those who succumb. The result in the most favourable case is a tendency to disease, or some check in development, and consequent less than normal vigour of the constitution. A nine-years-old child of a factory operative that has grown up in want, privation, and changing conditions, in cold and damp, with insufficient clothing and unwholesome dwellings, is far from having the working force of a child brought up under healthier conditions. At nine years of age it is sent into the mill to work 6½ hours (formerly 8, earlier still, 12 to 14, even 16 hours) daily, until the thirteenth year; then twelve hours until the eighteenth year. The old enfeebling influences continue, while the work is added to them. It is not to be denied that a child of nine years, even an operative's child, can hold out through 6½ hours' daily work, without anyone being able to trace visible bad results in its development directly to this cause; but in no case can its presence in the damp, heavy air of the factory, often at once warm and wet, contribute to good health; and, in any case, it is unpardonable to sacrifice to the greed of an unfeeling bourgeoisie the time of children which should be devoted solely to their physical and mental development, with-draw them from school and the fresh air, in order to wear them out for the benefit of the manufacturers. The bourgeoisie says: 'If we do not employ the children in the mills, they only remain under conditions unfavourable to their development;' and this is true, on the whole. But what does this mean if it is not a confession that the bourgeoisie first places the children of the working class under unfavourable conditions, and then exploits these bad conditions for its own benefit, appeals to that which is as much its own fault as the factory system, excuses the sin of today with the sin of yesterday? And if the Factory Act did not in some measure fetter their hands, how this 'humane', this 'benevolent' bourgeoisie, which has built its factories solely for the good of the working class, would take care of the interests of these workers! Let us hear how they acted before the factory inspector was at their heels. Their own admitted testimony shall convict them in the report of the Factories' Inquiry Commission of 1833.

The report of the Central Commission relates that the manufacturers began to employ children rarely of five years, often of six, very often of seven, usually of eight to nine years; that the working day often lasted fourteen to sixteen hours, exclusive of meals and intervals; that the manufacturers permitted overlookers to flog and maltreat children, and often took an active part in so doing themselves. One case is related of a Scotch manufacturer, who rode after a sixteen years old runaway, forced him to return running after the employer as fast as the master's horse trotted, and beat him the whole way with a long whip.[68] In the large towns where the operatives resisted more vigorously, such things naturally happened less often. But even this long working day failed to satisfy the greed of the capitalists. Their aim was to make the capital invested in the building and machinery produce the highest return, by every available means, to make it work as actively as possible. Hence the manufacturers introduced the shameful system of night-work. Some of them employed two sets of operatives, each numerous enough to fill the whole mill, and let one set work the twelve hours of the day, and the other twelve hours of the night. It is needless to picture the effect upon the frames of young children, and even upon the health of young persons and adults, produced by permanent loss of sleep at night, which cannot be made good by any amount of sleep during the day. Irritation of the whole nervous system, with general lassitude and enfeeblement of the entire frame, were the inevitable results, with the fostering of temptation to drunkenness and unbridled sexual indulgence. One manufacturer testifies[69] that during the two years in which night-work was carried on in his factory, the number of illegitimate children born was doubled, and such general demoralisation prevailed that he was obliged to give up night-work. Other manufacturers were yet more barbarous, requiring many hands to work thirty to forty hours at a stretch, several times a week, letting them get a couple of hours sleep only, because the night-shift was not complete, but calculated to replace a part of the operatives only.

The reports of the Commission touching this barbarism surpass everything that is known to me in this line. Such infamies as are here related, are nowhere else to be found – yet we shall see that the bourgeoisie constantly appeals to the testimony of the Commission as being in its own favour. The consequences of these cruelties became evident quickly enough. The Commissioners mention a crowd of cripples who appeared before them, who clearly owed their distortion to the long working hours. This distortion usually consists of a curving of the spinal column and legs, and is described as follows by Francis Sharp, M.R.C.S., of Leeds:[70]

> I never saw the peculiar bending of the lower ends of the thigh bones before I came to Leeds. At first I thought it was rachitis, but I was soon led to change my opinion in consequence of the mass of patients who presented themselves at the hospital, and the appearances of the disease at an age (from the fourteenth to the eighteenth year) in which children are usually not subject to rachitis, as well as by the circumstance that the malady had first appeared after children began to work in the mills. Thus far I have seen about a hundred such cases, and can, most decidedly, express the opinion that they are the consequences of overwork. So far as I know they were all mill children, and themselves attributed the evil to this cause. The number of cases of curvature of the spine which have fallen under my observation, and which were evidently consequent upon too protracted standing, was not less than three hundred.

Precisely similar is the testimony of Dr Ray, for eighteen years physician in the hospital in Leeds:[71]

> Malformations of the spine are very frequent among mill-hands; some of them consequent upon mere overwork, others the effect of long work upon constitutions originally feeble, or weakened by bad food. Deformities seem even more frequent than these diseases; the knees were bent inward, the ligaments very often

relaxed and enfeebled, and the long bones of the legs bent. The thick ends of these long bones were especially apt to be bent and disproportionately developed, and these patients came from the factories in which long work-hours were of frequent occurrence.

Surgeons Beaumont and Sharp, of Bradford, bear the same testimony. The reports of Drinkwater, Power, and Dr Loudon contain a multitude of examples of such distortions, and those of Tufnell and Sir David Barry, which are less directed to this point, give single examples.[72] The Commissioners for Lancashire, Cowell, Tufnell, and Hawkins, have almost wholly neglected this aspect of the physiological results of the factory system, though this district rivals Yorkshire in the number of cripples. I have seldom traversed Manchester without meeting three or four of them, suffering from precisely the same distortions of the spinal columns and legs as that described, and I have often been able to observe them closely. I know one personally who corresponds exactly with the foregoing description of Dr Ray, and who got into this condition in Mr Douglas' factory in Pendleton, an establishment which enjoys an unenviable notoriety among the operatives by reason of the former long working periods continued night after night. It is evident, at a glance, whence the distortions of these cripples come; they all look exactly alike. The knees are bent inward and backwards, the ankles deformed and thick, and the spinal column often bent forwards or to one side. But the crown belongs to the philanthropic manufacturers of the Macclesfield silk district. They employed the youngest children of all, even from five to six years of age. In the supplementary testimony of Commissioner Tufnell, I find the statement of a certain factory manager Wright, both of whose sisters were most shamefully crippled, and who had once counted the cripples in several streets, some of them the cleanest and neatest streets of Macclesfield. He found in Townley Street ten, George Street five, Charlotte Street four, Watercots fifteen, Bank Top three, Lord Street seven, Mill Lane twelve, Great George Street two, in the workhouse two, Park Green one, Peckford Street two, whose families all unanimously declared that the cripples had become such in consequence of overwork in the silk-twisting mills. One boy is mentioned so crippled as not to be able to go upstairs, and girls deformed in back and hips.

Other deformities also have proceeded from this overwork, especially flattening of the foot, which Sir D. Barry [73] frequently observed, as did the physicians and surgeons in Leeds. [74] In cases in which a stronger constitution, better food, and other more favourable circumstances enabled the young operative to resist this effect of a barbarous exploitation, we find, at least, pain in the back, hips, and legs, swollen joints, varicose veins, and large, persistent ulcers in the thighs and calves. These affections are almost universal among the operatives. The reports of Stuart, Mackintosh, and Sir D. Barry contain hundreds of examples; indeed, they know almost no operative who did not suffer from some of these affections; and in the remaining reports, the occurrence of the same phenomena is attested by many physicians. The reports covering Scotland place it beyond all doubt, that a working day of thirteen hours, even for men and women from eighteen to twenty-two years of age, produces at least these consequences, both in the flax-spinning mills of Dundee and Dunfermline, and in the cotton mills of Glasgow and Lanark.

All these affections are easily explained by the nature of factory-work, which is, as the manufacturers say, very 'light', and precisely by reason of its lightness, more enervating than any other. The operatives have little to do, but must stand the whole time. Anyone who sits down, say upon a window-ledge or a basket, is fined, and this perpetual upright position, this constant mechanical pressure of the upper portions of the body upon spinal column, hips, and legs, inevitably produces the results mentioned. This standing is not required by the work itself, and at Nottingham chairs have been introduced, with the result that these affections disappeared, and the operatives ceased to object to the length of the working day. But in a factory where the operative works solely for the bourgeois, and has small interest in doing his work well, he would probably use the seats more than would be agreeable and profitable to the manufacturer; and in order that somewhat less raw material may be spoiled for the bourgeois, the operative must sacrifice health and strength. [75] This long protracted upright position, with the bad atmosphere prevalent in the mills, entails, besides the deformities mentioned, a marked relaxation of all vital energies, and, in consequence, all sorts of other affections general rather than local. The atmosphere of the factories is, as a rule, at

once damp and warm, unusually warmer than is necessary, and, when the ventilation is not *very* good, impure, heavy,
deficient in oxygen, filled with dust and the smell of the machine
oil, which almost everywhere smears the floor, sinks into it, and
becomes rancid. The operatives are lightly clad by reason of the
warmth, and would readily take cold in case of irregularity of the
temperature; a draught is distasteful to them, the general enervation which gradually takes possession of all the physical functions
diminishes the animal warmth: this must be replaced from without, and nothing is therefore more agreeable to the operative than
to have all the doors and windows closed, and to stay in his warm
factory-air. Then comes the sudden change of temperature on
going out into the cold and wet or frosty atmosphere, without the
means of protection from the rain, or of changing wet clothing for
dry, a circumstance which perpetually produces colds. And when
one reflects that, with all this, not one single muscle of the body
is really exercised, really called into activity, except perhaps those
of the legs; that nothing whatsoever counteracts the enervating,
relaxing tendency of all these conditions; that every influence is
wanting which might give the muscles strength, the fibres elast-
icity and consistency; that from youth up, the operative is deprived
of all fresh air recreation, it is impossible to wonder at the almost
unanimous testimony of the physicians in the Factories' Report,
that they find a great lack of ability to resist disease, a general
depression in vital activity, a constant relaxation of the mental and
physical powers. Let us hear Sir D. Barry first:[76]

The unfavourable influences of mill-work upon the hands are
the following: (1) The inevitable necessity of forcing their mental
and bodily effort to keep pace with a machine moved by a uniform and unceasing motive power. (2) Continuance in an upright
position during unnaturally long and quickly recurring periods.
(3) Loss of sleep in consequence of too long working hours, pain
in the legs, and general physical derangement. To these are often
added low, crowded, dusty, or damp workrooms, impure air, a
high temperature, and constant perspiration. Hence the boys
especially very soon and with but few exceptions, lose the rosy
freshness of childhood, and become paler and thinner than other
boys. Even the hand-weaver's bound boy, who sits before his

loom with his bare feet resting upon the clay-floor, retains a fresher appearance, because he occasionally goes into the fresh air for a time. But the mill child has not a moment free except for meals, and never goes into the fresh air except on its way to them. All adult male spinners are pale and thin, suffer from capricious appetite and indigestion; and as they are all trained in the mills from their youth up, and there are very few tall, athletic men among them, the conclusion is justified that their occupation is very unfavourable for the development of the male constitution; females bear this work far better. [Very naturally. But we shall see that they have their own diseases.]

So, too, Power:[77]

I can bear witness that the factory system in Bradford has engendered a multitude of cripples, and that the effect of long continued labour upon the physique is apparent, not alone in actual deformity, but also, and much more generally, in stunted growth, relaxation of the muscles, and delicacy of the whole frame.

So, too, F. Sharp, in Leeds, the surgeon[78] already quoted:

When I moved from Scarborough to Leeds, I was at once struck by the fact that the general appearance of the children was much paler, and their fibre less vigorous here than in Scarborough and its environs. I saw, too, that many children were exceptionally small for their age. I have met with numberless cases of scrofula, lung trouble, mesenteric affections, and indigestion, concerning which I, as a medical man, have no doubt that they arose from mill work. I believe that the nervous energy of the body is weakened by the long hours, and the foundation of many diseases laid. If people from the country were not constantly coming in, the race of mill-hands would soon be wholly degenerate.

So, too, Beaumont, surgeon in Bradford:

To my thinking, the system according to which work is done in the mills here, produces a peculiar relaxation of the whole organism, and thereby makes children in the highest degree susceptible to epidemic, as well as to incidental illness. I regard the absence of all appropriate regulations for ventilation and cleanliness in the mills very decidedly as the chief cause of that peculiar tendency or susceptibility to morbid affections which I have so frequently met in my practice.

Similar testimony is borne by Dr Ray:

(1) I have had opportunity of observing the effects of the factory system upon the health of children under the most favourable circumstances (in Wood's mill, in Bradford, the best arranged of the district, in which he was factory surgeon).

(2) These effects are decidedly, and to a very great extent, injurious, even under these most favourable circumstances.

(3) In the year 1842, three-fifths of all the children employed in Wood's mill were treated by me.

(4) The worst effect is not the predominance of deformities, but of enfeebled and morbid constitutions.

(5) All this is greatly improved since the working hours of children have been reduced at Wood's to ten.

The Commissioner, Dr Loudon himself, who cites these witnesses, says:

In conclusion, I think it has been clearly proved that children have been worked a most unreasonable and cruel length of time daily, and that even adults have been expected to do a certain quantity of labour which scarcely any human being is able to endure. The consequence is that many have died prematurely, and others are afflicted for life with defective constitutions, and the fear of a posterity enfeebled by the shattered constitution of the survivors is but too well founded, from a physiological point of view.

And, finally, Dr Hawkins, in speaking of Manchester:

I believe that most travellers are struck by the lowness of stature, the leanness and the paleness which present themselves so commonly to the eye at Manchester, and above all, among the factory classes. I have never been in any town in Great Britain, nor in Europe, in which degeneracy of form and colour from the national standard has been so obvious. Among the married women all the characteristic peculiarities of the English wife are conspicuously wanting. I must confess that all the boys and girls brought before me from the Manchester mills had a depressed appearance, and were very pale. In the expression of their faces lay nothing of the usual mobility, liveliness, and cheeriness of youth. Many of them told me that they felt not the slightest inclination to play out of doors on Saturday and Sunday, but preferred to be quiet at home.

I add, at once, another passage of Hawkins' report, which only half belongs here, but may be quoted here as well as anywhere else:

Intemperance, excess, and want of providence are the chief faults of the factory population, and these evils may be readily traced to the habits which are formed under the present system, and almost inevitably arise from it. It is universally admitted that indigestion, hypochondria, and general debility affect this class to a very great extent. After twelve hours of monotonous toil, it is but natural to look about for a stimulant of one sort or another; but when the above-mentioned diseased conditions are added to the customary weariness, people will quickly and repeatedly take refuge in spirituous liquors.

For all this testimony of the physicians and commissioners, the report itself offers hundreds of cases of proof. That the growth of young operatives is stunted, by their work, hundreds of statements testify; among others, Cowell gives the weight of 46 youths of 17 years of age, from one Sunday school, of whom 26 employed in mills, averaged 104.5 pounds, and 20 not employed in mills, 117.7 pounds. One of the largest manufacturers of Manchester, leader of the opposition against the working-men, I think Robert Hyde Greg himself, said, on one occasion, that if things went on as at present, the operatives of Lancashire would soon be a race of pigmies.[79] A recruiting officer [80] testified that operatives are little adapted for military service, looked thin and nervous, and were frequently rejected by the surgeons as unfit. In Manchester he could hardly get men of five feet eight inches; they were usually only five feet six to seven, whereas in the agricultural districts, most of the recruits were five feet eight.

The men wear out very early in consequence of the conditions under which they live and work. Most of them are unfit for work at forty years, a few hold out to forty-five, almost none to fifty years of age. This is caused not only by the general enfeeblement

of the frame, but also very often by a failure of the sight, which is
a result of mule-spinning, in which the operative is obliged to fix
his gaze upon a long row of fine, parallel threads, and so greatly to
strain the sight.

Of 1,600 operatives employed in several factories in Harpur and
Lanark, but 10 were over 45 years of age; of 22,094 operatives in
diverse factories in Stockport and Manchester, but 143 were over 45
years old. Of these 143, 16 were retained as a special favour, and one
was doing the work of a child. A list of 131 spinners contained but
seven over 45 years, and yet the whole 131 were rejected by the
manufacturers, to whom they applied for work, as 'too old', and
were without means of support by reason of old age! Mr Ashworth,
a large manufacturer, admits in a letter to Lord Ashley, that, towards
the fortieth year, the spinners can no longer prepare the required
quantity of yarn, and are therefore 'sometimes' discharged; he calls
operatives forty years of age 'old people!' Commissioner Mackintosh expresses himself in the same way in the report of 1833:
'Although I was prepared for it from the way the children are
employed, I still found it difficult to believe the statements of the
older hands as to their ages; they age so very early.'

Surgeon Smellie, of Glasgow, who treated operatives chiefly,
says that forty years is old age for them.[81] And similar evidence
may be found elsewhere.[82] In Manchester, this premature old age
among the operatives is so universal that almost every man of forty
would be taken for ten to fifteen years older, while the prosperous
classes, men as well as women, preserve their appearance exceedingly well if they do not drink too heavily.

The influence of factory-work upon the female physique also is
marked and peculiar. The deformities entailed by long hours of
work are much more serious among women. Protracted work
frequently causes deformities of the pelvis, partly in the shape of
abnormal position and development of the hip bones, partly of
malformation of the lower portion of the spinal column.

'Although', says Dr Loudon, in his report, 'no example of
malformation of the pelvis and of some other affections came
under my notice, these things are nevertheless so common, that
every physician must regard them as probable consequences of
such working hours, and as vouched for besides by men of the
highest medical credibility.'

That factory operatives undergo more difficult confinement than other women is testified to by several midwives and accoucheurs, and also that they are more liable to miscarriage.[83] Moreover, they suffer from the general enfeeblement common to all operatives, and, when pregnant, continue to work in the factory up to the hour of delivery, because otherwise they lose their wages and are made to fear that they may be replaced if they stop away too soon. It frequently happens that women are at work one evening and delivered the next morning, and the case is none too rare of their being delivered in the factory among the machinery. And if the gentlemen of the bourgeoisie find nothing particularly shocking in this, their wives will perhaps admit that it is a piece of cruelty, an infamous act of barbarism, indirectly to force a pregnant woman to work twelve or thirteen hours daily (formerly still longer), up to the day of her delivery, in a standing position, with frequent stoopings. But this is not all. If these women are not obliged to resume work within two weeks, they are thankful, and count themselves fortunate. Many come back to the factory after eight, and even after three to four days, to resume full work. I once heard a manufacturer ask an overlooker: 'Is so and so not back yet?' 'No.' 'How long since she was confined?' 'A week.' 'She might surely have been back long ago. That one over there only stays three days.' Naturally, fear of being discharged, dread of starvation drives her to the factory in spite of her weakness, in defiance of her pain. The interest of the manufacturer will not brook that his employees stay at home by reason of illness; they must not be ill, they must not venture to lie still through a long confinement, or he must stop his machinery or trouble his supreme head with a temporary change of arrangements, and rather than do this, he discharges his people when they begin to be ill. Listen:[84] 'A girl feels very ill, can scarcely do her work. Why does she not ask permission to go home? Ah! the master is very particular, and if we are away half a day, we risk being sent away altogether.'

Or Sir D. Barry:[85] 'Thomas McDurt, workman, has slight fever. Cannot stay at home longer than four days, because he would fear of losing his place.'

And so it goes on in almost all the factories. The employment of young girls produces all sorts of irregularities during the period of development. In some, especially those who are better fed, the heat of the factories hastens this process, so that in single cases, girls of thirteen and fourteen are wholly mature. Robertson, whom I have already cited (mentioned in the Factories' Inquiry Commission's Report as the 'eminent' gynaecologist of Manchester), relates in the North of England *Medical and Surgical Journal*, that he had seen a girl of eleven years who was not only a wholly developed woman, but pregnant, and that it was by no means rare in Manchester for women to be confined at fifteen years of age. In such cases, the influence of the warmth of the factories is the same as that of a tropical climate, and, as in such climates, the abnormally early development revenges itself by correspondingly premature age and debility. On the other hand, retarded development of the female constitution occurs, the breasts mature late or not at all. [86] Menstruation first appears in the seventeenth or eighteenth, sometimes in the twentieth year, and is often wholly wanting. [87] Irregular menstruation, coupled with great pain and numerous affections, especially with anaemia, is very frequent, as the medical reports unanimously state.

Children of such mothers, particularly of those who are obliged to work during pregnancy, cannot be vigorous. They are, on the contrary, described in the report, especially in Manchester, as very feeble; and Barry alone asserts that they are healthy, but says further, that in Scotland, where his inspection lay, almost no married women worked in factories. Moreover, most of the factories there are in the country (with the exception of Glasgow), a circumstance which contributes greatly to the invigoration of the children. The operatives' children in the neighbourhood of Manchester are nearly all thriving and rosy, while those within the city look pale and scrofulous; but with the ninth year the colour vanishes suddenly, because all are then sent into the factories, when it soon becomes impossible to distinguish the country from the city children.

But besides all this, there are some branches of factory-work which have an especially injurious effect. In many rooms of the cotton- and flax-spinning mills, the air is filled with fibrous dust, which produces chest affections, especially among workers in the carding- and combing-rooms. Some constitutions can bear it, some cannot; but the operative has no choice. He must take the room in which he finds work, whether his chest is sound or not. The most common effects of this breathing of dust are blood-spitting, hard, noisy breathing, pains in the chest, coughs, sleeplessness – in short, all the symptoms of asthma ending in the worst cases in consumption.[88] Especially unwholesome is the wet spinning of linen-yarn which is carried on by young girls and boys. The water spirts over them from the spindle, so that the front of their clothing is constantly wet through to the skin; and there is always water standing on the floor. This is the case to a less degree in the doubling-rooms of the cotton mills, and the result is a constant succession of colds and affections of the chest. A hoarse, rough voice is common to all operatives, but especially to wet spinners and doublers. Stuart, Mackintosh, and Sir D. Barry express themselves in the most vigorous terms as to the unwholesomeness of this work, and the small consideration shown by most of the manufacturers for the health of the girls who do it. Another effect of flax-spinning is a peculiar deformity of the shoulder, especially a projection of the right shoulder-blade, consequent upon the nature of the work. This sort of spinning and the throstle-spinning of cotton frequently produce diseases of the knee-pan, which is used to check the spindle during the joining of broken threads. The frequent stooping and the bending to the low machines common to both these branches of work have, in general, a stunting effect upon the growth of the operative. In the throstle-room of the cotton mill at Manchester, in which I was employed, I do not remember to have seen one single tall, well-built girl; they were all short, dumpy, and badly-formed, decidedly ugly in the whole development of the figure. But apart from all these diseases and malformations, the limbs of the operatives suffer in still another way. The work between the machinery gives rise to multitudes of accidents of more or less serious nature, which have for the operative the secondary effect of unfitting him for his work more or less completely. The most common accident is the squeezing off of a single joint of a finger, somewhat less common the loss of the whole finger, half or a whole hand, an arm, etc., in the machinery. Lockjaw very often follows, even upon the lesser among these injuries, and brings death with it. Besides the deformed persons, a great number of maimed ones may be seen going about in Manchester; this one has lost an arm or a part of one, that one a foot, the third half a leg; it is like living in the midst of an army just returned from a campaign. But the most dangerous portion of the machinery is the strapping which conveys motive power from the shaft to the separate machines, especially if it contains buckles, which, however, are rarely used now. Whoever is seized by the strap is carried up with lightning speed, thrown against the ceiling above and floor below with such force that there is rarely a whole bone left in the body, and death follows instantly. Between June 12th and August 3rd, 1843, the *Manchester Guardian* reported the following serious accidents (the trifling ones it does not notice): June 12th, a boy died in Manchester of lockjaw, caused by his hand being crushed between wheels. June 16th, a youth in Saddleworth seized by a wheel and carried away with it; died, utterly mangled. June 29th, a young man at Green Acres Moor, near Manchester, at work in a machine shop, fell under the grindstone, which broke two of his ribs and lacerated him terribly. July 24th, a girl in Oldham died, carried around fifty times by a strap; no bone unbroken. July 27th, a girl in Manchester seized by the blower (the first machine that receives the raw cotton), and died of injuries received. August 3rd, a bobbins turner died in Dukenfield, caught in a strap, every rib broken. In the year 1843, the Manchester Infirmary treated 962 cases of wounds and mutilations caused by machinery, while the number of all other accidents within the district of the hospital was 2,426, so that for five accidents from all other causes, two were caused by machinery. The accidents which happened in Salford are not included here, nor those treated by surgeons in private practice. In such cases, whether or not the accident unfits the victim for further work, the employer, at best, pays the doctor, or, in very exceptional cases, he may pay wages during treatment; what becomes of the operative afterwards, in case he cannot work, is no concern of the employer.

The Factory Report says on this subject, that employers must be made responsible for all cases, since children cannot take care, and adults will take care in their own interest. But the gentlemen who write the report are bourgeois, and so they must contradict themselves and bring up later all sorts of bosh on the subject of the culpable temerity of the operatives.

The state of the case is this: if children cannot take care, the employment of children must be forbidden. If adults are reckless,

they must be mere over-grown children on a plane of intelligence
which does not enable them to appreciate the danger in its full
scope; and who is to blame for this but the bourgeoisie which keeps
them in a condition in which their intelligence cannot develop?
Or the machinery is ill-arranged, and must be surrounded with
fencing, to supply which falls to the share of the bourgeoisie. Or
the operative is under inducements which outweigh the threatened
danger; he must work rapidly to earn his wages, has no time to take
care, and for this, too, the bourgeoisie is to blame. Many accidents
happen, for instance, while the operatives are cleaning machinery
in motion. Why? Because the bourgeois would otherwise oblige
the worker to clean the machinery during the free hours while it is
not going, and the worker naturally is not disposed to sacrifice any
part of his free time. Every free hour is so precious to the worker
that he often risks his life twice a week rather than sacrifice one
of them to the bourgeois. Let the employer take from working
hours the time required for cleaning the machinery, and it will
never again occur to an operative to clean machinery in motion.
In short, from whatever point of view, the blame falls ultimately
on the manufacturer, and of him should be required, at the very
least, life-long support of the incapacitated operative, and support
of the victim's family in case death follows the accident. In the
earliest period of manufacture, the accidents were much more
numerous in proportion than now, for the machinery was inferior,
smaller, more crowded, and almost never fenced. But the number
is still large enough, as the foregoing cases prove, to arouse grave
question as to a state of things which permits so many deformities
and mutilations for the benefit of a single class, and plunges so
many industrious working-people into want and starvation by
reason of injuries undergone in the service and through the fault of
the bourgeoisie.

A pretty list of diseases engendered purely by the hateful money
greed of the manufacturers! Women made unfit for childbearing,
children deformed, men enfeebled, limbs crushed, whole generations wrecked, afflicted with disease and infirmity, purely to fill
the purses of the bourgeoisie. And when one reads of the barbarism of single cases, how children are seized naked in bed by the
overlookers, and driven with blows and kicks to the factory, their
clothing over their arms, [89] how their sleepiness is driven off with

blows, how they fall asleep over their work nevertheless, how one poor child sprang up, still asleep, at the call of the overlooker, and mechanically went through the operations of its work after its machine was stopped; when one reads how children, too tired to go home, hide away in the wool in the drying-room to sleep there, and could only be driven out of the factory with straps; how many hundreds came home so tired every night, that they could eat no supper for sleepiness and want of appetite, that their parents found them kneeling by the bedside, where they had fallen asleep during their prayers; when one reads all this and a hundred other villainies and infamies in this one report, all testified to on oath, confirmed by several witnesses, deposed by men whom the commissioners themselves declare trustworthy; when one reflects that this is a Liberal report, a bourgeois report, made for the purpose of reversing the previous Tory report, and rehabilitating the pureness of heart of the manufacturers, that the commissioners themselves are on the side of the bourgeoisie, and report all these things against their own will, how can one be otherwise than filled with wrath and resentment against a class which boasts of philanthropy and self-sacrifice, while its one object is to fill its purse *à tout prix*? Meanwhile, let us listen to the bourgeoisie speaking through the mouth of its chosen apostle, Dr Ure, who relates in his *Philosophy of Manufactures* [90] that the workers have been told that their wages bore no proportion to their sacrifices, the good understanding between masters and men being thus disturbed. Instead of this, the working-men should have striven to recommend themselves by attention and industry, and should have rejoiced in the prosperity of their masters. They would then become overseers, superintendents, and finally partners, and would thus – (Oh! wisdom, thou speakest as the dove!) – 'have increased at the same time the demand for their companions' labour in the market!'

> Had it not been for the violent collisions and interruptions resulting from erroneous views among the operatives, the factory system would have been developed still more rapidly and beneficially. [91]

Hereupon follows a long Jeremiad upon the spirit of resistance of the operatives, and on the occasion of a strike of the best-paid workers, the fine spinners, the following naïve observation: [92]

In fact, it was their high wages which enabled them to maintain a stipendiary committee in affluence, and to pamper themselves into nervous ailments, by a diet too rich and exciting for their indoor employments.

Let us hear how the bourgeois describes the work of children: [93]

I have visited many factories, both in Manchester and in the surrounding districts, during a period of several months, entering the spinning-rooms unexpectedly, and often alone, at different times of the day, and I never saw a single instance of corporal chastisement inflicted on a child; nor, indeed, did I ever see children in ill-humour. They seemed to be always cheerful and alert; taking pleasure in the light play of their muscles, enjoying the mobility natural to their age. The scene of industry, so far from exciting sad emotions, in my mind, was always exhilarating. It was delightful to observe the nimbleness with which they pieced broken ends, as the mule carriage began to recede from the fixed roller beam, and to see them at leisure, after a few seconds' exercise of their tiny fingers, to amuse themselves in any attitude they chose, till the stretch and winding on were once more completed. The work of these lively elves seemed to resemble a sport, in which habit gave them a pleasing dexterity. Conscious of their skill, they were delighted to show it off to any stranger. As to exhaustion by the day's work, they evinced no trace of it on emerging from the mill in the evening; for they immediately began to skip about any neighbouring playground, and to commence their little games with the same alacrity as boys issuing from a school.

Naturally! As though the immediate movement of every muscle were not an urgent necessity for frames grown at once stiff and relaxed! But Ure should have waited to see whether this momentary excitement had not subsided after a couple of minutes. And besides, Ure could see this whole performance only in the afternoon after five or six hours' work, but not in the evening! As to the health of the operatives, the bourgeois has the boundless impudence to cite the report of 1833 just quoted in a thousand places, as testimony for the excellent health of these people; to try to prove by detached and garbled quotations that no trace of scrofula can be found among them, and, what is quite true, that the factory system frees them from all acute diseases (that they have every variety of chronic affection instead he naturally conceals). To explain the impudence with which our friend Ure palms off the grossest falsehoods upon the English public, it must be known that the report consists of three large folio volumes, which it never occurs to a well-fed English bourgeois to study through. Let us hear further how he expresses himself as to the Factory Act of 1834, passed by the Liberal bourgeoisie, and imposing only the most meagre limitations upon the manufacturers, as we shall see. This law, especially its compulsory education clause, he calls an absurd and despotic measure directed against the manufacturers, through which all children under twelve years of age have been thrown out of employment; and with what results? The children thus discharged from their light and useful occupation receive no education whatsoever; cast out from the warm spinning-room into a cold world, they subsist only by begging and stealing, a life in sad contrast with their steadily improving condition in the factory and in Sunday school. Under the mask of philanthropy, this law intensifies the sufferings of the poor, and will greatly restrict the conscientious manufacturer in his useful work, if, indeed, it does not wholly stop him.[94]

The ruinous influence of the factory system began at an early day to attract general attention. We have already alluded to the Apprentices' Act of 1802. Later, towards 1817, Robert Owen, then a manufacturer in New Lanark, in Scotland, afterwards founder of English Socialism, began to call the attention of the Government, by memorials and petitions, to the necessity of legislative guarantees for the health of the operatives, and especially of children. The late Sir Robert Peel and other philanthropists united with him, and gradually secured the Factory Acts of 1818, 1825, and 1831, of which the first two were never enforced, and the last only here and there. This law of 1831, based upon the motion of Sir J. C. Hobhouse, provided that in cotton mills no one under twenty-one should be employed between half-past seven at night and half-past five in the morning; and that in all factories young persons under eighteen should work no longer than twelve hours daily, and nine hours on Saturday. But since operatives could not testify against their masters without being discharged, this law helped matters very little. In the great cities, where the operatives were more restive, the larger manufacturers came to an agreement among themselves to obey the law; but even there, there were many who, like the employers in the country, did not trouble themselves about it. Meanwhile, the demand for a ten hours' law had become lively among the operatives; that is, for a law which should forbid all operatives under eighteen years of age to work longer than ten hours daily; the Trades Unions, by their agitation, made this demand general throughout the manufacturing population; the philanthropic section of the Tory party, then led by Michael Sadler, seized upon the plan, and brought it before Parliament. Sadler obtained a parliamentary committee for the investigation of the factory system, and this committee reported in 1832. Its report was emphatically partisan, composed by strong enemies of the factory system, for party ends. Sadler permitted himself to be betrayed by his noble enthusiasm into the most distorted and erroneous statements, drew from his witnesses by the very form of his questions, answers which contained the truth, but truth in a perverted form. The manufacturers themselves, incensed at a report which represented them as monsters, now demanded an official investigation; they knew that an exact report must, in this case, be advantageous to them; they knew that Whigs, genuine bourgeois, were at the helm, with whom they were upon good terms, whose principles were opposed to any restriction upon manufacture. They obtained a commission, in due order, composed of Liberal bourgeois, whose report I have so often cited. This comes somewhat nearer the truth than Sadler's, but its deviations therefrom are in the opposite direction. On every page it betrays sympathy with the manufacturers, distrust of the Sadler report, repugnance to the working-men agitating independently and the supporters of the Ten Hours' Bill. It nowhere recognises the right of the working-man to a life worthy of a human being, to independent activity, and opinions of his own. It reproaches the operatives that in sustaining the Ten Hours' Bill they thought, not of the children only, but of themselves as well; it calls the working-men engaged in the agitation demagogues, ill-intentioned, malicious, etc.; is written, in short, on the side of the bourgeoisie; and still it cannot whitewash the manufacturers, and still it leaves such a mass of infamies upon the shoulders of the employers, that even after this report, the agitation for the Ten Hours' Bill, the hatred against the manufacturers, and the committee's severest epithets applied to them, are all fully justified. But there was the one difference, that whereas the Sadler report accuses the manufacturers of open, undisguised brutality, it now became evident that this brutality was chiefly carried on under the mask of civilisation and humanity. Yet Dr Hawkins, the medical commissioner for Lancashire, expresses himself decidedly in favour of the Ten Hours' Bill in the opening lines of his report, and Commissioner Mackintosh explains that his own report does not contain the whole truth, because it is very difficult to induce the operatives to testify against their employers, and because the manufacturers, besides being forced into greater concessions towards their operatives by the excitement among the latter, are often prepared for the inspection of the factories, have them swept, the speed of the machinery reduced, etc. In Lancashire especially they resorted to the device of bringing the overlookers of workrooms before the commissioners, and letting them testify as working-men to the humanity of the employers, the wholesome effects of the work, and the indifference, if not the hostility of the operatives, towards the Ten Hours' Bill. But these are not genuine working-men; they are deserters from their class, who have entered the service of the bourgeoisie for better pay, and fight in the interests of the capitalists against the workers. Their interest is that of the capitalists, and they are, therefore, almost more hated by the workers than the manufacturers themselves.

And yet this report suffices wholly to exhibit the most shameful recklessness of the manufacturing bourgeoisie towards its employees, the whole infamy of the industrial exploiting system in its full inhumanity. Nothing is more revolting than to compare the long register of diseases and deformities engendered by overwork, in this report, with the cold, calculating political economy of the manufacturers, by which they try to prove that they, and with them all England, must go to ruin, if they should be forbidden to cripple so and so many children every year. The language of Dr Ure alone, which I have quoted, would be yet more revolting if it were not so preposterous.

The result of this report was the Factory Act of 1834, which forbade the employment of children under nine years of age (except in silk mills), limited the working hours of children between 9–13 years to 48 per week, or 9 hours in any one day at the utmost; that of young persons from 14–18 years of age to 69 per week, or 12 on any one day as the maximum, provided for an hour and a half as the minimum interval for meals, and repeated the total prohibition of night-work for persons under eighteen years of age. Compulsory school attendance two hours daily was prescribed for all children under fourteen years, and the manufacturer declared punishable in case of employing children without a certificate of age from the factory surgeon, and a certificate of school attendance from the teacher. As recompense, the employer was permitted to with-draw one penny from the child's weekly earnings to pay the teacher. Further, surgeons and inspectors were appointed to visit the factories at all times, take testimony of operatives on oath, and enforce the law by prosecution before a Justice of the Peace. This is the law against which Dr Ure inveighs in such unmeasured terms!

The consequence of this law, and especially of the appointment of inspectors, was the reduction of working hours to an average of twelve to thirteen, and the superseding of children as far as possible. Hereupon some of the most crying evils disappeared almost wholly. Deformities arose now only in cases of weak constitution, and the effects of overwork became much less con-spicuous. Nevertheless, enough testimony remains to be found in the Factory Report, that the lesser evils, swelling of the ankles, weakness and pain in the legs, hips, and back, varicose veins, ulcers on the lower extremities, general weakness, especially of the pelvic region, nausea, want of appetite alternating with unnatural hunger, indigestion, hypochondria, affections of the chest in consequence of the dust and foul atmosphere of the factories, etc. etc., all occur among employees subject to the provisions of Sir J. C. Hobhouse's law (of 1831), which prescribes twelve to thirteen hours as the maximum. The reports from Glasgow and Manchester are espec-ially worthy of attention in this respect. These evils remained too, after the law of 1834, and continue to undermine the health of the working class to this day. Care has been taken to give the brutal profit-greed of the bourgeoisie a hypocritical, civilised form, to restrain the manufacturers through the arm of the law from too conspicuous villainies, and thus to give them a pretext for self-complacently parading their sham philanthropy. That is all. If a new commission were appointed today, it would find things pretty

much as before. As to the extemporised compulsory attendance at
school, it remained wholly a dead letter, since the Government
failed to provide good schools. The manufacturers employed as
teachers worn-out operatives, to whom they sent the children
two hours daily, thus complying with the letter of the law; but
the children learned nothing. And even the reports of the factory
inspectors, which are limited to the scope of the inspector's
duties, i.e. the enforcement of the Factory Act, give data enough
to justify the conclusion that the old evils inevitably remain.
Inspectors Horner and Saunders, in their reports for October and
December, 1844, state that, in a number of branches in which the
employment of children can be dispensed with or superseded by
that of adults, the working day is still fourteen to sixteen hours,
or even longer. Among the operatives in these branches they
found numbers of young people who had just outgrown the
provisions of the law. Many employers disregard the law, shorten
the meal times, work children longer than is permitted, and risk
prosecution, knowing that the possible fines are trifling in comparison with the certain profits derivable from the offence. Just at
present especially, while business is exceptionally brisk, they are
under great temptation in this respect.

Meanwhile the agitation for the Ten Hours' Bill by no means
died out among the operatives; in 1839 it was under full headway
once more, and Sadler's place, he having died, was filled in the
House of Commons by Lord Ashley[95] and Richard Oastler, both
Tories. Oastler especially, who carried on a constant agitation in
the factory districts, and had been active in the same way during
Sadler's life, was the particular favourite of the working-men.
They called him their 'good old king', 'the king of the factory
children', and there is not a child in the factory districts that does
not know and revere him, that does not join the procession which
moves to welcome him when he enters a town. Oastler vigorously
opposed the New Poor Law also, and was therefore imprisoned
for debt by a Mr Thornley, on whose estate he was employed as
agent, and to whom he owed money. The Whigs offered repeatedly to pay his debt and confer other favours upon him if he would
only give up his agitation against the Poor Law. But in vain; he
remained in prison, whence he published his Fleet Papers against
the factory system and the Poor Law.

The Tory Government of 1841 turned its attention once more to the Factory Acts. The Home Secretary, Sir James Graham, proposed, in 1843, a bill restricting the working hours of children to six and one-half, and making the enactments for compulsory school attendance more effective; the principal point in this connection being a provision for better schools. This bill was, however, wrecked by the jealousy of the dissenters; for, although compulsory religious instruction was not extended to the children of dissenters, the schools provided for were to be placed under the general supervision of the Established Church, and the Bible made the general reading-book; religion being thus made the foundation of all instruction, whence the dissenters felt themselves threatened. The manufacturers and the Liberals generally united with them, the working-men were divided by the Church question, and therefore inactive. The opponents of the bill, though outweighed in the great manufacturing towns, such as Salford and Stockport, and able in others, such as Manchester, to attack certain of its points only, for fear of the working-men, collected nevertheless nearly two million signatures for a petition against it, and Graham allowed himself to be so far intimidated as to withdraw the whole bill. The next year he omitted the school clauses, and proposed that, instead of the previous provisions, children between eight and thirteen years should be restricted to six and one-half hours, and so employed as to have either the whole morning or the whole afternoon free; that young people between thirteen and eighteen years, and all females, should be limited to twelve hours; and that the hitherto frequent evasions of the law should be prevented. Hardly had he proposed this bill, when the ten hours' agitation was begun again more vigorously than ever. Oastler had just then regained his liberty; a number of his friends and a collection among the workers had paid his debt, and he threw himself into the movement with all his might. The defenders of the Ten Hours' Bill in the House of Commons had increased in numbers, the masses of petitions supporting it which poured in from all sides brought them allies, and on March 19th, 1844, Lord Ashley carried, with a majority of 179 to 170, a resolution that the word 'Night' in the Factory Act should express the time from six at night to six in the morning, whereby the prohibition of night-work came to mean the limitation of working hours to twelve, including free hours, or ten hours of actual work a day. But the ministry did not agree to this. Sir James Graham began to threaten resignation from the Cabinet, and at the next vote on the bill the House rejected by a small majority both ten and twelve hours! Graham and Peel now announced that they should introduce a new bill, and that if this failed to pass they should resign. The new bill was exactly the old Twelve Hours' Bill with some changes of form, and the same House of Commons which had rejected the principal points of this bill in March, now swallowed it whole. The reason of this was that most of the supporters of the Ten Hours' Bill were Tories who let fall the bill rather than the ministry; but be the motives what they may, the House of Commons by its votes upon this subject, each vote reversing the last, has brought itself into the greatest contempt among all the workers, and proved most brilliantly the Chartists' assertion of the necessity of its reform. Three members, who had formerly voted against the ministry, afterwards voted for it and rescued it. In all the divisions, the bulk of the opposition voted *for* and the bulk of its own party *against* the ministry.[96] The foregoing propositions of Graham touching the employment of children six and one-half and of all other operatives twelve hours are now legislative provisions, and by them and by the limitation of overwork for making up time lost through breakdown of machinery or insufficient water-power by reason of frost or drought, a working day of more than twelve hours has been made well-nigh impossible. There remains, however, no doubt that, in a very short time, the Ten Hours' Bill will really be adopted. The manufacturers are naturally all against it, there are perhaps not ten who are for it; they have used every honourable and dishonourable means against this dreaded measure, but with no other result than that of drawing down upon them the ever deepening hatred of the working-men. The bill will pass. What the working-men will do they can do, and that they will have this bill they proved last spring. The economic arguments of the manufacturers that a Ten Hours' Bill would increase the cost of production and incapacitate the English producers for competition in foreign markets, and that wages must fall, are all *half* true; but they prove nothing except this, that the industrial greatness of England can be maintained only through the barbarous treatment of the operatives, the destruction of their health, the social, physical, and mental decay of whole generations. Naturally, if the Ten Hours' Bill were a final measure, it must ruin England; but since it must inevitably bring with it other measures which must draw England into a path wholly different from that hitherto followed, it can only prove an advance.

Let us turn to another side of the factory system which cannot be remedied by legislative provisions so easily as the diseases now engendered by it. We have already alluded in a general way to the nature of the employment, and enough in detail to be able to draw certain inferences from the facts given. The supervision of machinery, the joining of broken threads, is no activity which claims the operative's thinking powers, yet it is of a sort which prevents him from occupying his mind with other things. We have seen, too, that this work affords the muscles no opportunity for physical activity. Thus it is, properly speaking, not work, but tedium, the most deadening, wearing process conceivable. The operative is condemned to let his physical and mental powers decay in this utter monotony, it is his mission to be bored every day and all day long from his eighth year. Moreover, he must not take a moment's rest; the engine moves unceasingly; the wheels, the straps, the spindles hum and rattle in his ears without a pause, and if he tries to snatch one instant, there is the overlooker at his back with the book of fines. This condemnation to be buried alive in the mill, to give constant attention to the tireless machine, is felt as the keenest torture by the operatives, and its action upon mind and body is in the long run stunting in the highest degree. There is no better means of inducing stupefaction than a period of factory work, and if the operatives have, nevertheless, not only rescued their intelligence, but cultivated and sharpened it more than other working-men, they have found this possible only in rebellion against their fate and against the bourgeoisie, the sole subject on which under all circumstances they can think and feel while at work. Or, if this indignation against the bourgeoisie does not become the supreme passion of the working-man, the inevitable consequence is drunkenness and all that is generally called demoralisation. The physical enervation and the sickness, universal in consequence of the factory system, were enough to induce Commissioner Hawkins to attribute this demoralisation thereto as inevitable; how much more when mental lassitude is added to them, and when the influences already mentioned which tempt every working-man to demoral-isation, make themselves felt here too! There is no cause for surprise, therefore, that in the manufacturing towns especially, drunkenness and sexual excesses have reached the pitch which I have already described.[97]

Further, the slavery in which the bourgeoisie holds the prolet-ariat chained, is nowhere more conspicuous than in the factory system. Here ends all freedom in law and in fact. The operative must be in the mill at half-past five in the morning; if he comes a couple of minutes too late, he is fined; if he comes ten minutes too late, he is not let in until breakfast is over, and a quarter of the day's wages is withheld, though he loses only two and one-half hours' work out of twelve. He must eat, drink, and sleep at command. For satisfying the most imperative needs, he is vouchsafed the least possible time absolutely required by them. Whether his dwelling is a half-hour or a whole one removed from the factory does not concern his employer. The despotic bell calls him from his bed, his breakfast, his dinner.

What a time he has of it, too, inside the factory! Here the employer is absolute law-giver; he makes regulations at will, changes and adds to his codex at pleasure, and even, if he inserts the craziest stuff, the courts say to the working-man: 'You were your own master, no one forced you to agree to such a contract if you did not wish to; but now, when you have freely entered into it, you must be bound by it.' And so the working-man only gets into the bargain the mockery of the Justice of the Peace who is a bourgeois himself, and of the law which is made by the bourgeoisie. Such decisions have been given often enough. In October, 1844, the operatives of Kennedy's mill, in Manchester struck. Kennedy prosecuted them on the strength of a regulation placarded in the mill, that at no time more than two operatives in one room may quit work at once. And the court decided in his favour, giving the working-men the explanation cited above.[98] And such rules as these usually are! For instance:

1. The doors are closed ten minutes after work begins, and thereafter no one is admitted until the breakfast hour; whoever is absent during this time forfeits 3d. per loom.
2. Every power-loom weaver detected absenting himself at

another time, while the machinery is in motion, forfeits for
each hour and each loom, 3d. Every person who leaves the
room during working hours, without obtaining permission
from the overlooker, forfeits 3d.

3. Weavers who fail to supply themselves with scissors forfeit,
per day, 1d.
4. All broken shuttles, brushes, oil-cans, wheels, window panes,
etc., must be paid for by the weaver.
5. No weaver to stop work without giving a week's notice. The
manufacturer may dismiss any employee without notice for
bad work or improper behaviour.
6. Every operative detected speaking to another, singing or
whistling, will be fined 6d.; for leaving his place during
working hours, 6d.[99]

Another copy of factory regulations lies before me, according to
which every operative who comes three minutes too late, forfeits
the wages for a quarter of an hour, and everyone who comes
twenty minutes too late, for a quarter of a day. Everyone who
remains absent until breakfast forfeits a shilling on Monday, and
sixpence every other day of the week, etc, etc. This last is the
regulation of the Phoenix Works in Jersey Street, Manchester. It
may be said that such rules are necessary in a great, complicated
factory, in order to insure the harmonious working of the different
parts; it may be asserted that such a severe discipline is as necessary
here as in an army. This may be so, but what sort of a social order
is it which cannot be maintained without such shameful tyranny?
Either the end sanctifies the means, or the inference of the badness
of the end from the badness of the means is justified. Everyone
who has served as a soldier knows what it is to be subjected even
for a short time to military discipline. But these operatives are
condemned from their ninth year to their death to live under the
sword, physically and mentally. They are worse slaves than the
negroes in America, for they are more sharply watched, and yet it
is demanded of them that they shall live like human beings, shall
think and feel like men! Verily, this they can do only under
glowing hatred towards their oppressors, and towards that order of
things which place them in such a position, which degrades them
to machines. But it is far more shameful yet, that according to the

universal testimony of the operatives, numbers of manufacturers collect the fines imposed upon the operatives with the most heartless severity, and for the purpose of piling up extra profits out of the farthings thus extorted from the impoverished proletarians. Leach asserts, too, that the operatives often find the factory clock moved forward a quarter of an hour and the doors shut, while the clerk moves about with the fines-book inside, noting the many names of the absentees. Leach claims to have counted ninety-five operatives thus shut out, standing before a factory, whose clock was a quarter of an hour slower than the town clocks at night, and a quarter of an hour faster in the morning. The Factory Report relates similar facts. In one factory the clock was set back during working hours, so that the operatives worked overtime without extra pay; in another, a whole quarter of an hour overtime was worked; in a third, there were two clocks, an ordinary one and a machine clock, which registered the revolutions of the main shaft; if the machinery went slowly, working hours were measured by the machine clock until the number of revolutions due in twelve hours was reached; if work went well, so that the number was reached before the usual working hours were ended, the operatives were forced to toil on to the end of the twelfth hour. The witness adds that he had known girls who had good work, and who had worked overtime, who, nevertheless, betook themselves to a life of prostitution rather than submit to this tyranny.[100] To return to the fines, Leach relates having repeatedly seen women in the last period of pregnancy fined 6d. for the offence of sitting down a moment to rest. Fines for bad work are wholly arbitrary; the goods are examined in the ware-room, and the supervisor charges the fines upon a list without even summoning the operative, who only learns that he has been fined when the overlooker pays his wages, and the goods have perhaps been sold, or certainly been placed beyond his reach. Leach has in his possession such a fines list, ten feet long, and amounting to £35 17s. 10d. He relates that in the factory where this list was made, a new supervisor was dismissed for fining too little, and so bringing in £5 too little weekly.[101] And I repeat that I know Leach to be a thoroughly trustworthy man incapable of a falsehood.

But the operative is his employer's slave in still other respects. If his wife or daughter finds favour in the eyes of the master, a command, a hint suffices, and she must place herself at his disposal. When the employer wishes to supply with signatures a petition in favour of bourgeois interests, he need only send it to his mill. If he wishes to decide a Parliamentary election, he sends his enfranchised operatives in rank and file to the polls, and they vote for the bourgeois candidate whether they will or no. If he desires a majority in a public meeting, he dismisses them half-an-hour earlier than usual, and secures them places close to the platform, where he can watch them to his satisfaction.

Two further arrangements contribute especially to force the operative under the dominion of the manufacturer; the Truck system and the Cottage system. The truck system, the payment of the operatives in goods, was formerly universal in England. The manufacturer opens a shop, 'for the convenience of the operatives, and to protect them from the high prices of the petty dealers'. Here goods of all sorts are sold to them on credit; and to keep the operatives from going to the shops where they could get their goods more cheaply – the 'Tommy shops' usually charging twenty-five to thirty per cent. more than others – wages are paid in requisitions on the shop instead of money. The general indignation against this infamous system led to the passage of the Truck Act in 1831, by which, for most employees, payment in truck orders was declared void and illegal, and was made punishable by fine; but, like most other English laws, this has been enforced only here and there. In the towns it is carried out comparatively efficiently; but in the country, the truck system, disguised or undisguised, flourishes. In the town of Leicester, too, it is very common. There lie before me nearly a dozen convictions for this offence, dating from the period between November, 1843, and June, 1844, and reported, in part, in the *Manchester Guardian* and, in part, in the *Northern Star*. The system is, of course, less openly carried on at present; wages are usually paid in cash, but the employer still has means enough at command to force him to purchase his wares in the truck shop and nowhere else. Hence it is difficult to combat the truck system, because it can now be carried on under cover of the law, provided only that the operative receives his wages in money. The *Northern Star* of April 27th, 1843, publishes a letter from an operative of Holmfirth, near Huddersfield, in Yorkshire, which refers to a manufacturer of the name of Bowers, as follows [retranslated from the German]:

It is very strange to think that the accursed truck system should exist to such an extent as it does in Holmfirth, and nobody be found who has the pluck to make the manufacturer stop it. There are here a great many honest hand-weavers suffering through this damned system; here is one sample from a good many out of the noble-hearted Free Trade Clique. There is a manufacturer who has upon himself the curses of the whole district on account of his infamous conduct towards his poor weavers; if they have got a piece ready which comes to 34 or 36 shillings, he gives them 20s. in money and the rest in cloth or goods, and 40 to 50 per cent. dearer than at the other shops, and often enough the goods are rotten into the bargain. But, what says the *Free Trade Mercury*, the *Leeds Mercury*? They are not bound to take them; they can please themselves. Oh, yes, but they must take them or else starve. If they ask for another 20s. in money, they must wait eight or fourteen days for a warp; but if they take the 20s. and the goods, then there is always a warp ready for them. And that is Free Trade. Lord Brougham said we ought to put by something in our young days, so that we need not go to the parish when we are old. Well, are we to put by the rotten goods? If this did not come from a lord, one would say his brains were as rotten as the goods that our work is paid in. When the unstamped papers came out 'illegally', there was a lot of them to report it to the police in Holmfirth, the Blythes, the Edwards, etc.; but where are they now? But this is different. Our truck manufacturer belongs to the pious Free Trade lot; he goes to church twice every Sunday, and repeats devoutly after the parson: 'We have left undone the things we ought to have done, and we have done the things we ought not to have done, and there is no good in us; but, good Lord, deliver us.' Yes, deliver us till tomorrow, and we will pay our weavers again in rotten goods.

The Cottage system looks much more innocent and arose in a much more harmless way, though it has the same enslaving influence upon the employee. In the neighbourhood of the mills in the country, there is often a lack of dwelling accommodation for the operatives. The manufacturer is frequently obliged to build such dwellings and does so gladly, as they yield great advantages, besides the interest upon the capital invested. If any owner of working-men's dwellings averages about six per cent. on his invested capital, it is safe to calculate that the manufacturer's cottages yield twice this rate; for so long as his factory does not stand perfectly idle he is sure of occupants, and of occupants who pay punctually. He is therefore spared the two chief disadvantages under which other house-owners labour; his cottages never stand empty, and he runs no risk. But the rent of the cottages is as high as though these disadvantages were in full force, and by obtaining the same rent as the ordinary house-owner, the manufacturer, at cost of the oper-atives, makes a brilliant investment at twelve to fourteen per cent. For it is clearly unjust that he should make twice as much profit as other competing house-owners, who at the same time are ex-cluded from competing with him. But it implies a double wrong, when he draws his fixed profit from the pockets of the non-possessing class, which must consider the expenditure of every penny. He is used to that, however, he whose whole wealth is gained at the cost of his employees. But this injustice becomes an infamy when the manufacturer, as often happens, forces his oper-atives, who must occupy his houses on pain of dismissal, to pay a higher rent than the ordinary one, or even to pay rent for houses in which they do not live! The *Halifax Guardian,* quoted by the Liberal *Sun,* asserts that hundreds of operatives in Ashton-under-Lyne, Oldham, and Rochdale, etc., are forced by their employers to pay house-rent whether they occupy the house or not.[102] The cottage system is universal in the country districts; it has created whole villages, and the manufacturer usually has little or no competition against his houses, so that he can fix his price regard-less of any market rate, indeed at his pleasure. And what power does the cottage system give the employer over his operatives in disagreements between master and men? If the latter strike, he need only give them notice to quit his premises, and the notice need only be a week; after that time the operative is not only without bread but without a shelter, a vagabond at the mercy of the law which sends him, without fail, to the treadmill.

Such is the factory system sketched as fully as my space permits, and with as little partisan spirit as the heroic deeds of the bour-geoisie against the defenceless workers permit – deeds towards

which it is impossible to remain indifferent, towards which indifference were a crime. Let us compare the condition of the free
Englishman of 1845 with the Saxon serf under the lash of the
Norman barons of 1145. The serf was *glebae adscriptus*, bound to
the soil, so is the free working-man through the cottage system.
The serf owed his master the *jus primae noctis*, the right of the first
night – the free working-man must, on demand, surrender to his
master not only that, but the right of every night. The serf could
acquire no property; everything that he gained, his master could
take from him; the free working-man has no property, can gain
none by reason of the pressure of competition, and what even
the Norman baron did not do, the modern manufacturer does.
Through the truck system, he assumes every day the administration in detail of the things which the worker requires for
his immediate necessities. The relation of the lord of the soil to
the serf was regulated by the prevailing customs and bye-laws
which were obeyed, because they corresponded to them. The free
working-man's relation to his master is regulated by laws which
are *not* obeyed, because they correspond neither with the interests
of the employer nor with the prevailing customs. The lord of the
soil could not separate the serf from the land, nor sell him apart
from it, and since almost all the land was fief and there was no
capital, practically could not sell him at all. The modern bourgeois
forces the working-man to sell himself. The serf was the slave of
the piece of land on which he was born, the working-man is the
slave of his own necessaries of life and of the money with which
he has to buy them – both are *slaves of a thing*. The serf had a
guarantee for the means of subsistence in the feudal order of
society in which every member had his own place. The free
working-man has no guarantee whatsoever, because he has a
place in society only when the bourgeoisie can make use of him;
in all other cases he is ignored, treated as non-existent. The serf
sacrificed himself for his master in war, the factory operative in
peace. The lord of the serf was a barbarian who regarded his
villein as a head of cattle; the employer of operatives is civilised
and regards his 'hand' as a machine. In short, the position of the
two is not far from equal, and if either is at a disadvantage, it is the
free working-man. Slaves they both are, with the single difference
that the slavery of the one is undissembled, open, honest; that

of the other cunning, sly, disguised, deceitfully concealed from himself and everyone else, a hypocritical servitude worse than the old. The philanthropic Tories were right when they gave the operatives the name white slaves. But the hypocritical disguised slavery recognises the right to freedom, at least in outward form; bows before a freedom-loving public opinion, and herein lies the historic progress as compared with the old servitude, that the *principle* of freedom is affirmed, and the oppressed will one day see to it that this principle is carried out.[103]

The Remaining Branches of Industry

We were compelled to deal with the factory system somewhat at length, as it is an entirely novel creation of the industrial period; we shall be able to treat the other workers the more briefly, because what has been said either of the industrial proletariat in general, or of the factory system in particular, will wholly, or in part, apply to them. We shall, therefore, merely have to record how far the factory system has succeeded in forcing its way into each branch of industry, and what other peculiarities these may reveal.

The four branches comprised under the Factory Act are engaged in the production of clothing stuffs. We shall do best if we deal next with those workers who receive their materials from these factories; and, first of all, with the stocking-weavers of Nottingham, Derby, and Leicester. Touching these workers, the Children's Employment Commission reports that the long working hours, imposed by low wages, with a sedentary life and the strain upon the eyes involved in the nature of the employment, usually enfeeble the whole frame, and especially the eyes. Work at night is impossible without a very powerful light produced by concentrating the rays of the lamp, making them pass through glass globes, which is most injurious to the sight. At forty years of age, nearly all wear spectacles. The children employed at spooling and hemming usually suffer grave injuries to the health and constitution. They work from the sixth, seventh, or eighth year ten to twelve hours daily in small, close rooms. It is not uncommon for them to faint at their work, to become too feeble for the most ordinary household occupation, and so near-sighted as to be obliged to wear glasses during childhood. Many were found by the commissioners to exhibit all the symptoms of a scrofulous constitution, and the manufacturers usually refuse to employ girls who have worked in this way as being too weak. The condition of these children is characterised as 'a disgrace to a Christian country', and the wish expressed for legislative inter-ference. The Factory Report[104] adds that the stocking-weavers are the worst-paid workers in Leicester, earning six, or with great effort, seven shillings a week, for sixteen to eighteen hours' daily work. Formerly they earned twenty to twenty-one shillings, but the introduction of enlarged frames has ruined their business; the great majority still work with old, small, single frames, and compete with difficulty with the progress of machinery. Here, too, every progress is a disadvantage for the workers. Nevertheless, Commissioner Power speaks of the pride of the stocking-weavers that they are free, and had no factory bell to measure out the time for their eating, sleeping, and working. Their position today is no better than in 1833, when the Factory Commission made the foregoing statements; the competition of the Saxon stocking-weavers, who have scarcely anything to eat, takes care of that. This competition is too strong for the English in nearly all foreign markets, and for the lower qualities of goods even in the English market. It must be a source of rejoicing for the patriotic German stocking-weaver that his starvation wages force his English brother to starve too! And, verily, will he not starve on, proud and happy, for the greater glory of German industry, since the honour of the Fatherland demands that his table should be bare, his dish half empty? Ah! it is a noble thing this competition, this 'race of the nations'. In the *Morning Chronicle*, another Liberal sheet, the organ of the bourgeoisie par excellence, there were published some letters from a stocking-weaver in Hinckley, describing the condition of his fellow-workers. Among other things, he reports 50 families, 321 persons, who were supported by 109 frames; each frame yielded on an average 5½ shillings; each family earned an average of 11s. 4d. weekly. Out of this there was required for house rent, frame rent, fuel, light, soap, and needles, together 5s. 10d., so that there remained for food, per head daily, 1½d., and for clothing nothing. 'No eye', says the stocking-weaver, 'has seen, no ear heard, and no heart felt the half of the sufferings that these poor people endure.' Beds were wanting either wholly or in part, the children ran about ragged and barefoot; the men said, with tears in their eyes: 'It's a long time since we had any meat; we have almost forgotten how it tastes;' and, finally, some of them worked on Sunday, though public opinion pardons anything else more readily than this, and the rattling noise of the frame is audible throughout the neighbourhood. 'But', said one of them, 'look at my children and ask no questions. My poverty forces me to it; I can't and won't hear my children forever crying for bread, without trying the last means of winning it honestly. Last Monday I got up at two in the morning and worked to near midnight; the other days from six in the morning to between eleven and twelve at night. I have had enough of it; I shan't kill myself; so now I go to bed at ten o'clock, and make up the lost time on Sundays.' Neither in Leicester, Nottingham, nor Derby have wages risen since 1833; and the worst of it is that in Leicester the truck system prevails to a great extent, as I have mentioned. It is therefore not to be wondered at that the weavers of this region take a very active part in all working-men's movements, the more active and effective because the frames are worked chiefly by men.

In this stocking-weavers' district the lace industry also has its headquarters. In the three counties mentioned there are in all 2,760 lace frames in use, while in all the rest of England there are but 786. The manufacture of lace is greatly complicated by a rigid division of labour, and embraces a multitude of branches. The yarn is first spooled by girls fourteen years of age and upwards, winders; then the spools are set up on the frames by boys, eight years old and upwards, threaders, who pass the thread through fine openings, of which each machine has an average of 1,800, and bring it towards its destination; then the weaver weaves the lace which comes out of the machine like a broad piece of cloth and is taken apart by very little children who draw out the connecting threads. This is called running or drawing lace, and the children themselves lace-runners. The lace is then made ready for sale. The winders, like the threaders, have no specified working-time, being called upon whenever the spools on a frame are empty, and are liable, since the weavers work at night, to be required at any time in the factory or workroom. This irregularity, the frequent night-work, the disorderly way of living consequent upon it, engender a multitude of physical and moral ills, especially early and unbridled sexual licence, upon which point all witnesses are unanimous. The work is very bad for the eyes, and although a permanent injury in the case of the threaders is not universally observable, inflammations of the eye, pain, tears, and momentary uncertainty of vision during the act of threading are engendered. For the winders, however, it is certain that their work seriously affects the eye, and produces, besides the frequent inflammations of the cornea, many cases of amaurosis and cataract. The work of the weavers themselves is very difficult, as the frames have constantly been made wider, until those now in use are almost all worked by three men in turn, each working eight hours, and the frame being kept in use the whole twenty-four. Hence it is that the winders and threaders are so often called upon during the night, and must work to prevent the frame from standing idle. The filling in of 1,800 openings with thread occupies three children at least two hours. Many frames are moved by steam-power, and the work of men thus superseded; and, as the Children's Employment Commission's Report mentions only lace factories to which the children are summoned, it seems to follow either that the work of the weavers has been removed to great factory rooms of late, or that steam-weaving has become pretty general; a forward movement of the factory system in either case. Most unwholesome of all is the work of the runners, who are usually children of seven, and even of five and four, years old. Commissioner Grainger actually found one child of two years old employed at this work. Following a thread which is to be withdrawn by a needle from an intricate texture, is very bad for the eyes, especially when, as is usually the case, the work is continued fourteen to sixteen hours. In the least unfavourable case, aggravated near-sightedness follows; in the worst case, which is frequent enough, incurable blindness from amaurosis. But, apart from that, the children, in consequence of sitting perpetually bent up, become feeble, narrow-chested, and scrofulous from bad digestion. Disordered functions of the uterus are almost universal among the girls, and curvature of the spine also, so that 'all the runners may be recognised from their gait.' The same consequences for the eyes and the whole constitution are produced by the embroidery of lace. Medical witnesses are unanimously of the opinion that the health of all children employed in the production of lace suffers seriously, that they are pale, weak, delicate, undersized, and much less able than other children to resist disease. The affections from which they usually suffer are general debility, frequent fainting, pains in the head, sides, back, and hips, palpitation of the heart, nausea, vomiting and want of appetite, curvature of the spine, scrofula, and consumption. The health of the female lacemakers especially, is constantly and deeply undermined; complaints are universal of anaemia, difficult childbirth, and miscarriage.[105] The same subordinate official of the Children's Employment Commission reports further that the children are very often ill-clothed and ragged, and receive insufficient food, usually only bread and tea, often no meat for months together. As to their moral condition, he reports:[106]

All the inhabitants of Nottingham, the police, the clergy, the manufacturers, the working-people, and the parents of the children are all unanimously of opinion that the present system of labour is a most fruitful source of immorality. The threaders, chiefly boys, and the winders, usually girls, are called for in the factory at the same time; and as their parents cannot know how long they are wanted there, they have the finest opportunity to form improper connections and remain together after the close of the work. This has contributed, in no small degree, to the immorality which, according to general opinion, exists to a terrible extent in Nottingham. Apart from this, the quiet of home life, and the comfort of the family to which these children and young people belong, is wholly sacrificed to this most unnatural state of things.

Another branch of lace-making, bobbin-lacework, is carried on in the agricultural shires of Northampton, Oxford, and Bedford, chiefly by children and young persons, who complain universally of bad food, and rarely taste meat. The employment itself is most unwholesome. The children work in small, ill-ventilated, damp rooms, sitting always bent over the lace cushion. To support the body in this wearying position, the girls wear stays with a wooden busk, which, at the tender age of most of them, when the bones are still very soft, wholly displace the ribs, and make narrow chests universal. They usually die of consumption after suffering the severest forms of digestive disorders, brought on by sedentary work in a bad atmosphere. They are almost wholly without education, least of all do they receive moral training. They love finery, and in consequence of these two influences their moral condition is most deplorable, and prostitution almost epidemic among them.[107]

This is the price at which society purchases for the fine ladies of the bourgeoisie the pleasure of wearing lace; a reasonable price truly! Only a few thousand blind working-men, some consumptive labourers' daughters, a sickly generation of the vile multitude bequeathing its debility to its equally 'vile' children and children's children. But what does that come to? Nothing, nothing whatsoever! Our English bourgeoisie will lay the report of the Government Commission aside indifferently, and wives and daughters will deck themselves with lace as before. It is a beautiful thing, the composure of an English bourgeois.

A great number of operatives are employed in the cotton-printing establishments of Lancashire, Derbyshire, and the West of Scotland. In no branch of English industry has mechanical ingenuity produced such brilliant results as here, but in no other has it so crushed the workers. The application of engraved cylinders driven by steam-power, and the discovery of a method of printing four to six colours at once with such cylinders, has as completely superseded hand-work as did the application of machinery to the spinning and weaving of cotton, and these new arrangements in the printing-works have superseded the hand-workers much more than was the case in the production of the fabrics. One man, with the assistance of one child, now does with a machine the work done formerly by 200 block printers; a single machine yields 28 yards of printed cloth per minute. The calico printers are in a very bad way in consequence; the shires of Lancaster, Derby, and Chester produced (according to a petition of the printers to the House of Commons), in the year 1842, 11,000,000 pieces of printed cotton goods: of these, 100,000 were printed by hand exclusively, 900,000 in part with machinery and in part by hand, and 10,000,000 by machinery alone, with four to six colours. As the machinery is chiefly new and undergoes constant improvement, the number of hand-printers is far too great for the available quantity of work, and many of them are therefore starving; the petition puts the number at one-quarter of the whole, while the rest are employed but one or two, in the best case three days in the week, and are ill-paid. Leach [108] asserts of one print-work (Deeply Dale, near Bury, in Lancashire), that the hand-printers did not earn on an average more than five shillings, though he knows that the machine-printers were pretty well paid. The print-works are thus wholly affiliated with the factory system, but without being subject to the legislative restrictions placed upon it. They produce an article subject to fashion, and have therefore no regular work. If they have small orders, they work half time; if they make a hit with a pattern, and business is brisk, they work twelve hours, perhaps all night. In the neighbourhood of my home, near Manchester, there was a print-work that was often lighted when I returned late at night; and I have heard that the children were obliged at times to work so long there, that they would try to catch a moment's rest and sleep on the stone steps and in the corners of the lobby. I have no legal proof of the truth of the statement, or I should name the firm. The Report of the Children's Employment Commission is very cursory upon this subject, stating merely that in England, at least, the children are mostly pretty well clothed and fed (relatively, according to the wages of the parents), that they receive no education whatsoever, and are morally on a low plane. It is only necessary to remember that these children are subject to the factory system, and then, referring the reader to what has already been said of that, we can pass on.

Of the remaining workers employed in the manufacture of clothing stuffs little remains to be said; the bleachers' work is very unwholesome, obliging them to breathe chlorine, a gas injurious to the lungs. The work of the dyers is in many cases very healthful, since it requires the exertion of the whole body; how these workers are paid is little known, and this is ground enough for the inference that they do not receive less than the average wages, otherwise they would make complaint. The fustian cutters, who, in consequence of the large consumption of cotton velvet, are comparatively numerous, being estimated at from 3,000 to 4,000, have suffered very severely, indirectly, from the influence of the factory system. The goods formerly woven with hand-looms, were not perfectly uniform, and required a practised hand in cutting the single rows of threads. Since power-looms have been used, the rows run regularly; each thread of the weft is exactly parallel with the preceding one, and cutting is no longer an art. The workers thrown out of employment by the introduction of machinery turn to fustian cutting, and force down wages by their competition; the manufacturers discovered that they could employ women and children, and the wages sank to the rate paid them, while hundreds of men were thrown out of employment. The manufacturers found that they could get the work done in the factory itself more cheaply than in the cutters' workroom, for which they indirectly paid the rent. Since this discovery, the low upper-storey cutters' rooms stand empty in many a cottage, or are let for dwellings, while the cutter has lost his freedom of choice of his working hours, and is brought under the dominion of the factory bell. A cutter of perhaps forty-five years of age told me that he could remember a time when he had received 8d. a yard for work, for which he now received 1d.; true, he can cut the more regular texture more quickly than the old, but he can by no means do twice as much in an hour as formerly, so that his wages have sunk to less than a quarter of what they were. Leach [109] gives a list of wages paid in 1827 and in 1843 for various goods, from which it appears that articles paid in 1827 at the rates of 4d., 2¼d., 2¾d., and 1d. per yard, were paid in 1843 at the rate of 1½d., 1d., ¼d., and ⅜d. per yard, cutters' wages. The average weekly wage, according to Leach, was as follows: 1827, £1 6s. 6d.; £1 2s. 6d.; £1; £1 6s. 6d.; and for the same goods in 1843, 10s. 6d.; 7s. 6d.; 6s. 8d.; 10s.; while there are hundreds of workers who cannot find employment even at these last-named rates. Of the hand-weavers of the cotton industry we have already spoken; the other woven fabrics are almost exclusively produced on hand-looms. Here most of the workers have suffered as the weavers have done from the crowding in of competitors displaced by machinery, and are, moreover, subject like the factory operatives to a severe fine system for bad work. Take, for instance, the silk weavers. Mr Brocklehurst, one of the largest silk manufacturers in all England, laid before a committee of members of Parliament lists taken from his books, from which it appears that for goods for which he paid wages in 1821 at the rate of 30s., 14s., 3s. 6d., 9d., 1s. 6d., 10s., he paid in 1839 but 9s., 7s. 3d., 2s. 3d., 4d., 6d., 6s. 3d, while in this case no improvement in the machinery has taken place. But what Mr Brocklehurst does may very well be taken as a standard for all. From the same lists it appears that the average weekly wage of his weavers, after all deductions, was, in 1821, 16s. 6d., and, in 1831, but 6s. Since that time wages have fallen still further. Goods which brought in 4d. weavers' wages in 1831, bring in but 2½d. in 1843 (single sarsnets), and a great number of weavers in the country can get work only when they undertake these goods at 1½d.–2d. Moreover, they are subject to arbitrary deductions from their wages. Every weaver who receives materials is given a card, on which is usually to be read that the work is to be returned at a specified hour of the day; that a weaver who cannot work by reason of illness must make the fact known at the office within three days, or sickness will not be regarded as an excuse; that it will not be regarded as a sufficient excuse if the weaver claims to have been obliged to wait for yarn; that for certain faults in the work (if, for example, more weft-threads are found within a given space than are prescribed), not less than half the wages will be deducted; and that if the goods should not be ready at the time specified, one penny will be deducted for every yard returned. The deductions in accordance with these cards are so considerable that, for instance, a man who comes twice a week to Leigh, in Lancashire, to gather up woven goods, brings his employer at least £15 fines every time. He asserts this himself, and he is regarded as one of the most lenient. Such things were formerly settled by arbitration; but as the workers were usually dismissed if they insisted upon that, the custom has been almost wholly abandoned, and the manufacturer acts arbitrarily as prosecutor, witness, judge, law-giver, and executive in one person. And if the workman goes to a Justice of the Peace, the answer is: 'When you accepted your card you entered upon a contract, and you must abide by it.' The case is the same as that of the factory operatives. Besides, the employer obliges the workman to sign a document in which he declares that he agrees to the deductions made. And if a workman rebels, all the manufacturers in the town know at once that he is a man who, as Leach says,[110] 'resists the lawful order as established by weavers' cards, and, moreover, has the impudence to doubt the wisdom of those who are, as he ought to know, his superiors in society.'

Naturally, the workers are perfectly free; the manufacturer does not force them to take his materials and his cards, but he says to them what Leach translates into plain English with the words: 'If you don't like to be frizzled in my frying-pan, you can take a walk into the fire.' The silk weavers of London, and especially of Spitalfields, have lived in periodic distress for a long time, and that they still have no cause to be satisfied with their lot is proved by their taking a most active part in English labour movements in general, and in London ones in particular. The distress prevailing among them gave rise to the fever which broke out in East

London, and called forth the Commission for Investigating the Sanitary Condition of the Labouring Class. But the last report of the London Fever Hospital shows that this disease is still raging.

After the textile fabrics, by far the most important products of English industry are the metal-wares. This trade has its head-quarters at Birmingham, where the finer metal goods of all sorts are produced, at Sheffield for cutlery, and in Staffordshire, especially at Wolverhampton, where the coarser articles, locks, nails, etc., are manufactured. In describing the position of the workers employed in these trades, let us begin with Birmingham. The disposition of the work has retained in Birmingham, as in most places where metals are wrought, something of the old handicraft character; the small employers are still to be found, who work with their apprentices in the shop at home, or when they need steam-power, in great factory buildings which are divided into little shops, each rented to a small employer, and supplied with a shaft moved by the engine, and furnishing motive power for the machinery. Leon Faucher, author of a series of articles in the *Revue des Deux Mondes*, which at least betray study, and are better than what has hitherto been written upon the subject by Englishmen or Germans, characterises this relation in contrast with the manufacture of Lancashire as '*démocratie industrielle*', and observes that it produces no very favourable results for master or men. This observation is perfectly correct, for the many small employers cannot well subsist on the profit divided amongst them, determined by competition, a profit under other circumstances absorbed by a single manufacturer. The centralising tendency of capital holds them down. For one who grows rich ten are ruined, and a hundred placed at a greater disadvantage than ever, by the pressure of the one upstart who can afford to sell more cheaply than they. And in the cases where they have to compete from the beginning against great capitalists, it is self-evident that they can only toil along with the greatest difficulty. The apprentices are, as we shall see, quite as badly off under the small employers as under the manufacturers, with the single difference that they, in turn, may become small employers, and so attain a certain independence – that is to say, they are at best less directly exploited by the bourgeoisie than under the factory system. Thus these small employers are neither genuine proletarians, since they live in part upon the work of their apprentices, nor genuine bourgeois, since their principal means of support is their own work. This peculiar midway position of the Birmingham iron-workers is to blame for their having so rarely joined wholly and unreservedly in the English labour movements. Birmingham is a politically radical, but not a Chartist, town. There are, however, numerous larger fact-ories belonging to capitalists; and in these the factory system reigns supreme. The division of labour, which is here carried out to the last detail (in the needle industry, for example), and the use of steam-power, admit of the employment of a great multitude of women and children, and we find here [111] precisely the same features reappearing which the Factories' Report presented – the work of women up to the hour of confinement, incapacity as housekeepers, neglect of home and children, indifference, actual dislike to family life, and demoralisation; further, the crowding out of men from employment, the constant improvement of machin-ery, early emancipation of children, husbands supported by their wives and children, etc. etc. The children are described as half-starved and ragged, the half of them are said not to know what it is to have enough to eat, many of them get nothing to eat before the midday meal, or even live the whole day upon a pennyworth of bread for a noonday meal – there were actually cases in which children received no food from eight in the morning until seven at night. Their clothing is very often scarcely sufficient to cover their nakedness, many are barefoot even in winter. Hence they are all small and weak for their age, and rarely develop with any degree of vigour. And when we reflect that with these insufficient means of reproducing the physical forces, hard and protracted work in close rooms is required of them, we cannot wonder that there are few adults in Birmingham fit for military service. 'The working men', says a recruiting surgeon, 'are small, delicate, and of very slight physical power; many of them deformed, too, in the chest or spinal column.' According to the assertion of a recruiting sergeant, the people of Birmingham are smaller than those anywhere else, being usually 5 feet 4 to 5 inches tall; out of 613 recruits, but 238 were found fit for service. As to education, a series of depositions and specimens taken from the metal districts have already been given, [112] to which the reader is referred. It appears further, from the Children's Employment Commission's Report, that in Birmingham more than half the children between five and fifteen years attend no school whatsoever, that those who do are constantly changing, so that it is impossible to give them any training of an enduring kind, and that they are all withdrawn from school very early and set to work. The report makes it clear what sort of teachers are employed. One teacher, in answer to the question whether she gave moral instruction, said, No, for threepence a week school fees that was too much to require, but that she took a great deal of trouble to instil good principles into the children. (And she made a decided slip in her English in saying it.) In the schools the commissioner found constant noise and disorder. The moral state of the children is in the highest degree deplorable. Half of all the criminals are children under fifteen, and in a single year ninety ten-years'-old offenders, among them forty-four serious criminal cases, were sentenced. Unbridled sexual intercourse seems, according to the opinion of the commissioner, almost universal, and that at a very early age.[113]

In the iron district of Staffordshire the state of things is still worse. For the coarse wares made here neither much division of labour (with certain exceptions) nor steam-power or machinery can be applied. In Wolverhampton, Willenhall, Bilston, Sedgeley, Wednesfield, Darlaston, Dudley, Walsall, Wednesbury, etc., there are, therefore, fewer factories, but chiefly single forges, where the small masters work alone, or with one or more apprentices, who serve them until reaching the twenty first year. The small employers are in about the same situation as those of Birmingham; but the apprentices, as a rule, are much worse off. They get almost exclusively meat from diseased animals or such as have died a natural death, or tainted meat, or fish to eat, with veal from calves killed too young, and pork from swine smothered during transportation, and such food is furnished not by small employers only, but by large manufacturers, who employ from thirty to forty apprentices. The custom seems to be universal in Wolverhampton, and its natural consequence is frequent bowel complaints and other diseases. Moreover, the children usually do not get enough to eat, and have rarely other clothing than their working rags, for which reason, if for no other, they cannot go to Sunday school. The dwellings are bad and filthy, often so much so that they give rise to disease; and in spite of the not materially unhealthy work, the children are puny, weak, and, in many cases, severely crippled. In Willenhall, for instance, there are countless persons who have, from perpetually filing at the lathe, crooked backs and one leg crooked, 'hind-leg' as they call it, so that the two legs have the form of a K; while it is said that more than one-third of the working-men there are ruptured. Here, as well as in Wolverhampton, numberless cases were found of retarded puberty among girls (for girls, too, work at the forges) as well as among boys, extending even to the nineteenth year. In Sedgeley and its surrounding district, where nails form almost the sole product, the nailers live and work in the most wretched stable-like huts, which for filth can scarcely be equalled. Girls and boys work from the tenth or twelfth year, and are accounted fully skilled only when they make a thousand nails a day. For twelve hundred nails the pay is 5¾d. Every nail receives twelve blows, and since the hammer weighs 1¼ pounds, the nailer must lift 18,000 pounds to earn this miserable pay. With this hard work and insufficient food, the children inevitably develop ill-formed, undersized frames, and the commissioners depositions confirm this. As to the state of education in this district, data have already been furnished in the foregoing chapters. It is upon an incredibly low plane; half the children do not even go to Sunday school, and the other half go irregularly; very few, in comparison with the other districts, can read, and in the matter of writing the case is much worse. Naturally, for between the seventh and tenth years, just when they are beginning to get some good out of going to school, they are set to work, and the Sunday school teachers, smiths or miners, frequently cannot read, and write their names with difficulty. The prevailing morals correspond with these means of education. In Willenhall, Commissioner Horne asserts, and supplies ample proofs of his assertion, that there exists absolutely no moral sense among the workers. In general, he found that the children neither recognised duties to their parents nor felt any affection for them. They were so little capable of thinking of what they said, so stolid, so hopelessly stupid, that they often asserted that they were well treated, were coming on famously, when they were forced to work twelve to fourteen hours, were clad in rags, did not get enough to eat, and were beaten so that they felt it several days afterwards. They knew nothing of a different kind of life than that in which they toil from morning until they are allowed to stop at night, and did not even understand the question, never heard before, whether they were tired.[114]

In Sheffield wages are better, and the external state of the workers also. On the other hand, certain branches of work are to be noticed here, because of their extraordinarily injurious influence upon health. Certain operations require the constant pressure of tools against the chest, and engender consumption in many cases; others, file-cutting among them, retard the general development of the body and produce digestive disorders; bone-cutting for knife handles brings with it headache, biliousness, and among girls, of whom many are employed, anaemia. By far the most unwholesome work is the grinding of knife-blades and forks, which, especially when done with a dry stone, entails certain early death. The unwholesomeness of this work lies in part in the bent posture, in which chest and stomach are cramped; but especially in the quantity of sharp-edged metal dust particles freed in the cutting, which fill the atmosphere, and are necessarily inhaled. The dry grinders' average life is hardly thirty-five years, the wet grinders' rarely exceeds forty-five. Dr Knight, in Sheffield, says:[115]

I can convey some idea of the injuriousness of this occupation only by asserting that the hardest drinkers among the grinders are the longest lived among them, because they are longest and oftenest absent from their work. There are, in all, some 2,500 grinders in Sheffield. About 150 (80 men and 70 boys) are fork grinders; these die between the twenty-eighth and thirty-second years of age. The razor grinders, who grind wet as well as dry, die between forty and forty-five years, and the table cutlery grinders, who grind wet, die between the fortieth and fiftieth year.

The same physician gives the following description of the course of the disease called grinders' asthma:

They usually begin their work with the fourteenth year, and, if they have good constitutions, rarely notice any symptoms before the twentieth year. Then the symptoms of their peculiar disease appear. They suffer from shortness of breath at the slightest effort in going up hill or up stairs, they habitually raise the shoulders to relieve the permanent and increasing want of breath; they bend forward, and seem, in general, to feel most comfortable in the

crouching position in which they work. Their complexion becomes dirty yellow, their features express anxiety, they complain
of pressure upon the chest. Their voices become rough and hoarse,
they cough loudly, and the sound is as if air were driven through
a wooden tube. From time to time they expectorate considerable
quantities of dust, either mixed with phlegm or in balls or
cylindrical masses, with a thin coating of mucus. Spitting blood,
inability to lie down, night sweat, colliquative diarrhoea, unusual
loss of flesh, and all the usual symptoms of consumption of the
lungs finally carry them off, after they have lingered months, or
even years, unfit to support themselves or those dependent upon
them. I must add that all attempts which have hitherto been made
to prevent grinders' asthma, or to cure it, have wholly failed.

All this Knight wrote ten years ago; since then the number of
grinders and the violence of the disease have increased, though
attempts have been made to prevent it by covered grindstones and
carrying off the dust by artificial draught. These methods have
been at least partially successful, but the grinders do not desire their
adoption, and have even destroyed the contrivance here and there,
in the belief that more workers may be attracted to the business
and wages thus reduced; they are for a short life and a merry one.
Dr Knight has often told grinders who came to him with the first
symptoms of asthma that a return to grinding means certain death,
but with no avail. He who is once a grinder falls into despair, as
though he had sold himself to the devil. Education in Sheffield is
upon a very low plane; a clergyman, who had occupied himself
largely with the statistics of education, was of the opinion that of
16,500 children of the working class who are in a position to
attend school, scarcely 6,500 can read. This comes of the fact that
the children are taken from school in the seventh, and, at the very
latest, in the twelfth year, and that the teachers are good for
nothing; one was a convicted thief who found no other way of
supporting himself after being released from jail than teaching
school! Immorality among young people seems to be more prevalent in Sheffield than anywhere else. It is hard to tell which town
ought to have the prize, and in reading the report one believes of
each one that this certainly deserves it! The younger generation
spend the whole of Sunday lying in the street tossing coins or

fighting dogs, go regularly to the gin palace, where they sit with their sweethearts until late at night, when they take walks in solitary couples. In an ale-house which the commissioner visited, there sat forty to fifty young people of both sexes, nearly all under seventeen years of age, and each lad beside his lass. Here and there cards were played, at other places dancing was going on, and everywhere drinking. Among the company were openly avowed professional prostitutes. No wonder, then, that, as all the witnesses testify, early, unbridled sexual intercourse, youthful prostitution, beginning with persons of fourteen to fifteen years, is extraordinarily frequent in Sheffield. Crimes of a savage and desperate sort are of common occurrence; one year before the commissioner's visit, a band, consisting chiefly of young persons, was arrested when about to set fire to the town, being fully equipped with lances and inflammable substances. We shall see later that the labour movement in Sheffield has this same savage character.[116]

Besides these two main centres of the metal industry, there are needle factories in Warrington, Lancashire, where great want, immorality, and ignorance prevail among the workers, and especially among the children; and a number of nail forges in the neighbourhood of Wigan, in Lancashire, and in the east of Scotland. The reports from these latter districts tell almost precisely the same story as those of Staffordshire. There is one more branch of this industry carried on in the factory districts, especially in Lancashire, the essential peculiarity of which is the production of machinery by machinery, whereby the workers, crowded out elsewhere, are deprived of their last refuge, the creation of the very enemy which supersedes them. Machinery for planing and boring, cutting screws, wheels, nuts, etc., with power lathes, has thrown out of employment a multitude of men who formerly found regular work at good wages; and whoever wishes to do so may see crowds of them in Manchester.

North of the iron district of Staffordshire lies an industrial region to which we shall now turn our attention, the Potteries, whose headquarters are in the borough of Stoke, embracing Henley, Burslem, Lane End, Lane Delph, Etruria, Coleridge, Langport, Tunstall, and Golden Hill, containing together 60,000 inhabitants. The Children's Employment Commission reports upon this subject that in some branches of this industry, in the production of stoneware, the children have light employment in warm, airy rooms; in others, on the contrary, hard, wearing labour is required, while they receive neither sufficient food nor good clothing. Many children complain: 'Don't get enough to eat, get mostly potatoes with salt, never meat, never bread, don't go to school, haven't got no clothes.' 'Haven't got nothin' to eat today for dinner, don't never have dinner at home, get mostly potatoes and salt, sometimes bread.' 'These is all the clothes I have, no Sunday suit at home.' Among the children whose work is especially injurious are the mould-runners, who have to carry the moulded article with the form to the drying-room, and afterwards bring back the empty form, when the article is properly dried. Thus they must go to and fro the whole day, carrying burdens heavy in proportion to their age, while the high temperature in which they have to do this increases very considerably the exhaustiveness of the work. These children, with scarcely a single exception, are lean, pale, feeble, stunted; nearly all suffer from stomach troubles, nausea, want of appetite, and many of them die of consumption. Almost as delicate are the boys called 'jiggers', from the 'jigger' wheel which they turn. But by far the most injurious is the work of those who dip the finished article into a fluid containing great quantities of lead, and often of arsenic, or have to take the freshly-dipped article up with the hand. The hands and clothing of these workers, adults and children, are always wet with this fluid, the skin softens and falls off under the constant contact with rough objects, so that the fingers often bleed, and are constantly in a state most favourable for the absorption of this dangerous substance. The consequence is violent pain, and serious disease of the stomach and intestines, obstinate constipation, colic, sometimes consumption, and, most common of all, epilepsy among children. Among men, partial paralysis of the hand muscles, *colica pictorum*, and paralysis of whole limbs are ordinary phenomena. One witness relates that two children who worked with him died of convulsions at their work; another who had helped with the dipping two years while a boy, relates that he had violent pains in the bowels at first, then convulsions, in consequence of which he was confined to his bed two months, since when the attacks of convulsions have increased in frequency, are now daily, accompanied often by ten to twenty epileptic fits, his right arm is paralysed, and the physicians tell him that he can never regain the use of his limbs. In one factory were found in the dipping-house four men, all epileptic and afflicted with severe colic, and eleven boys, several of whom were already epileptic. In short, this frightful disease follows this occupation universally: and that, too, to the greater pecuniary profit of the bourgeoisie! In the rooms in which the stoneware is scoured, the atmosphere is filled with pulverised flint, the breathing of which is as injurious as that of the steel dust among the Sheffield grinders. The workers lose breath, cannot lie down, suffer from sore throat and violent coughing, and come to have so feeble a voice that they can scarcely be heard. They, too, all die of consumption. In the Potteries district, the schools are said to be comparatively numerous, and to offer the children opportunities for instruction; but as the latter are so early set to work for twelve hours and often more per day, they are not in a position to avail themselves of the schools, so that three-fourths of the children examined by the commissioner could neither read nor write, while the whole district is plunged in the deepest ignorance. Children who have attended Sunday school for years could not tell one letter from another, and the moral and religious education, as well as the intellectual, is on a very low plane.[117]

In the manufacture of glass, too, work occurs which seems little injurious to men, but cannot be endured by children. The hard labour, the irregularity of the hours, the frequent night-work, and especially the great heat of the working place (100 to 130 Fahrenheit), engender in children general debility and disease, stunted growth, and especially affections of the eye, bowel complaint, and rheumatic and bronchial affections. Many of the children are pale, have red eyes, often blind for weeks at a time, suffer from violent nausea, vomiting, coughs, colds, and rheumatism. When the glass is withdrawn from the fire, the children must often go into such heat that the boards on which they stand catch fire under their feet. The glassblowers usually die young of debility and chest affections.[118]

As a whole, this report testifies to the gradual but sure introduction of the factory system into all branches of industry, recognisable especially by the employment of women and children. I have not thought it necessary to trace in every case the progress of machinery and the superseding of men as workers. Everyone who is in any degree acquainted with the nature of manufacture can fill this out for himself, while space fails me to describe in detail an aspect of our present system of production, the result of which I have already sketched in dealing with the factory system. In all directions machinery is being introduced, and the last trace of the working-man's independence thus destroyed. In all directions the family is being dissolved by the labour of wife and children, or inverted by the husband's being thrown out of employment and made dependent upon them for bread; everywhere the inevitable machinery bestows upon the great capitalist command of trade and of the workers with it. The centralisation of capital strides forward without interruption, the division of society into great capitalists and non-possessing workers is sharper every day, the industrial development of the nation advances with giant strides towards the inevitable crisis.

I have already stated that in the handicrafts the power of capital, and in some cases the division of labour too, has produced the same results, crushed the small tradesmen, and put great capitalists and non-possessing workers in their place. As to these handicrafts-men there is little to be said, since all that relates to them has already found its place where the proletariat in general was under discussion. There has been but little change here in the nature of the work and its influence upon health since the beginning of the industrial movement. But the constant contact with the factory operatives, the pressure of the great capitalists, which is much more felt than that of the small employer to whom the apprentice still stood in a more or less personal relation, the influences of life in towns, and the fall of wages, have made nearly all the handicraftsmen active participators in labour movements. We shall soon have more to say on this point, and turn mean-while to one section of workers in London who deserve our attention by reason of the extraordinary barbarity with which they are exploited by the money-greed of the bourgeoisie. I mean the dressmakers and sewing-women.

It is a curious fact that the production of precisely those articles which serve the personal adornment of the ladies of the bourgeoisie involves the saddest consequences for the health of the workers. We have already seen this in the case of the lacemakers, and come now to the dressmaking establishments of London for further proof. They employ a mass of young girls – there are said to be

15,000 of them in all – who sleep and eat on the premises, come usually from the country, and are therefore absolutely the slaves of their employers. During the fashionable season, which lasts some four months, working hours, even in the best establishments, are fifteen, and, in very pressing cases, eighteen a day; but in most shops work goes on at these times without any set regulation, so that the girls never have more than six, often not more than three or four, sometimes, indeed, not more than two hours in the twenty-four, for rest and sleep, working nineteen to twenty hours, if not the whole night through, as frequently happens! The only limit set to their work is the absolute physical inability to hold the needle another minute. Cases have occurred in which these helpless creatures did not undress during nine consecutive days and nights, and could only rest a moment or two here and there upon a mattress, where food was served them ready cut up in order to require the least possible time for swallowing. In short, these unfortunate girls are kept by means of the moral whip of the modern slave-driver, the threat of discharge, to such long and unbroken toil as no strong man, much less a delicate girl of fourteen to twenty years, can endure. In addition to this, the foul air of the workroom and sleeping places, the bent posture, the often bad and indigestible food, all these causes, combined with almost total exclusion from fresh air, entail the saddest consequences for the health of the girls. Enervation, exhaustion, debility, loss of appetite, pains in the shoulders, back, and hips, but especially headache, begin very soon; then follow curvatures of the spine, high, deformed shoulders, leanness, swelled, weeping, and smarting eyes, which soon become short-sighted; coughs, narrow chests, and shortness of breath, and all manner of disorders in the development of the female organism. In many cases the eyes suffer, so severely that incurable blindness follows; but if the sight remains strong enough to make continued work possible, consumption usually soon ends the sad life of these milliners and dressmakers. Even those who leave this work at an early age retain permanently injured health, a broken constitution; and, when married, bring feeble and sickly children into the world. All the medical men interrogated by the commissioner agreed that no method of life could be invented better calculated to destroy health and induce early death.

With the same cruelty, though somewhat more indirectly, the rest of the needle-women of London are exploited. The girls employed in stay-making have a hard, wearing occupation, trying to the eyes. And what wages do they get? I do not know; but this I know, that the middle-man who has to give security for the material delivered, and who distributes the work among the needle-women, receives 1½d. per piece. From this he deducts his own pay, at least ½d., so that 1d. at most reaches the pocket of the girl. The girls who sew neckties must bind themselves to work sixteen hours a day, and receive 4s. 6d. a week.[119] But the shirt-makers' lot is the worst. They receive for an ordinary shirt 1½d., formerly 2d.–3d.; but since the workhouse of St Pancras, which is administered by a Radical board of guardians, began to undertake work at 1½d., the poor women outside have been compelled to do the same. For fine, fancy shirts, which can be made in one day of eighteen hours, 6d. is paid. The weekly wage of these sewing-women, according to this and according to testimony from many sides, including both needle-women and employers, is 2s. 6d. to 3s. for most strained work continued far into the night. And what crowns this shameful barbarism is the fact that the women must give a money deposit for a part of the materials entrusted to them, which they naturally cannot do unless they pawn a part of them (as the employers very well know), redeeming them at a loss; or if they cannot redeem the materials, they must appear before a Justice of the Peace, as happened to a sewing-woman in November, 1843. A poor girl who got into this strait and did not know what to do next, drowned herself in a canal in 1844. These women usually live in little garret rooms in the utmost distress, where as many crowd together as the space can possibly admit, and where, in winter, the animal warmth of the workers is the only heat obtainable. Here they sit bent over their work, sewing from four or five in the morning until midnight, destroying their health in a year or two and ending in an early grave, without being able to obtain the poorest necessities of life meanwhile.[120] And below them roll the brilliant equipages of the upper bourgeoisie, and perhaps ten steps away some pitiable dandy loses more money in one evening at faro than they can earn in a year.

*   *   *

Such is the condition of the English manufacturing proletariat. In all directions, whithersoever we may turn, we find want and disease permanent or temporary, and demoralisation arising from the condition of the workers; in all directions slow but sure undermining, and final destruction of the human being physically as well as mentally. Is this a state of things which can last? It cannot and will not last. The workers, the great majority of the nation, will not endure it. Let us see what they say of it.

Labour Movements

It must be admitted, even if I had not proved it so often in detail, that the English workers cannot feel happy in this condition; that theirs is not a state in which a man or a whole class of men can think, feel, and live as human beings. The workers must therefore strive to escape from this brutalising condition, to secure for themselves a better, more human position; and this they cannot do without attacking the interest of the bourgeoisie which consists in exploiting them. But the bourgeoisie defends its interests with all the power placed at its disposal by wealth and the might of the State. In proportion as the working-man determines to alter the present state of things, the bourgeois becomes his avowed enemy.

Moreover, the working-man is made to feel at every moment that the bourgeoisie treats him as a chattel, as its property, and for this reason, if for no other, he must come forward as its enemy. I have shown in a hundred ways in the foregoing pages, and could have shown in a hundred others, that, in our present society, he can save his manhood only in hatred and rebellion against the bourgeoisie. And he can protest with most violent passion against the tyranny of the propertied class, thanks to his education, or rather want of education, and to the abundance of hot Irish blood that flows in the veins of the English working class. The English working-man is no Englishman nowadays; no calculating money-grabber like his wealthy neighbour. He possesses more fully developed feelings, his native northern coldness is overborne by the unrestrained development of his passions and their control over him. The cultivation of the understanding which so greatly strengthens the selfish tendency of the English bourgeois, which has made selfishness his predominant trait and concentrated all his emotional power upon the single point of money-greed, is wanting in the working-man, whose passions are therefore strong and mighty as those of the foreigner. English nationality is annihilated in the working-man.

Since, as we have seen, no single field for the exercise of his manhood is left him, save his opposition to the whole conditions of his life, it is natural that exactly in this opposition he should be most manly, noblest, most worthy of sympathy. We shall see that all the energy, all the activity of the working-men is directed to this point, and that even their attempts to attain general education all stand in direct connection with this. True, we shall have single acts of violence and even of brutality to report, but it must always be kept in mind that the social war is avowedly raging in England; and that, whereas it is in the interest of the bourgeoisie to conduct this war hypocritically, under the disguise of peace and even of philanthropy, the only help for the working-men consists in laying bare the true state of things and destroying this hypocrisy; that the most violent attacks of the workers upon the bourgeoisie and its servants are only the open, undisguised expression of that which the bourgeoisie perpetrates secretly, treacherously against the workers.

The revolt of the workers began soon after the first industrial development, and has passed through several phases. The investigation of their importance in the history of the English people I must reserve for separate treatment, limiting myself meanwhile to such bare facts as serve to characterise the condition of the English proletariat.

The earliest, crudest, and least fruitful form of this rebellion was that of crime. The working-man lived in poverty and want, and saw that others were better off than he. It was not clear to his mind why he, who did more for society than the rich idler, should be the one to suffer under these conditions. Want conquered his inherited respect for the sacredness of property, and he stole. We have seen how crime increased with the extension of manufacture; how the yearly number of arrests bore a constant relation to the number of bales of cotton annually consumed.

The workers soon realised that crime did not help matters. The criminal could protest against the existing order of society only singly, as one individual; the whole might of society was brought to bear upon each criminal, and crushed him with its immense superiority. Besides, theft was the most primitive form of protest, and for this reason, if for no other, it never became the universal expression of the public opinion of the working-men, however much they might approve of it in silence. As a class, they first manifested opposition to the bourgeoisie when they resisted the introduction of machinery at the very beginning of the industrial period. The first inventors, Arkwright and others, were persecuted in this way and their machines destroyed. Later, there took place a number of revolts against machinery, in which the occurrences were almost precisely the same as those of the printers' disturbances in Bohemia in 1844; factories were demolished and machinery destroyed.

This form of opposition also was isolated, restricted to certain localities, and directed against one feature only of our present social arrangements. When the momentary end was attained, the whole weight of social power fell upon the unprotected evildoers and punished them to its heart's content, while the machinery was introduced none the less. A new form of opposition had to be found.

At this point help came in the shape of a law enacted by the old, unreformed, oligarchic-Tory parliament, a law which never could have passed the House of Commons later, when the Reform Bill had legally sanctioned the distinction between bourgeoisie and proletariat, and made the bourgeoisie the ruling class. This was enacted in 1824, and repealed all laws by which coalitions between working-men for labour purposes had hitherto been forbidden. The working-men obtained a right previously restricted to the aristocracy and bourgeoisie, the right of free association. Secret coalitions had, it is true, previously existed, but could never achieve great results. In Glasgow, as Symonds [121] relates, a general strike of weavers had taken place in 1812, which was brought about by a secret association. It was repeated in 1822, and on this occasion vitriol was thrown into the faces of the two working-men who would not join the association, and were therefore regarded by the members as traitors to their class. Both the assaulted lost the use of their eyes in consequence of the injury. So, too, in 1818, the association of Scottish miners was powerful enough to carry on a general strike. These associations required their members to take an oath of fidelity and secrecy, had regular lists, treasurers, bookkeepers, and local branches. But the secrecy with which everything was conducted crippled their growth. When, on the other hand, the working-man received in 1824 the right of free association, these combinations were very soon spread over all England and attained great power. In all branches of industry Trades Unions were formed with the outspoken intention of protecting the single working-man against the tyranny and neglect of the bourgeoisie. Their objects were to deal, *en masse*, as a power, with the employers; to regulate the rate of wages according to the profit of the latter, to raise it when opportunity offered, and to keep it uniform in each trade throughout the country. Hence they tried to settle with the capitalists a scale of wages to be universally adhered to, and ordered out on strike the employees of such individuals as refused to accept the scale. They aimed further to keep up the demand for labour by limiting the number of apprentices, and so to keep wages high; to counteract, as far as possible, the indirect wages reductions which the manufacturers brought about by means of new tools and machinery; and finally, to assist unemployed working-men financially. This they do either directly or by means of a card to legitimate the bearer as a 'society man', and with which the working-man wanders from place to place, supported by his fellow-workers, and instructed as to the best opportunity for finding employment. This is tramping, and the wanderer a tramp. To attain these ends, a President and Secretary are engaged at a salary (since it is to be expected that no manufacturer will employ such persons), and a committee collects the weekly contributions and watches over their expenditure for the purposes of the association. When it proved possible and advantageous, the various trades of single districts united in a federation and held delegate conventions at set times. The attempt has been made in single cases to unite the workers of one branch over all England in one great Union; and several times (in 1830 for the first time) to form one universal trades association for the whole United Kingdom, with a separate organisation for each trade. These associations, however, never held together long, and were seldom realised even for the moment, since an exceptionally universal excitement is necessary to make such a federation possible and effective.

The means usually employed by these Unions for attaining their ends are the following: if one or more employers refuse to pay the wage specified by the Union, a deputation is sent or a petition forwarded (the working-men, you see, know how to recognise the absolute power of the lord of the factory in his little State); if this proves unavailing, the Union commands the employees to stop work, and all hands go home. This strike is either partial when one or several, or general when all employers in the trade refuse to regulate wages according to the proposals of the Union. So far go the lawful means of the Union, assuming the strike to take effect after the expiration of the legal notice, which is not always the case. But these lawful means are very weak when there are workers outside the Union, or when members separate from it for the sake of the momentary advantage offered by the bourgeoisie. Especially in the case of partial strikes can the manufacturer readily secure recruits from these black sheep (who are known as knobsticks), and render fruitless the efforts of the united workers. Knobsticks are usually threatened, insulted, beaten, or otherwise maltreated by the members of the Union; intimidated, in short, in every way. Prosecution follows, and as the law-abiding bourgeoisie has the power in its own hands, the force of the Union is broken almost every time by the first unlawful act, the first judicial procedure against its members.

The history of these Unions is a long series of defeats of the working-men, interrupted by a few isolated victories. All these efforts naturally cannot alter the economic law according to which wages are determined by the relation between supply and demand in the labour market. Hence the Unions remain powerless against all *great* forces which influence this relation. In a commercial crisis the Union itself must reduce wages or dissolve wholly; and in a time of considerable increase in the demand for labour, it cannot fix the rate of wages higher than would be reached spontaneously by the competition of the capitalists among themselves. But in dealing with minor, single influences they are powerful. If the employer had no concentrated, collective opposition to expect, he would in his own interest gradually reduce wages to a lower and lower point; indeed, the battle of competition which he has to wage against his fellow-manufacturers would force him to do so, and wages would soon reach the minimum. But this competition of the manufacturers among themselves is, *under average conditions*, somewhat restricted by the opposition of the working-men.

Every manufacturer knows that the consequence of a reduction not justified by conditions to which his competitors also are subjected, would be a strike, which would most certainly injure him, because his capital would be idle as long as the strike lasted, and his machinery would be rusting, whereas it is very doubtful whether he could, in such a case, enforce his reduction. Then he has the certainty that if he should succeed, his competitors would follow him, reducing the price of the goods so produced, and thus depriving him of the benefit of his policy. Then, too, the Unions often bring about a more rapid increase of wages after a crisis than would otherwise follow. For the manufacturer's interest is to delay raising wages until forced by competition, but now the working-men demand an increased wage as soon as the market improves, and they can carry their point by reason of the smaller supply of workers at his command under such circumstances. But, for resistance to more considerable forces which influence the labour market, the Unions are powerless. In such cases hunger gradually drives the strikers to resume work on any terms, and when once a few have begun, the force of the Union is broken, because these few knobsticks, with the reserve supplies of goods in the market, enable the bourgeoisie to overcome the worst effects of the interruption of business. The funds of the Union are soon exhausted by the great numbers requiring relief, the credit which the shopkeepers give at high interest is withdrawn after a time, and want compels the working-man to place himself once more under the yoke of the bourgeoisie. But strikes end disastrously for the workers mostly because the manufacturers, in their own interest (which has, be it said, become their interest only through the resistance of the workers), are obliged to avoid all useless reductions, while the workers feel in every reduction imposed by the state of trade a deterioration of their condition, against which they must defend themselves as far as in them lies.

It will be asked, 'Why, then, do the workers strike in such cases, when the uselessness of such measures is so evident?' Simply because they *must* protest against every reduction, even if dictated by necessity; because they feel bound to proclaim that they, as human beings, shall not be made to bow to social circumstances, but social conditions ought to yield to them as human beings; because silence on their part would be a recognition of these social conditions, an admission of the right of the bourgeoisie to exploit the workers in good times and let them starve in bad ones. Against this the working-men must rebel so long as they have not lost all human feeling, and that they protest in this way and no other, comes of their being practical English people, who express themselves in *action*, and do not, like German theorists, go to sleep as soon as their protest is properly registered and placed *ad acta*, there to sleep as quietly as the protesters themselves. The active resistance of the English working-men has its effect in holding the money greed of the bourgeoisie within certain limits, and keeping alive the opposition of the workers to the social and political omnipotence of the bourgeoisie, while it compels the admission that something more is needed than Trades Unions and strikes to break the power of the ruling class. But what gives these Unions and the strikes arising from them their real importance is this, that they are the first attempt of the workers to abolish competition. They imply the recognition of the fact that the supremacy of the bourgeoisie is based wholly upon the competition of the workers among themselves; i.e. upon their want of cohesion. And precisely because the Unions direct themselves against the vital nerve of the present social order, however one-sidedly, in however narrow a way, are they so dangerous to this social order. The working-men cannot attack the bourgeoisie, and with it the whole existing order of society, at any sorer point than this. If the competition of the workers among themselves is destroyed, if all determine not to be further exploited by the bourgeoisie, the rule of property is at an end. Wages depend upon the relation of demand to supply, upon the accidental state of the labour market, simply because the workers have hitherto been content to be treated as chattels, to be bought and sold. The moment the workers resolve to be bought and sold no longer, when in the determination of the value of labour, they take the part of men possessed of a will as well as of working-power, at that moment the whole Political Economy of today is at an end.

The laws determining the rate of wages would, indeed, come into force again in the long run, if the working-men did not go beyond this step of abolishing competition among themselves. But they must go beyond that unless they are prepared to recede again and to allow competition among themselves to reappear. Thus once advanced so far, necessity compels them to go farther; to abolish not only one kind of competition, but competition itself altogether, and that they will do.

The workers are coming to perceive more clearly with every day how competition affects them; they see far more clearly than the bourgeois that competition of the capitalists among themselves presses upon the workers too, by bringing on commercial crises, and that this kind of competition, too, must be abolished. They will soon learn *how* they have to go about it.

That these Unions contribute greatly to nourish the bitter hatred of the workers against the property-holding class need hardly be said. From them proceed, therefore, with or without the connivance of the leading members, in times of unusual excitement, individual actions which can be explained only by hatred wrought to the pitch of despair, by a wild passion overwhelming all restraints. Of this sort are the attacks with vitriol mentioned in the foregoing pages, and a series of others, of which I shall cite several. In 1831, during a violent labour movement, young Ashton, a manufacturer in Hyde, near Manchester, was shot one evening when crossing a field, and no trace of the assassin discovered. There is no doubt that this was a deed of vengeance of the working-men. Incendiarisms and attempted explosions are very common. On Friday, September 29th, 1843, an attempt was made to blow up the saw-works of Padgin, in Howard Street, Sheffield. A closed iron tube filled with powder was the means employed, and the damage was considerable. On the following day, a similar attempt was made in Ibbetson's knife and file works at Shales Moor, near Sheffield. Mr Ibbetson had made himself obnoxious by an active participation in bourgeois movements, by low wages, the exclusive employment of knobsticks, and the exploitation of the Poor Law for his own benefit. He had reported, during the crisis of 1842, such operatives as refused to accept reduced wages, as persons who could find work but would not take it, and were, therefore, not deserving of relief, so compelling the acceptance of a reduction. Considerable damage was inflicted by the explosion, and all the working-men who came to view it regretted only 'that the whole concern was not blown into the air'. On Friday, October 6th, 1844, an attempt to set fire to the factory of Ainsworth and Crompton, at Bolton, did no damage; it was the third or fourth attempt in the same factory within a very short time. In the meeting of the Town Council of Sheffield, on Wednesday, January 10th, 1844, the Commissioner of Police exhibited a cast-iron machine, made for the express purpose of producing an explosion, and found filled with four pounds of powder, and a fuse which had been lighted but had not taken effect, in the works of Mr Kitchen, Earl Street, Sheffield. On Sunday, January 20th, 1844, an explosion caused by a package of powder took place in the sawmill of Bently & White, at Bury, in Lancashire, and produced considerable damage. On Thursday, February 1st, 1844, the Soho Wheel Works, in Sheffield, were set on fire and burnt up.

Here are six such cases in four months, all of which have their sole origin in the embitterment of the working-men against the employers. What sort of a social state it must be in which such things are possible I need hardly say. These facts are proof enough that in England, even in good business years, such as 1843, the social war is avowed and openly carried on, and still the English bourgeoisie does not stop to reflect! But the case which speaks most loudly is that of the Glasgow Thugs,[122] which came up before the Assizes from the 3rd to the 11th of January, 1838. It appears from the proceedings that the Cotton-Spinners' Union, which existed here from the year 1816, possessed rare organisation and power. The members were bound by an oath to adhere to the decision of the majority, and had during every turnout a secret committee which was unknown to the mass of the members, and controlled the funds of the Union absolutely. This committee fixed a price upon the heads of knobsticks and obnoxious manu-facturers and upon incendiarisms in mills. A mill was thus set on fire in which female knobsticks were employed in spinning in the place of men; a Mrs McPherson, mother of one of these girls, was murdered, and both murderers sent to America at the expense of the association. As early as 1820, a knobstick named McQuarry was shot at and wounded, for which deed the doer received twenty pounds from the Union, but was discovered and trans-ported for life. Finally, in 1837, in May, disturbances occurred in consequence of a turnout in the Oatbank and Mile End factories, in which perhaps a dozen knobsticks were maltreated. In July of the same year, the disturbances still continued, and a certain Smith, a knobstick, was so maltreated that he died. The committee was now arrested, an investigation begun, and the leading members found guilty of participation in conspiracies, maltreatment of knobsticks, and incendiarism in the mill of James and Francis Wood, and they were transported for seven years. What do our good Germans say to this story? [123]

The property-holding class, and especially the manufacturing portion of it which comes into direct contact with the working-men, declaims with the greatest violence against these Unions, and is constantly trying to prove their uselessness to the working-men upon grounds which are economically perfectly correct, but for that very reason partially mistaken, and for the working-man's understanding totally without effect. The very zeal of the bourgeoisie shows that it is not disinterested in the matter; and apart from the indirect loss involved in a turnout, the state of the case is such that whatever goes into the pockets of the manufacturers comes of necessity out of those of the worker. So that even if the working-men did not know that the Unions hold the emulation of their masters in the reduction of wages, at least in a measure, in check, they would still stand by the Unions, simply to the injury of their enemies, the manufacturers. In war the injury of one party is the benefit of the other, and since the working-men are on a war-footing towards their employers, they do merely what the great potentates do when they get into a quarrel. Beyond all other bourgeois is our friend Dr Ure, the most furious enemy of the Unions. He foams with indignation at the 'secret tribunals' of the cotton-spinners, the most powerful section of the workers, tribunals which boast their ability to paralyse every disobedient manu-facturer,[124] 'and so bring ruin on the man who had given them profitable employment for many a year.' He speaks of a time [125] 'when the inventive head and the sustaining heart of trade were held in bondage by the unruly lower members.' A pity that the English working-men will not let themselves be pacified so easily with thy fable as the Roman Plebs, thou modern Menenius Agrippa! Finally, he relates the following: at one time the coarse mule-spinners had misused their power beyond all endurance. High wages, instead of awakening thankfulness towards the manu-facturers and leading to intellectual improvement (in harmless study of sciences useful to the bourgeoisie, of course), in many cases produced pride and supplied funds for supporting rebellious spirits in strikes, with which a number of manufacturers were visited one after the other in a purely arbitrary manner. During an unhappy disturbance of this sort in Hyde, Dukinfield, and the surrounding neighbourhood, the manufacturers of the district, anxious lest they should be driven from the market by the French, Belgians, and Americans, addressed themselves to the machine-works of Sharp, Roberts & Co., and requested Mr Sharp to turn his inventive mind to the construction of an automatic mule in order 'to emancipate the trade from galling slavery and impending ruin'.[126]

'He produced in the course of a few months a machine apparently instinct with the thought, feeling, and tact of the experienced workman – which even in its infancy displayed a new principle of regulation, ready in its mature state to fulfil the functions of a finished spinner. Thus the Iron Man, as the operatives fitly call it, sprung out of the hands of our modern Prometheus at the bidding of Minerva – a creation destined to restore order among the industrious classes, and to confirm to Great Britain the empire of art. The news of this Herculean prodigy spread dismay through the Union, and even long before it left its cradle, so to speak, it strangled the Hydra of misrule.' [127]

Ure proves further that the invention of the machine, with which four and five colours are printed at once, was a result of the disturbances among the calico printers; that the refractoriness of the yarn-dressers in the power-loom weaving mills gave rise to a new and perfected machine for warp-dressing, and mentions several other such cases. A few pages earlier this same Ure gives himself a great deal of trouble to prove in detail that machinery is beneficial to the workers! But Ure is not the only one; in the Factory Report, Mr Ashworth, the manufacturer, and many another, lose no opportunity to express their wrath against the Unions. These wise bourgeois, like certain governments, trace every movement which they do not understand, to the influence of ill-intentioned agitators, demagogues, traitors, spouting idiots, and ill-balanced youth. They declare that the paid agents of the Unions are interested in the agitation because they live upon it, as though the necessity for this payment were not forced upon them by the bourgeois, who will give such men no employment!

The incredible frequency of these strikes proves best of all to what extent the social war has broken out all over England. No week passes, scarcely a day, indeed, in which there is not a strike in some direction, now against a reduction, then against a refusal to raise the rate of wages, again by reason of the employment of knobsticks or the continuance of abuses, sometimes against new machinery, or for a hundred other reasons. These strikes, at first skirmishes, sometimes result in weighty struggles; they decide nothing, it is true, but they are the strongest proof that the decisive battle between bourgeoisie and proletariat is approaching. They are the military school of the working-men in which they prepare themselves for the great struggle which cannot be avoided; they are the pronunciamentos of single branches of industry that these too have joined the labour movement. And when one examines a year's file of the *Northern Star*, the only sheet which reports all the movements of the proletariat, one finds that all the proletarians of the towns and of country manufacture have united in associations, and have protested from time to time, by means of a general strike, against the supremacy of the bourgeoisie. And as schools of war, the Unions are unexcelled. In them is developed the peculiar courage of the English. It is said on the Continent that the English, and especially the working-men, are cowardly, that they cannot carry out a revolution because, unlike the French, they do not riot at intervals, because they apparently accept the bourgeois *régime* so quietly. This is a complete mistake. The English working-men are second to none in courage; they are quite as restless as the French, but they fight differently. The French, who are by nature political, struggle against social evils with political weapons; the English, for whom politics exist only as a matter of interest, solely in the interest of bourgeois society, fight, not against the Government, but directly against the bourgeoisie; and for the time, this can be done only in a peaceful manner. Stagnation in business, and the want consequent upon it, engendered the revolt at Lyons, in 1834, in favour of the Republic: in 1842, at Manchester, a similar cause gave rise to a universal turnout for the Charter and higher wages. That courage is required for a turnout, often indeed much loftier courage, much bolder, firmer determination than for an insurrection, is self-evident. It is, in truth, no trifle for a working-man who knows want from experience, to face it with wife and children, to endure hunger and wretchedness for months together, and stand firm and unshaken through it all. What is death, what the galleys which await the French revolutionist, in comparison with gradual starvation, with the daily sight of a starving family, with the certainty of future revenge on the part of the bourgeoisie, all of which the English working-man chooses in preference to subjection under the yoke of the property-holding class? We shall meet later an example of this obstinate, unconquerable courage of men who surrender to force only when all resistance would be aimless and unmeaning. And precisely in this quiet perseverance, in this lasting determination which undergoes a hundred tests every day, the English working-man develops that side of his character which commands most respect. People who endure so much to bend one single bourgeois will be able to break the power of the whole bourgeoisie.

But apart from that, the English working-man has proved his courage often enough. That the turnout of 1842 had no further results came from the fact that the men were in part forced into it by the bourgeoisie, in part neither clear nor united as to its object. But aside from this, they have shown their courage often enough when the matter in question was a specific social one. Not to mention the Welsh insurrection of 1839, a complete battle was waged in Manchester in May, 1843, during my residence there. Pauling & Henfrey, a brick firm, had increased the size of the bricks without raising wages, and sold the bricks, of course, at a higher price. The workers, to whom higher wages were refused, struck work, and the Brickmakers' Union declared war upon the firm. The firm, meanwhile, succeeded with great difficulty in securing hands from the neighbourhood, and among the knobsticks, against whom in the beginning intimidation was used, the proprietors set twelve men to guard the yard, all ex-soldiers and policemen, armed with guns. When intimidation proved unavailing, the brick-yard, which lay scarcely a hundred paces from an infantry barracks, was stormed at ten o'clock one night by a crowd of brickmakers, who advanced in military order, the first ranks armed with guns. They forced their way in, fired upon the watchmen as soon as they saw them, stamped out the wet bricks spread out to dry, tore down the piled-up rows of those already dry, demolished everything which came in their way, pressed into a building, where they destroyed the furniture and maltreated the wife of the overlooker who was living there. The watchmen, meanwhile, had placed themselves behind a hedge, whence they could fire safely and without interruption. The assailants stood before a burning brick-kiln, which threw a bright light upon them, so that every ball of their enemies struck home, while every one of their own shots missed its mark. Nevertheless, the firing lasted half-an-hour, until the ammunition was exhausted, and the object of the visit – the demolition of all the destructible objects in the yard – was attained. Then the military approached, and the brickmakers withdrew to Eccles, three miles from Manchester. A short time before reaching Eccles they held roll-call, and each man was called according to his number in the section when they separated, only to fall the more certainly into the hands of the police, who were approaching from all sides. The number of the wounded must have been very considerable, but those only could be counted who were arrested. One of these had received three bullets (in the thigh, the calf, and the shoulder), and had travelled in spite of them more than four miles on foot. These people have proved that they, too, possess revolutionary courage, and do not shun a rain of bullets. And when an unarmed multitude, without a precise aim common to them all, are held in check in a shut-off market-place, whose outlets are guarded by a couple of policemen and dragoons, as happened in 1842, this by no means proves a want of courage. On the contrary, the multitude would have stirred quite as little if the servants of public (i.e. of the bourgeois) order had not been present. Where the working-people have a specific end in view, they show courage enough; as, for instance, in the attack upon Birley's mill, which had later to be protected by artillery.

In this connection, a word or two as to the respect for the law in England. True, the law is sacred to the bourgeois, for it is his own composition, enacted with his consent, and for his benefit and protection. He knows that, even if an individual law should injure him, the whole fabric protects his interests; and more than all, the sanctity of the law, the sacredness of order as established by the active will of one part of society, and the passive acceptance of the other, is the strongest support of his social position. Because the English bourgeois finds himself reproduced in his law, as he does in his God, the policeman's truncheon which, in a certain measure, is his own club, has for him a wonderfully soothing power. But for the working-man quite otherwise! The working-man knows too well, has learned from too oft-repeated experience, that the law is a rod which the bourgeois has prepared for him; and when he is not compelled to do so, he never appeals to the law. It is ridiculous to assert that the English working-man fears the police, when every week in Manchester policemen are beaten, and last year an attempt was made to storm a station-house secured by iron doors and shutters. The power of the police in the turnout of 1842 lay, as I have already said, in the want of a clearly defined object on the part of the working-men themselves.

Since the working-men do not respect the law, but simply submit to its power when they cannot change it, it is most natural that they should at least propose alterations in it, that they should wish to put a proletarian law in the place of the legal fabric of the bourgeoisie. This proposed law is the People's Charter, which in form is purely political, and demands a democratic basis for the House of Commons. Chartism is the compact form of their opposition to the bourgeoisie. In the Unions and turnouts opposition always remained isolated: it was single working-men or sections who fought a single bourgeois. If the fight became general, this was scarcely by the intention of the working-men; or, when it did happen intentionally, Chartism was at the bottom of it. But in Chartism it is the whole working class which arises against the bourgeoisie, and attacks, first of all, the political power, the legislative rampart with which the bourgeoisie has surrounded itself. Chartism has proceeded from the Democratic party which arose between 1780 and 1790 with and in the proletariat, gained strength during the French Revolution, and came forth after the peace as the Radical party. It had its headquarters then in Birmingham and Manchester, and later in London; extorted the Reform Bill from the Oligarchs of the old Parliament by a union with the Liberal bourgeoisie, and has steadily consolidated itself, since then, as a more and more pronounced working-men's party in opposition to the bourgeoisie In 1835 a committee of the General Workingmen's Association of London, with William Lovett at its head, drew up the People's Charter, whose six points are as follows:

(1) Universal suffrage for every man who is of age, sane and unconvicted of crime;

(2) Annual Parliaments;

(3) Payment of members of Parliament, to enable poor men to stand for election;

(4) Voting by ballot to prevent bribery and intimidation by the bourgeoisie;

(5) Equal electoral districts to secure equal representation; and

(6) Abolition of the even now merely nominal property qualification of 300 pounds in land for candidates in order to make every voter eligible. These six points, which are all limited to the reconstitution of the House of Commons, harmless as they seem, are sufficient to overthrow the whole English Constitution, Queen and Lords included. The so-called monarchical and aristocratic elements of the Constitution can maintain themselves only because the bourgeoisie has an interest in the continuance of their sham existence; and more than a sham existence neither possesses today. But as soon as real public opinion in its totality backs the House of Commons, as soon as the House of Commons incorporates the will, not of the bourgeoisie alone, but of the whole nation, it will absorb the whole power so completely that the last halo must fall from the head of the monarch and the aristocracy. The English working-man respects neither Lords nor Queen. The bourgeois, while in reality allowing them but little influence, yet offers to them personally a sham worship. The English Chartist is politically a republican, though he rarely or never mentions the word, while he sympathises with the republican parties of all countries, and calls himself in preference a democrat. But he is more than a mere republican, his democracy is not simply political.

Chartism was from the beginning in 1835 chiefly a movement among the working-men, though not yet sharply separated from the bourgeoisie. The Radicalism of the workers went hand in hand with the Radicalism of the bourgeoisie; the Charter was the shibboleth of both. They held their National Convention every year in common, seeming to be one party. The lower middle class was just then in a very bellicose and violent state of mind in consequence of the disappointment over the Reform Bill and of the bad business years of 1837–39, and viewed the boisterous Chartist agitation with a very favourable eye. Of the vehemence of this agitation no one in Germany has any idea. The people were called upon to arm themselves, were frequently urged to revolt; pikes were got ready, as in the French Revolution, and in 1838, one Stephens, a Methodist parson, said to the assembled working-people of Manchester: 'You have no need to fear the power of Government, the soldiers, bayonets, and cannon that are at the disposal of your oppressors; you have a weapon that is far mightier than all these, a weapon against which bayonets and cannon are powerless, and a child of ten years can wield it. You have only to take a couple of matches and a bundle of straw dipped in pitch, and I will see what the Government and its hundreds of thousands of soldiers will do against this one weapon if it is used boldly.'

As early as that year the peculiarly social character of the working-men's Chartism manifested itself. The same Stephens said, in a meeting of 200,000 men on Kersall Moor, the Mons Sacer of Manchester: 'Chartism, my friends, is no political movement, where the main point is your getting the ballot. Chartism is a knife and fork question: the Charter means a good house, good food and drink, prosperity, and short working hours.'

The movements against the new Poor Law and for the Ten Hours' Bill were already in the closest relation to Chartism. In all the meetings of that time the Tory Oastler was active, and hundreds of petitions for improvements of the social condition of the workers were circulated along with the national petition for the People's Charter adopted in Birmingham. In 1839 the agitation continued as vigorously as ever, and when it began to relax somewhat at the end of the year, Bussey, Taylor, and Frost hastened to call forth uprisings simultaneously in the North of England, in Yorkshire, and Wales. Frost's plan being betrayed, he was obliged to open hostilities prematurely. Those in the North heard of the failure of his attempt in time to withdraw. Two months later, in January, 1840, several so-called spy outbreaks took place in Sheffield and Bradford, in Yorkshire, and the excitement gradually subsided. Meanwhile the bourgeoisie turned its attention to more practical projects, more profitable for itself, namely the Corn Laws. The Anti-Corn Law Association was formed in Manchester, and the consequence was a relaxation of the tie between the Radical bourgeoisie and the proletariat. The working-men soon perceived that for them the abolition of the Corn Laws could be of little use, while very advantageous to the bourgeoisie; and they could therefore not be won for the project.

The crisis of 1842 came on. Agitation was once more as vigorous as in 1839. But this time the rich manufacturing bourgeoisie, which was suffering severely under this particular crisis, took part in it. The Anti-Corn Law League, as it was now called, assumed a decidedly revolutionary tone. Its journals and agitators used undisguisedly revolutionary language, one very good reason for which was the fact that the Conservative party had been in power since 1841. As the Chartists had previously done, these bourgeois leaders called upon the people to rebel; and the working-men who had most to suffer from the crisis were not inactive, as the year's national petition for the charter with its three and a half million signatures proves. In short, if the two Radical parties had been somewhat estranged, they allied themselves once more. At a meeting of Liberals and Chartists held in Manchester, February 15th, 1842, a petition urging the repeal of the Corn Laws and the adoption of the Charter was drawn up. The next day it was adopted by both parties. The spring and summer passed amidst violent agitation and increasing distress. The bourgeoisie was determined to carry the repeal of the Corn Laws with the help of the crisis, the want which it entailed, and the general excitement. At this time, the Conservatives being in power, the Liberal bourgeoisie half abandoned their law-abiding habits; they wished to bring about a revolution with the help of the workers. The working-men were to take the chestnuts from the fire to save the bourgeoisie from burning their own fingers. The old idea of a 'holy month', a general strike, broached in 1839 by the Chartists, was revived. This time, however, it was not the working-men who wished to quit work, but the manufacturers who wished to close their mills and send the operatives into the country parishes upon the property of the aristocracy, thus forcing the Tory Parliament and the Tory Ministry to repeal the Corn Laws. A revolt would naturally have followed, but the bourgeoisie stood safely in the background and could await the result without compromising itself if the worst came to the worst. At the end of July business began to improve; it was high time. In order not to lose the opportunity, three firms in Staleybridge reduced wages in spite of the improvement.[128] Whether they did so of their own motion or in agreement with other manufacturers, especially those of the League, I do not know. Two withdrew after a time, but the third, William Bailey & Brothers, stood firm, and told the objecting operatives that 'if this did not please them, they had better go and play a bit.' This contemptuous answer the hands received with cheers. They left the mill, paraded through the town, and called upon all their fellows to quit work. In a few hours every mill stood idle, and the operatives marched to Mottram Moor to hold a meeting. This was on August 5th. August 8th they proceeded to Ashton and Hyde five thousand strong, closed all the mills and coal-pits, and held meetings, in which, however, the question discussed was not, as the bourgeoisie had hoped, the repeal of the Corn Laws, but, 'a fair day's wages for a fair day's work.' August 9th they proceeded to Manchester, unresisted by the authorities (all Liberals), and closed the mills; on the 11th they were in Stockport, where they met with the first resistance as they were storming the workhouse, the favourite child of the bourgeoisie. On the same day there was a general strike and disturbance in Bolton, to which the authorities here, too, made no resistance. Soon the uprising spread throughout the whole manufacturing district, and all employments, except harvesting and the production of food, came to a standstill. But the rebellious operatives were quiet. They were driven into this revolt without wishing it. The manufacturers, with the single exception of the Tory Birley, in Manchester, had, *contrary to their custom*, not opposed it. The thing had begun without the working-men's having any distinct end in view, for which reason they were all united in the determination not to be shot at for the benefit of the Corn Law repealing bourgeoisie. For the rest, some wanted to carry the Charter, others who thought this premature wished merely to secure the wages rate of 1840. On this point the whole insurrection was wrecked. If it had been from the beginning an intentional, determined working-men's insurrection, it would surely have carried its point; but these crowds who had been driven into the streets by their masters, against their own will, and with no definite purpose, could do nothing. Meanwhile the bourgeoisie, which had not moved a finger to carry the alliance of February 10th into effect, soon perceived that the working-men did not propose to become its tools, and that the illogical manner in which it had abandoned its law-abiding standpoint threatened danger. It therefore resumed its law-abiding attitude, and placed itself upon the side of Government as against the working-men.

It swore in trusty retainers as special constables (the German merchants in Manchester took part in this ceremony, and marched in an entirely superfluous manner through the city with their cigars in their mouths and thick truncheons in their hands). It gave the command to fire upon the crowd in Preston, so that the unintentional revolt of the people stood all at once face to face, not only with the whole military power of the Government, but with the whole property-holding class as well. The working-men, who had no especial aim, separated gradually, and the insurrection came to an end without evil results. Later, the bourgeoisie was guilty of one shameful act after another, tried to whitewash itself by expressing a horror of popular violence by no means consistent with its own revolutionary language of the spring; laid the blame of insurrection upon Chartist instigators, whereas it had itself done more than all of them together to bring about the uprising; and resumed its old attitude of sanctifying the name of the law, with a shamelessness perfectly unequalled. The Chartists, who were all but innocent of bringing about this uprising, who simply did what the bourgeoisie meant to do when they made the most of their opportunity, were prosecuted and convicted, while the bourgeoisie escaped without loss, and had, besides, sold off its old stock of goods with advantage during the pause in work.

The fruit of the uprising was the decisive separation of the proletariat from the bourgeoisie. The Chartists had not hitherto concealed their determination to carry the Charter at all costs, even that of a revolution; the bourgeoisie, which now perceived, all at once, the danger with which any violent change threatened its position, refused to hear anything further of physical force, and proposed to attain its end by moral force, as though this were anything else than the direct or indirect threat of physical force. This was one point of dissension, though even this was removed later by the assertion of the Chartists (who are at least as worthy of being believed as the bourgeoisie) that they, too, refrained from appealing to physical force. The second point of dissension and the main one, which brought Chartism to light in its purity, was the repeal of the Corn Laws. In this the bourgeoisie was directly interested, the proletariat not. The Chartists therefore divided into two parties whose political programmes agreed literally, but which were nevertheless thoroughly different and incapable of union. At the Birmingham National Convention, in January, 1843, Sturge, the representative of the Radical bourgeoisie, proposed that the name of the Charter be omitted from the rules of the Chartist Association, nominally because this name had become connected with recollections of violence during the insurrection, a connection, by the way, which had existed for years, and against which Mr Sturge had hitherto advanced no objection. The working-men refused to drop the name, and when Mr Sturge was outvoted, that worthy Quaker suddenly became loyal, betook himself out of the hall, and founded a 'Complete Suffrage Association' within the Radical bourgeoisie. So repugnant had these recollections become to the Jacobinical bourgeoisie, that he altered even the name Universal Suffrage into the ridiculous title, Complete Suffrage. The working-men laughed at him and quietly went their way.

From this moment Chartism was purely a working-man's cause freed from all bourgeois elements. The 'Complete' journals, the Weekly Dispatch, Weekly Chronicle, Examiner, etc., fell gradually into the sleepy tone of the other Liberal sheets, espoused the cause of Free Trade, attacked the Ten Hours' Bill and all exclusively working-men's demands, and let their Radicalism as a whole fall rather into the background. The Radical bourgeoisie joined hands with the Liberals against the working-men in every collision, and in general made the Corn Law question, which for the English is the Free Trade question, their main business. They thereby fell under the dominion of the Liberal bourgeoisie, and now play a most pitiful role.

The Chartist working-men, on the contrary, espoused with redoubled zeal all the struggles of the proletariat against the bourgeoisie. Free competition has caused the workers suffering enough to be hated by them; its apostles, the bourgeoisie, are their declared enemies. The working-man has only disadvantages to await from the complete freedom of competition. The demands hitherto made by him, the Ten Hours' Bill, protection of the workers against the capitalist, good wages, a guaranteed position, repeal of the new Poor Law, all of the things which belong to Chartism quite as essentially as the 'Six Points', are directly opposed to free competition and Free Trade. No wonder, then, that the working-men will not hear of Free Trade and the repeal of the Corn Laws (a fact incomprehensible to the whole English bourgeoisie), and while at least wholly indifferent to the Corn Law question, are most deeply embittered against its advocates. This question is precisely the point at which the proletariat separates from the bourgeoisie, Chartism from Radicalism; and the bourgeois understanding cannot comprehend this, because it cannot comprehend the proletariat.

Therein lies the difference between Chartist democracy and all previous political bourgeois democracy. Chartism is of an essentially social nature, a class movement. The 'Six Points' which for the Radical bourgeois are the beginning and end of the matter, which are meant, at the utmost, to call forth certain further reforms of the Constitution, are for the proletarian a mere means to further ends. 'Political power our means, social happiness our end', is now the clearly formulated war-cry of the Chartists. The 'knife and fork question' of the preacher Stephens was a truth for a part of the Chartists only, in 1838; it is a truth for all of them in 1845. There is no longer a mere politician among the Chartists, and even though their Socialism is very little developed, though their chief remedy for poverty has hitherto consisted in the land-allotment system, which was superseded[129] by the introduction of manufacture, though their chief practical propositions are apparently of a reactionary nature, yet these very measures involve the alternative that they must either succumb to the power of competition once more and restore the old state of things, or they must themselves entirely overcome competition and abolish it. On the other hand, the present indefinite state of Chartism, the separation from the purely political party, involves that precisely the characteristic feature, its social aspect, will have to be further developed. The approach to Socialism cannot fail, especially when the next crisis directs the working-men by force of sheer want to social instead of political remedies. And a crisis must follow the present active state of industry and commerce in 1847 at the latest, and probably in 1846; one, too, which will far exceed in extent and violence all former crises. The working-men will carry their Charter, naturally; but meanwhile they will learn to see clearly with regard to many points which they can make by means of it and of which they now know very little.

Meanwhile the socialist agitation also goes forward. English Socialism comes under our consideration so far only as it affects the working class. The English Socialists demand the gradual introduction of possession in common in home colonies embracing two to three thousand persons who shall carry on both agriculture and manufacture and enjoy equal rights and equal education. They demand greater facility of obtaining divorce, the establishment of a rational government, with complete freedom of conscience and the abolition of punishment, the same to be replaced by a rational treatment of the offender. These are their practical measures, their theoretical principles do not concern us here. English Socialism arose with Owen, a manufacturer, and proceeds therefore with great consideration toward the bourgeoisie and great injustice toward the proletariat in its methods, although it culminates in demanding the abolition of the class antagonism between bourgeoisie and proletariat.

The Socialists are thoroughly tame and peaceable, accept our existing order, bad as it is, so far as to reject all other methods but that of winning public opinion. Yet they are so dogmatic that success by this method is for them, and for their principles as at present formulated, utterly hopeless. While bemoaning the demoralisation of the lower classes, they are blind to the element of progress in this dissolution of the old social order, and refuse to acknowledge that the corruption wrought by private interests and hypocrisy in the property-holding class is much greater. They acknowledge no historic development, and wish to place the nation in a state of Communism at once, overnight, not by the unavoidable march of its political development up to the point at which this transition becomes both possible and necessary. They understand, it is true, why the working-man is resentful against the bourgeois, but regard as unfruitful this class hatred, which is, after all, the only moral incentive by which the worker can be brought nearer the goal. They preach instead, a philanthropy and universal love far more unfruitful for the present state of England. They acknowledge only a psychological development, a development of man in the abstract, out of all relation to the Past, whereas the whole world rests upon that Past, the individual man included. Hence they are too abstract, too metaphysical, and accomplish little. They are recruited in part from the working class, of which they have enlisted but a very small fraction representing, however, its most educated and solid elements. In its present form, Socialism can never become the common creed of the working class; it must condescend to return for a moment to the Chartist standpoint. But the true proletarian Socialism having passed through Chartism, purified of its bourgeois elements, assuming the form which it has already reached in the minds of many Socialists and Chartist leaders (who are nearly all Socialists), must, within a short time, play a weighty part in the history of the development of the English people. English Socialism, the basis of which is much more ample than that of the French, is behind it in theoretical development, will have to recede for a moment to the French standpoint in order to proceed beyond it later. Meanwhile the French, too, will develop farther. English Socialism affords the most pronounced expression of the prevailing absence of religion among the working-men, an expression so pronounced indeed that the mass of the working-men, being unconsciously and mere-ly practically irreligious, often draw back before it. But here, too, necessity will force the working-men to abandon the remnants of a belief which, as they will more and more clearly perceive, serves only to make them weak and resigned to their fate, obedient and faithful to the vampire property-holding class.

Hence it is evident that the working-men's movement is divided into two sections, the Chartists and the Socialists. The Chartists are theoretically the more backward, the less developed, but they are genuine proletarians all over, the representatives of their class. The Socialists are more far-seeing, propose practical remedies against distress, but, proceeding originally from the bourgeoisie, are for this reason unable to amalgamate completely with the working class. The union of Socialism with Chartism, the reproduction of French Communism in an English manner, will be the next step, and has already begun. Then only, when this has been achieved, will the working class be the true intellectual leader of England. Meanwhile, political and social development will proceed, and will foster this new party, this new departure of Chartism.

These different sections of working-men, often united, often separated, Trades Unionists, Chartists, and Socialists, have founded on their own hook numbers of schools and reading-rooms for the advancement of education. Every Socialist, and almost every

Chartist institution, has such a place, and so too have many trades. Here the children receive a purely proletarian education, free from all the influences of the bourgeoisie; and, in the reading-rooms, proletarian journals and books alone, or almost alone, are to be found. These arrangements are very dangerous for the bourgeoisie, which has succeeded in withdrawing several such institutes, 'Mechanics' Institutes', from proletarian influences, and making them organs for the dissemination of the sciences useful to the bourgeoisie. Here the natural sciences are now taught, which may draw the working-men away from the opposition to the bourgeoisie, and perhaps place in their hands the means of making inventions which bring in money for the bourgeoisie; while for the working-man the acquaintance with the natural sciences is utterly useless *now* when it too often happens that he never gets the slightest glimpse of Nature in his large town with his long working hours. Here Political Economy is preached, whose idol is free competition, and whose sum and substance for the working-man is this, that he cannot do anything more rational than resign himself to starvation. Here all education is tame, flabby, subservient to the ruling politics and religion, so that for the working-man it is merely a constant sermon upon quiet obedience, passivity, and resignation to his fate.

The mass of working-men naturally have nothing to do with these institutes, and betake themselves to the proletarian reading-rooms and to the discussion of matters which directly concern their own interests, whereupon the self-sufficient bourgeoisie says its *Dixi et Salvavi*, and turns with contempt from a class which 'prefers the angry ranting of ill-meaning demagogues to the advantages of solid education'. That, however, the working-men appreciate solid education when they can get it unmixed with the interested cant of the bourgeoisie, the frequent lectures upon scientific, aesthetic, and economic subjects prove which are delivered especially in the Socialist institutes, and very well attended. I have often heard working-men, whose fustian jackets scarcely held together, speak upon geological, astronomical, and other subjects, with more knowledge than most 'cultivated' bourgeois in Germany possess. And in how great a measure the English proletariat has succeeded in attaining independent education is shown especially by the fact that the epoch-making products of modern philosophical, political, and poetical literature are read by working-men almost exclusively. The bourgeois, enslaved by social conditions and the prejudices involved in them, trembles, blesses, and crosses himself before everything which really paves the way for progress; the proletarian has open eyes for it, and studies it with pleasure and success. In this respect the Socialists, especially, have done wonders for the education of the proletariat. They have translated the French materialists, Helvetius, Holbach, Diderot, etc., and disseminated them, with the best English works, in cheap editions. Strauss's *Life of Jesus* and Proudhon's *Property* also circulate among the working-men only. Shelley, the genius, the prophet, Shelley, and Byron, with his glowing sensuality and his bitter satire upon our existing society, find most of their readers in the proletariat; the bourgeoisie owns only castrated editions, family editions, cut down in accordance with the hypocritical morality of today. The two great practical philosophers of latest date, Bentham and Godwin, are, especially the latter, almost exclusively the property of the proletariat; for though Bentham has a school within the Radical bourgeoisie, it is only the proletariat and the Socialists who have succeeded in developing his teachings a step forward. The proletariat has formed upon this basis a literature, which consists chiefly of journals and pamphlets, and is far in advance of the whole bourgeois literature in intrinsic worth. On this point more later.

One more point remains to be noticed. The factory operatives, and especially those of the cotton district, form the nucleus of the labour movement. Lancashire, and especially Manchester, is the seat of the most powerful Unions, the central point of Chartism, the place which numbers most Socialists. The more the factory system has taken possession of a branch of industry, the more the working-men employed in it participate in the labour movement; the sharper the opposition between working-men and capitalists, the clearer the proletarian consciousness in the working-men. The small masters of Birmingham, though they suffer from the crises, still stand upon an unhappy middle ground between proletarian Chartism and shopkeepers' Radicalism. But, in general, all the workers employed in manufacture are won for one form or the other of resistance to capital and bourgeoisie; and all are united upon this point, that they, as working-men, a title of which they are proud, and which is the usual form of address in Chartist meetings, form a separate class, with separate interests and principles, with a separate way of looking at things in contrast with that of all property-owners; and that in this class reposes the strength and the capacity of development of the nation.

The Mining Proletariat

The production of raw materials and fuel for a manufacture so colossal as that of England requires a considerable number of workers. But of all the materials needed for its industries (except wool, which belongs to the agricultural districts), England produces only the minerals: the metals and the coal. While Cornwall possesses rich copper, tin, zinc, and lead mines, Staffordshire, Wales, and other districts yield great quantities of iron, and almost the whole North and West of England, central Scotland, and certain districts of Ireland, produce a superabundance of coal.[130]

In the Cornish mines about 19,000 men, and 11,000 women and children are employed, in part above and in part below ground. Within the mines below ground, men and boys above twelve years old are employed almost exclusively. The condition of these workers seems, according to the Children's Employment Commission's Reports, to be comparatively endurable, materially, and the English often enough boast of their strong, bold miners, who follow the veins of mineral below the bottom of the very sea. But in the matter of the health of these workers, this same Children's Employment Commission's Report judges differently. It shows in Dr Barham's intelligent report how the inhalation of an atmosphere containing little oxygen, and mixed with dust and the smoke of blasting powder, such as prevails in the mines, seriously affects the lungs, disturbs the action of the heart, and diminishes the activity of the digestive organs; that wearing toil, and especially the climbing up and down of ladders, upon which even vigorous young men have to spend in some mines more than an hour a day, and which precedes and follows daily work, contributes greatly to the development of these evils, so that men who begin this work in early youth are far from reaching the stature of women who work above ground; that many die young of galloping consumption, and most miners at middle age of slow consumption, that they age prematurely and become unfit for work between the thirty-fifth and forty-fifth years, that many are attacked by acute inflammations of the respiratory organs when exposed to the sudden change from the warm air of the shaft (after climbing the ladder in profuse perspiration), to the cold wind above ground, and that these acute inflammations are very frequently fatal. Work above ground, breaking and sorting the ore, is done by girls and children, and is described as very wholesome, being done in the open air.

In the North of England, on the borders of Northumberland and Durham, are the extensive lead mines of Alston Moor. The reports from this district [131] agree almost wholly with those from Cornwall. Here, too, there are complaints of want of oxygen, excessive dust, powder smoke, carbonic acid gas, and sulphur, in the atmosphere of the workings. In consequence, the miners here, as in Cornwall, are small of stature, and nearly all suffer from the thirtieth year throughout life from chest affections, which end, especially when this work is persisted in, as is almost always the case, in consumption, so greatly shortening the average of life of these people. If the miners of this district are somewhat longer-lived than those of Cornwall, this is the case, because they do not enter the mines before reaching the nineteenth year, while in Cornwall, as we have seen, this work is begun in the twelfth year. Nevertheless, the majority die here, too, between forty and fifty years of age, according to medical testimony. Of 79 miners, whose death was entered upon the public register of the district, and who attained an average of 45 years, 37 had died of consumption and 6 of asthma. In the surrounding districts, Allendale, Stanhope, and Middleton, the average length of life was 49, 48, and 47 years respectively, and the deaths from chest affections composed 48, 54, and 56 per cent. of the whole number. Let us compare these figures with the so-called Swedish tables, detailed tables of mortality embracing all the inhabitants of Sweden, and recognised in England as the most correct standard hitherto attainable for the average length of life of the British working class. According to them, male persons who survive the nineteenth year attain an average of 57.5 years; but, according to this, the North of England miners are robbed by their work of an average of ten years of life. Yet the Swedish tables are accepted as the standard of longevity of the *workers* and present, therefore, the average chances of life as affected by the unfavourable conditions in which the proletariat lives, a standard of longevity less than the normal one. In this district we find again the lodging-houses and sleeping-places with which we have already become acquainted in the towns, and in quite as filthy, disgusting, and overcrowded a state as there. Commissioner Mitchell visited one such sleeping barrack, 18 feet long, 13 feet wide, and arranged for the reception of 42 men and 14 boys, or 56 persons altogether, one-half of whom slept above the other in berths as on shipboard. There was no opening for the escape of the foul air; and, although no one had slept in this pen for three nights preceding the visit, the smell and the atmosphere were such that Commissioner Mitchell could not endure it a moment. What must it be through a hot summer night, with fifty-six occupants? And this is not the steerage of an American slave ship, it is the dwelling of free-born Britons!

Let us turn now to the most important branch of British mining, the iron and coal mines, which the Children's Employment Commission treats in common, and with all the detail which the importance of the subject demands. Nearly the whole of the first part of this report is devoted to the condition of the workers employed in these mines. After the detailed description which I have furnished of the state of the industrial workers, I shall, however, be able to be as brief in dealing with this subject as the scope of the present work requires.

In the coal and iron mines which are worked in pretty much the same way, children of four, five, and seven years are employed. They are set to transporting the ore or coal loosened by the miner from its place to the horse-path or the main shaft, and to opening and shutting the doors (which separate the divisions of the mine and regulate its ventilation) for the passage of workers and material. For watching the doors the smallest children are usually employed, who thus pass twelve hours daily, in the dark, alone, sitting usually in damp passages without even having work enough to save them from the stupefying, brutalising tedium of doing nothing. The transport of coal and iron-stone, on the other hand, is very hard labour, the stuff being shoved in large tubs, without wheels, over the uneven floor of the mine; often over moist clay, or through water, and frequently up steep inclines and through paths so low-roofed that the workers are forced to creep on hands and knees. For this more wearing labour, therefore, older children and half-grown girls are employed. One man or two boys per tub are employed, according to circumstances; and, if two boys, one pushes and the other pulls. The loosening of the ore or coal, which is done by men or strong youths of sixteen years or more, is also very weary work. The usual working day is eleven to twelve hours, often longer; in Scotland it reaches fourteen hours, and double time is frequent, when all the employees are at work below ground twenty-four, and even thirty-six hours at a stretch. Set times for meals are almost unknown, so that these people eat when hunger and time permit.

The standard of living of the miners is in general described as fairly good and their wages high in comparison with those of the agricultural labourers surrounding them (who, however, live at starvation rates), except in certain parts of Scotland and in the Irish mines, where great misery prevails. We shall have occasion to return later to this statement, which, by the way, is merely relative, implying comparison to the poorest class in all England. Meanwhile, we shall consider the evils which arise from the present method of mining, and the reader may judge whether any pay in money can indemnify the miner for such suffering.

The children and young people who are employed in transporting coal and iron-stone all complain of being over-tired. Even in the most recklessly conducted industrial establishments there is no such universal and exaggerated overwork. The whole report proves this, with a number of examples on every page. It is constantly happening that children throw themselves down on the stone hearth or the floor as soon as they reach home, fall asleep at once without being able to take a bite of food, and have to be washed and put to bed while asleep; it even happens that they lie down on the way home, and are found by their parents late at night asleep on the road. It seems to be a universal practice among these children to spend Sunday in bed to recover in some degree from the over-exertion of the week. Church and school are visited by but few, and even of these the teachers complain of their great sleepiness and the want of all eagerness to learn. The same thing is true of the elder girls and women. They are overworked in the most brutal manner. This weariness, which is almost always carried to a most painful pitch, cannot fail to affect the constitution. The

first result of such over-exertion is the diversion of vitality to the
one sided development of the muscles, so that those especially of
the arms, legs, and back, of the shoulders and chest, which are
chiefly called into activity in pushing and pulling, attain an un-
commonly vigorous development, while all the rest of the body
suffers and is atrophied from want of nourishment. More than
all else the stature suffers, being stunted and retarded; nearly all
miners are short, except those of Leicestershire and Warwickshire,
who work under exceptionally favourable conditions. Further,
among boys as well as girls, puberty is retarded, among the former
often until the eighteenth year; indeed, a nineteen years old boy
appeared before Commissioner Symonds, showing no evidence
beyond that of the teeth, that he was more than eleven or twelve
years old. This prolongation of the period of childhood is at
bottom nothing more than a sign of checked development, which
does not fail to bear fruit in later years. Distortions of the legs,
knees bent inwards and feet bent outwards, deformities of the
spinal column and other malformations, appear the more readily in
constitutions thus weakened, in consequence of the almost universally constrained position during work; and they are so frequent
that in Yorkshire and Lancashire, as in Northumberland and
Durham, the assertion is made by many witnesses, not only by
physicians, that a miner may be recognised by his shape among a
hundred other persons. The women seem to suffer especially from
this work, and are seldom, if ever, as straight as other women.
There is testimony here, too, to the fact that deformities of the
pelvis and consequent difficult, even fatal, childbearing arise from
the work of women in the mines. But apart from these local
deformities, the coal miners suffer from a number of special
affections easily explained by the nature of the work. Diseases of
the digestive organs are first in order; want of appetite, pains in the
stomach, nausea, and vomiting, are most frequent, with violent
thirst, which can be quenched only with the dirty, lukewarm
water of the mine; the digestion is checked and all the other
affections are thus invited. Diseases of the heart, especially hyper-
trophy, inflammation of the heart and pericardium, contraction
of the *auriculo-ventricular* communications and the entrance of
the *aorta* are also mentioned repeatedly as diseases of the miners,
and are readily explained by overwork; and the same is true of

the almost universal rupture which is a direct consequence of protracted over-exertion. In part from the same cause and in part from the bad, dust-filled atmosphere mixed with carbonic acid and hydrocarbon gas, which might so readily be avoided, there arise numerous painful and dangerous affections of the lungs, especially asthma, which in some districts appears in the fortieth, in others in the thirtieth year in most of the miners, and makes them unfit for work in a short time. Among those employed in wet workings the oppression in the chest naturally appears much earlier; in some districts of Scotland between the twentieth and thirtieth years, during which time the affected lungs are especially susceptible to inflammations and diseases of a feverish nature. The peculiar disease of workers of this sort is 'black spittle', which arises from the saturation of the whole lung with coal particles, and manifests itself in general debility, headache, oppression of the chest, and thick, black mucous expectoration. In some districts this disease appears in a mild form; in others, on the contrary, it is wholly incurable, especially in Scotland. Here, besides the symptoms just mentioned, which appear in an intensified form, short, wheezing, breathing, rapid pulse (exceeding 100 per minute), and abrupt coughing, with increasing leanness and debility, speedily make the patient unfit for work. Every case of this disease ends fatally. Dr Mackellar, in Pencaitland, East Lothian, testified that in all the coal mines which are properly ventilated this disease is unknown, while it frequently happens that miners who go from well- to ill-ventilated mines are seized by it. The profit-greed of mine-owners which prevents the use of ventilators is therefore responsible for the fact that this working-men's disease exists at all. Rheumatism too, is, with the exception of the Warwick and Leicestershire workers, a universal disease of the coal miners, and arises especially from the frequently damp working-places. The consequence of all these diseases is that, in all districts *without exception*, the coal miners age early and become unfit for work soon after the fortieth year, though this is different in different places. A coal miner who can follow his calling after the 45th or 50th year is a very great rarity indeed. It is universally recognised that such workers enter upon old age at forty. This applies to those who loosen the coal from the bed; the loaders, who have constantly to lift heavy blocks of coal into the tubs, age with the twenty-eighth or thirtieth year, so that it is proverbial in the coal mining districts that the loaders are old before they are young. That this premature old age is followed by the early death of the colliers is a matter of course, and a man who reaches sixty is a great exception among them. Even in South Staffordshire, where the mines are comparatively wholesome, few men reach their fifty-first year. Along with this early superannuation of the workers we naturally find, just as in the case of the mills, frequent lack of employment of the elder men, who are often supported by very young children. If we sum up briefly the results of the work in coal mines, we find, as Dr Southwood Smith, one of the commissioners, does, that through prolonged childhood on the one hand and premature age on the other, that period of life in which the human being is in full possession of his powers, the period of manhood, is greatly shortened, while the length of life in general is below the average. This, too, on the debit side of the bourgeoisie's reckoning!

All this deals only with the average of the English coal mines. But there are many in which the state of things is much worse, those, namely, in which thin seams of coal are worked. The coal would be too expensive if a part of the adjacent sand and clay were removed; so the mine-owners permit only the seams to be worked; whereby the passages which elsewhere are four or five feet high and more are here kept so low that to stand upright in them is not to be thought of. The working-man lies on his side and loosens the coal with his pick; resting upon his elbow as a pivot, whence follow inflammations of the joint, and in cases where he is forced to kneel, of the knee also. The women and children who have to transport the coal crawl upon their hands and knees, fastened to the tub by a harness and chain (which frequently passes between the legs), while a man behind pushes with hands and head. The pushing with the head engenders local irritations, painful swellings, and ulcers. In many cases, too, the shafts are wet, so that these workers have to crawl through dirty or salt water several inches deep, being thus exposed to a special irritation of the skin. It can be readily imagined how greatly the diseases already peculiar to the miners are fostered by this especially frightful, slavish toil.

But these are not all the evils which descend upon the head of the coal miner. In the whole British Empire there is no occupation in which a man may meet his end in so many diverse ways as in this one. The coal mine is the scene of a multitude of the most terrifying calamities, and these come directly from the selfishness of the bourgeoisie. The hydrocarbon gas which develops so freely in these mines, forms, when combined with atmospheric air, an explosive which takes fire upon coming into contact with a flame, and kills everyone within its reach. Such explosions take place, in one mine or another, nearly every day; on September 28th, 1844, one killed 96 men in Haswell Colliery, Durham. The carbonic acid gas, which also develops in great quantities, accumulates in the deeper parts of the mine, frequently reaching the height of a man, and suffocates everyone who gets into it. The doors which separate the sections of the mines are meant to prevent the propagation of explosions and the movement of the gases; but since they are entrusted to small children, who often fall asleep or neglect them, this means of prevention is illusory. A proper ventilation of the mines by means of fresh air-shafts could almost entirely remove the injurious effects of both these gases. But for this purpose the bourgeoisie has no money to spare, preferring to command the working-men to use the Davy lamp, which is wholly useless because of its dull light, and is, therefore, usually replaced by a candle. If an explosion occurs, the recklessness of the miner is blamed, though the bourgeois might have made the explosion well-nigh impossible by supplying good ventilation. Further, every few days the roof of a working falls in, and buries or mangles the workers employed in it. It is the interest of the bourgeois to have the seams worked out as completely as possible, and hence the accidents of this sort. Then, too, the ropes by which the men descend into the mines are often rotten, and break, so that the unfortunates fall, and are crushed. All these accidents, and I have no room for special cases, carry off yearly, according to the *Mining Journal*, some fourteen hundred human beings. The *Manchester Guardian* reports at least two or three accidents every week for Lancashire alone. In nearly all mining districts the people composing the coroner's juries are, in almost all cases, dependent upon the mine-owners, and where this is not the case, immemorial custom ensures that the verdict shall be: 'Accidental Death'. Besides, the jury takes very little interest in the state of the mine, because it does not understand anything about the matter. But the Children's Employment Commission does not hesitate to make the mine-owners directly responsible for the greater number of these cases.

As to the education and morals of the mining population, they are, according to the Children's Employment Commission, pretty good in Cornwall, and excellent in Alston Moor; in the coal districts, in general, they are, on the contrary, reported as on an excessively low plane. The workers live in the country in neglected regions, and if they do their weary work, no human being outside the police force troubles himself about them. Hence, and from the tender age at which children are put to work, it follows that their mental education is wholly neglected. The day schools are not within their reach, the evening and Sunday schools mere shams, the teachers worthless. Hence, few can read and still fewer write. The only point upon which their eyes are as yet open is the fact that their wages are far too low for their hateful and dangerous work. To church they go seldom or never; all the clergy complain of their irreligion as beyond comparison. As a matter of fact, their ignorance of religious and of secular things, alike, is such that the ignorance of the factory operatives, shown in numerous examples in the foregoing pages, is trifling in comparison with it. The categories of religion are known to them only from the terms of their oaths. Their morality is destroyed by their work itself. That the overwork of all miners must engender drunkenness is self-evident. As to their sexual relations, men, women, and children work in the mines, in many cases, wholly naked, and in most cases, nearly so, by reason of the prevailing heat, and the consequences in the dark, lonely mines may be imagined. The number of illegitimate children is here disproportionately large, and indicates what goes on among the half-savage population below ground; but proves too, that the illegitimate intercourse of the sexes has not here, as in the great cities, sunk to the level of prostitution. The labour of women entails the same consequences as in the factories, dissolves the family, and makes the mother totally incapable of household work.

When the Children's Employment Commission's Report was laid before Parliament, Lord Ashley hastened to bring in a bill wholly forbidding the work of women in the mines, and greatly limiting that of children. The bill was adopted, but has remained a dead letter in most districts, because no mine inspectors were appointed to watch over its being carried into effect. The evasion of the law is very easy in the country districts in which the mines are situated; and no one need be surprised that the Miners' Union laid before the Home Secretary an official notice, last year, that in the Duke of Hamilton's coal mines in Scotland, more than sixty women were at work; or that the *Manchester Guardian* reported that a girl perished in an explosion in a mine near Wigan, and no one troubled himself further about the fact that an infringement of the law was thus revealed. In single cases the employment of women may have been discontinued, but in general the old state of things remains as before.

These are, however, not all the afflictions known to the coal miners. The bourgeoisie, not content with ruining the health of these people, keeping them in danger of sudden loss of life, robbing them of all opportunity for education, plunders them in other directions in the most shameless manner. The truck system is here the rule, not the exception, and is carried on in the most direct and undisguised manner. The cottage system, likewise, is universal, and here almost a necessity; but it is used here, too, for the better plundering of the workers. To these means of oppression must be added all sorts of direct cheating. While coal is sold by weight, the worker's wages are reckoned chiefly by measure; and when his tub is not perfectly full he receives no pay whatever, while he gets not a farthing for over-measure. If there is more than a specified quantity of dust in the tub, a matter which depends much less upon the miner than upon the nature of the seam, he not only loses his whole wage but is fined besides. The fine system in general is so highly perfected in the coal mines, that a poor devil who has worked the whole week and comes for his wages, sometimes learns from the overseer, who fine at discretion and without summoning the workers, that he not only has no wages but must pay so and so much in fines extra! The overseer has, in general, absolute power over wages; he notes the work done, and can please himself as to what he pays the worker, who is forced to take his word. In some mines, where the pay is according to weight, false decimal scales are used, whose weights are not subject to the inspection of the authorities; in one coal mine there was actually a regulation that any workman who intended to complain of the falseness of the scales *must give notice to the overseer*

three weeks in advance! In many districts, especially in the North of
England, it is customary to engage the workers by the year; they
pledge themselves to work for no other employer during that
time, but the mine-owner by no means pledges himself to give
them work, so that they are often without it for months together,
and if they seek elsewhere, they are sent to the treadmill for six
weeks for breach of contract. In other contracts, work to the
amount of 26s. every 14 days, is promised the miners, but not
furnished, in others still, the employers advance the miners small
sums to be worked out afterwards, thus binding the debtors to
themselves. In the North, the custom is general of keeping the
payment of wages one week behindhand, chaining the miners in
this way to their work. And to complete the slavery of these
enthralled workers, nearly all the Justices of the Peace in the coal
districts are mine-owners themselves, or relatives or friends of
mine-owners, and possess almost unlimited power in these poor,
uncivilised regions where there are few newspapers, these few in
the service of the ruling class, and but little other agitation. It is
almost beyond conception how these poor coal miners have been
plundered and tyrannised over by Justices of the Peace acting as
judges in their own cause.

So it went on for a long time. The workers did not know any
better than that they were there for the purpose of being swindled
out of their very lives. But gradually, even among them, and
especially in the factory districts, where contact with the more
intelligent operatives could not fail of its effect, there arose a spirit of
opposition to the shameless oppression of the 'coal kings'. The men
began to form Unions and strike from time to time. In civilised
districts they joined the Chartists body and soul. The great coal
district of the North of England, shut off from all industrial intercourse, remained backward until, after many efforts, partly of the
Chartists and partly of the more intelligent miners themselves, a
general spirit of opposition arose in 1843. Such a movement seized
the workers of Northumberland and Durham that they placed
themselves at the forefront of a general Union of coal miners
throughout the kingdom, and appointed W. P. Roberts, a Chartist
solicitor, of Bristol, their 'Attorney General', he having distinguished himself in earlier Chartist trials. The Union soon spread
over a great majority of the districts; agents were appointed in

all directions, who held meetings everywhere and secured new members; at the first conference of delegates, in Manchester, in 1844, there were 60,000 members represented, and at Glasgow, six months later, at the second conference, 100,000. Here all the affairs of the coal miners were discussed and decisions as to the greater strikes arrived at. Several journals were founded, especially the *Miners' Advocate*, at Newcastle-upon-Tyne, for defending the rights of the miners. On March 31st, 1844, the contracts of all the miners of Northumberland and Durham expired. Roberts was empowered to draw up a new agreement, in which the men demanded:

(1) Payment by weight instead of measure;
(2) Determination of weight by means of ordinary scales subject to the public inspectors;
(3) Half-yearly renewal of contracts;
(4) Abolition of the fines system and payment according to work actually done;
(5) The employers to guarantee to miners in their exclusive service at least four days' work per week, or wages for the same.

This agreement was submitted to the 'coal kings', and a deputation appointed to negotiate with them; they answered, however, that for them the Union did not exist, that they had to deal with single workmen only, and should never recognise the Union. They also submitted an agreement of their own which ignored all the foregoing points, and was, naturally, refused by the miners. War was thus declared. On March 31st, 1844, 40,000 miners laid down their picks, and every mine in the county stood empty. The funds of the Union were so considerable that for several months a weekly contribution of 2s. 6d. could be assured to each family. While the miners were thus putting the patience of their masters to the test, Roberts organised with incomparable perseverance both strike and agitation, arranged for the holding of meetings, traversed England from one end to the other, preached peaceful and legal agitation, and carried on a crusade against the despotic Justices of the Peace and truck masters, such as had never been known in England. This he had begun at the beginning of the year. Wherever a miner had been condemned by a Justice of the Peace, he obtained a *habeas corpus* from the Court of Queen's bench, brought his client to London, and always secured an acquittal. Thus, January 13th, Judge

Williams of Queen's bench acquitted three miners condemned by
the Justices of the Peace of Bilston, South Staffordshire; the offence
of these people was that they refused to work in a place which
threatened to cave in, and had actually caved in before their return!
On an earlier occasion, Judge Patteson had acquitted six working-
men, so that the name Roberts began to be a terror to the mine-
owners. In Preston four of his clients were in jail. In the first week
of January he proceeded thither to investigate the case on the spot,
but found, when he arrived, the condemned all released before the
expiration of the sentence. In Manchester there were seven in jail;
Roberts obtained a *habeas corpus* and acquittal for all from Judge
Wightman. In Prescott nine coal miners were in jail, accused of
creating a disturbance in St Helen's, South Lancashire, and awaiting
trial; when Roberts arrived upon the spot, they were released at
once. All this took place in the first half of February. In April,
Roberts released a miner from jail in Derby, four in Wakefield, and
four in Leicester. So it went on for a time until these Dogberries
came to have some respect for the miners. The truck system shared
the same fate. One after another Roberts brought the disreputable
mine-owners before the courts, and compelled the reluctant Justices of the Peace to condemn them; such dread of this 'lightning'
'Attorney General' who seemed to be everywhere at once spread
among them, that at Belper, for instance, upon Roberts's arrival, a
truck firm published the following notice:

NOTICE
PENTRICH COAL MINE

The Messrs. Haslam think it necessary, in order to prevent all
mistakes, to announce that all persons employed in their colliery
will receive their wages wholly in cash, and may expend them
when and as they choose to do. If they purchase goods in the
shops of Messrs. Haslam they will receive them as heretofore at
wholesale prices, but they are not expected to make their purchases there, and work and wages will be continued as usual
whether purchases are made in these shops or elsewhere.

This triumph aroused the greatest jubilation throughout the
English working class, and brought the Union a mass of new
members. Meanwhile the strike in the North was proceeding.
Not a hand stirred, and Newcastle, the chief coal port, was so

stripped of its commodity that coal had to be brought from the Scotch coast, in spite of the proverb. At first, while the Union's funds held out, all went well, but towards summer the struggle became much more painful for the miners. The greatest want prevailed among them; they had no money, for the contributions of the workers of all branches of industry in England availed little among the vast number of strikers, who were forced to borrow from the small shopkeepers at a heavy loss. The whole press, with the single exception of the few proletarian journals, was against them; the bourgeois, even the few among them who might have had enough sense of justice to support the miners, learnt from the corrupt Liberal and Conservative sheets only lies about them. A deputation of twelve miners who went to London received a sum from the proletariat there, but this, too, availed little among the mass who needed support. Yet, in spite of all this, the miners remained steadfast, and what is even more significant, were quiet and peaceable in the face of all the hostilities and provocation of the mine-owners and their faithful servants. No act of revenge was carried out, not a renegade was maltreated, not one single theft committed. Thus the strike had continued well on towards four months, and the mine-owners still had no prospect of getting the upper hand. One way was, however, still open to them. They remembered the cottage system; it occurred to them that the houses of the rebellious spirits were *their* property. In July, notice to quit was served the workers, and, in a week, the whole forty thousand were put out of doors. This measure was carried out with revolting cruelty. The sick, the feeble, old men and little children, even women in childbirth, were mercilessly turned from their beds and cast into the roadside ditches. One agent dragged by the hair from her bed, and into the street, a woman in the pangs of childbirth. Soldiers and police in crowds were present, ready to fire at the first symptom of resistance, on the slightest hint of the Justices of the Peace, who had brought about the whole brutal procedure. This, too, the working-men endured without resistance. The hope had been that the men would use violence; they were spurred on with all force to infringements of the laws, to furnish an excuse for making an end of the strike by the intervention of the military. The homeless miners, remembering the warnings of their Attorney General, remained unmoved, set up their household goods upon the moors or the harvested fields, and held out. Some, who had no other place, encamped on the roadsides and in ditches, others upon land belonging to other people, whereupon they were prosecuted, and, having caused 'damage of the value of a halfpenny', were fined a pound, and, being unable to pay it, worked it out on the treadmill. Thus they lived eight weeks and more of the wet fag-end of last summer under the open sky with their families, with no further shelter for themselves and their little ones than the calico curtains of their beds; with no other help than the scanty allowances of their Union and the fast shrinking credit with the small dealers. Hereupon Lord Londonderry, who owns consider-able mines in Durham, threatened the small tradesmen in 'his' town of Seaham with his most high displeasure if they should continue to give credit to 'his' rebellious workers. This 'noble' lord made himself the first clown of the turnout in consequence of the ridiculous, pompous, ungrammatical ukases addressed to the workers, which he published from time to time, with no other result than the merriment of the nation. When none of their efforts produced any effect, the mine-owners imported, at great expense, hands from Ireland and such remote parts of Wales as have as yet no labour movement. And when the competition of workers against workers was thus restored, the strength of the strikers collapsed. The mine-owners obliged them to renounce the Union, abandon Roberts, and accept the conditions laid down by the employers. Thus ended at the close of September the great five months' battle of the coal miners against the mine-owners, a battle fought on the part of the oppressed with an endurance, courage, intelligence, and coolness which demands the highest admiration. What a degree of true human culture, of enthusiasm and strength of character, such a battle implies on the part of men who, as we have seen in the Children's Employment Commission's Report, were described as late as 1840, as being thoroughly brutal and wanting in moral sense! But how hard, too, must have been the pressure which brought these forty thousand colliers to rise as one man and to fight out the battle like an army not only well-disciplined but enthusiastic, an army possessed of one single determination, with the greatest coolness and composure, to a point beyond which further resistance would have been madness. And what a battle! Not against visible, mortal enemies, but against hunger, want, misery, and homelessness, against their own passions provoked to madness by the brutality of wealth. If they had revolted with violence, they, the unarmed and defenceless, would have been shot down, and a day or two would have decided the victory of the owners. This law-abiding reserve was no fear of the constable's staff, it was the result of deliberation, the best proof of the intelligence and self-control of the working-men.

Thus were the working-men forced once more, in spite of their unexampled endurance, to succumb to the might of capital. But the fight had not been in vain. First of all, this nineteen weeks' strike had torn the miners of the North of England forever from the intellectual death in which they had hitherto lain; they have left their sleep, are alert to defend their interests, and have entered the movement of civilisation, and especially the movement of the workers. The strike, which first brought to light the whole cruelty of the owners, has established the opposition of the workers here, forever, and made at least two-thirds of them Chartists; and the acquisition of thirty thousand such determined, experienced men is certainly of great value to the Chartists. Then, too, the endurance and law-abiding which characterised the whole strike, coupled with the active agitation which accompanied it, has fixed public attention upon the miners. On the occasion of the debate upon the export duty on coal, Thomas Duncombe, the only decidedly Chartist member of the House of Commons, brought up the condition of the coal miners, had their petition read, and by his speech forced the bourgeois journals to publish, at least in their reports of Parliamentary proceedings, a correct statement of the case. Immediately after the strike, occurred the explosion at Haswell; Roberts went to London, demanded an audience with Peel, insisted as representative of the miners upon a thorough investigation of the case, and succeeded in having the first geological and chemical notabilities of England, Professors Lyell and Faraday, commissioned to visit the spot. As several other explosions followed in quick succession, and Roberts again laid the details before the Prime Minister, the latter promised to propose the necessary measures for the protection of the workers, if possible, in the next session of Parliament, i.e. the present one of 1845. All this would not have been accomplished if these workers had not, by means of the strike, proved themselves freedom-loving men worthy of all respect, and if they had not engaged Roberts as their counsel.

Scarcely had it become known that the coal miners of the North had been forced to renounce the Union and discharge Roberts, when the miners of Lancashire formed a Union of some ten thousand men, and guaranteed their Attorney General a salary of £1200 a year. In the autumn of last year they collected more than £700, rather more than £200 of which they expended upon salaries and judicial expenses, and the rest chiefly in support of men out of work, either through want of employment or through dissensions with their employers. Thus the working-men are constantly coming to see more clearly that, united, they too are a respectable power, and can, in the last extremity, defy even the might of the bourgeoisie. And this insight, the gain of all labour movements, has been won for all the miners of England by the Union and the strike of 1844. In a very short time the difference of intelligence and energy which now exists in favour of the factory operatives will have vanished, and the miners of the kingdom will be able to stand abreast of them in every respect. Thus one piece of standing ground after another is undermined beneath the feet of the bourgeoisie; and how long will it be before their whole social and political edifice collapses with the basis upon which it rests?[132]

But the bourgeoisie will not take warning. The resistance of the miners does but embitter it the more. Instead of appreciating this forward step in the general movement of the workers, the property-holding class saw in it only a source of rage against a class of people who are fools enough to declare themselves no longer submissive to the treatment they had hitherto received. It saw in the just demands of the non-possessing workers only impertinent discontent, mad rebellion against 'Divine and human order'; and, in the best case, a success (to be resisted by the bourgeoisie with all its might) won by 'ill-intentioned demagogues who live by agitation and are too lazy to work'. It sought, of course, without success, to represent to the workers that Roberts and the Union's agents whom the Union very naturally had to pay, were insolent swindlers, who drew the last farthing from the working-men's pockets. When such insanity prevails in the property-holding class, when it is so blinded by its momentary profit that it no longer has eyes for the most conspicuous signs of the times, surely all hope of a peaceful solution of the social question for England must be abandoned. The only possible solution is a violent revolution, which cannot fail to take place.

The Agricultural Proletariat

We have seen in the introduction how, simultaneously with the small bourgeoisie and the modest independence of the former workers, the small peasantry also was ruined when the former union of industrial and agricultural work was dissolved, the abandoned fields thrown together into large farms, and the small peasants superseded by the overwhelming competition of the large farmers. Instead of being landowners or leaseholders, as they had been hitherto, they were now obliged to hire themselves as labourers to the large farmers or the landlords. For a time this position was endurable, though a deterioration in comparison with their former one. The extension of industry kept pace with the increase of population until the progress of manufacture began to assume a slower pace, and the perpetual improvement of machinery made it impossible for manufacture to absorb the whole surplus of the agricultural population. From this time forward, the distress which had hitherto existed only in the manufacturing districts, and then only at times, appeared in the agricultural districts too. The twenty-five years' struggle with France came to an end at about the same time; the diminished production at the various seats of the wars, the shutting off of imports, and the necessity of providing for the British army in Spain, had given English agriculture an artificial prosperity, and had besides withdrawn to the army vast numbers of workers from their ordinary occupations. This check upon the import trade, the opportunity for exportation, and the military demand for workers, now suddenly came to an end; and the necessary consequence was what the English call agricultural distress. The farmers had to sell their corn at low prices, and could, therefore, pay only low wages. In 1815, in order to keep up prices, the Corn Laws were passed, prohibiting the importation of corn so long as the price of wheat continued less than 80 shillings per quarter. These naturally ineffective laws were several times modified, but did not succeed in ameliorating the distress in the agricultural districts. All that they did was to change the disease, which, under free competition from abroad, would have assumed an acute form, culminating in a series of crises, into a chronic one which bore heavily but uniformly upon the farm labourers.

For a time after the rise of the agricultural proletariat, the patriarchal relation between master and man, which was being destroyed for manufacture, developed here the same relation of the farmer to his hands which still exists almost everywhere in Germany. So long as this lasted, the poverty of the farm hands was less conspicuous; they shared the fate of the farmer, and were discharged only in cases of the direst necessity. But now all this is changed. The farm hands have become day-labourers almost everywhere, are employed only when needed by the farmers, and, therefore, often have no work for weeks together, especially in winter. In the patriarchal time, the hands and their families lived on the farm, and their children grew up there, the farmer trying to find occupation on the spot for the oncoming generation; day-labourers, then, were the exception, not the rule. Thus there was, on every farm, a larger number of hands than were strictly necessary. It became, therefore, the interest of the farmers to dissolve this relation, drive the farm hand from the farm, and transform him into a day-labourer. This took place pretty generally towards the year 1830, and the consequence was that the hitherto latent over-population was set free, the rate of wages forced down, and the poor-rate enormously increased. From this time the agricultural districts became the headquarters of permanent, as the manufacturing districts had long been of periodic, pauperism; and the modification of the Poor Law was the first measure which the State was obliged to apply to the daily increasing impoverishment of the country parishes. Moreover, the constant extension of farming on a large scale, the introduction of threshing and other machines, and the employment of women and children (which is now so general that its effects have recently been investigated by a special official commission), threw a large number of men out of employment. It is manifest, therefore, that here, too, the system of industrial production has made its entrance, by means of farming on a large scale, by the abolition of the patriarchal relation, which is of the greatest importance just here, by the introduction of machinery, steam, and the labour of women and children. In so doing, it has swept the last and most stationary portion of working humanity into the revolutionary movement. But the longer agriculture had remained stationary, the heavier now became the burden upon the worker, the more violently broke forth the results of the disorganisation of the old social fabric. The 'overpopulation' came to light all at once, and could not, as in the manufacturing districts, be absorbed by the needs of an increasing production. New factories could always be built, if there were consumers for their products, but new land could not be created. The cultivation of waste common land was too daring a speculation for the bad times following the conclusion of peace. The necessary consequence was that the competition of the workers among each other reached the highest point of intensity, and wages fell to the minimum. So long as the old Poor Law existed, the workers received relief from the rates; wages naturally fell still lower, because the farmers forced the largest possible number of labourers to claim relief. The higher poor-rate, necessitated by the surplus population, was only increased by this measure, and the new Poor Law, of which we shall have more to say later, was now enacted as a remedy. But this did not improve matters. Wages did not rise, the surplus population could not be got rid of, and the cruelty of the new law did but serve to embitter the people to the utmost. Even the poor-rate, which diminished at first after the passage of the new law, attained its old height after a few years. Its only effect was that whereas previously three to four million half-paupers had existed, a million of total paupers now appeared, and the rest, still half-paupers, merely went without relief. The poverty in the agricultural districts has increased every year. The people live in the greatest want, whole families must struggle along with 6, 7, or 8 shillings a week, and at times have nothing. Let us hear a description of this population given by a Liberal member of Parliament as early as 1830.[133]

An English agricultural labourer and an English pauper, these words are synonymous. His father was a pauper and his mother's milk contained no nourishment. From his earliest childhood he had bad food, and only half enough to still his hunger, and even yet he undergoes the pangs of unsatisfied hunger almost all the time that he is not asleep. He is half-clad, and has not more fire than barely suffices to cook his scanty meal. And so cold and damp are always at home with him, and leave him only in fine weather. He is married, but he knows nothing of the joys of the husband and father. His wife and children, hungry, rarely warm, often ill and helpless, always careworn and hopeless like himself, are naturally grasping, selfish, and troublesome, and so, to use his own expression, he hates the sight of them, and enters his cot only because it offers him a trifle more shelter from rain and wind than a hedge. He must support his family, though he cannot do so, whence come beggary, deceit of all sorts, ending in fully developed craftiness. If he were so inclined, he yet has not the courage which makes of the more energetic of his class wholesale poachers and smugglers. But he pilfers when occasion offers, and teaches his children to lie and steal. His abject and submissive demeanour towards his wealthy neighbours shows that they treat him roughly and with suspicion; hence he fears and hates them, but he never will injure them by force. He is depraved through and through, too far gone to possess even the strength of despair. His wretched existence is brief, rheumatism and asthma bring him to the workhouse, where he will draw his last breath without a single pleasant recollection, and will make room for another luckless wretch to live and die as he has done.

Our author adds that besides this class of agricultural labourers, there is still another, somewhat more energetic and better endowed physically, mentally, and morally; those, namely, who live as wretchedly, but were not born to this condition. These he represents as better in their family life, but smugglers and poachers who get into frequent bloody conflicts with the gamekeepers and revenue officers of the coast, become more embittered against society during the prison life which they often undergo, and so stand abreast of the first class in their hatred of the property-holders. 'And,' he says, in closing, 'this whole class is called, by courtesy, the bold peasantry of England.'

Down to the present time, this description applies to the greater portion of the agricultural labourers of England. In June, 1844, the *Times* sent a correspondent into the agricultural districts to report upon the condition of this class, and the report which he furnished agreed wholly with the foregoing. In certain districts

wages were not more than six shillings a week; not more, that
is, that in many districts in Germany, while the prices of all the
necessaries of life are at least twice as high. What sort of life these
people lead may be imagined; their food scanty and bad, their
clothing ragged, their dwellings cramped and desolate, small,
wretched huts, with no comforts whatsoever; and, for young
people, lodging-houses where men and women are scarcely separated, and illegitimate intercourse thus provoked. One or two days
without work in the course of a month must inevitably plunge
such people into the direst want. Moreover, they cannot combine
to raise wages, because they are scattered, and if one alone refuses
to work for low wages, there are dozens out of work, or supported
by the rates, who are thankful for the most trifling offer, while to
him who declines work, every other form of relief than the hated
workhouse is refused by the Poor Law guardians as to a lazy
vagabond; for the guardians are the very farmers from whom
or from whose neighbours and acquaintances alone he can get
work. And not from one or two special districts of England do
such reports come. On the contrary, the distress is general, equally
great in the North and South, the East and West. The condition
of the labourers in Suffolk and Norfolk corresponds with that of
Devonshire, Hampshire, and Sussex. Wages are as low in Dorset-
shire and Oxfordshire as in Kent and Surrey, Buckinghamshire
and Cambridgeshire.

One especially barbaric cruelty against the working class is em-
bodied in the Game Laws, which are more stringent than in any
other country, while the game is plentiful beyond all conception.
The English peasant who, according to the old English custom and
tradition, sees in poaching only a natural and noble expression of
courage and daring, is stimulated still further by the contrast
between his own poverty and the *car tel est notre plaisir* of the lord,
who preserves thousands of hares and game birds for his private
enjoyment. The labourer lays snares, or shoots here and there a
piece of game. It does not injure the landlord as a matter of fact, for
he has a vast superfluity, and it brings the poacher a meal for
himself and his starving family. But if he is caught he goes to jail,
and for a second offence receives at the least seven years' transportation. From the severity of these laws arise the frequent
bloody conflicts with the gamekeepers, which lead to a number of

murders every year Hence the post of gamekeeper is not only dangerous, but of ill-repute and despised. Last year, in two cases, gamekeepers shot themselves rather than continue their work. Such is the moderate price at which the landed aristocracy purchases the noble sport of shooting; but what does it matter to the lords of the soil? Whether one or two more or less of the 'surplus' live or die matters nothing, and even if in consequence of the Game Laws half the surplus population could be put out of the way, it would be all the better for the other half – according to the philanthropy of the English landlords.

Although the conditions of life in the country, the isolated dwellings, the stability of the surroundings and occupations, and consequently of the thoughts, are decidedly unfavourable to all development, yet poverty and want bear their fruits even here. The manufacturing and mining proletariat emerged early from the first stage of resistance to our social order, the direct rebellion of the individual by the perpetration of crime; but the peasants are still in this stage at the present time. Their favourite method of social warfare is incendiarism. In the winter which followed the Revolution of July, in 1830–31, these incendiarisms first became general. Disturbances had taken place, and the whole region of Sussex and the adjacent counties has been brought into a state of excitement in October, in consequence of an increase of the coastguard (which made smuggling much more difficult and 'ruined the coast' – in the words of a farmer), changes in the Poor Law, low wages, and the introduction of machinery. In the winter the farmers' hay- and corn-stacks were burnt in the fields, and the very barns and stables under their windows. Nearly every night a couple of such fires blazed up, and spread terror among the farmers and landlords. The offenders were rarely discovered, and the workers attributed the incendiarism to a mythical person whom they named 'Swing'. Men puzzled their brains to discover who this Swing could be and whence this rage among the poor of the country districts. Of the great motive power, Want, Oppression, only a single person here and there thought, and certainly no one in the agricultural districts. Since that year the incendiarisms have been repeated every winter, with each recurring unemployed season of the agricultural labourers. In the winter of 1843–44, they were once more extraordinarily frequent. There lies before me a series of numbers of the *Northern Star* of that time, each one of which contains a report of several incendiarisms, stating in each case its authority. The numbers wanting in the following list I have not at hand; but they, too, doubtless contain a number of cases. Moreover, such a sheet cannot possibly ascertain all the cases which occur. November 25th, 1843, two cases; several earlier ones are discussed. December 16th, in Bedfordshire, general excitement for a fortnight past in consequence of frequent incendiarisms, of which several take place every night. Two great farmhouses burnt down within the last few days; in Cambridgeshire four great farmhouses, Hertfordshire one, and besides these, fifteen other incendiarisms in different districts. December 30th, in Norfolk one, Suffolk two, Essex two, Cheshire one, Lancashire one, Derby, Lincoln, and the South twelve. January 6th, 1844, in all ten. January 13th, seven. January 20th, four incendiarisms. From this time forward, three or four incendiarisms per week are reported, and not as formerly until the spring only, but far into July and August. And that crimes of this sort are expected to increase in the approaching hard season of 1844–45, the English papers already indicate.

What do my readers think of such a state of things in the quiet, idyllic country districts of England? Is this social war, or is it not? Is it a natural state of things which can last? Yet here the landlords and farmers are as dull and stupefied, as blind to everything which does not directly put money into their pockets, as the manufacturers and the bourgeoisie in general in the manufacturing districts. If the latter promise their employees salvation through the repeal of the Corn Laws, the landlords and a great part of the farmers promise theirs Heaven upon earth from the maintenance of the same laws. But in neither case do the property-holders succeed in winning the workers to the support of their pet hobby. Like the operatives, the agricultural labourers are thoroughly indifferent to the repeal or non-repeal of the Corn Laws. Yet the question is an important one for both. That is to say – by the repeal of the Corn Laws, free competition, the present social economy is carried to its extreme point; all further development within the present order comes to an end, and the only possible step farther is a radical transformation of the social order.[134] For the agricultural labourers the question has, further, the following important bearing: free importation of corn involves (how, I cannot explain *here*)

the emancipation of the farmers from the landlords, their transformation into Liberals. Towards this consummation the Anti-
Corn Law League has already largely contributed, and this is its
only real service. When the farmers become Liberals, i.e. conscious bourgeois, the agricultural labourers will inevitably become
Chartists and Socialists; the first change involves the second. And
that a new movement is already beginning among the agricultural
labourers is proved by a meeting which Earl Radnor, a Liberal
landlord, caused to be held in October, 1844, near Highworth,
where his estates lie, to pass resolutions against the Corn Laws. At
this meeting, the labourers, perfectly indifferent as to these laws,
demanded something wholly different, namely smallholdings, at
low rent, for themselves, telling Earl Radnor all sorts of bitter
truths to his face. Thus the movement of the working class is
finding its way into the remote, stationary, mentally dead agricultural districts; and, thanks to the general distress, will soon be as
firmly rooted and energetic as in the manufacturing districts.[135] As
to the religious state of the agricultural labourers, they are, it is
true, more pious than the manufacturing operatives; but they, too,
are greatly at odds with the Church – for in these districts members
of the Established Church almost exclusively are to be found. A
correspondent of the *Morning Chronicle*, who, over the signature
'One who has whistled at the plough', reports his tour through the
agricultural districts, relates, among other things, the following
conversation with some labourers after service: 'I asked one of
these people whether the preacher of the day was their own
clergyman. "Yes, blast him! He is our own parson, and begs the
whole time. He's been always a-begging as long as I've known
him." (The sermon had been upon a mission to the heathen.)
"And as long as I've known him too," added another; "and I never
knew a parson but what was begging for this or the other." "Yes,"
said a woman, who had just come out of the church, "and look
how wages are going down, and see the rich vagabonds with
whom the parsons eat and drink and hunt. So help me God, we are
more fit to starve in the workhouse than pay the parsons as go
among the heathen." "And why," said another, "don't they send
the parsons as drones every day in Salisbury Cathedral, for nobody
but the bare stones? Why don't *they* go among the heathen?"
"They don't go," said the old man whom I had first asked,

"because they are rich, they have all the land they need, they want the money in order to get rid of the poor parsons. I know what they want. I know them too long for that." "But, good friends," I asked, "you surely do not always come out of the church with such bitter feelings towards the preacher? Why do you go at all?" "What for do we go?" said the woman. "We must, if we do not want to lose everything, work and all, we must." I learned later that they had certain little privileges of firewood and potato land (which they paid for!) on condition of going to church.' After describing their poverty and ignorance, the correspondent closes by saying: 'And now I boldly assert that the condition of these people, their poverty, their hatred of the church, their external submission and inward bitterness against the ecclesiastical dignit-aries, is the rule among the country parishes of England, and its opposite is the exception.'

If the peasantry of England shows the consequences which a numerous agricultural proletariat in connection with large farming involves for the country districts, Wales illustrates the ruin of the smallholders. If the English country parishes reproduce the antag-onism between capitalist and proletarian, the state of the Welsh peasantry corresponds to the progressive ruin of the small bour-geoisie in the towns. In Wales are to be found, almost exclusively, smallholders, who cannot with like profit sell their products as cheaply as the larger, more favourably situated English farmers, with whom, however, they are obliged to compete. Moreover, in some places the quality of the land admits of the raising of livestock only, which is but slightly profitable. Then, too, these Welsh farmers, by reason of their separate nationality, which they retain pertinaciously, are much more stationary than the English farmers. But the competition among themselves and with their English neighbours (and the increased mortgages upon their land con-sequent upon this) has reduced them to such a state that they can scarcely live at all; and because they have not recognised the true cause of their wretched condition, they attribute it to all sorts of small causes, such as high tolls, etc, which do check the develop-ment of agriculture and commerce, but are taken into account as standing charges by everyone who takes a holding, and are there-fore really ultimately paid by the landlord. Here, too, the new Poor Law is cordially hated by the tenants, who hover in perpetual danger of coming under its sway. In 1843, the famous 'Rebecca' disturbances broke out among the Welsh peasantry; the men dressed in women's clothing, blackened their faces, and fell in armed crowds upon the toll-gates, destroyed them amidst great rejoicing and firing of guns, demolished the toll-keepers' houses, wrote threatening letters in the name of the imaginary 'Rebecca', and once went so far as to storm the workhouse of Carmarthen. Later, when the militia was called out and the police strengthened, the peasants drew them off with wonderful skill upon false scents, demolished toll-gates at one point while the militia, lured by false signal bugles, was marching in some opposite direction; and betook themselves finally, when the police was too thoroughly reinforced, to single incendiarisms and attempts at murder. As usual, these greater crimes were the end of the movement. Many withdrew from disapproval, others from fear, and peace was restored of itself. The Government appointed a commission to investigate the affair and its causes, and there was an end of the matter. The poverty of the peasantry continues, however, and will one day, since it cannot under existing circumstances grow less, but must go on intensifying, produce more serious manifestations than these humorous Rebecca masquerades.

If England illustrates the results of the system of farming on a large scale and Wales on a small one, Ireland exhibits the consequences of overdividing the soil. The great mass of the population of Ireland consists of small tenants who occupy a sorry hut without partitions, and a potato patch just large enough to supply them most scantily with potatoes through the winter. In consequence of the great competition which prevails among these small tenants, the rent has reached an unheard-of height, double, treble, and quadruple that paid in England. For every agricultural labourer seeks to become a tenant-farmer, and though the division of land has gone so far, there still remain numbers of labourers in competition for plots. Although in Great Britain 32,000,000 acres of land are cultivated, and in Ireland but 14,000,000; although Great Britain produces agricultural products to the value of £150,000,000, and Ireland of but £36,000,000, there are in Ireland 75,000 agricultural proletarians *more* than in the neighbouring island.[136] How great the competition for land in Ireland must be is evident from this extraordinary disproportion, especially when one reflects that the labourers in

Great Britain are living in the utmost distress. The consequence of this competition is that it is impossible for the tenants to live much better than the labourers, by reason of the high rents paid. The Irish people is thus held in crushing poverty, from which it cannot free itself under our present social conditions. These people live in the most wretched clay huts, scarcely good enough for cattle-pens, have scant food all winter long, or, as the report above quoted expresses it, they have potatoes half enough thirty weeks in the year, and the rest of the year nothing. When the time comes in the spring at which this provision reaches its end, or can no longer be used because of its sprouting, wife and children go forth to beg and tramp the country with their kettle in their hands. Meanwhile the husband, after planting potatoes for the next year, goes in search of work either in Ireland or England, and returns at the potato harvest to his family. This is the condition in which nine-tenths of the Irish country folks live. They are poor as church mice, wear the most wretched rags, and stand upon the lowest plane of intelligence possible in a half-civilised country. According to the report quoted, there are, in a population of 8.5 millions, 585,000 heads of families in a state of total destitution; and according to other authorities, cited by Sheriff Alison,[137] there are in Ireland 2,300,000 persons who could not live without public or private assistance – or 27 per cent. of the whole population paupers!

The cause of this poverty lies in the existing social conditions, especially in competition here found in the form of the subdivision of the soil. Much effort has been spent in finding other causes. It has been asserted that the relation of the tenant to the landlord who lets his estate in large lots to tenants, who again have their sub-tenants, and sub-sub-tenants, in turn, so that often ten middlemen come between the landlord and the actual cultivator – it has been asserted that the shameful law which gives the landlord the right of expropriating the cultivator who may have paid his rent duly, if the first tenant fails to pay the landlord, that this law is to blame for all this poverty. But all this determines only the form in which the poverty manifests itself. Make the small tenant a landowner himself and what follows? The majority could not live upon their holdings even if they had no rent to pay, and any slight improvement which might take place would be lost again in a few years in consequence of the rapid increase of population. The children would then live to grow up under the improved conditions who now die in consequence of poverty in early childhood. From another side comes the assertion that the shameless oppression inflicted by the English is the cause of the trouble. It is the cause of the somewhat earlier appearance of this poverty, but not of the poverty itself. Or the blame is laid on the Protestant Church forced upon a Catholic nation; but divide among the Irish what the Church takes from them, and it does not reach six shillings a head. Besides, tithes are a tax upon landed property, not upon the tenant, though he may nominally pay them; now, since the Commutation Bill of 1838, the landlord pays the tithes directly and reckons so much higher rent, so that the tenant is none the better off. And in the same way a hundred other causes of this poverty are brought forward, all proving as little as these. This poverty is the result of our social conditions; apart from these, causes may be found for the manner in which it manifests itself, but not for the fact of its existence. That poverty manifests itself in Ireland thus and not otherwise, is owing to the character of the people, and to their historical development. The Irish are a people related in their whole charac-ter to the Latin nations, to the French, and especially to the Italians. The bad features of their character we have already had depicted by Carlyle. Let us now hear an Irishman, who at least comes nearer to the truth than Carlyle, with his prejudice in favour of the Teutonic character:[138]

They are restless, yet indolent, clever and indiscreet, stormy, impatient, and improvident; brave by instinct, generous without much reflection, quick to revenge and forgive insults, to make and to renounce friendships, gifted with genius prodigally, spar-ingly with judgment.

With the Irish, feeling and passion predominate; reason must bow before them. Their sensuous, excitable nature prevents reflection and quiet, persevering activity from reaching development – such a nation is utterly unfit for manufacture as now conducted. Hence they held fast to agriculture, and remained upon the lowest plane even of that. With the small subdivisions of land, which were not here artificially created, as in France and on the Rhine, by the division of great estates, but have existed from time immemorial, an improvement of the soil by the investment of capital was not to be thought of; and it would, according to Alison, require £120 million sterling to bring the soil up to the not very high state of fertility already attained in England. The English immigration, which might have raised the standard of Irish civilisation, has contented itself with the most brutal plundering of the Irish people; and while the Irish, by their immigration into England, have furnished England a leaven which will produce its own results in the future, they have little for which to be thankful to the English immigration.

The attempts of the Irish to save themselves from their present ruin, on the one hand, take the form of crimes. These are the order of the day in the agricultural districts, and are nearly always directed against the most immediate enemies, the landlord's agents, or their obedient servants, the Protestant intruders, whose large farms are made up of the potato patches of hundreds of ejected families. Such crimes are especially frequent in the South and West. On the other hand, the Irish hope for relief by means of the agitation for the repeal of the Legislative Union with England. From all the foregoing, it is clear that the uneducated Irish must see in the English their worst enemies; and their first hope of improvement in the conquest of national independence. But quite as clear is it, too, that Irish distress cannot be removed by any Act of Repeal. Such an Act would, however, at once lay bare the fact that the cause of Irish misery, which now seems to come from abroad, is really to be found at home. Meanwhile, it is an open question whether the accomplishment of repeal will be necessary to make this clear to the Irish. Hitherto, neither Chartism nor Socialism has had marked success in Ireland.

I close my observations upon Ireland at this point the more readily, as the Repeal Agitation of 1843 and O'Connell's trial have been the means of making the Irish distress more and more known in Germany.

We have now followed the proletariat of the British Islands through all branches of its activity, and found it everywhere living in want and misery under totally inhuman conditions. We have seen discontent arise with the rise of the proletariat, grow, develop, and organise; we have seen open bloodless and bloody battles of the proletariat against the bourgeoisie. We have investigated the principles according to which the fate, the hopes, and fears of the proletariat are determined, and we have found that there is no prospect of improvement in their condition.

We have had an opportunity, here and there, of observing the conduct of the bourgeoisie towards the proletariat, and we have found that it considers only itself, has only its own advantage in view. However, in order not to be unjust, let us investigate its mode of action somewhat more exactly.

The Attitude of the Bourgeoisie
towards the Proletariat

In speaking of the bourgeoisie I include the so-called aristocracy, for this is a privileged class, an aristocracy, only in contrast with the bourgeoisie, not in contrast with the proletariat. The proletarian sees in both only the property-holder – i.e. the bourgeois. Before the privilege of property all other privileges vanish. The sole difference is this, that the bourgeois proper stands in active relations with the manufacturing, and, in a measure, with the mining proletarians, and, as farmer, with the agricultural labourers, whereas the so-called aristocrat comes into contact with the agricultural labourer only.

I have never seen a class so deeply demoralised, so incurably debased by selfishness, so corroded within, so incapable of progress, as the English bourgeoisie; and I mean by this, especially the bourgeoisie proper, particularly the Liberal, Corn Law repealing bourgeoisie. For it nothing exists in this world, except for the sake of money, itself not excluded. It knows no bliss save that of rapid gain, no pain save that of losing gold.[139] In the presence of this avarice and lust of gain, it is not possible for a single human sentiment or opinion to remain untainted. True, these English bourgeois are good husbands and family men, and have all sorts of other private virtues, and appear, in ordinary intercourse, as decent and respectable as all other bourgeois; even in business they are better to deal with than the Germans; they do not higgle and haggle so much as our own pettifogging merchants; but how does this help matters? Ultimately it is self-interest, and especially money gain, which alone determines them. I once went into Manchester with such a bourgeois, and spoke to him of the bad, unwholesome method of building, the frightful condition of the working-people's quarters, and asserted that I had never seen so ill-built a city. The man listened quietly to the end, and said at the corner where we parted: 'And yet there is a great deal of money made here; good morning, sir.' It is utterly indifferent to the English bourgeois whether his working-men starve or not, if only he makes money. All the conditions of life are measured by money, and what brings no money is nonsense, unpractical, idealistic bosh. Hence, Political Economy, the Science of Wealth, is the favourite study of these bartering Jews. Every one of them is a Political Economist. The relation of the manufacturer to his operatives has nothing human in it; it is purely economic. The manufacturer is Capital, the operative Labour. And if the operative will not be forced into this abstraction, if he insists that he is not Labour, but a man, who possesses, among other things, the attribute of labour force, if he takes it into his head that he need not allow himself to be sold and bought in the market, as the commodity 'Labour', the bourgeois reason comes to a standstill. He cannot comprehend that he holds any other relation to the operatives than that of purchase and sale; he sees in them not human beings, but hands, as he constantly calls them to their faces; he insists, as Carlyle says, that 'Cash Payment is the only nexus between man and man.' Even the relation between himself and his wife is, in ninety-nine cases out of a hundred, mere 'Cash Payment'. Money determines the worth of the man; he is 'worth ten thousand pounds'. He who has money is of 'the better sort of people', is 'influential', and what *he* does counts for something in his social circle. The huckstering spirit penetrates the whole language, all relations are expressed in business terms, in economic categories. Supply and demand are the formulas according to which the logic of the English bourgeois judges all human life. Hence free competition in every respect, hence the *régime* of *laissez-faire, laissez-aller* in government, in medicine, in education, and soon to be in religion, too, as the State Church collapses more and more. Free competition will suffer no limitation, no State supervision; the whole State is but a burden to it. It would reach its highest perfection in a *wholly* ungoverned anarchic society, where each might exploit the other to his heart's content. Since, however, the bourgeoisie cannot dispense with government, but must have it to hold the equally indispensable proletariat in check, it turns the power of government against the proletariat and keeps out of its way as far as possible.

Let no one believe, however, that the 'cultivated' Englishman openly brags with his egotism. On the contrary, he conceals it under the vilest hypocrisy. What? The wealthy English fail to remember the poor? They who have founded philanthropic institutions, such as no other country can boast of! Philanthropic institutions forsooth! As though you rendered the proletarians a service in first sucking out their very life-blood and then practising your self-complacent, Pharisaic philanthropy upon them, placing yourselves before the world as mighty benefactors of humanity when you give back to the plundered victims the hundredth part of what belongs to them! Charity which degrades him who gives more than him who takes; charity which treads the downtrodden still deeper in the dust, which demands that the degraded, the pariah cast out by society, shall first surrender the last that remains to him, his very claim to manhood, shall first beg for mercy before your mercy deigns to press, in the shape of alms, the brand of degradation upon his brow. But let us hear the English bourgeoisie's own words. It is not yet a year since I read in the *Manchester Guardian* the following letter to the editor, which was published without comment as a perfectly natural, reasonable thing:

MR EDITOR – For some time past our main streets are haunted by swarms of beggars, who try to awaken the pity of the passers-by in a most shameless and annoying manner, by exposing their tattered clothing, sickly aspect, and disgusting wounds and deformities. I should think that when one not only pays the poor-rate, but also contributes largely to the charitable institutions, one had done enough to earn a right to be spared such disagreeable and impertinent molestations. And why else do we pay such high rates for the maintenance of the municipal police, if they do not even protect us so far as to make it possible to go to or out of town in peace? I hope the publication of these lines in your widely-circulated paper may induce the authorities to remove this nuisance; and I remain –

Your obedient servant,

A LADY

There you have it! The English bourgeoisie is charitable out of self-interest; it gives nothing outright, but regards its gifts as a business matter, makes a bargain with the poor, saying: 'If I spend this much upon benevolent institutions, I thereby purchase the

right not to be troubled any further, and you are bound thereby
to stay in your dusky holes and not to irritate my tender nerves
by exposing your misery. You shall despair as before, but you shall
despair unseen, this I require, this I purchase with my subscription
of twenty pounds for the infirmary!' It is infamous, this charity of
a Christian bourgeois! And so writes 'A Lady'; she does well to
sign herself such, well that she has lost the courage to call herself a
woman! But if the 'Ladies' are such as this, what must the 'Gentlemen' be? It will be said that this is a single case; but no, the
foregoing letter expresses the temper of the great majority of the
English bourgeoisie, or the editor would not have accepted it, and
some reply would have been made to it, which I watched for in vain
in the succeeding numbers. And as to the efficiency of this philanthropy, Canon Parkinson himself says that the poor are relieved
much more by the poor than by the bourgeoisie; and such relief
given by an honest proletarian who knows himself what it is to be
hungry, for whom sharing his scanty meal is really a sacrifice, but a
sacrifice borne with pleasure, such help has a wholly different ring
to it from the carelessly-tossed alms of the luxurious bourgeois.

In other respects, too, the bourgeoisie assumes a hypocritical,
boundless philanthropy, but only when its own interests require it;
as in its Politics and Political Economy. It has been at work now
well on towards five years to prove to the working-men that it
strives to abolish the Corn Laws solely in their interest. But the
long and short of the matter is this: the Corn Laws keep the price
of bread higher than in other countries, and thus raise wages, but
these high wages render difficult competition of the manufacturers
against other nations in which bread, and consequently wages, are
cheaper. The Corn Laws being repealed, the price of bread falls,
and wages gradually approach those of other European countries,
as must be clear to everyone from our previous exposition of the
principles according to which wages are determined. The manufacturer can compete more readily, the demand for English goods
increases, and, with it, the demand for labour. In consequence of
this increased demand wages would actually rise somewhat, and the
unemployed workers be re-employed; but for how long? The
'surplus population' of England, and especially of Ireland, is sufficient to supply English manufacture with the necessary operatives,
even if it were doubled; and, in a few years, the small advantage of

the repeal of the Corn Laws would be balanced, a new crisis would follow, and we should be back at the point from which we started, while the first stimulus to manufacture would have increased population meanwhile. All this the proletarians understand very well, and have told the manufacturers to their faces; but, in spite of that, the manufacturers have in view solely the immediate advantage which the Corn Laws would bring them. They are too narrow-minded to see that, even for themselves, no permanent advantage can arise from this measure, because their competition with each other would soon force the profit of the individual back to its old level; and thus they continue to shriek to the working-men that it is purely for the sake of the starving millions that the rich members of the Liberal party pour hundreds and thousands of pounds into the treasury of the Anti-Corn Law League, while everyone knows that they are only sending the butter after the cheese, that they calculate upon earning it all back in the first ten years after the repeal of the Corn Laws. But the workers are no longer to be misled by the bourgeoisie, especially since the insurrection of 1842. They demand of everyone who presents himself as interested in their welfare, that he should declare himself in favour of the People's Charter as proof of the sincerity of his professions, and in so doing, they protest against all outside help, for the Charter is a demand for the power to help themselves. Whoever declines so to declare himself they pronounce their enemy, and are perfectly right in so doing, whether he be a declared foe or a false friend. Besides, the Anti-Corn Law League has used the most despicable falsehoods and tricks to win the support of the workers. It has tried to prove to them that the money price of labour is in inverse proportion to the price of corn; that wages are high when grain is cheap, and *vice versa*, an assertion which it pretends to prove with the most ridiculous arguments, and one which is, in itself, more ridiculous than any other that has proceeded from the mouth of an Economist. When this failed to help matters, the workers were promised bliss supreme in consequence of the increased demand in the labour market; indeed, men went so far as to carry through the streets two models of loaves of bread, on one of which, by far the larger, was written: 'American Eightpenny Loaf, Wages Four Shillings per Day', and upon the much smaller one: 'English Eightpenny

Loaf, Wages Two Shillings a Day.' But the workers have not allowed themselves to be misled. They know their lords and masters too well.

But rightly to measure the hypocrisy of these promises, the practice of the bourgeoisie must be taken into account. We have seen in the course of our report how the bourgeoisie exploits the proletariat in every conceivable way for its own benefit! We have, however, hitherto seen only how the single bourgeois maltreats the proletariat upon his own account. Let us turn now to the manner in which the bourgeoisie as a party, as the power of the State, conducts itself towards the proletariat. Laws are necessary only because there are persons in existence who own nothing; and although this is directly expressed in but few laws, as, for instance, those against vagabonds and tramps, in which the proletariat as such is outlawed, yet enmity to the proletariat is so emphatically the basis of the law that the judges, and especially the Justices of the Peace, who are bourgeois themselves, and with whom the proletariat comes most in contact, find this meaning in the laws without further consideration. If a rich man is brought up, or rather summoned, to appear before the court, the judge regrets that he is obliged to impose so much trouble, treats the matter as favourably as possible, and, if he is forced to condemn the accused, does so with extreme regret, etc. etc., and the end of it all is a miserable fine, which the bourgeois throws upon the table with contempt and then departs. But if a poor devil gets into such a position as involves appearing before the Justice of the Peace – he has almost always spent the night in the station-house with a crowd of his peers – he is regarded from the beginning as guilty; his defence is set aside with a contemptuous 'Oh! we know the excuse', and a fine imposed which he cannot pay and must work out with several months on the treadmill. And if nothing can be proved against him, he is sent to the treadmill, none the less, 'as a rogue and a vagabond'. The partisanship of the Justices of the Peace, especially in the country, surpasses all description, and it is so much the order of the day that all cases which are not too utterly flagrant are quietly reported by the newspapers, without comment. Nor is anything else to be expected. For on the one hand, these Dog-berries do merely construe the law according to the intent of the farmers, and, on the other, they are themselves bourgeois, who see the foundation of all true order in the interests of their class. And the conduct of the police corresponds to that of the Justices of the Peace. The bourgeois may do what he will and the police remain ever polite, adhering strictly to the law, but the proletarian is roughly, brutally treated; his poverty both casts the suspicion of every sort of crime upon him and cuts him off from legal redress against any caprice of the administrators of the law; for him, therefore, the protecting forms of the law do not exist, the police force their way into his house without further ceremony, arrest and abuse him; and only when a working-men's association, such as the miners, engages a Roberts, does it become evident how little the protective side of the law exists for the working-men, how frequently he has to bear all the burdens of the law without enjoying its benefits.

Down to the present hour, the property-holding class in Parliament still struggles against the better feelings of those not yet fallen a prey to egotism, and seeks to subjugate the proletariat still further. One piece of common land after another is appropriated and placed under cultivation, a process by which the general cultivation is furthered, but the proletariat greatly injured. Where there were still commons, the poor could pasture an ass, a pig, or geese, the children and young people had a place where they could play and live out of doors; but this is gradually coming to an end. The earnings of the worker are less, and the young people, deprived of their playground, go to the beer-shops. A mass of acts for enclosing and cultivating commons is passed at every session of Parliament. When the Government determined during the session of 1844 to force the all monopolising railways to make travelling possible for the workers by means of charges proportionate to their means, a penny a mile, and proposed therefore to introduce such a third class train upon every railway daily, the 'Reverend Father in God', the Bishop of London, proposed that Sunday, the only day upon which working-men in work *can* travel, be exempted from this rule, and travelling thus be left open to the rich and shut off from the poor. This proposition was, however, too direct, too undisguised to pass through Parliament, and was dropped. I have no room to enumerate the many concealed attacks of even one single session upon the proletariat. One from the session of 1844 must suffice. An obscure member of Parliament, a Mr Miles, proposed a bill regulating the relation of master and servant which seemed comparatively unobjectionable. The Government became interested in the bill, and it was referred to a committee. Meanwhile the strike among the miners in the North broke out, and Roberts made his triumphal passage through England with his acquitted working-men. When the bill was reported by the committee, it was discovered that certain most despotic provisions had been interpolated in it, especially one conferring upon the employer the power to bring before any Justice of the Peace every working-man who had contracted verbally or in writing to do any work whatsoever, in case of refusal to work or other misbehaviour, and have him condemned to prison with hard labour for two months, upon the oath of the employer or his agent or overlooker, i.e. upon the oath of the accuser. This bill aroused the working-men to the utmost fury, the more so as the Ten Hours' Bill was before Parliament at the same time, and had called forth a considerable agitation. Hundreds of meetings were held, hundreds of working-men's petitions forwarded to London to Thomas Duncombe, the representative of the interests of the proletariat. This man was, except Ferrand, the representative of 'Young England', the only vigorous opponent of the bill; but when the other Radicals saw that the people were declaring against it, one after the other crept forward and took his place by Duncombe's side; and as the Liberal bourgeoisie had not the courage to defend the bill in the face of the excitement among the working-men, it was ignominiously lost.

Meanwhile the most open declaration of war of the bourgeoisie upon the proletariat is Malthus's Law of Population and the New Poor Law framed in accordance with it. We have already alluded several times to the theory of Malthus. We may sum up its final result in these few words, that the earth is perennially overpopulated, whence poverty, misery, distress, and immorality must prevail; that it is the lot, the eternal destiny of mankind, to exist in too great numbers, and therefore in diverse classes, of which some are rich, educated, and moral, and others more or less poor, distressed, ignorant, and immoral. Hence it follows in practice, and Malthus himself drew this conclusion, that charities and poor-rates are, properly speaking, nonsense, since they serve only to maintain, and stimulate the increase of, the surplus population whose competition crushes down wages for the employed; that the employment of the poor by the Poor Law Guardians is equally unreasonable, since only a fixed quantity of the products of labour can be consumed, and for every unemployed labourer thus furnished employment, another hitherto employed must be driven into enforced idleness, whence private undertakings suffer at cost of Poor Law industry; that, in other words, the whole problem is not how to support the surplus population, but how to restrain it as far as possible. Malthus declares in plain English that the right to live, a right previously asserted in favour of every man in the world, is nonsense. He quotes the words of a poet, that the poor man comes to the feast of Nature and finds no cover laid for him, and adds that 'she bids him begone', for he did not before his birth ask of society whether or not he is welcome. This is now the pet theory of all genuine English bourgeois, and very naturally, since it is the most specious excuse for them, and has, moreover, a good deal of truth in it under existing conditions. If, then, the problem is not to make the 'surplus population' useful, to transform it into available population, but merely to let it starve to death in the least objectionable way and to prevent its having too many children, this, of course, is simple enough, provided the surplus population perceives its own super-fluousness and takes kindly to starvation. There is, however, in spite of the violent exertions of the humane bourgeoisie, no immediate prospect of its succeeding in bringing about such a disposition among the workers. The workers have taken it into their heads that they, with their busy hands, are the necessary, and the rich capitalists, who do nothing, the surplus population.

Since, however, the rich hold all the power, the proletarians must submit, if they will not good-temperedly perceive it for themselves, to have the law actually declare them superfluous. This has been done by the New Poor Law. The Old Poor Law which rested upon the Act of 1601 (the 43rd of Elizabeth), naïvely started from the notion that it is the duty of the parish to provide for the maintenance of the poor. Whoever had no work received relief, and the poor man regarded the parish as pledged to protect him from starvation. He demanded his weekly relief as his right, not as a favour, and this became, at last, too much for the bourgeoisie. In 1833, when the bourgeoisie had just come into power through the Reform Bill, and pauperism in the country districts had just reached its full development, the bourgeoisie began the reform of the Poor Law according to its own point of view. A commission was appointed, which investigated the administration of the Poor Laws, and revealed a multitude of abuses. It was discovered that the whole working class in the country was pauperised and more or less dependent upon the rates, from which they received relief when wages were low; it was found that this system by which the unemployed were maintained, the ill-paid and the parents of large families relieved, fathers of illegitimate children required to pay alimony, and poverty, in general, recognised as needing protection, it was found that this system was ruining the nation, was –

. . . a check upon industry, a reward for improvident marriage, a stimulus to increased population, and a means of counterbalancing the effect of an increased population upon wages; a national provision for discouraging the honest and industrious, and protecting the lazy, vicious, and improvident; calculated to destroy the bonds of family life, hinder systematically the accumulation of capital, scatter that which is already accumulated, and ruin the taxpayers. Moreover, in the provision of aliment, it sets a premium upon illegitimate children. [words of the Report of the Poor Law Commissioners.] [140]

This description of the action of the Old Poor Law is certainly correct; relief fosters laziness and increase of 'surplus population'. Under present social conditions it is perfectly clear that the poor man is compelled to be an egotist, and when he can choose, living equally well in either case, he prefers doing nothing to working. But what follows therefrom? That our present social conditions are good for nothing, and not as the Malthusian Commissioners conclude, that poverty is a crime, and, as such, to be visited with heinous penalties which may serve as a warning to others.

But these wise Malthusians were so thoroughly convinced of the infallibility of their theory that they did not for one moment hesitate to cast the poor into the Procrustean bed of their economic notions and treat them with the most revolting cruelty. Convinced with Malthus and the rest of the adherents of free competition that it is best to let each one take care of himself, they would have preferred to abolish the Poor Laws altogether. Since, however, they had neither the courage nor the authority to do this, they proposed a Poor Law constructed as far as possible in harmony with the doctrine of Malthus, which is yet more barbarous than that of *laissez-faire*, because it interferes actively in cases in which the latter is passive. We have seen how Malthus characterises poverty, or rather the want of employment, as a crime under the title 'superfluity', and recommends for it punishment by starvation. The commissioners were not quite so barbarous; death outright by starvation was something too terrible even for a Poor Law Commissioner. 'Good', said they, 'we grant you poor a right to exist, but only to exist; the right to multiply you have not, nor the right to exist as befits human beings. You are a pest, and if we cannot get rid of you as we do of other pests, you shall feel, at least, that you are a pest, and you shall at least be held in check, kept from bringing into the world other 'surplus', either directly or through inducing in others laziness and want of employment. Live you shall, but live as an awful warning to all those who might have inducements to become 'superfluous'.

They accordingly brought in the New Poor Law, which was passed by Parliament in 1834, and continues in force down to the present day. All relief in money and provisions was abolished; the only relief allowed was admission to the workhouses immediately built. The regulations for these workhouses, or, as the people call them, Poor Law Bastilles, is such as to frighten away everyone who has the slightest prospect of life without this form of public charity. To make sure that relief be applied for only in the most extreme cases and after every other effort had failed, the workhouse has been made the most repulsive residence which the refined ingenuity of a Malthusian can invent. The food is worse than that of the most ill-paid working-man while employed, and the work harder, or they might prefer the workhouse to their wretched existence outside. Meat, especially fresh meat, is rarely furnished, chiefly potatoes, the worst possible bread and oatmeal porridge, little or no beer. The food of criminal prisoners is better, as a rule, so that the paupers frequently commit some offence for the purpose of getting into jail. For the workhouse is a jail too; he who does not finish his task gets nothing to eat; he who wishes to go out must ask permission, which is granted or not, according to his behaviour or the inspector's whim, tobacco is forbidden, also the receipt of gifts from relatives or friends outside the house; the paupers wear a workhouse uniform, and are handed over, helpless and without redress, to the caprice of the inspectors. To prevent their labour from competing with that of outside concerns, they are set to rather useless tasks: the men break stones, 'as much as a strong man can accomplish with effort in a day'; the women, children, and aged men pick oakum, for I know not what insignificant use. To prevent the 'superfluous' from multiplying, and 'demoralised' parents from influencing their children, families are broken up, the husband is placed in one wing, the wife in another, the children in a third, and they are permitted to see one another only at stated times after long intervals, and then only when they have, in the opinion of the officials, behaved well. And in order to shut off the external world from contamination by pauperism within these bastilles, the inmates are permitted to receive visits only with the consent of the officials, and in the reception-rooms; to communicate in general with the world outside only by leave and under supervision.

Yet the food is supposed to be wholesome and the treatment humane with all this. But the intent of the law is too loudly outspoken for this requirement to be in any wise fulfilled. The Poor Law Commissioners and the whole English bourgeoisie deceive themselves if they believe the administration of the law possible without these results. The treatment, which the letter of the law prescribes, is in direct contradiction of its spirit. If the law in its essence proclaims the poor criminals, the workhouses prisons, their inmates beyond the pale of the law, beyond the pale of humanity, objects of disgust and repulsion, then all commands to the contrary are unavailing. In practice, the spirit and not the letter of the law is followed in the treatment of the poor, as in the following few examples:

In the workhouse at Greenwich, in the summer of 1843, a boy five years old was punished by being shut into the dead-room, where he had to sleep upon the lids of the coffins. In the workhouse at Herne, the same punishment was inflicted upon a little girl for wetting the bed at night, and this method of punishment seems to be a favourite one. This workhouse, which stands in one of the most beautiful regions of Kent, is peculiar, in so far as its windows open only upon the court, and but two, newly introduced, afford the inmates a glimpse of the outer world.'

The author who relates this in the *Illuminated Magazine*, closes his description with the words: 'If God punished men for crimes as man punishes man for poverty, then woe to the sons of Adam!'

In November, 1843, a man died at Leicester, who had been dismissed two days before from the workhouse at Coventry. The details of the treatment of the poor in this institution are revolting. The man, George Robson, had a wound upon the shoulder, the treatment of which was wholly neglected; he was set to work at the pump, using the sound arm; was given only the usual workhouse fare, which he was utterly unable to digest by reason of the unhealed wound and his general debility; he naturally grew weaker, and the more he complained, the more brutally he was treated. When his wife tried to bring him her drop of beer, she was reprimanded, and forced to drink it herself in the presence of the female warder. He became ill, but received no better treatment. Finally, at his own request, and under the most insulting epithets, he was discharged, accompanied by his wife. Two days later he died at Leicester, in consequence of the neglected wound and of the food given him, which was utterly indigestible for one in his condition, as the surgeon present at the inquest testified. When he was discharged, there were handed to him letters containing money, which had been kept back six weeks, and opened, according to a rule of the establishment, by the inspector! In Birmingham such scandalous occurrences took place, that finally, in 1843, an official was sent to investigate the case. He found that four tramps had been shut up naked under a staircase in a black hole, eight to ten days, often deprived of food until noon, and that at the severest season of the year. A little boy had been passed through all grades of punishment known to the institution; first locked up in a damp, vaulted, narrow, lumber-room; then in the dog-hole twice, the second time three days and three nights; then the same length of time in the old dog-hole, which was still worse; then the tramp-room, a stinking, disgustingly filthy hole, with wooden sleeping stalls, where the official, in the course of his inspection, found two other tattered boys, shrivelled with cold, who had been spending three days there. In the dog-hole there were often seven, and in the tramp-room, twenty men huddled together. Women, also, were placed in the dog-hole, because they refused to go to church; and one was shut four days into the tramp-room, with God knows what sort of company, and that while she was ill and receiving medicine! Another woman was placed in the insane department for punishment, though she was perfectly sane. In the workhouse at Bacton, in Suffolk, in January, 1844, a similar investigation revealed the fact that a feeble-minded woman was employed as nurse, and took care of the patients accordingly; while sufferers, who were often restless at night, or tried to get up, were tied fast with cords passed over the covering and under the bedstead, to save the nurses the trouble of sitting up at night. One patient was found dead, bound in this way. In the St Pancras workhouse in London (where the cheap shirts already mentioned are made), an epileptic died of suffocation during an attack in bed, no one coming to his relief; in the same house, four to six, sometimes eight children, slept in one bed. In Shoreditch workhouse a man was placed, together with a fever patient violently ill, in a bed teeming with vermin. In Bethnal Green workhouse, London, a woman in the sixth month of pregnancy was shut up in the reception-room with her two-year-old child, from February 28th to March 20th, without being admitted into the workhouse itself, and without a trace of a bed or the means of satisfying the most natural wants. Her husband, who was brought into the workhouse, begged to have his wife released from this imprisonment, whereupon he received twenty-four hours imprisonment, with bread and water, as the penalty of his insolence. In the workhouse at Slough, near Windsor, a man lay dying in September, 1844. His wife journeyed to him, arriving at midnight; and hastening to the workhouse, was refused admission. She was not permitted to see her husband until the next morning, and then only in the presence of a female warder, who forced herself upon the wife at every succeeding visit, sending her away at the end of half-an-hour. In the workhouse at Middleton, in Lancashire, twelve, and at times eighteen, paupers, of both sexes, slept in one room. This institution is not embraced by the New Poor Law, but is administered under an old special act (Gilbert's Act). The inspector had instituted a brewery in the house for his own benefit. In Stockport, July 31st, 1844, a man, seventy-two years old, was brought before the Justice of the Peace for refusing to break stones, and insisting that, by reason of his age and a stiff knee, he was unfit for his work. In vain did he offer to undertake any work adapted to his physical strength; he was sentenced to two weeks upon the treadmill. In the workhouse at Basford, an inspecting official found that the sheets had not been changed in thirteen weeks, shirts in four weeks, stockings in two to ten months, so that of forty-five boys but three had stockings, and all their shirts were in tatters. The beds swarmed with vermin, and the tableware was washed in the slop-pails. In the west of London workhouse, a porter who had infected four girls with syphilis was not discharged, and another who had concealed a deaf and dumb girl four days and nights in his bed was also retained.

As in life, so in death. The poor are dumped into the earth like infected cattle. The pauper burial-ground of St Brides, London, is a bare morass, in use as a cemetery since the time of Charles II, and filled with heaps of bones; every Wednesday the paupers are thrown into a ditch fourteen feet deep; a curate rattles through the Litany at the top of his speed; the ditch is loosely covered in, to be re-opened the next Wednesday, and filled with corpses as long as one more can be forced in. The putrefaction thus engendered contaminates the whole neighbourhood. In Manchester, the pauper burial-ground lies opposite to the Old Town, along the Irk: this, too, is a rough, desolate place. About two years ago a railroad was carried through it. If it had been a respectable cemetery, how the bourgeoisie and the clergy would have shrieked over the desecration! But it was a pauper burial-ground, the resting-place of the outcast and superfluous, so no one concerned himself about the matter. It was not even thought worth while to convey the partially decayed bodies to the other side of the cemetery; they were heaped up just as it happened, and piles were driven into newly-made graves, so that the water oozed out of the swampy ground, pregnant with putrefying matter, and filled the neighbourhood with the most revolting and injurious gases. The disgusting brutality which accompanied this work I cannot describe in further detail.

Can anyone wonder that the poor decline to accept public relief under these conditions? That they starve rather than enter these bastilles? I have the reports of five cases in which persons actually starving, when the guardians refused them outdoor relief, went back to their miserable homes and died of starvation rather than enter these hells. Thus far have the Poor Law Commissioners attained their object. At the same time, however, the workhouses have intensified, more than any other measure of the party in power, the hatred of the working class against the property-holders, who very generally admire the New Poor Law.

From Newcastle to Dover, there is but one voice among the workers − the voice of hatred against the new law. The bourgeoisie has formulated so clearly in this law its conception of its duties towards the proletariat, that it has been appreciated even by the dullest. So frankly, so boldly had the conception never yet been formulated, that the non-possessing class exists solely for the purpose of being exploited, and of starving when the property-holders can no longer make use of it. Hence it is that this new Poor Law has contributed so greatly to accelerate the labour movement, and especially to spread Chartism; and, as it is carried out most extensively in the country, it facilitates the development of the proletarian movement which is arising in the agricultural districts. Let me add that a similar law in force in Ireland since 1838, affords a similar refuge for eighty thousand paupers. Here, too, it has made itself disliked, and would have been intensely hated if it had attained anything like the same importance as in England. But what difference does the ill-treatment of eighty thousand proletarians make in a country in which there are two and a half millions of them? In Scotland there are, with local exceptions, no Poor Laws.

I hope that after this picture of the New Poor Law and its results, no word which I have said of the English bourgeoisie will be thought too stern. In this public measure, in which it acts *in corpore* as the ruling power, it formulates its real intentions, reveals the animus of those smaller transactions with the proletariat, of which the blame apparently attaches to individuals. And that this measure did not originate with any one section of the bourgeoisie, but enjoys the approval of the whole class, is proved by the Parlia-mentary debates of 1844. The Liberal party had enacted the New Poor Law; the Conservative party, with its Prime Minister Peel at the head, defends it, and only alters some petty-fogging trifles in the Poor Law Amendment Bill of 1844. A Liberal majority carried the bill, a Conservative majority approved it, and the 'Noble Lords' gave their consent each time. Thus is the expulsion of the proletariat from State and society outspoken, thus is it publicly proclaimed that proletarians are not human beings, and do not deserve to be treated as such. Let us leave it to the proletarians of the British Empire to re-conquer their human rights.[141]

Such is the state of the British working class as I have come to know it in the course of twenty-one months, through the medium of my own eyes, and through official and other trustworthy reports. And when I call this condition, as I have frequently enough done in the foregoing pages, an utterly unbearable one, I am not alone in so doing. As early as 1833, Gaskell declared that he despaired of a peaceful issue, and that a revolution can hardly fail to follow. In 1838, Carlyle explained Chartism and the revolutionary activity of the working-men as arising out of the misery in which they live, and only wondered that they have sat so quietly eight long years at the Barmecide feast, at which they have been regaled by the Liberal bourgeoisie with empty promises. And in 1844 he declared that the work of organising labour must be begun at once 'if Europe or at least England, is long to remain inhabitable'. And the *Times*, the 'first journal of Europe', said in June, 1844: 'War to palaces, peace unto cabins – that is a battle-cry of terror which may come to resound throughout our country. Let the wealthy beware!'

* * *

Meanwhile, let us review once more the chances of the English bourgeoisie. In the worst case, foreign manufacture, especially that of America, may succeed in withstanding English competition, even after the repeal of the Corn Laws, inevitable in the course of a few years. German manufacture is now making great efforts, and that of America has developed with giant strides. America, with its inexhaustible resources, with its unmeasured coal and iron fields, with its unexampled wealth of water-power and its navigable rivers, but especially with its energetic, active population, in comparison with which the English are phlegmatic dawdlers – America has in less than ten years created a manufacture which already competes with England in the coarser cotton goods, has excluded the English from the markets of North and South

America, and holds its own in China, side by side with England. If any country is adapted to holding a monopoly of manufacture, it is America. Should English manufacture be thus vanquished – and in the course of the next twenty years, if the present conditions remain unchanged, this is inevitable – the majority of the proletariat must become forever superfluous, and has no other choice than to starve or to rebel. Does the English bourgeoisie reflect upon this contingency? On the contrary; its favourite economist, McCulloch, teaches from his student's desk, that a country so young as America, which is not even properly populated, cannot carry on manufacture successfully or dream of competing with an old manufacturing country like England. It were madness in the Americans to make the attempt, for they could only lose by it; better far for them to stick to their agriculture, and when they have brought their whole territory under the plough, a time may perhaps come for carrying on manufacture with a profit. So says the wise economist, and the whole bourgeoisie worships him, while the Americans take possession of one market after another, while a daring American speculator recently even sent a shipment of American cotton goods to England, where they were sold for re-exportation!

But assuming that England retained the monopoly of manufactures, that its factories perpetually multiply, what must be the result? The commercial crises would continue, and grow more violent, more terrible, with the extension of industry and the multiplication of the proletariat. The proletariat would increase in geometrical proportion, in consequence of the progressive ruin of the lower middle class and the giant strides with which capital is concentrating itself in the hands of the few; and the proletariat would soon embrace the whole nation, with the exception of a few millionaires. But in this development there comes a stage at which the proletariat perceives how easily the existing power may be overthrown, and then follows a revolution.

Neither of these supposed conditions may, however, be expected to arise. The commercial crises, the mightiest levers for all independent development of the proletariat, will probably shorten the process, acting in concert with foreign competition and the deepening ruin of the lower middle class. I think the people will not endure more than one more crisis. The next one, in 1846 or

1847, will probably bring with it the repeal of the Corn Laws [142] and the enactment of the Charter. What revolutionary movements the Charter may give rise to remains to be seen. But, by the time of the next following crisis, which, according to the analogy of its predecessors, must break out in 1852 or 1853, unless delayed perhaps by the repeal of the Corn Laws or hastened by other influences, such as foreign competition – by the time this crisis arrives, the English people will have had enough of being plundered by the capitalists and left to starve when the capitalists no longer require their services. If, up to that time, the English bourgeoisie does not pause to reflect – and to all appearance it certainly will not do so – a revolution will follow with which none hitherto known can be compared. The proletarians, driven to despair, will seize the torch which Stephens has preached to them; the vengeance of the people will come down with a wrath of which the rage of 1793 gives no true idea. The war of the poor against the rich will be the bloodiest ever waged. Even the union of a part of the bourgeoisie with the proletariat, even a general reform of the bourgeoisie, would not help matters. Besides, the change of heart of the bourgeoisie could only go as far as a luke-warm *juste-milieu*; the more determined, uniting with the workers, would only form a new Gironde, and succumb in the course of the mighty development. The prejudices of a whole class cannot be laid aside like an old coat: least of all, those of the stable, narrow, selfish English bourgeoisie. These are all inferences which may be drawn with the greatest certainty: conclusions, the premises for which are undeniable facts, partly of historical development, partly facts inherent in human nature. Prophecy is nowhere so easy as in England, where all the component elements of society are clearly defined and sharply separated. The revolution must come; it is already too late to bring about a peaceful solution; but it can be made more gentle than that prophesied in the foregoing pages. This depends, however, more upon the development of the proletariat than upon that of the bourgeoisie. In proportion as the proletariat absorbs socialistic and communistic elements, will the revolution diminish in bloodshed, revenge, and savagery. Communism stands, in principle, above the breach between bourgeoisie and proletariat, recognises only its historic significance for the present, but not its justification for the future: wishes, indeed, to bridge over this chasm, to do away with all class antagonisms. Hence it recognises as justified, so long as the struggle exists, the exasperation of the proletariat towards its oppressors as a necessity, as the most important lever for a labour movement just beginning; but it goes beyond this exasperation, because Communism is a question of humanity and not of the workers alone. Besides, it does not occur to any Communist to wish to revenge himself upon individuals, or to believe that, in general, the single bourgeois can act otherwise, under existing circumstances, than he does act. English Socialism, i.e. Communism, rests directly upon the irresponsibility of the individual. Thus the more the English workers absorb communistic ideas, the more superfluous becomes their present bitterness, which, should it continue so violent as at present, could accomplish nothing; and the more their action against the bourgeoisie will lose its savage cruelty. If, indeed, it were possible to make the whole proletariat communistic before the war breaks out, the end would be very peaceful; but that is no longer possible, the time has gone by. Meanwhile, I think that before the outbreak of open, declared war of the poor against the rich, there will be enough intelligent comprehension of the social question among the proletariat, to enable the communistic party, with the help of events, to conquer the brutal element of the revolution and prevent a 'Ninth Thermidor'. In any case, the experience of the French will not have been undergone in vain, and most of the Chartist leaders are, moreover, already Communists. And as Communism stands above the strife between bourgeoisie and proletariat, it will be easier for the better elements of the bourgeoisie (which are, however, deplorably few, and can look for recruits only among the rising generation) to unite with it than with purely proletarian Chartism.

If these conclusions have not been sufficiently established in the course of the present work, there may be other opportunities for demonstrating that they are necessary consequences of the historical development of England. But this I maintain, the war of the poor against the rich now carried on in detail and indirectly will become direct and universal. It is too late for a peaceful solution. The classes are divided more and more sharply, the spirit of resistance penetrates the workers, the bitterness intensifies, the guerilla skirmishes become concentrated in more important battles, and soon a slight impulse will suffice to set the avalanche in motion. Then, indeed, will the war-cry resound through the land: 'War to the palaces, peace to the cottages!' – but then it will be too late for the rich to beware.

ENGELS'S NOTES TO *THE CONDITION OF THE WORKING CLASS IN ENGLAND IN 1844*

1 According to Porter's *Progress of the Nation*, London, 1836, vol. i., 1838, vol. ii., 1843, vol. iii. (official data), and other sources chiefly official.

2 cf. on this point my 'Outlines for a Critique of Political Economy' in the *Deutsch-Französische Jahrbucher*.

3 This applies to the time of sailing vessels. The Thames now is a dreary collection of ugly steamers. — F. E.

4 *The Times*, Oct. 12th, 1843.

5 Quoted by Dr W. P. Alison, F.R.S.E, Fellow and late President of the Royal College of Physicians, etc. etc. *Observations on the Management of the Poor in Scotland and its Effects on the Health of Great Towns*. Edinburgh, 1840. The author is a religious Tory, brother of the historian, Archibald Alison.

6 *Report to the Home Secretary from the Poor-Law Commissioners on an Inquiry into the Sanitary Condition of the Labouring Classes in Great Britain with Appendix*. Presented to both Houses of Parliament in July 1842, 3 vols. Folio.

7 *The Artisan*, October, 1842.

8 *Arts and Artisan at Home and Abroad*, by J. C. Symonds, Edinburgh, 1839. The author, as it seems, himself a Scotchman, is a Liberal, and consequently fanatically opposed to every independent movement of working-men. The passages here cited are to be found pp. 116 *et seq.*

9 It must be borne in mind that these cellars are not mere storing-rooms for rubbish, but dwellings of human beings.

10 cf. 'Report of the Town Council' in the *Statistical Journal*, vol. 2, p. 404.

11 *The Moral and Physical Condition of the Working-Classes Employed in the Cotton Manufacture in Manchester*. By James Ph. Kay, M.D. 2nd Ed. 1832.

Dr Kay confuses the working class in general with the factory workers, otherwise an excellent pamphlet.

12 And yet an English Liberal wiseacre asserts, in the Report of the Children's Employment Commission, that these courts are the masterpiece of municipal architecture, because, like a multitude of little parks, they improve ventilation, the circulation of air! Certainly, if each court had two or four broad open entrances facing each other, through which the air could pour; but they never have two, rarely one, and usually only a narrow covered passage.

13 Nassau W. Senior. *Letters on the Factory Act to the Rt. Hon. the President of the Board of Trade*. (Chas. Poulett Thompson, Esq.), London, 1837, p.24.

14 Kay, loc. cit., p.32.

15 P. Gaskell. 'The Manufacturing Population of England: its Moral, Social and Physical Condition, and the Changes which have arisen from the Use of Steam Machinery; with an Examination of Infant Labour', *Fiat Justitia*, 1833. – Depicting chiefly the state of the working class in Lanca-shire. The author is a Liberal, but wrote at a time when it was not a feature of Liberalism to chant the happiness of the workers. He is therefore un-prejudiced, and can afford to have eyes for the evils of the present state of things, and especially for the factory system. On the other hand, he wrote before the Factories Enquiry Commission, and adopts from un-trustworthy sources many assertions afterwards refuted by the Report of the Commission. This work, although on the whole a valuable one, can therefore only be used with discretion, especially as the author, like Kay, confuses the whole working class with the mill hands. The history of the development of the proletariat contained in the introduction to the present work, is chiefly taken from this work of Gaskell's.

16 Thomas Carlyle. *Chartism*, London, 1840, p.28.

17 Adam Smith. *Wealth of Nations* i, McCulloch's edition in one volume, sect. 8, p.36: 'The wear and tear of a slave, it has been said, is at the ex-pense of his master, but that of a free servant is at his own expense. The wear and tear of the latter, however, is, in reality, as much at the expense of his master as that of the former. The wages paid to journeymen and servants of every kind, must be such as may enable them, one with another, to continue the race of journeymen and servants, according as the increasing, diminishing, or stationary demand of the society may happen to require. But though the wear and tear of a free servant be equally at the expense of his master, it generally costs him much less than that of a slave. The fund for replacing or repairing, if I may say so, the wear and tear of the slave, is commonly managed by a negligent master or careless overseer.'

18 And it came in 1847.

19 Archibald Alison. *Principles of Population and their Connection with Human Happiness*, two vols., 1840. This Alison is the historian of the French Rev-olution, and, like his brother, Dr W. P. Alison, a religious Tory.

20 *Chartism*, pp.28, 31, etc.

21 When as here and elsewhere I speak of society as a responsible whole, having rights and duties, I mean, of course, the ruling power of society, the class which at present holds social and political control, and bears, therefore, the responsibility for the condition of those to whom it grants no share in such control. This ruling class in England, as in all other civilised countries, is the bourgeoisie. But that this society, and especially the bourgeoisie, is charged with the duty of protecting every member of society, at least in his life, to see to it, for example, that no one starves, I

need not now prove to my *German* readers. If I were writing for the English bourgeoisie, the case would be different. [And so it is now in Germany. Our German capitalists are fully up to the English level, in this respect at least, in the year of grace, 1886.]

22 Dr Alison. *Management of the Poor in Scotland.*

23 Alison. *Principles of Population*, vol. ii.

24 Dr Alison in an article read before the British Association for the Advancement of Science. October, 1844, in York.

25 'The Manufacturing Population of England', ch 8.

26 *Report of Commission of Inquiry into the Employment of Children and Young Persons in Mines and Collieries and in the Trades and Manufactures in which numbers of them work together, not being included under the terms of the Factories' Regulation Act. First and Second Reports, Grainger's Report.* Second Report usually cited as 'Children's Employment Commission's Report'. First Report, 1841; Second Report, 1843.

27 *Fifth Annual Report of the Registrar General of Births, Deaths, and Marriages.*

28 Dr Cowen. *Vital Statistics of Glasgow.*

29 *Report of Commission of Inquiry into the State of Large Towns and Populous Districts.* First Report, 1844. Appendix.

30 Factories' Inquiry Commission's Reports, 3rd volume. Report of Dr Hawkins on Lancashire, in which Dr Robertson is cited – the 'Chief Authority for Statistics in Manchester'.

31 Quoted by Dr Wade from the Report of the Parliamentary Factories' Commission of 1832, in his *History of the Middle and Working Classes.* London, 1835, 3rd ed.

32 'Children's Employment Commission's Report'. App. Part II. Q. 18, No. 216, 217, 226, 233, etc. Horne.

33 *Ibid.* evidence, pp.9, 39; 133.

34 *Ibid.* pp.9, 36; 146.

35 *Ibid.* p.34; 158.

36 Symonds' Report. Appendix Part I., pp. E, 22 *et seq.*

37 *Arts and Artisans.*

38 *Principles of Population*, vol. ii. pp.136, 197.

39 We shall see later how the rebellion of the working class against the bourgeoisie in England is legalised by the right of coalition.

40 *Chartism*, pp.34 *et seq.*

41 *Ibid.*, p.40.

42 Shall I call bourgeois witnesses to bear testimony for me here, too? I select one only, whom everyone may read, namely, Adam Smith. *Wealth of Nations* (McCulloch's four-volume edition), vol. iii., book 5, chap.8, p.297.

43 *Principles of Population*, vol. ii., pp.76 *et seq.* p.82, p.135.

44 *Philosophy of Manufacture*, London, 1835, pp.406 *et seq.* We shall have occasion to refer further to this reputable work.

45 *On the Present Condition of the Labouring Poor in Manchester*, etc. By the Rev. Rd. Parkinson, Canon of Manchester, 3d ed., London and Manchester, 1841, pamphlet.

46 'The Manufacturing Population of England', chap. 10.

47 The total of population, about fifteen millions, divided by the number of convicted criminals (22,733).

48 *The Cotton Manufacture of Great Britain*, by Dr A. Ure, 1836.

49 *History of the Cotton Manufacture of Great Britain*, by E. Baines, Esq.

50 *Stubborn Facts from the Factories by a Manchester Operative.* Published and dedicated to the working classes, by Wm. Rashleigh, M.P., London, Ollivier, 1844, p.28 *et seq.*

51 cf. Factories' Inquiry Commission's Report.

52 L. Symonds, in *Arts and Artisans*.

53 See Dr Ure in *Philosophy of Manufacture*.

54 Report of Factory Inspector, L. Homer, October, 1844: 'The state of things in the matter of wages is greatly perverted in certain branches of cotton manufacture in Lancashire; there are hundreds of young men, between twenty and thirty, employed as piecers and otherwise, who do not get more than 8 or 9 shillings a week, while children under thirteen years, working under the same roof, earn 5 shillings, and young girls, from sixteen to twenty years, 10–12 shillings per week.'

55 Report of Factories' Inquiry Commission. Testimony of Dr Hawkins, p.3.

56 In 1843, among the accidents brought to the Infirmary in Manchester, one hundred and eighty-nine were from burning.

57 Factories' Inquiry Commission's Report, Power's Report on Leeds, *passim.* Tufnell Report on Manchester, p.17. etc.

58 This letter is re-translated from the German, no attempt being made to reproduce either the spelling or the original Yorkshire dialect.

59 How numerous married women are in the factories is seen from information furnished by a manufacturer: in 412 factories in Lancashire, 10,721 of them were employed; of the husbands of these women, but 5,314 were also employed in the factories, 3,927 were otherwise employed, 821 were unemployed, and information was wanting as to 659. Or, two if not three men for each factory are supported by the work of their wives.

60 House of Commons, March 15th, 1844.

61 Factories' Inquiry Commission's Report, p.4.

62 For further examples and information cf. Factories' Inquiry Commission's Report. Cowell Evidence, pp.37–39, 72, 77, 59; Tufnell Evidence, pp.9, 15, 45, 54, etc.

63 Cowell Evidence, pp.35, 37, and elsewhere.

64 Power Evidence, p.8.

65 Cowell Evidence, p.57

66 Cowell Evidence, p.82.

67 Factories' Inquiry Commission's Report, p.4, Hawkins.

68 Stuart Evidence, p.35.

69 Tufnell Evidence, p.91.

70 Dr Loudon Evidence, pp.12, 13.

71 Dr Loudon Evidence, p.16.

72 Drinkwater Evidence, pp.72, 80, 146, 148, 150 (two brothers); 69 (two brothers); 155, and many others.
Power Evidence, pp.63, 66, 67 (two cases); 68 (three cases); 69 (two cases); in Leeds, pp.29, 31, 40, 43, 53 *et seq.*
Loudon Evidence, pp.4, 7 (four cases); 8 (several cases), etc.
Sir D. Barry Evidence, pp.6, 8, 13, 21, 22, 44, 55 (three cases), etc.
Tufnell Evidence, pp.5, 6, 16, etc.

73 Factories' Inquiry Commission's Report, 1836, Sir D. Barry Evidence, p.21 (two cases).

74 Factories' Inquiry Commission's Report, 1836, Loudon Evidence, pp.13, 16, etc.

75 In the spinning-room of a mill at Leeds, too, chairs had been introduced. Drinkwater Evidence, p.80.

76 General report by Sir D. Barry.

77 Power Report, p.74.

78 The surgeons in England are scientifically educated as well as the physicians, and have, in general, medical as well as surgical practice. They are in general, for various reasons, preferred to the physicians.

79 This statement is not taken from the report.

80 Tufnell, p.59.

81 Stuart Evidence, p.101.

82 Tufnell Evidence, pp.3, 9, 15.

83 Hawkins Report, p.4; Evidence, p.14, etc. etc. Hawkins Evidence, pp.11, 13.

84 Cowell Evidence, p.77.

85 Sir D. Barry Evidence, p.44.

86 Cowell, p.35.

87 Dr Hawkins Evidence, p.11; Dr Loudon, p.14, etc.; Sir D. Barry, p.5, etc.

88 cf. Stuart, pp.13, 70, 101; Mackintosh, p.24, etc.; Power Report on Nottingham, on Leeds; Cowell, p.33, etc.; Barry, p.12 (five cases in one factory), pp.17, 44, 52, 60, etc.; Loudon, p.13.

89 Stuart, p.39.

90 *Philosophy of Manufacture*, by Dr Andrew Ure, pp.277 *et seq.*

91 *Ibid.*, p.277.

92 *Ibid.*, p.298.

93 *Ibid.*, p.301.

94 *Ibid.*, pp.405, 406 *et seq.*

95 Afterwards Earl of Shaftesbury, died 1885.

96 It is notorious that the House of Commons made itself ridiculous a second time in the same session in the same way on the Sugar Question, when it first voted against the ministry and then for it, after an application of the ministerial whip.

97 Let us hear another competent judge: 'If we consider the example of the Irish in connection with the ceaseless toil of the cotton operative class, we shall wonder less at their terrible demoralisation. Continuous exhausting toil, day after day, year after year, is not calculated to develop the intellectual and moral capabilities of the human being. The wearisome routine of endless drudgery, in which the same mechanical process is ever repeated, is like the torture of Sisyphus; the burden of toil, like the rock, is ever falling back upon the worn-out drudge. The mind attains neither knowledge nor the power of thought from the eternal employment of the same muscles. The intellect dozes off in dull indolence, but the coarser part of our nature reaches a luxuriant development. To condemn a human being to such work is to cultivate the animal quality in him. He grows indifferent, he scorns the impulses and customs which distinguish his kind. He neglects the conveniences and finer pleasures of life, lives in filthy poverty with scanty nourishment, and squanders the rest of his earnings in debauchery.' – Dr J. Kay.

98 *Manchester Guardian*, October 30th.

99 *Stubborn Facts*, p.9 *et seq.*

100 Drinkwater Evidence; p.80.

101 *Stubborn Facts*, pp.13–17.

102 *Sun*, a London daily; end of November, 1844.

103 I have neither time nor space to deal in detail with the replies of the manufacturers to the charges made against them for twelve years past. These men will not learn because their supposed interest blinds them. As, moreover, many of their objections have been met in the foregoing, the following is all that it is necessary for me to add.

You come to Manchester, you wish to make yourself acquainted with the state of affairs in England. You naturally have good introductions to respectable people. You drop a remark or two as to the condition of the workers. You are made acquainted with a couple of the first Liberal manufacturers, Robert Hyde Greg, perhaps, Edmund Ashworth, Thomas Ashton, or others. They are told of your wishes. The manufacturer understands you, knows what he has to do. He accompanies you to his factory in the country; Mr Greg to Quarrybank in Cheshire, Mr Ashworth to Turton near Bolton, Mr Ashton to Hyde. He leads you through a superb, admirably arranged building, perhaps supplied with ventilators, he calls your attention to the lofty, airy rooms, the fine machinery, here and there a healthy-looking operative. He gives you an excellent lunch, and proposes to you to visit the operatives' homes; he conducts you to the cottages, which look new, clean and neat, and goes with you into this one and that one, naturally only to overlookers, mechanics, etc., so that you may see 'families who live wholly from the factory'. Among other families you might find that only wife and children work, and the husband darns stockings. The presence of the employer keeps you from asking indiscreet questions; you find everyone well-paid, comfortable, comparatively healthy by reason of the country air; you begin to be converted from your exaggerated ideas of misery and starvation. But, that the cottage system makes slaves of the operatives, that there may be a truck shop in the neighbourhood, that the people hate the manufacturer, this they do not point out to you, because he is present. He has built a school, church, reading-room, etc. That he uses the school to train children to subordination, that he tolerates in the reading-room such prints only as represent the interests of the bourgeoisie, that he dismisses his employees if they read Chartist or Socialist papers or books, this is all concealed from you. You see an easy, patriarchal relation, you see the life of the overlookers, you see what the bourgeoisie *promises* the workers if they become its slaves, mentally and morally. This 'country manufacture' has always been what the employers like to show, because in it the disadvantages of the factory system, especially from the point of view of health, are, in part, done away with by the free air and surroundings, and because the patriarchal servitude of the workers can here be longest maintained. Dr Ure sings a dithyramb upon the theme. But woe to the operatives to whom it occurs to think for themselves and become Chartists! For them the paternal affection of the manufacturer comes to a sudden end. Further, if you should wish to be accompanied through the working-people's quarters of Manchester, if you should desire to see the development of the factory system in a factory town, you may wait long before these rich bourgeoisie will help you! These gentlemen do not know in what condition their employees are nor what they want, and they dare not know things which would make them uneasy or even oblige them to act in opposition to their own interests. But, fortunately, that is of no consequence: what the working-men have to carry out, they carry out for themselves.

104 Grainger Report. Appendix, Part I., pp. 7, 15 *et seq.*, 132–42.

105 Grainger's whole Report.

106 Grainger, Children's Employment Commission's Report.

107 Burns, Children's Employment Commission's Report.

108 Leach. *Stubborn Facts from the Factories*, p.47.

109 Leach. *Stubborn Facts from the Factories*, p.33.

110 Leach. *Stubborn Facts from the Factories*, pp. 37–40.

111 Children's Employment Commission's Report.

112 See p.149.

113 Grainger Report and Evidence.

114 Horne Report and Evidence.

115 Dr Knight, *Sheffield*.

116 Symonds Report and Evidence.

117 Scriven Report and Evidence.

118 Leifchild Report Append., Part II., p. L 2, ss. 11,12; Franks Report Append., Part II., p.K 7, s. 48, Tancred Evid. Append., Part II., p.I, 76, etc. – Children's Employment Commission's Rep't.

119 See *Weekly Dispatch*, March 16th, 1844.

120 Thomas Hood, the most talented of all the English humorists now living, and, like all humorists, full of human feeling, but wanting in mental energy, published at the beginning of 1844 a beautiful poem, 'The Song of the Shirt', which drew sympathetic but unavailing tears from the eyes of the daughters of the bourgeoisie. Originally published in *Punch*, it made the round of all the papers. As discussions of the condition of the sewing-women filled all the papers at the time, special extracts are needless.

121 *Arts and Artisans*, p.137 *et seq*.

122 So called from the East Indian tribe, whose only trade is the murder of all the strangers who fall into its hands.

123 'What kind of wild justice must it be in the hearts of these men that prompts them, with cold deliberation, in conclave assembled, to doom their brother workman, as the deserter of his order and his order's cause, to die a traitor's and a deserter's death, have him executed, in default of any public judge and hangman, then by a secret one; like your old Chivalry *Fehmgericht* and Secret Tribunal, suddenly revived in this strange guise; suddenly rising once more on the astonished eye, dressed not now in mail shirts, but in fustian jackets, meeting not in Westphalian forests, but in the paved Gallowgate of Glasgow! Such a temper must be widespread and virulent among the many when, even in its worst acme, it can take such form in the few.' – Carlyle. *Chartism*, p.40.

124 Dr Ure, *Philosophy of Manufacture*, p.282.

125 *Ibid.*, p.282.

126 *Ibid.*, p.367.

127 *Ibid.*, pp.366 *et seq*.

128 cf. Report of Chambers of Commerce of Manchester and Leeds at the end of July and beginning of August.

129 See Introduction, pp.117–121.

130 According to the census of 1841, the number of working-men employed in mines in Great Britain, without Ireland, was:

	Men over 20 years	Men under 20 years	Women over 20 years	Women under 20 Years	Together
A	83,408	32,475	1,185	1,165	118,233
B	9,866	3,428	913	1,200	15,407
C	9,427	1,932	40	20	11,419
D	7,733	2,679	424	73	10,949
E	4,602	1,349	68	82	6,101
F	24,162	6,591	472	491	31,616
Total	137,398	48,454	3,102	3,031	193,725

A Coal mines   B Copper mines   C Lead mines   D Iron mines
E Tin mines   F Various, the mineral not specified

As the coal and iron mines are usually worked by the same people, a part of the miners attributed to the coal mines, and a very considerable part of those mentioned under the last heading, are to be attributed to the iron mines.

131 Also found in the Children's Employment Commission's Report: Commissioner Mitchell's Report.

132 The coal miners have at this moment, 1886, six of their body sitting in the House of Commons.

133 E. G. Wakefield, M.P. *Swing Unmasked; or, The Cause of Rural Incendiarism.* London, 1831. Pamphlet. The foregoing extracts may be found pp. 9–13, the passages dealing in the original with the then still existing Old Poor Law being here omitted.

134 This has been literally fulfilled. After a period of unexampled extension of trade, Free Trade has landed England in a crisis, which began in 1878, and is still increasing in energy in 1886.

135 The agricultural labourers have now a Trades' Union; their most energetic representative, Joseph Arch, was elected M.P. in 1885.

136 Report of the Poor Law Commission upon Ireland.

137 *Principles of Population*, vol. ii.

138 *The State of Ireland.* London, 1807; 2nd ed., 1821. Pamphlet.

139 Carlyle gives in his *Past and Present* (London, 1843) a splendid description of the English bourgeoisie and its disgusting money greed.

140 Extracts from Information received from the Poor Law Commissioners. Published by authority. London, 1833.

141 To prevent misconstructions and consequent objections, I would observe that I have spoken of the bourgeoisie as a *class*, and that all such facts as refer to individuals serve merely as evidence of the way of thinking and acting of a *class*. Hence I have not entered upon the distinctions between the divers sections, subdivisions and parties of the bourgeoisie, which have a mere historical and theoretical significance. And I can, for the same reason, mention but casually the few members of the bourgeoisie who have shown themselves honourable exceptions. These are, on the one hand, the pronounced Radicals, who are almost Chartists, such as a few members of the House of Commons, the manufacturers

Hindly of Ashton, and Fielden of Todmordon (Lancashire), and, on the other hand, the philanthropic Tories, who have recently constituted themselves 'Young England', among whom are the members of Parliament, Disraeli, Borthwick, Ferrand, Lord John Manners, etc. Lord Ashley, too, is in sympathy with them. The hope of Young England is a restoration of the old 'Merry England' with its brilliant features and its romantic feudalism. This object is of course unattainable and ridiculous, a satire upon all historic development; but the good intention, the courage to resist the existing state of things and prevalent prejudices, and to recognise the vileness of our present condition, is worth something anyhow. Wholly isolated is the half-German Englishman, Thomas Carlyle, who, originally a Tory, goes beyond all those hitherto mentioned. He has sounded the social disorder more deeply than any other English bourgeois, and demands the organisation of labour.

142 And it did.

SOCIALISM: UTOPIAN
AND SCIENTIFIC

Introduction to the 1892 English Edition

General introduction and the history of materialism

The present little book is, originally, part of a larger whole. About 1875, Dr E. Dühring, privatdocent at Berlin University, suddenly and rather clamorously announced his conversion to Socialism, and presented the German public not only with an elaborate Socialist theory, but also with a complete practical plan for the reorganisation of society. As a matter of course, he fell foul of his predecessors; above all, he honoured Marx by pouring out upon him the full vials of his wrath.

This took place about the same time when the two sections of the Socialist party in Germany – Eisenachers and Lasselleans – had just effected their fusion [at the Gotha Unification Congress], and thus obtained not only an immense increase of strength, but, was what more, the faculty of employing the whole of this strength against the common enemy. The Socialist party in Germany was fast becoming a power. But, to make it a power, the first condition was that the newly-conquered unity should not be imperilled. And Dr Dühring openly proceeded to form around himself a sect, the nucleus of a future separate party. It thus became necessary to take up the gauntlet thrown down to us, and to fight out the struggle, whether we liked it or not.

This, however, though it might not be an over-difficult, was evidently a long-winded business. As is well known, we Germans are of a terribly ponderous *Gründlichkeit*, radical profundity or profound radicality, whatever you may like to call it. Whenever any one of us expounds what he considers a new doctrine, he has first to elaborate it into an all-comprising system. He has to prove that both the first principles of logic and the fundamental laws of the universe had existed from all eternity for no other purpose than to ultimately lead to this newly-discovered, crowning theory. And Dr Dühring, in this respect, was quite up to the national mark. Nothing less than a complete *System of Philosophy*, mental, moral, natural, and historical; a complete *System of Political Economy and Socialism*; and, finally, a *Critical History of Political Economy* – three big volumes in octavo, heavy extrinsically and intrinsically, three army-corps of arguments mobilised against all previous philosophers and economists in general, and against Marx in particular – in fact, an attempt at a complete 'revolution in science' – these were what I should have to tackle. I had to treat of all and every possible subject, from concepts of time and space to Bimetallism; from the eternity of matter and motion, to the perishable nature of moral ideas; from Darwin's natural selection to the education of youth in a future society. Anyhow, the systematic comprehensiveness of my opponent gave me the opportunity of developing, in opposition to him, and in a more connected form than had previously been done, the views held by Marx and myself on this great variety of subjects. And that was the principal reason which made me undertake this otherwise ungrateful task.

My reply was first published in a series of articles in the Leipzig *Vorwärts*, the chief organ of the Socialist party, and later on as a book: *Herrn Eugen Dührings Umwälzung der Wissenchaft* (Mr E. Dühring's *Revolution in Science*), a second edition of which appeared in Zurich, 1886.

At the request of my friend, Paul Lafargue, now representative of Lille in the French Chamber of Deputies, I arranged three chapters of this book as a pamphlet, which he translated and published in 1880, under the title: *Socialisme utopique et Socialisme scientifique*. From this French text, a Polish and a Spanish edition were prepared. In 1883, our German friends brought out the pamphlet in the original language. Italian, Russian, Danish, Dutch, and Roumanian translations, based upon the German text, have since been published. Thus, with the present English edition, this little book circulates in 10 languages. I am not aware that any other Socialist work, not even our *Communist Manifesto* of 1848, or Marx's *Capital*, has been so often translated. In Germany, it has had four editions of about 20,000 copies in all.

The Appendix, 'The Mark', was written with the intention of spreading among the German Socialist party some elementary knowledge of the history and development of landed property in Germany. This seemed all the more necessary at a time when the assimilation by that party of the working-people of the towns was in a fair way of completion, and when the agricultural labourers and peasants had to be taken in hand. This appendix has been included in the translation,* as the original forms of tenure of land common to all Teutonic tribes, and the history of their decay, are even less known in England than in Germany. I have left the text as it stands in the original, without alluding to the hypothesis recently started by Maxim Kovalevsky, according to which the partition of the arable and meadow lands among the members of the Mark was preceded by their being cultivated for joint-account by a large patriarchal family community, embracing several generations (as exemplified by the still existing South Slavonian Zadruga), and that the partition, later on, took place when the community had increased, so as to become too unwieldy for joint-account management. Kovalevsky is probably quite right, but the matter is still *sub judice*.

The economic terms used in this work, as far as they are new, agree with those used in the English edition of Marx's *Capital*. We call 'production of commodities' that economic phase where articles are produced not only for the use of the producers, but also for the purpose of exchange; that is, *as commodities*, not as use values. This phase extends from the first beginnings of production for exchange down to our present time; it attains its full development under capitalist production only, that is, under conditions where the capitalist, the owner of the means of production, employs, for wages, labourers, people deprived of all means of production except their own labour-power, and pockets the excess of the selling price of the products over his outlay. We divide the history of industrial production since the Middle Ages into three periods:

1. Handicraft, small master craftsman with a few journeymen and apprentices, where each labourer produces a complete article.
2. Manufacture, where greater numbers of workmen, grouped in one large establishment, produce the complete article on the principle of division of labour, each workman performing only one partial operation, so that the product is complete only after having passed successively through the hands of all.
3. Modern industry, where the product is produced by machinery driven by power, and where the work of the labourer is limited to superintending and correcting the performance of the mechanical agent.

* Not reproduced in this edition.

I am perfectly aware that the contents of this work will meet with objection from a considerable portion of the British public. But, if we Continentals had taken the slightest notice of the prejudices of British 'respectability', we should be even worse off than we are. This book defends what we call 'historical materialism', and the word materialism grates upon the ears of the immense majority of British readers. 'Agnosticism' might be tolerated, but materialism is utterly inadmissible.

And yet, the original home of all modern materialism, from the seventeenth century onwards, is England.

Materialism is the natural-born son of Great Britain. Already the British schoolman, Duns Scotus, asked, 'whether it was impossible for matter to think?'

In order to effect this miracle, he took refuge in God's omnipotence – i.e. he made theology preach materialism. Moreover, he was a nominalist. Nominalism, the first form of materialism, is chiefly found among the English schoolmen.

The real progenitor of English materialism is Bacon. To him, natural philosophy is the only true philosophy, and physics based upon the experience of the senses is the chiefest part of natural philosophy. Anaxagoras and his *homoiomeriae*, Democritus and his atoms, he often quotes as his authorities. According to him, the senses are infallible and the source of all knowledge. All science is based on experience, and consists in subjecting the data furnished by the senses to a rational method of investigation. Induction, analysis, comparison, observation, experiment, are the principal forms of such a rational method. Among the qualities inherent in matter, motion is the first and foremost, not only in the form of mechanical and mathematical motion, but chiefly in the form of an impulse, a vital spirit, a tension – or a 'qual', to use a term of Jakob Böhme's * – of matter.

In Bacon, its first creator, materialism still occludes within itself the germs of a many-sided development. On the one hand,

---

* A philosophical play on words. Qual literally means torture, a pain which drives to action of some kind; at the same time, the mystic Böhme puts into the German word something of the meaning of the Latin *qualitas*; his 'qual' was the activating principle arising from, and promoting in its turn, the spontaneous development of the thing, relation, or person subject to it, in contradistinction to a pain inflicted from without. [Note by Engels to the English Edition]

matter, surrounded by a sensuous, poetic glamour, seems to attract man's whole entity by winning smiles. On the other, the aphoristically formulated doctrine pullulates with inconsistencies imported from theology.

In its further evolution, materialism becomes one-sided. Hobbes is the man who systematises Baconian materialism. Knowledge based upon the senses loses its poetic blossom, it passes into the abstract experience of the mathematician; geometry is proclaimed as the queen of sciences. Materialism takes to misanthropy. If it is to overcome its opponent, misanthropic, fleshless spiritualism, and that on the latter's own ground, materialism has to chastise its own flesh and turn ascetic. Thus, from a sensual, it passes into an intellectual, entity; but thus, too, it evolves all the consistency, regardless of consequences, characteristic of the intellect.

Hobbes, as Bacon's continuator, argues thus: if all human knowledge is furnished by the senses, then our concepts and ideas are but the phantoms, divested of their sensual forms, of the real world. Philosophy can but give names to these phantoms. One name may be applied to more than one of them. There may even be names of names. It would imply a contradiction if, on the one hand, we maintained that all ideas had their origin in the world of sensation, and, on the other, that a word was more than a word; that, besides the beings known to us by our senses, beings which are one and all individuals, there existed also beings of a general, not individual, nature. An unbodily substance is the same absurdity as an unbodily body. Body, being, substance, are but different terms for the same reality. *It is impossible to separate thought from matter that thinks.* This matter is the substratum of all changes going on in the world. The word infinite is meaningless, unless it states that our mind is capable of performing an endless process of addition. Only material things being perceptible to us, we cannot know anything about the existence of God. My own existence alone is certain. Every human passion is a mechanical movement, which has a beginning and an end. The objects of impulse are what we call good. Man is subject to the same laws as nature. Power and freedom are identical.

Hobbes had systematised Bacon, without, however, furnishing a proof for Bacon's fundamental principle, the origin of all human knowledge from the world of sensation. It was Locke who, in his *Essay on the Human Understanding*, supplied this proof.

Hobbes had shattered the theistic prejudices of Baconian materialism; Collins, Dodwell, Coward, Hartley, Priestley, similarly shattered the last theological bars that still hemmed in Locke's sensationalism. At all events, for practical materialists, Deism is but an easy-going way of getting rid of religion.

                         Karl Marx, *The Holy Family*, pp. 201–204

Thus Karl Marx wrote about the British origin of modern materialism. If Englishmen nowadays do not exactly relish the compliment he paid their ancestors, more's the pity. It is none the less undeniable that Bacon, Hobbes and Locke are the fathers of that brilliant school of French materialism which made the eighteenth century, in spite of all battles on land and sea won over Frenchmen by Germans and Englishmen, a pre-eminently French century, even before that crowning French Revolution, the results of which we outsiders, in England as well as Germany, are still trying to acclimatise.

There is no denying it. About the middle of this century, what struck every cultivated foreigner who set up his residence in England, was what he was then bound to consider the religious bigotry and stupidity of the English respectable middle class. We, at that time, were all materialists, or, at least, very advanced freethinkers, and to us it appeared inconceivable that almost all educated people in England should believe in all sorts of impossible miracles, and that even geologists like Buckland and Mantell should contort the facts of their science so as not to clash too much with the myths of the book of Genesis; while, in order to find people who dared to use their own intellectual faculties with regard to religious matters, you had to go amongst the uneducated, the 'great unwashed', as they were then called, the working people, especially the Owenite Socialists.

But England has been 'civilised' since then. The exhibition of 1851 sounded the knell of English insular exclusiveness. England became gradually internationalised, in diet, in manners, in ideas; so much so that I begin to wish that some English manners and customs had made as much headway on the Continent as other Continental habits have made here. Anyhow, the introduction and spread of salad-oil (before 1851 known only to the aristocracy) has been accompanied by a fatal spread of Continental scepticism in matters religious, and it has come to this, that agnosticism, though not yet considered 'the thing' quite as much as the Church of England, is yet very nearly on a par, as far as respectability goes, with Baptism, and decidedly ranks above the Salvation Army. And I cannot help believing that under those circumstances it will be consoling to many who sincerely regret and condemn this progress of infidelity to learn that these 'new-fangled notions' are not of foreign origin, are not 'made in Germany', like so many other articles of daily use, but are undoubtedly Old English, and that their British originators 200 years ago went a good deal further than their descendants now dare to venture.

What, indeed, is agnosticism but, to use an expressive Lancashire term, 'shamefaced' materialism? The agnostic's conception of Nature is materialistic throughout. The entire natural world is governed by law, and absolutely excludes the intervention of action from without. But, he adds, we have no means either of ascertaining or of disproving the existence of some Supreme Being beyond the known universe. Now, this might hold good at the time when Laplace, to Napoleon's question, why, in the great astronomer's *Treatise on Celestial Mechanics*, the Creator was not even mentioned, proudly replied, 'I had no need of this hypothesis.' But, nowadays, in our evolutionary conception of the universe, there is absolutely no room for either a Creator or a Ruler; and to talk of a Supreme Being shut out from the whole existing world, implies a contradiction in terms, and, as it seems to me, a gratuitous insult to the feelings of religious people.

Again, our agnostic admits that all our knowledge is based upon the information imparted to us by our senses. But, he adds, how do we know that our senses give us correct representations of the objects we perceive through them? And he proceeds to inform us that, whenever he speaks of objects, or their qualities, he does in reality not mean those objects and qualities, of which he cannot know anything for certain, but merely the impressions which they have produced on his senses. Now, this line of reasoning seems undoubtedly hard to beat by mere argumentation. But before there was argumentation, there was action. *Im Anfang war die Tat.**

* Goethe, *Faust*: 'In the beginning was the deed.'

And human action had solved the difficulty long before human ingenuity invented it. The proof of the pudding is in the eating. From the moment we turn to our own use these objects, according to the qualities we perceive in them, we put to an infallible test the correctness or otherwise of our sense-perception. If these perceptions have been wrong, then our estimate of the use to which an object can be turned must also be wrong, and our attempt must fail. But, if we succeed in accomplishing our aim, if we find that the object does agree with our idea of it, and does answer the purpose we intended it for, then that is proof positive that our perceptions of it and of its qualities, *so far*, agree with reality outside ourselves. And, whenever we find ourselves face-to-face with a failure, then we generally are not long in making out the cause that made us fail; we find that the perception upon which we acted was either incomplete and superficial, or combined with the results of other perceptions in a way not warranted by them – what we call defective reasoning. So long as we take care to train our senses properly, and to keep our action within the limits prescribed by perceptions properly made and properly used, so long we shall find that the result of our action proves the conformity of our perceptions with the objective nature of the things perceived. Not in one single instance, so far, have we been led to the conclusion that our sense-perceptions, scientifically controlled, induce in our minds ideas respecting the outer world that are, by their very nature, at variance with reality, or that there is an inherent incompatibility between the outer world and our sense-perceptions of it.

But then come the Neo-Kantian agnostics and say: We may correctly perceive the qualities of a thing, but we cannot by any sensible or mental process grasp the thing-in-itself. This 'thing-in-itself' is beyond our ken. To this Hegel, long since, has replied: if you know all the qualities of a thing, you know the thing itself; nothing remains but the fact that the said thing exists without us; and, when your senses have taught you that fact, you have grasped the last remnant of the thing-in-itself, Kant's celebrated unknowable *Ding an sich*. To which it may be added that in Kant's time our knowledge of natural objects was indeed so fragmentary that he might well suspect, behind the little we knew about each of them, a mysterious 'thing-in-itself'. But one after another these ungraspable things have been grasped, analysed, and, what is more, *reproduced* by the giant progress of science; and what we can produce we certainly cannot consider as unknowable. To the chemistry of the first half of this century, organic substances were such mysterious objects; now we learn to build them up one after another from their chemical elements without the aid of organic processes. Modern chemists declare that as soon as the chemical constitution of no-matter-what body is known, it can be built up from its elements. We are still far from knowing the constitution of the highest organic substances, the albuminous bodies; but there is no reason why we should not, if only after centuries, arrive at the knowledge and, armed with it, produce artificial albumen. But, if we arrive at that, we shall at the same time have produced organic life, for life, from its lowest to its highest forms, is but the normal mode of existence of albuminous bodies.

As soon, however, as our agnostic has made these formal mental reservations, he talks and acts as the rank materialist he at bottom is. He may say that, as far as we know, matter and motion, or as it is now called, energy, can neither be created nor destroyed, but that we have no proof of their not having been created at some time or other. But if you try to use this admission against him in any particular case, he will quickly put you out of court. If he admits the possibility of spiritualism *in abstracto*, he will have none of it *in concreto*. As far as we know and can know, he will tell you, there is no creator and no Ruler of the universe; as far as we are concerned, matter and energy can neither be created nor annihilated; for us, mind is a mode of energy, a function of the brain; all we know is that the material world is governed by immutable laws, and so forth. Thus, as far as he is a scientific man, as far as he *knows* anything, he is a materialist; outside his science, in spheres about which he knows nothing, he translates his ignorance into Greek and calls it agnosticism.

At all events, one thing seems clear: even if I was an agnostic, it is evident that I could not describe the conception of history sketched out in this little book as 'historical agnosticism'. Religious people would laugh at me, agnostics would indignantly ask, was I making fun of them? And thus, I hope even British respectability will not be overshocked if I use, in English as well as in so many other languages, the term 'historical materialism', to designate that view of the course of history which seeks the ultimate cause and the great moving power of all important historic events in the economic development of society, in the changes in the modes of production and exchange, in the consequent division of society into distinct classes, and in the struggles of these classes against one another.

This indulgence will, perhaps, be accorded to me all the sooner if I show that historical materialism may be of advantage even to British respectability. I have mentioned the fact that, about 40 or 50 years ago, any cultivated foreigner settling in England was struck by what he was then bound to consider the religious bigotry and stupidity of the English respectable middle class. I am now going to prove that the respectable English middle class of that time was not quite as stupid as it looked to the intelligent foreigner. Its religious leanings can be explained.

History (the role of religion) in the English middle class

When Europe emerged from the Middle Ages, the rising middle class of the towns constituted its revolutionary element. It had conquered a recognised position within medieval feudal organisation, but this position, also, had become too narrow for its expansive power. The development of the middle class, the *bourgeoisie*, became incompatible with the maintenance of the feudal system; the feudal system, therefore, had to fall.

But the great international centre of feudalism was the Roman Catholic Church. It united the whole of feudalised Western Europe, in spite of all internal wars, into one grand political system, opposed as much to the schismatic Greeks as to the Mohammedan countries. It had organised its own hierarchy on the feudal model, and, lastly, it was itself by far the most powerful feudal lord, holding, as it did, fully one-third of the soil of the Catholic world. Before profane feudalism could be successfully attacked in each country and in detail, this, its sacred central organisation, had to be destroyed.

Moreover, parallel with the rise of the middle class went on the great revival of science; astronomy, mechanics, physics, anatomy, physiology were again cultivated. And the bourgeoisie, for the development of its industrial production, required a science which ascertained the physical properties of natural objects and the modes

INTRODUCTION 341

of action of the forces of Nature. Now up to then science had
but been the humble handmaid of the Church, had not been
allowed to overlap the limits set by faith, and for that reason had
been no science at all. Science rebelled against the Church; the
bourgeoisie could not do without science, and, therefore, had to
join in the rebellion.

The above, though touching but two of the points where the
rising middle class was bound to come into collision with the
established religion, will be sufficient to show, first, that the class
most directly interested in the struggle against the pretensions of
the Roman Church was the bourgeoisie; and second, that every
struggle against feudalism, at that time, had to take on a religious
disguise, had to be directed against the Church in the first
instance. But if the universities and the traders of the cities started
the cry, it was sure to find, and did find, a strong echo in the
masses of the country people, the peasants, who everywhere had
to struggle for their very existence with their feudal lords, spiritual and temporal.

The long fight of the bourgeoisie against feudalism culminated
in three great, decisive battles.

The first was what is called the Protestant Reformation in
Germany. The war cry raised against the Church, by Luther, was
responded to by two insurrections of a political nature; first, that of
the lower nobility under Franz von Sickingen (1523), then the
great Peasants' War, 1525. Both were defeated, chiefly in consequence of the indecision of the parties most interested, the
burghers of the towns – an indecision into the causes of which we
cannot here enter. From that moment, the struggle degenerated
into a fight between the local princes and the central power, and
ended by blotting out Germany, for 200 years, from the politically
active nations of Europe. The Lutheran Reformation produced a
new creed indeed, a religion adapted to absolute monarchy. No
sooner were the peasants of North-east Germany converted to
Lutheranism than they were from freemen reduced to serfs.

But where Luther failed, Calvin won the day. Calvin's creed was
one fit for the boldest of the bourgeoisie of his time. His predest-
ination doctrine was the religious expression of the fact that in
the commercial world of competition success or failure does not
depend upon a man's activity or cleverness, but upon circumstances

uncontrollable by him. It is not of him that willeth or of him that runneth, but of the mercy of unknown superior economic powers; and this was especially true at a period of economic revolution, when all old commercial routes and centres were replaced by new ones, when India and America were opened to the world, and when even the most sacred economic articles of faith – the value of gold and silver – began to totter and to break down. Calvin's church constitution was thoroughly democratic and republican; and where the kingdom of God was republicanised, could the kingdoms of this world remain subject to monarchs, bishops, and lords? While German Lutheranism became a willing tool in the hands of princes, Calvinism founded a republic in Holland, and active republican parties in England, and, above all, Scotland.

In Calvinism, the second great bourgeois upheaval found its doctrine ready cut and dried. This upheaval took place in England. The middle class of the towns brought it on, and the yeomanry of the country districts fought it out. Curiously enough, in all the three great bourgeois risings, the peasantry furnishes the army that has to do the fighting; and the peasantry is just the class that, the victory once gained, is most surely ruined by the economic consequences of that victory. A hundred years after Cromwell, the yeomanry of england had almost disappeared. Anyhow, had it not been for that yeomanry and for the *plebeian* element in the towns, the bourgeoisie alone would never have fought the matter out to the bitter end, and would never have brought Charles I to the scaffold. In order to secure even those conquests of the bourgeoisie that were ripe for gathering at the time, the revolution had to be carried considerably further – exactly as in 1793 in France and 1848 in Germany. This seems, in fact, to be one of the laws of evolution of bourgeois society.

Well, upon this excess of revolutionary activity there necessarily followed the inevitable reaction which, in its turn, went beyond the point where it might have maintained itself. After a series of oscillations, the new centre of gravity was at last attained and became a new starting-point. The grand period of English history, known to respectability under the name of 'the Great Rebellion', and the struggles succeeding it, were brought to a close by the comparatively puny events entitled by Liberal historians 'the Glorious Revolution'.

The new starting-point was a compromise between the rising middle class and the ex-feudal landowners. The latter, though called, as now, the aristocracy, had been long since on the way which led them to become what Louis Philippe in France became at a much later period: 'the first bourgeois of the kingdom'. Fortunately for England, the old feudal barons had killed one another during the War of the Roses. Their successors, though mostly scions of the old families, had been so much out of the direct line of descent that they constituted quite a new body, with habits and tendencies far more bourgeois than feudal. They fully understood the value of money, and at once began to increase their rents by turning hundreds of small farmers out and replacing them with sheep. Henry VIII, while squandering the Church lands, created fresh bourgeois landlords by wholesale; the innumerable confiscation of estates, regranted to absolute or relative upstarts, and continued during the whole of the seventeenth century, had the same result. Consequently, ever since Henry VII, the English 'aristocracy', far from counteracting the development of industrial production, had, on the contrary, sought to indirectly profit thereby; and there had always been a section of the great landowners willing, from economical or political reasons, to cooperate with the leading men of the financial and industrial bourgeoisie. The compromise of 1689 was, therefore, easily accomplished. The political spoils of 'pelf and place' were left to the great landowning families, provided the economic interests of the financial, manufacturing, and commercial middle class were sufficiently attended to. And these economic interests were at that time powerful enough to determine the general policy of the nation. There might be squabbles about matters of detail, but, on the whole, the aristocratic oligarchy knew too well that its own economic prosperity was irretrievably bound up with that of the industrial and commercial middle class.

From that time, the bourgeoisie was a humble, but still a recognised, component of the ruling classes of England. With the rest of them, it had a common interest in keeping in subjection the great working mass of the nation. The merchant or manufacturer himself stood in the position of master, or, as it was until lately called, of 'natural superior' to his clerks, his work-people, his domestic servants. His interest was to get as much and as good work out of them as he could; for this end, they had to be trained to proper submission. He was himself religious; his religion had supplied the standard under which he had fought the king and the lords; he was not long in discovering the opportunities this same religion offered him for working upon the minds of his natural inferiors, and making them submissive to the behests of the masters it had pleased God to place over them. In short, the English bourgeoisie now had to take a part in keeping down the 'lower orders', the great producing mass of the nation, and one of the means employed for that purpose was the influence of religion.

There was another factor that contributed to strengthen the religious leanings of the bourgeoisie. That was the rise of materialism in England. This new doctrine not only shocked the pious feelings of the middle class; it announced itself as a philosophy fit only for scholars and cultivated men of the world, in contrast to religion, which was good enough for the uneducated masses, including the bourgeoisie. With Hobbes, it stepped on the stage as a defender of royal prerogative and omnipotence; it called upon absolute monarchy to keep down that *puer robustus sed malitiosus* * – to wit, the people. Similarly, with the successors of Hobbes, with Bolingbroke, Shaftesbury, etc., the new deistic form of materialism remained an aristocratic, esoteric doctrine, and, therefore, hateful to the middle class both for its religious heresy and for its anti-bourgeois political connections. Accordingly, in opposition to the materialism and deism of the aristocracy, those Protestant sects which had furnished the flag and the fighting contingent against the Stuarts continued to furnish the main strength of the progressive middle class, and form even today the backbone of 'the Great Liberal Party'.

In the meantime, materialism passed from England to France, where it met and coalesced with another materialistic school of philosophers, a branch of Cartesianism. In France, too, it remained at first an exclusively aristocratic doctrine. But, soon, its revolutionary character asserted itself. The French materialists did not limit their criticism to matters of religious belief; they extended it to whatever scientific tradition or political institution they met with; and to prove the claim of their doctrine to universal application, they took the shortest cut, and boldly applied it to all

* Vigorous but malicious child.

subjects of knowledge in the giant work after which they were named – the *Encyclopédie*. Thus, in one or the other of its two forms – avowed materialism or deism – it became the creed of the whole cultured youth of France; so much so that, when the Great Revolution broke out, the doctrine hatched by English Royalists gave a theoretical flag to French Republicans and Terrorists, and furnished the text for the Declaration of the Rights of Man.

The Great French Revolution was the third uprising of the bourgeoisie, but the first that had entirely cast off the religious cloak, and was fought out on undisguised political lines; it was the first, too, that was really fought out up to the destruction of one of the combatants, the aristocracy, and the complete triumph of the other, the bourgeoisie. In England, the continuity of pre-revolutionary and post-revolutionary institutions, and the compromise between landlords and capitalists, found its expression in the continuity of judicial precedents and in the religious preservation of the feudal forms of the law. In France, the Revolution constituted a complete breach with the traditions of the past; it cleared out the very last vestiges of feudalism, and created in the *Code Civil* a masterly adaptation of the old Roman law – that almost perfect expression of the juridical relations corresponding to the economic stage called by Marx the production of commodities – to modern capitalist conditions; so masterly that this French revolutionary code still serves as a model for reforms of the law of property in all other countries, not excepting England. Let us, however, not forget that if English law continues to express the economic relations of capitalist society in that barbarous feudal language which corresponds to the thing expressed, just as English spelling corresponds to English pronunciation – *vous écrivez Londres et vous prononcez Constantinople*, said a Frenchman – that same English law is the only one which has preserved through ages, and transmitted to America and the Colonies, the best part of that old Germanic personal freedom, local self-government, and independence from all interference but that of the law courts, which on the Continent has been lost during the period of absolute monarchy, and has nowhere been as yet fully recovered.

To return to our British bourgeois. The French Revolution gave him a splendid opportunity, with the help of the Continental monarchies, to destroy French maritime commerce, to annex French colonies, and to crush the last French pretensions to maritime rivalry. That was one reason why he fought it. Another was that the ways of this revolution went very much against his grain. Not only its 'execrable' terrorism, but the very attempt to carry bourgeois rule to extremes. What should the British bourgeois do without his aristocracy, that taught him manners, such as they were, and invented fashions for him – that furnished officers for the army, which kept order at home, and the navy, which conquered colonial possessions and new markets aboard? There was, indeed, a progressive minority of the bourgeoisie, that minority whose interests were not so well attended to under the compromise; this section, composed chiefly of the less wealthy middle class, did sympathise with the Revolution, but it was powerless in Parliament.

Thus, if materialism became the creed of the French Revolution, the God-fearing English bourgeois held all the faster to his religion. Had not the reign of terror in Paris proved what was the upshot, if the religious instincts of the masses were lost? The more materialism spread from France to neighbouring countries, and was reinforced by similar doctrinal currents, notably by German philosophy, the more, in fact, materialism and free thought generally became, on the Continent, the necessary qualifications of a cultivated man, the more stubbornly the English middle class stuck to its manifold religious creeds. These creeds might differ from one another, but they were, all of them, distinctly religious, Christian creeds.

While the Revolution ensured the political triumph of the bourgeoisie in France, in England Watt, Arkwright, Cartwright, and others, initiated an industrial revolution, which completely shifted the centre of gravity of economic power. The wealth of the bourgeoisie increased considerably faster than that of the landed aristocracy. Within the bourgeoisie itself, the financial aristocracy, the bankers, etc., were more and more pushed into the background by the manufacturers. The compromise of 1689, even after the gradual changes it had undergone in favour of the bourgeoisie, no longer corresponded to the relative position of the parties to it. The character of these parties, too, had changed; the bourgeoisie of 1830 was very different from that of the preceding century. The political power still left to the aristocracy, and used by them to resist the pretensions of the new industrial bourgeoisie, became incompatible with the new economic interests. A fresh struggle with the aristocracy was necessary; it could end only in a victory of the new economic power. First, the Reform Act was pushed through, in spite of all resistance, under the impulse of the French Revolution of 1830. It gave to the bourgeoisie a recognised and powerful place in Parliament. Then the Repeal of the Corn Laws, which settled, once and for all, the supremacy of the bourgeoisie, and especially of its most active portion, the manufacturers, over the landed aristocracy. This was the greatest victory of the bourgeoisie; it was, however, also the last it gained in its own exclusive interest. Whatever triumphs it obtained later on, it had to share with a new social power – first its ally, but soon its rival.

The industrial revolution had created a class of large manufacturing capitalists, but also a class – and a far more numerous one – of manufacturing work-people. This class gradually increased in numbers, in proportion as the industrial revolution seized upon one branch of manufacture after another, and in the same proportion it increased its power. This power it proved as early as 1824, by forcing a reluctant Parliament to repeal the acts forbidding combinations of workmen. During the Reform agitation, the working-men constituted the Radical wing of the Reform party; the Act of 1832 having excluded them from the suffrage, they formulated their demands in the People's Charter, and constituted themselves, in opposition to the great bourgeois Anti-Corn Law party, into an independent party, the Chartists, the first working-men's party of modern times.

Then came the Continental revolutions of February and March 1848, in which the working people played such a prominent part, and, at least in Paris, put forward demands which were certainly inadmissible from the point of view of capitalist society. And then came the general reaction. First, the defeat of the Chartists on April 10, 1848; then the crushing of the Paris working men's insurrection in June of the same year; then the disasters of 1849 in Italy, Hungary, South Germany, and at last the victory of Louis Bonaparte over Paris, December 2, 1851. For a time, at least, the bugbear of working-class pretensions was put down, but at what cost! If the British bourgeois had been convinced before of the necessity of maintaining the common people in a religious mood, how much more must he feel that necessity after all these experiences? Regardless of the sneers of his Continental compeers, he continued to spend thousands and tens of thousands, year after year, upon the evangelisation of the lower orders; not content with his own native religious machinery, he appealed to Brother Jonathan, the greatest organiser in existence of religion as a trade, and imported from America revivalism, Moody and Sankey, and the like; and, finally, he accepted the dangerous aid of the Salvation Army, which revives the propaganda of early Christianity, appeals to the poor as the elect, fights capitalism in a religious way, and thus fosters an element of early Christian class antagonism, which one day may become troublesome to the well-to-do people who now find the ready money for it.

It seems a law of historical development that the bourgeoisie can in no European country get hold of political power — at least for any length of time — in the same exclusive way in which the feudal aristocracy kept hold of it during the Middle Ages. Even in France, where feudalism was completely extinguished, the bourgeoisie as a whole has held full possession of the Government for very short periods only. During Louis Philippe's reign, 1830–48, a very small portion of the bourgeoisie ruled the kingdom; by far the larger part were excluded from the suffrage by the high qualification. Under the Second Republic, 1848–51, the whole bourgeoisie ruled but for three years only; their incapacity brought on the Second Empire. It is only now, in the Third Republic, that the bourgeoisie as a whole have kept possession of the helm for more than 20 years; and they are already showing lively signs of decadence. A durable reign of the bourgeoisie has been possible only in countries like America, where feudalism was unknown, and society at the very beginning started from a bourgeois basis. And even in France and America, the successors of the bourgeoisie, the working people, are already knocking at the door.

In England, the bourgeoisie never held undivided sway. Even the victory of 1832 left the landed aristocracy in almost exclusive possession of all the leading Government offices. The meekness with which the middle class submitted to this remained inconceivable to me until the great Liberal manufacturer, Mr W. A. Forster, in a public speech, implored the young men of Bradford to learn French, as a means to get on in the world, and quoted from his own experience how sheepish he looked when, as a Cabinet Minister, he had to move in society where French was, at least, as necessary as English! The fact was, the English middle class of that time were, as a rule, quite uneducated upstarts, and could not help leaving to the aristocracy those superior Government places where other qualifications were required than mere insular narrowness and insular conceit, seasoned by business sharpness.* Even now the endless newspaper debates about middle-class education show that the English middle class does not yet consider itself good enough for the best education, and looks to something more modest. Thus, even after the repeal of the Corn Laws, it appeared a matter of course that the men who had carried the day – the Cobdens, Brights, Forsters, etc. – should remain excluded from a share in the official government of the country, until 20 years afterwards a new Reform Act opened to them the door of the Cabinet. The English bourgeoisie are, up to the present day, so deeply penetrated by a sense of their social inferiority that they keep up, at their own expense and that of the nation, an ornamental caste of drones to represent the nation worthily at all State functions; and they consider themselves highly honoured whenever one of themselves is found worthy of admission into this select and privileged body, manufactured, after all, by themselves.

The industrial and commercial middle class had, therefore, not yet succeeded in driving the landed aristocracy completely from political power when another competitor, the working class, appeared on the stage. The reaction after the Chartist movement and

---

* And even in business matters, the conceit of national Chauvinism is but a sorry adviser. Up to quite recently, the average English manufacturer considered it derogatory for an Englishman to speak any language but his own, and felt rather proud than otherwise of the fact that 'poor devils' of foreigners settled in England and took off his hands the trouble of disposing of his products abroad. He never noticed that these foreigners, mostly Germans, thus got command of a very large part of British foreign trade, imports and exports, and that the direct foreign trade of Englishmen became limited, almost entirely, to the colonies, China, the United States, and South America. Nor did he notice that these Germans traded with other Germans abroad, who gradually organised a complete network of commercial colonies all over the world. But, when Germany, about 40 years ago [c.1850], seriously began manufacturing for export, this network served her admirably in her transformation, in so short a time, from a corn-exporting into a first-rate manufacturing country. Then, about 10 years ago, the British manufacturer got frightened, and asked his ambassadors and consuls how it was that he could no longer keep his customers together. The unanimous answer was:
(1) You don't learn your customer's language but expect him to speak your own;
(2) You don't even try to suit your customer's wants, habits, and tastes, but expect him to conform to your English ones.

the Continental revolutions, as well as the unparalleled extension of English trade from 1848–66 (ascribed vulgarly to Free Trade alone, but due far more to the colossal development of railways, ocean steamers, and means of intercourse generally), had again driven the working class into the dependency of the Liberal party, of which they formed, as in pre-Chartist times, the Radical wing. Their claims to the franchise, however, gradually became irresistible; while the Whig leaders of the Liberals 'funked', Disraeli showed his superiority by making the Tories seize the favourable moment and introduce household suffrage in the boroughs, along with a redistribution of seats. Then followed the ballot; then, in 1884, the extension of household suffrage to the counties and a fresh redistribution of seats, by which electoral districts were, to some extent, equalised. All these measures considerably increased the electoral power of the working class, so much so that in at least 150 to 200 constituencies that class now furnished the majority of the voters. But parliamentary government is a capital school for teaching respect for tradition; if the middle class look with awe and veneration upon what Lord John Manners playfully called 'our old nobility', the mass of the working-people then looked up with respect and deference to what used to be designated as 'their betters', the middle class. Indeed, the British workman, some 15 years ago, was the model workman, whose respectful regard for the position of his master, and whose self-restraining modesty in claiming rights for himself, consoled our German economists of the *Katheder-Socialist* school for the incurable communistic and revolutionary tendencies of their own working-men at home.

But the English middle class – good men of business as they are – saw farther than the German professors. They had shared their powers but reluctantly with the working class. They had learnt, during the Chartist years, what that *puer robustus sed malitiosus*, the people, is capable of. And since that time, they had been compelled to incorporate the better part of the People's Charter in the Statutes of the United Kingdom. Now, if ever, the people must be kept in order by moral means, and the first and foremost of all moral means of action upon the masses is and remains – religion. Hence the parsons' majorities on the School Boards, hence the increasing self-taxation of the bourgeoisie for the support of all sorts of revivalism, from ritualism to the Salvation Army.

And now came the triumph of British respectability over the free thought and religious laxity of the Continental bourgeois. The workmen of France and Germany had become rebellious. They were thoroughly infected with Socialism, and, for very good reasons, were not at all particular as to the legality of the means by which to secure their own ascendancy. The *puer robustus*, here, turned from day to day more *malitiosus*. Nothing remained to the French and German bourgeoisie as a last resource but to silently drop their free thought, as a youngster, when sea-sickness creeps upon him, quietly drops the burning cigar he brought swaggeringly on board; one by one, the scoffers turned pious in outward behaviour, spoke with respect of the Church, its dogmas and rites, and even conformed with the latter as far as could not be helped. French bourgeois dined *maigre* on Fridays, and German ones sat out long Protestant sermons in their pews on Sundays. They had come to grief with materialism. '*Die Religion muss dem Volk erhalten werden*' – religion must be kept alive for the people – that was the only and the last means to save society from utter ruin. Unfortunately for themselves, they did not find this out until they had done their level best to break up religion for ever. And now it was the turn of the British bourgeoisie to sneer and to say: 'Why, you fools, I could have told you that 200 years ago!'

However, I am afraid neither the religious stolidity of the British, nor the *post festum* conversion of the Continental bourgeois will stem the rising Proletarian tide. Tradition is a great retarding force, is the *vis inertiae* of history, but, being merely passive, is sure to be broken down; and thus religion will be no lasting safeguard to capitalist society. If our juridical, philosophical, and religious ideas are the more or less remote offshoots of the economical relations prevailing in a given society, such ideas cannot, in the long run, withstand the effects of a complete change in these relations. And, unless we believe in supernatural revelation, we must admit that no religious tenets will ever suffice to prop up a tottering society.

In fact, in England too, the working-people have begun to move again. They are, no doubt, shackled by traditions of various kinds. Bourgeois traditions, such as the widespread belief that there can be but two parties, Conservatives and Liberals, and that the working class must work out its salvation by and through the great Liberal Party. Working-men's traditions, inherited from their first tentative efforts at independent action, such as the exclusion, from ever so many old Trade Unions, of all applicants who have not gone through a regular apprenticeship; which means the breeding, by every such union, of its own blacklegs. But, for all that, the English working class is moving, as even Professor Brentano has sorrowfully had to report to his brother *Katheder-Socialists*. It moves, like all things in England, with a slow and measured step, with hesitation here, with more or less un-fruitful, tentative attempts there; it moves now and then with an over-cautious mistrust of the name of Socialism, while it gradually absorbs the substance, and the movement spreads and seizes one layer of the workers after another. It has now shaken out of their torpor the unskilled labourers of the East End of London, and we all know what a splendid impulse these fresh forces have given it in return. And if the pace of the movement is not up to the impatience of some people, let them not forget that it is the working class which keeps alive the finest qualities of the English character, and that, if a step in advance is once gained in England, it is, as a rule, never lost afterwards. If the sons of the old Chartists, for reasons unexplained above, were not quite up to the mark, the grandsons bid fair to be worthy of their forefathers.

But the triumph of the European working class does not depend upon England alone. It can only be secured by the cooperation of, at least, England, France and Germany. In both the latter countries, the working-class movement is well ahead of England. In Germany, it is even within measurable distance of success. The progress it has there made during the last 25 years is unparalleled. It advances with ever-increasing velocity. If the German middle class have shown themselves lamentably deficient in political capacity, discipline, courage, energy, and perseverance, the German working class have given ample proof of all these qualities. Four hundred years ago, Germany was the starting-point of the first upheaval of the European middle class; as things are now, is it outside the limits of possibility that Germany will be the scene, too, of the first great victory of the European proletariat?

FREDERICK ENGELS
London, April 20, 1892

Chapter 1

The Development of Utopian Socialism

Modern Socialism is, in its essence, the direct product of the recognition, on the one hand, of the class antagonisms existing in the society of today between proprietors and non-proprietors, between capitalists and wage-workers; on the other hand, of the anarchy existing in production. But, in its theoretical form, modern Socialism originally appears ostensibly as a more logical extension of the principles laid down by the great French philosophers of the eighteenth century. Like every new theory, modern Socialism had, at first, to connect itself with the intellectual stock-in-trade ready to its hand, however deeply its roots lay in material economic facts.

The great men, who in France prepared men's minds for the coming revolution, were themselves extreme revolutionists. They recognised no external authority of any kind whatever. Religion, natural science, society, political institutions — everything was subjected to the most unsparing criticism: everything must justify its existence before the judgment-seat of reason or give up existence. Reason became the sole measure of everything. It was the time when, as Hegel says, the world stood upon its head;* first

* This is a passage on the French Revolution:
'Thought, the concept of law, all at once made itself felt, and against this the old scaffolding of wrong could make no stand. In this conception of law, therefore, a constitution has now been established, and henceforth everything must be based upon this. Since the Sun had been in the firmament, and the planets circled around him, the sight had never been seen of man standing upon his head – i.e., on the Idea – and building reality after this image. Anaxagoras first said that the *Nous*, reason, rules the world; but now, for the first time, had men come to recognise that the Idea must rule the mental reality. And this was a magnificent sunrise. All thinking Beings have participated in celebrating this holy day. A sublime emotion swayed men at that time, an enthusiasm of reason pervaded the world, as if now had come the reconciliation of the Divine Principle with the world.' Hegel, *Philosophy of History*, 1840, p.535.

Is it not high time to set the anti-Socialist law in action against such teachings, subversive and to the common danger, by the late Professor Hegel?

in the sense that the human head, and the principles arrived at by its thought, claimed to be the basis of all human action and association; but by and by, also, in the wider sense that the reality which was in contradiction to these principles had, in fact, to be turned upside down. Every form of society and government then existing, every old traditional notion, was flung into the lumber-room as irrational; the world had hitherto allowed itself to be led solely by prejudices; everything in the past deserved only pity and contempt. Now, for the first time, appeared the light of day, the kingdom of reason; henceforth superstition, injustice, privilege, oppression, were to be superseded by eternal truth, eternal Right, equality based on Nature and the inalienable rights of man.

We know today that this kingdom of reason was nothing more than the idealised kingdom of the bourgeoisie; that this eternal Right found its realisation in bourgeois justice; that this equality reduced itself to bourgeois equality before the law; that bourgeois property was proclaimed as one of the essential rights of man; and that the government of reason, the Contrat Social of Rousseau, came into being, and only could come into being, as a democratic bourgeois republic. The great thinkers of the eighteenth century could no more than their predecessors, go beyond the limits imposed upon them by their epoch.

But, side by side with the antagonisms of the feudal nobility and the burghers, who claimed to represent all the rest of society, was the general antagonism of exploiters and exploited, of rich idlers and poor workers. It was this very circumstance that made it possible for the representatives of the bourgeoisie to put themselves forward as representing not one special class, but the whole of suffering humanity. Still further. From its origin the bourgeoisie was saddled with its antithesis: capitalists cannot exist without wage-workers, and, in the same proportion as the medieval burgher of the guild developed into the modern bourgeois, the guild journeyman and the day-labourer, outside the guilds, developed into the proletarian. And although, upon the whole, the bourgeoisie, in their struggle with the nobility, could claim to represent at the same time the interests of the different working classes of that period, yet in every great bourgeois movement there were independent outbursts of that class which was the forerunner, more or less developed, of the modern proletariat. For example, at the time of the German

Reformation and the Peasants' War, the Anabaptists and Thomas Münzer; in the great English Revolution, the Levellers; in the great French Revolution, Babeuf.

There were theoretical enunciations, corresponding with these revolutionary uprisings of a class not yet developed; in the sixteenth and seventeenth centuries, Utopian pictures of ideal social conditions;* in the eighteenth century, actual communistic theories (Morelly and Mably). The demand for equality was no longer limited to political rights; it was extended also to the social conditions of individuals. It was not simply class privileges that were to be abolished, but class distinctions themselves. A Communism, ascetic, denouncing all the pleasures of life, Spartan, was the first form of the new teaching. Then came the three great Utopians: Saint-Smon, to whom the middle-class movement, side by side with the proletarian, still had a certain significance; Fourier; and Owen, who in the country where capitalist production was most developed, and under the influence of the antagonisms begotten of this, worked out his proposals for the removal of class distinction systematically and in direct relation to French materialism.

One thing is common to all three. Not one of them appears as a representative of the interests of that proletariat which historical development had, in the meantime, produced. Like the French philosophers, they do not claim to emancipate a particular class to begin with, but all humanity at once. Like them, they wish to bring in the kingdom of reason and eternal justice, but this kingdom, as they see it, is as far as Heaven from Earth, from that of the French philosophers.

For, to our three social reformers, the bourgeois world, based upon the principles of these philosophers, is quite as irrational and unjust, and, therefore, finds its way to the dust-hole quite as readily as feudalism and all the earlier stages of society. If pure reason and justice have not, hitherto, ruled the world, this has been the case only because men have not rightly understood them. What was wanted was the individual man of genius, who has now arisen and who understands the truth. That he has now arisen, that the truth has now been clearly understood, is not an inevitable event, following of necessity in the chains of historical development,

---

* Engels refers here to the works of the utopian Socialists Thomas More (16th century) and Tommaso Campanella (17th century).

but a mere happy accident. He might just as well have been born 500 years earlier, and might then have spared humanity 500 years of error, strife, and suffering.

We saw how the French philosophers of the eighteenth century, the forerunners of the Revolution, appealed to reason as the sole judge of all that is. A rational government, rational society, were to be founded; everything that ran counter to eternal reasons was to be remorselessly done away with. We saw also that this eternal reason was in reality nothing but the idealised understanding of the eighteenth century citizen, just then evolving into the bourgeois. The French Revolution had realised this rational society and government.

But the new order of things, rational enough as compared with earlier conditions, turned out to be by no means absolutely rational. The state based upon reason completely collapsed. Rousseau's Contrat Social had found its realisation in the Reign of Terror, from which the bourgeoisie, who had lost confidence in their own political capacity, had taken refuge first in the corruption of the Directorate, and, finally, under the wing of the Napoleonic despotism. The promised eternal peace was turned into an endless war of conquest. The society based upon reason had fared no better. The antagonism between rich and poor, instead of dissolving into general prosperity, had become intensified by the removal of the guild and other privileges, which had to some extent bridged it over, and by the removal of the charitable institutions of the Church. The 'freedom of property' from feudal fetters, now veritably accomplished, turned out to be, for the small capitalists and small proprietors, the freedom to sell their small property, crushed under the overmastering competition of the large capitalists and landlords, to these great lords, and thus, as far as the small capitalists and peasant proprietors were concerned, became 'freedom from property'. The development of industry upon a capitalistic basis made poverty and misery of the working masses conditions of existence of society. Cash payment became more and more, in Carlyle's phrase, the sole nexus between man and man. The number of crimes increased from year to year. Formerly, the feudal vices had openly stalked about in broad daylight; though not eradicated, they were now at any rate thrust into the background. In their stead, the bourgeois vices, hitherto practised in secret, began to blossom all the more luxuriantly.

Trade became to a greater and greater extent cheating. The 'fraternity' of the revolutionary motto was realised in the chicanery and rivalries of the battle of competition. Oppression by force was replaced by corruption; the sword, as the first social lever, by gold. The right of the first night was transferred from the feudal lords to the bourgeois manufacturers. Prostitution increased to an extent never head of. Marriage itself remained, as before, the legally recognised form, the official cloak of prostitution, and, moreover, was supplemented by rich crops of adultery.

In a word, compared with the splendid promises of the philosophers, the social and political institutions born of the 'triumph of reason' were bitterly disappointing caricatures. All that was wanting was the men to formulate this disappointment, and they came with the turn of the century. In 1802, Saint-Simon's Geneva letters appeared; in 1808 appeared Fourier's first work, although the groundwork of his theory dated from 1799; on January 1, 1800, Robert Owen undertook the direction of New Lanark.

At this time, however, the capitalist mode of production, and with it the antagonism between the bourgeoisie and the proletariat, was still very incompletely developed. Modern Industry, which had just arisen in England, was still unknown in France. But Modern Industry develops, on the one hand, the conflicts which make absolutely necessary a revolution in the mode of production, and the doing away with its capitalistic character – conflicts not only between the classes begotten of it, but also between the very productive forces and the forms of exchange created by it. And, on the other hand, it develops, in these very gigantic productive forces, the means of ending these conflicts. If, therefore, about the year 1800, the conflicts arising from the new social order were only just beginning to take shape, this holds still more fully as to the means of ending them. The 'have-nothing' masses of Paris, during the Reign of Terror, were able for a moment to gain the mastery, and thus to lead the bourgeois revolution to victory in spite of the bourgeoisie themselves. But, in doing so, they only proved how impossible it was for their domination to last under the conditions then obtaining. The proletariat, which then for the first time evolved itself from these 'have-nothing' masses as the nucleus of a new class, as yet quite incapable of independent political action, appeared as an oppressed, suffering order, to whom, in its incapacity to help itself, help could, at best, be brought in from without or down from above.

This historical situation also dominated the founders of Socialism. To the crude conditions of capitalistic production and the crude class conditions correspond crude theories. The solution of the social problems, which as yet lay hidden in undeveloped economic conditions, the Utopians attempted to evolve out of the human brain. Society presented nothing but wrongs; to remove these was the task of reason. It was necessary, then, to discover a new and more perfect system of social order and to impose this upon society from without by propaganda, and, wherever it was possible, by the example of model experiments. These new social systems were foredoomed as Utopian; the more completely they were worked out in detail, the more they could not avoid drifting off into pure fantasies.

These facts once established, we need not dwell a moment longer upon this side of the question, now wholly belonging to the past. We can leave it to the literary small fry to solemnly quibble over these fantasies, which today only make us smile, and to crow over the superiority of their own bald reasoning, as compared with such 'insanity'. For ourselves, we delight in the stupendously grand thoughts and germs of thought that everywhere break out through their fantastic covering, and to which these Philistines are blind.

Saint-Simon was a son of the great French Revolution, at the outbreak of which he was not yet 30. The Revolution was the victory of the third estate – i.e. of the great masses of the nation, working in production and in trade, over the privileged idle classes, the nobles and the priests. But the victory of the third estate soon revealed itself as exclusively the victory of a smaller part of this 'estate', as the conquest of political power by the socially privileged section of it – i.e. the propertied bourgeoisie. And the bourgeoisie had certainly developed rapidly during the Revolution, partly by speculation in the lands of the nobility and of the Church, confiscated and afterwards put up for sale, and partly by frauds upon the nation by means of army contracts. It was the domination of these swindlers that, under the Directorate, brought France to the verge of ruin, and thus gave Napoleon the pretext for his *coup d'état*.

Hence, to Saint-Simon the antagonism between the third estate and the privileged classes took the form of an antagonism between 'workers' and 'idlers'. The idlers were not merely the old privileged classes, but also all who, without taking any part in production or distribution, lived on their incomes. And the workers were not only the wage-workers, but also the manufacturers, the merchants, the bankers. That the idlers had lost the capacity for intellectual leadership and political supremacy had been proved, and was by the Revolution finally settled. That the non-possessing classes had not this capacity seemed to Saint-Simon proved by the experiences of the Reign of Terror. Then, who was to lead and command? According to Saint-Simon, science and industry, both united by a new religious bond, destined to restore that unity of religious ideas which had been lost since the time of the Reformation – a necessarily mystic and rigidly hierarchic 'new Christianity'. But science, that was the scholars; and industry, that was, in the first place, the working bourgeois, manufacturers, merchants, bankers. These bourgeois were, certainly, intended by Saint-Simon to transform themselves into a kind of public officials, of social trustees; but they were still to hold, vis-à-vis the workers, a commanding and economically privileged position. The bankers especially were to be called upon to direct the whole of social production by the regulation of credit. This conception was in exact keeping with a time in which Modern Industry in France and, with it, the chasm between bourgeoisie and proletariat was only just coming into existence. But what Saint-Simon especially lays stress upon is this: what interests him first, and above all other things, is the lot of the class that is the most numerous and the most poor ('la classe la plus nombreuse et la plus pauvre').

Already in his Geneva letters, Saint-Simon lays down the proposition that 'all men ought to work'. In the same work he recognises also that the Reign of Terror was the reign of the non-possessing masses. 'See,' says he to them, 'what happened in France at the time when your comrades held sway there; they brought about a famine.'

But to recognise the French Revolution as a class war, and not simply one between nobility and bourgeoisie, but between nobility, bourgeoisie, and the non-possessors, was, in the year 1802, a most pregnant discovery. In 1816, he declares that politics is the science of production, and foretells the complete absorption of politics by economics. The knowledge that economic conditions are the basis of political institutions appears here only in embryo. Yet what is here already very plainly expressed is the idea of the future conversion of political rule over men into an administration of things and a direction of processes of production – that is to say, the 'abolition of the state', about which recently there has been so much noise.

Saint-Simon shows the same superiority over his contemporaries when in 1814, immediately after the entry of the allies into Paris, and again in 1815, during the Hundred Days' War, he proclaims the alliance of France and England, and then of both of these countries with Germany, as the only guarantee for the prosperous development and peace of Europe. To preach to the French in 1815 an alliance with the victors of Waterloo required as much courage as historical foresight.

If in Saint-Simon we find a comprehensive breadth of view, by virtue of which almost all the ideas of later Socialists that are not strictly economic are found in him in embryo, we find in Fourier a criticism of the existing conditions of society, genuinely French and witty, but not upon that account any the less thorough. Fourier takes the bourgeoisie, their inspired prophets before the Revolution, and their interested eulogists after it, at their own word. He lays bare remorselessly the material and moral misery of the bourgeois world. He confronts it with the earlier philosophers' dazzling promises of a society in which reason alone should reign, of a civilisation in which happiness should be universal, of an illimitable human perfectibility, and with the rose-colored phraseology of the bourgeois ideologists of his time. He points out how everywhere the most pitiful reality corresponds with the most high-sounding phrases, and he overwhelms this hopeless fiasco of phrases with his mordant sarcasm.

Fourier is not only a critic; his imperturbably serene nature makes him a satirist, and assuredly one of the greatest satirists of all time. He depicts, with equal power and charm, the swindling speculations that blossomed out upon the downfall of the Revolution, and the shopkeeping spirit prevalent in, and characteristic of, French commerce at that time. Still more masterly is his criticism of the bourgeois form of the relations between sexes, and the position of woman in bourgeois society. He was the first to declare that in any given society the degree of woman's emancipation is the natural measure of the general emancipation.

But Fourier is at his greatest in his conception of the history of society. He divides its whole course, thus far, into four stages of evolution – savagery, barbarism, the patriarchate, civilisation. This last is identical with the so-called civil, or bourgeois, society of today – i.e. with the social order that came in with the sixteenth century. He proves 'that the civilised stage raises every vice practised by barbarism in a simple fashion into a form of existence, complex, ambiguous, equivocal, hypocritical' – that civilisation moves 'in a vicious circle', in contradictions which it constantly reproduces without being able to solve them; hence it constantly arrives at the very opposite to that which it wants to attain, or pretends to want to attain, so that, e.g., 'under civilisation poverty is born of superabundance itself'.

Fourier, as we see, uses the dialectic method in the same masterly way as his contemporary, Hegel. Using these same dialectics, he argues against talk about illimitable human perfectibility, that every historical phase has its period of ascent and also its period of descent, and he applies this observation to the future of the whole human race. As Kant introduced into natural science the idea of the ultimate destruction of the Earth, Fourier introduced into historical science that of the ultimate destruction of the human race.

Whilst in France the hurricane of the Revolution swept over the land, in England a quieter, but not on that account less tremendous, revolution was going on. Steam and the new tool-making machinery were transforming manufacture into modern industry, and thus revolutionising the whole foundation of bourgeois society. The sluggish march of development of the manufacturing period changed into a veritable storm and stress period of production. With constantly increasing swiftness the splitting-up into large capitalists and non-possessing proletarians went on. Between these, instead of the former stable middle class, an unstable mass of artisans and small shopkeepers, the most fluctuating portion of the population, now led a precarious existence.

The new mode of production was, as yet, only at the beginning of its period of ascent; as yet it was the normal, regular method of production – the only one possible under existing conditions. Nevertheless, even then it was producing crying social abuses – the herding together of a homeless population in the worst quarters of the large towns; the loosening of all traditional moral bonds, of patriarchal subordination, of family relations; overwork, especially of women and children, to a frightful extent; complete demoralisation of the working class, suddenly flung into altogether new conditions, from the country into the town, from agriculture into modern industry, from stable conditions of existence into insecure ones that change from day to day.

At this juncture, there came forward as a reformer a manufacturer 29 years old – a man of almost sublime, childlike simplicity of character, and at the same time one of the few born leaders of men. Robert Owen had adopted the teaching of the materialistic philosophers: that man's character is the product, on the one hand, of heredity; on the other, of the environment of the individual during his lifetime, and especially during his period of development. In the industrial revolution most of his class saw only chaos and confusion, and the opportunity of fishing in these troubled waters and making large fortunes quickly. He saw in it the opportunity of putting into practice his favourite theory, and so of bringing order out of chaos. He had already tried it with success, as superintendent of more than 500 men in a Manchester factory. From 1800 to 1829, he directed the great cotton mill at New Lanark, in Scotland, as managing partner, along the same lines, but with greater freedom of action and with a success that made him a European reputation. A population, originally consisting of the most diverse and, for the most part, very demoralised elements, a population that gradually grew to 2,500, he turned into a model colony, in which drunkenness, police, magistrates, lawsuits, poor laws, charity, were unknown. And all this simply by placing the people in conditions worthy of human beings, and especially by carefully bringing up the rising generation. He was the founder of infant schools, and introduced them first at New Lanark. At the age of two, the children came to school, where they enjoyed themselves so much that they could scarely be got home again. Whilst his competitors worked their people 13 or 14 hours a day, in New Lanark the working day was only 10 and a half hours. When a crisis in cotton stopped work for four months, his workers received their full wages all the time. And with all this the business more than doubled in value, and to the last yielded large profits to its proprietors.

In spite of all this, Owen was not content. The existence which he secured for his workers was, in his eyes, still far from being worthy of human beings. 'The people were slaves at my mercy.' The relatively favourable conditions in which he had placed them were still far from allowing a rational development of the character and of the intellect in all directions, much less of the free exercise of all their faculties.

And yet, the working part of this population of 2,500 persons was daily producing as much real wealth for society as, less than half a century before, it would have required the working part of a population of 600,000 to create. I asked myself, what became of the difference between the wealth consumed by 2,500 persons and that which would have been consumed by 600,000? [*]

The answer was clear. It had been used to pay the proprietors of the establishment 5 per cent on the capital they had laid out, in addition to over 300,000 pounds clear profit. And that which held for New Lanark held to a still greater extent for all the factories in England.

If this new wealth had not been created by machinery, imperfectly as it has been applied, the wars of Europe, in opposition to Napoleon, and to support the aristocratic principles of society, could not have been maintained. And yet this new power was the creation of the working classes.[†]

To them, therefore, the fruits of this new power belonged. The newly-created gigantic productive forces, hitherto used only to enrich individuals and to enslave the masses, offered to Owen the foundations for a reconstruction of society; they were destined, as the common property of all, to be worked for the common good of all.

[*] From *The Revolution in Mind and Practice*, p.21, a memorial addressed to all the 'red Republicans, Communists and Socialists of Europe', and sent to the provisional government of France, 1848, and also 'to Queen Victoria and her responsible advisers.'
[†] Note, l.c. p.22.

Owen's communism was based upon this purely business foundation, the outcome, so to say, of commercial calculation. Throughout, it maintained this practical character. Thus, in 1823, Owen proposed the relief of the distress in Ireland by Communist colonies, and drew up complete estimates of costs of founding them, yearly expenditure, and probable revenue. And in his definite plan for the future, the technical working out of details is managed with such practical knowledge – ground plan, front and side and bird's-eye views all included – that the Owen method of social reform once accepted, there is from the practical point of view little to be said against the actual arrangement of details.

His advance in the direction of Communism was the turning-point in Owen's life. As long as he was simply a philanthropist, he was rewarded with nothing but wealth, applause, honour, and glory. He was the most popular man in Europe. Not only men of his own class, but statesmen and prince listened to him approvingly. But when he came out with his Communist theories, that was quite another thing. Three great obstacles seemed to him especially to block the path to social reform: private property, religion, the present form of marriage.

He knew what confronted him if he attacked these – outlawry, excommunication from official society, the loss of his whole social position. But nothing of this prevented him from attacking them without fear of consequences, and what he had foreseen happened. Banished from official society, with a conspiracy of silence against him in the press, ruined by his unsuccessful Communist experiments in America, in which he sacrificed all his fortune, he turned directly to the working class and continued working in their midst for 30 years. Every social movement, every real advance in England on behalf of the workers links itself to the name of Robert Owen. He forced through in 1819, after five years' fighting, the first law limiting the hours of labour of women and children in factories. He was president of the first Congress at which all the Trade Unions of England united in a single great trade association. He introduced as transition measures to the complete communistic organisation of society, on the one hand, cooperative societies for retail trade and production. These have since that time, at least, given practical proof that the merchant and the manufacturer are socially quite unnecessary. On the other hand, he introduced labour bazaars for the exchange of the products of labour through the medium of labour-notes, whose unit was a single hour of work; institutions necessarily doomed to failure, but completely anticipating Proudhon's bank of exchange of a much later period, and differing entirely from this in that it did not claim to be the panacea for all social ills, but only a first step towards a much more radical revolution of society.

The Utopians' mode of thought has for a long time governed the Socialist ideas of the nineteenthth century, and still governs some of them. Until very recently, all French and English Socialists did homage to it. The earlier German Communism, including that of Weitling, was of the same school. To all these, Socialism is the expression of absolute truth, reason and justice, and has only to be discovered to conquer all the world by virtue of its own power. And as absolute truth is independent of time, space, and of the historical development of man, it is a mere accident when and where it is discovered. With all this, absolute truth, reason, and justice are different with the founder of each different school. And as each one's special kind of absolute truth, reason, and justice is again conditioned by his subjective understanding, his conditions of existence, the measure of his knowledge and his intellectual training, there is no other ending possible in this conflict of absolute truths than that they shall be mutually exclusive of one another. Hence, from this nothing could come but a kind of eclectic, average Socialism, which, as a matter of fact, has up to the present time dominated the minds of most of the socialist workers in France and England. Hence, a mish-mash allowing of the most manifold shades of opinion: a mish-mash of such critical statements, economic theories, pictures of future society by the founders of different sects, as excite a minimum of opposition; a mish-mash which is the more easily brewed the more the definite sharp edges of the individual constituents are rubbed down in the stream of debate, like rounded pebbles in a brook.

To make a science of Socialism, it had first to be placed upon a real basis.

Chapter 2
The Science of Dialectics

In the meantime, along with and after the French philosophy of the eighteenth century, had arisen the new German philosophy, culminating in Hegel.

Its greatest merit was the taking up again of dialectics as the highest form of reasoning. The old Greek philosophers were all born natural dialecticians, and Aristotle, the most encyclopedic of them, had already analysed the most essential forms of dialectic thought. The newer philosophy, on the other hand, although in it also dialectics had brilliant exponents (e.g. Descartes and Spinoza), had, especially through English influence, become more and more rigidly fixed in the so-called metaphysical mode of reasoning, by which also the French of the eighteenth century were almost wholly dominated, at all events in their special philosophical work. Outside philosophy in the restricted sense, the French nevertheless produced masterpieces of dialectic. We need only call to mind Diderot's *Le Neveu de Rameau*, and Rousseau's *Discours sur l'origine et les fondements de l'inégalité parmi less hommes*. We give here, in brief, the essential character of these two modes of thought.

When we consider and reflect upon Nature at large, or the history of mankind, or our own intellectual activity, at first we see the picture of an endless entanglement of relations and reactions, permutations and combinations, in which nothing remains what, where and as it was, but everything moves, changes, comes into being and passes away. We see, therefore, at first the picture as a whole, with its individual parts still more or less kept in the background; we observe the movements, transitions, connections, rather than the things that move, combine, and are connected. This primitive, naïve but intrinsically correct conception of the world is that of ancient Greek philosophy, and was first clearly formulated by Heraclitus: everything is and is not, for everything is fluid, is constantly changing, constantly coming into being and passing away.

But this conception, correctly as it expresses the general character of the picture of appearances as a whole, does not suffice to explain the details of which this picture is made up, and so long as we do not understand these, we have not a clear idea of the whole picture. In order to understand these details, we must detach them from their natural, special causes, effects, etc. This is, primarily, the task of natural science and historical research: branches of science which the Greek of classical times, on very good grounds, relegated to a subordinate position, because they had first of all to collect materials for these sciences to work upon. A certain amount of natural and historical material must be collected before there can be any critical analysis, comparison, and arrangement in classes, orders, and species. The foundations of the exact natural sciences were, therefore, first worked out by the Greeks of the Alexandrian period,* and later on, in the Middle Ages, by the Arabs. Real natural science dates from the second half of the fifteenth century, and thence onward it had advanced with constantly increasing rapidity. The analysis of Nature into its individual parts, the grouping of the different natural processes and objects in definite classes, the study of the internal anatomy of organised bodies in their manifold forms – these were the fundamental conditions of the gigantic strides in our knowledge of Nature that have been made during the last 400 years. But this method of work has also left us as legacy the habit of observing natural objects and processes in isolation, apart from their connection with the vast whole; of observing them in repose, not in motion; as constraints, not as essentially variables; in their death, not in their life. And when this way of looking at things was transferred by Bacon and Locke from natural science to philosophy, it begot the narrow, metaphysical mode of thought peculiar to the last century.

* The Alexandrian period of the development of science comprises the period extending from the third century B.C. to the seventeenth century A.D. It derives its name from the town of Alexandria in Egypt, which was one of the most important centres of international economic intercourses at that time. In the Alexandrian period, mathematics (Euclid and Archimedes), geography, astronomy, anatomy, physiology, etc., attained considerable development.

To the metaphysician, things and their mental reflexes, ideas, are isolated, are to be be considered one after the other and apart from each other, are objects of investigation fixed, rigid, given once for all. He thinks in absolutely irreconcilable antitheses. His communication is 'yea, yea; nay, nay'; for whatsoever is more than these cometh of evil. For him, a thing either exists or does not exist; a thing cannot at the same time be itself and something else. Positive and negative absolutely exclude one another; cause and effect stand in a rigid antithesis, one to the other.

At first sight, this mode of thinking seems to us very luminous, because it is that of so-called sound common sense. Only sound common sense, respectable fellow that he is, in the homely realm of his own four walls, has very wonderful adventures directly he ventures out into the wide world of research. And the metaphysical mode of thought, justifiable and necessary as it is in a number of domains whose extent varies according to the nature of the particular object of investigation, sooner or later reaches a limit, beyond which it becomes one-sided, restricted, abstract, lost in insoluble contradictions. In the contemplation of individual things, it forgets the connection between them; in the contemplation of their existence, it forgets the beginning and end of that existence, of their repose; it forgets their motion. It cannot see the woods for the trees.

For everyday purposes, we know and can say, e.g., whether an animal is alive or not. But, upon closer inquiry, we find that this is, in many cases, a very complex question, as the jurists know very well. They have cudgelled their brains in vain to discover a rational limit beyond which the killing of the child in its mother's womb is murder. It is just as impossible to determine absolutely the moment of death, for physiology proves that death is not an instantaneous, momentary phenomenon, but a very protracted process.

In like manner, every organised being is every moment the same and not the same; every moment, it assimilates matter supplied from without, and gets rid of other matter; every moment, some cells of its body die and others build themselves anew; in a longer or shorter time, the matter of its body is completely renewed, and is replaced by other molecules of matter, so that every organised being is always itself, and yet something other than itself.

Further, we find upon closer investigation that the two poles of an antithesis, positive and negative, e.g., are as inseparable as they are opposed, and that despite all their opposition, they mutually interpenetrate. And we find, in like manner, that cause and effect are conceptions which only hold good in their application to individual cases; but as soon as we consider the individual cases in their general connection with the universe as a whole, they run into each other, and they become confounded when we contemplate that universal action and reaction in which causes and effects are eternally changing places, so that what is effect here and now will be cause there and then, and vice versa.

None of these processes and modes of thought enters into the framework of metaphysical reasoning. Dialectics, on the other hand, comprehends things and their representations, ideas, in their essential connection, concatenation, motion, origin and ending. Such processes as those mentioned above are, therefore, so many corroborations of its own method of procedure.

Nature is the proof of dialectics, and it must be said for modern science that it has furnished this proof with very rich materials increasing daily, and thus has shown that, in the last resort, Nature works dialectically and not metaphysically; that she does not move in the eternal oneness of a perpetually recurring circle, but goes through a real historical evolution. In this connection, Darwin must be named before all others. He dealt the metaphysical conception of Nature the heaviest blow by his proof that all organic beings, plants, animals, and man himself, are the products of a process of evolution going on through millions of years. But the naturalists who have learned to think dialectically, are few and far between, and this conflict of the results of discovery with preconceived modes of thinking, explains the endless confusion now reigning in theoretical natural science, the despair of teachers as well as learners, of authors and readers alike.

An exact representation of the universe, of its evolution, of the development of mankind, and of the reflection of this evolution in the minds of men, can therefore only be obtained by the methods of dialectics with its constant regard to the innumerable actions and reactions of life and death, of progressive or retrogressive changes. And in this spirit the new German philosophy has worked. Kant began his career by resolving the stable solar system of Newton and its eternal duration, after the famous initial impulse had once been given, into the result of a historical process, the formation of the sun and all the planets out of a rotating, nebulous mass. From this, he at the same time drew the conclusion that, given this origin of the solar system, its future death followed of necessity. His theory, half a century later, was established mathematically by Laplace, and half a century after that, the spectroscope proved the existence in space of such incandescent masses of gas in various stages of condensation.

This new German philosophy culminated in the Hegelian system. In this system – and herein is its great merit – for the first time the whole world, natural, historical, intellectual, is represented as a process – i.e. as in constant motion, change, transformation, development; and the attempt is made to trace out the internal connection that makes a continuous whole of all this movement and development. From this point of view, the history of mankind no longer appeared as a wild whirl of senseless deeds of violence, all equally condemnable at the judgment seat of mature philosophic reason and which are best forgotten as quickly as possible, but as the process of evolution of man himself. It was now the task of the intellect to follow the gradual march of this process through all its devious ways, and to trace out the inner law running through all its apparently accidental phenomena.

That the Hegelian system did not solve the problem it propounded is here immaterial. Its epoch-making merit was that it propounded the problem. This problem is one that no single individual will ever be able to solve. Although Hegel was – with Saint-Simon – the most encyclopedic mind of his time, yet he was limited, first, by the necessarily limited extent of his own knowledge and, second, by the limited extent and depth of the knowledge and conceptions of his age. To these limits, a third must be added. Hegel was an idealist. To him, the thoughts within his brain were not the more or less abstract pictures of actual things and processes, but, conversely, things and their evolution were only the realised pictures of the 'Idea', existing somewhere from eternity before the world was. This way of thinking turned everything upside down, and completely reversed the actual connection of things in the world. Correctly and ingeniously as many groups of facts were grasped by Hegel, yet, for the reasons just given, there is much that is botched, artificial, laboured, in a word, wrong in point of detail. The

Hegelian system, in itself, was a colossal miscarriage – but it was also the last of its kind.

It was suffering, in fact, from an internal and incurable contradiction. Upon the one hand, its essential proposition was the conception that human history is a process of evolution, which, by its very nature, cannot find its intellectual final term in the discovery of any so-called absolute truth. But, on the other hand, it laid claim to being the very essence of this absolute truth. A system of natural and historical knowledge, embracing everything, and final for all time, is a contradiction to the fundamental law of dialectic reasoning. This law, indeed, by no means excludes, but, on the contrary, includes the idea that the systematic knowledge of the external universe can make giant strides from age to age.

The perception of the the fundamental contradiction in German idealism led necessarily back to materialism, but – *nota bene* – not to the simply metaphysical, exclusively mechanical materialism of the eighteenth century. Old materialism looked upon all previous history as a crude heap of irrationality and violence; modern materialism sees in it the process of evolution of humanity, and aims at discovering the laws thereof. With the French of the eighteenth century, and even with Hegel, the conception obtained of Nature as a whole – moving in narrow circles, and forever immutable, with its eternal celestial bodies, as Newton, and unalterable organic species, as Linnaeus, taught. Modern materialism embraces the more recent discoveries of natural science, according to which Nature also has its history in time, the celestial bodies, like the organic species that, under favourable conditions, people them, being born and perishing. And even if Nature, as a whole, must still be said to move in recurrent cycles, these cycles assume infinitely larger dimensions. In both aspects, modern materialism is essentially dialectic, and no longer requires the assistance of that sort of philo-sophy which, queen-like, pretended to rule the remaining mob of sciences. As soon as each special science is bound to make clear its position in the great totality of things and of our knowledge of things, a special science dealing with this totality is superfluous or unnecessary. That which still survives of all earlier philosophy is the science of thought and its law – formal logic and dialectics. Everything else is subsumed in the positive science of Nature and history.

Whilst, however, the revolution in the conception of Nature could only be made in proportion to the corresponding positive materials furnished by research, already much earlier certain historical facts had occurred which led to a decisive change in the conception of history. In 1831, the first working-class rising took place in Lyons; between 1838 and 1842, the first national working-class movement, that of the English Chartists, reached its height. The class struggle between proletariat and bourgeoisie came to the front in the history of the most advanced countries in Europe, in proportion to the development, upon the one hand, of modern industry, upon the other, of the newly-acquired political supremacy of the bourgeoisie. Facts more and more strenuously gave the lie to the teachings of bourgeois economy as to the identity of the interests of capital and labour, as to the universal harmony and universal prosperity that would be the consequence of unbridled competition. All these things could no longer be ignored, any more than the French and English Socialism, which was their theoretical, though very imperfect, expression. But the old idealist conception of history, which was not yet dislodged, knew nothing of class struggles based upon economic interests, knew nothing of economic interests; production and all economic relations appeared in it only as incidental, subordinate elements in the 'history of civilisation'.

The new facts made imperative a new examination of all past history. Then it was seen that all past history, with the exception of its primitive stages, was the history of class struggles; that these warring classes of society are always the products of the modes of production and of exchange – in a word, of the economic conditions of their time; that the economic structure of society always furnishes the real basis, starting from which we can alone work out the ultimate explanation of the whole superstructure of juridical and political institutions as well as of the religious, philosophical, and other ideas of a given historical period. Hegel has freed history from metaphysics – he made it dialectic; but his conception of history was essentially idealistic. But now idealism was driven from its last refuge, the philosophy of history; now a materialistic treatment of history was propounded, and a method found of explaining man's 'knowing' by his 'being', instead of, as heretofore, his 'being' by his 'knowing'.

From that time forward, Socialism was no longer an accidental discovery of this or that ingenious brain, but the necessary outcome of the struggle between two historically developed classes – the proletariat and the bourgeoisie. Its task was no longer to manufacture a system of society as perfect as possible, but to examine the historico-economic succession of events from which these classes and their antagonism had of necessity sprung, and to discover in the economic conditions thus created the means of ending the conflict. But the Socialism of earlier days was as incompatible with this materialist conception as the conception of Nature of the French materialists was with dialectics and modern natural science. The Socialism of earlier days certainly criticised the existing capitalistic mode of production and its consequences. But it could not explain them, and, therefore, could not get the mastery of them. It could only simply reject them as bad. The more strongly this earlier Socialism denounced the exploitations of the working class, inevitable under Capitalism, the less able was it clearly to show in what this exploitation consisted and how it arose. But for this it was necessary –

1. to present the capitalistic mode of production in its historical connection and its inevitableness during a particular historical period, and therefore, also, to present its inevitable downfall, and
2. to lay bare its essential character, which was still a secret. This was done by the discovery of surplus-value.

It was shown that the appropriation of unpaid labour is the basis of the capitalist mode of production and of the exploitation of the worker that occurs under it; that even if the capitalist buys the labour power of his labourer at its full value as a commodity on the market, he yet extracts more value from it than he paid for; and that in the ultimate analysis, this surplus-value forms those sums of value from which are heaped up constantly increasing masses of capital in the hands of the possessing classes. The genesis of capitalist production and the production of capital were both explained.

These two great discoveries, the materialistic conception of history and the revelation of the secret of capitalistic production through surplus-value, we owe to Marx. With these discoveries, Socialism became a science. The next thing was to work out all its details and relations.

Chapter 3

Historical Materialism

The materialist conception of history starts from the proposition that the production of the means to support human life and, next to production, the exchange of things produced, is the basis of all social structure; that in every society that has appeared in history, the manner in which wealth is distributed and society divided into classes or orders is dependent upon what is produced, how it is produced, and how the products are exchanged. From this point of view, the final causes of all social changes and political revolutions are to be sought, not in men's brains, not in men's better insights into eternal truth and justice, but in changes in the modes of production and exchange. They are to be sought, not in the philosophy, but in the economics of each particular epoch. The growing perception that existing social institutions are unreasonable and unjust, that reason has become unreason, and right wrong,* is only proof that in the modes of production and exchange changes have silently taken place with which the social order, adapted to earlier economic conditions, is no longer in keeping. From this it also follows that the means of getting rid of the incongruities that have been brought to light must also be present, in a more or less developed condition, within the changed modes of production themselves. These means are not to be invented by deduction from fundamental principles, but are to be discovered in the stubborn facts of the existing system of production.

What is, then, the position of modern Socialism in this connection?

The present situation of society – this is now pretty generally conceded – is the creation of the ruling class of today, of the bourgeoisie. The mode of production peculiar to the bourgeoisie, known, since Marx, as the capitalist mode of production, was

* Mephistopheles, in Goethe's *Faust*

incompatible with the feudal system, with the privileges it conferred upon individuals, entire social ranks and local corporations, as well as with the hereditary ties of subordination which constituted the framework of its social organisation. The bourgeoisie broke up the feudal system and built upon its ruins the capitalist order of society, the kingdom of free competition, of personal liberty, of the equality, before the law, of all commodity owners, of all the rest of the capitalist blessings. Thenceforward, the capitalist mode of production could develop in freedom. Since steam, machinery, and the making of machines by machinery transformed the older manufacture into modern industry, the productive forces evolved under the guidance of the bourgeoisie, developed with a rapidity and in a degree unheard of before. But just as the older manufacture, in its time, and handicraft, becoming more developed under its influence, had come into collision with the feudal trammels of the guilds, so now modern industry, in its complete development, comes into collision with the bounds within which the capitalist mode of production holds it confined. The new productive forces have already outgrown the capitalistic mode of using them. And this conflict between productive forces and modes of production is not a conflict engendered in the mind of man, like that between original sin and divine justice. It exists, in fact, objectively, outside us, independently of the will and actions even of the men that have brought it on. Modern Socialism is nothing but the reflex, in thought, of this conflict in fact, its ideal reflection in the minds, first, of the class directly suffering under it, the working class.

Now, in what does this conflict consist?

Before capitalist production – i.e. in the Middle Ages – the system of petty industry obtained generally, based upon the private property of the labourers in their means of production; in the country, the agriculture of the small peasant, freeman, or serf; in the towns, the handicrafts organised in guilds. The instruments of labour – land, agricultural implements, the workshop, the tool – were the instruments of labour of single individuals, adapted for the use of one worker, and, therefore, of necessity, small, dwarfish, circumscribed. But, for this very reason, they belonged as a rule to the producer himself. To concentrate these scattered, limited means of production, to enlarge them, to turn them into the powerful levers of production of the present day – this was precisely the historic role of capitalist production and of its upholder, the bourgeoisie. In the fourth section of *Capital*, Marx has explained in detail how since the fifteenth century this has been historically worked out through the three phases of simple co-operation, manufacture, and modern industry. But the bourgeoisie, as is shown there, could not transform these puny means of production into mighty productive forces without transforming them, at the same time, from means of production of the individual into social means of production only workable by a collectivity of men. The spinning-wheel, the hand-loom, the blacksmith's hammer, were replaced by the spinning-machine, the power-loom, the steam-hammer; the individual workshop, by the factory implying the co-operation of hundreds and thousands of workmen. In like manner, production itself changed from a series of individual into a series of social acts, and the production from individual to social products. The yarn, the cloth, the metal articles that now come out of the factory were the joint product of many workers, through whose hands they had successively to pass before they were ready. No one person could say of them: 'I made that; this is *my* product.'

But where, in a given society, the fundamental form of production is that spontaneous division of labour which creeps in gradually and not upon any preconceived plan, there the products take on the form of commodities, whose mutual exchange, buying and selling, enable the individual producers to satisfy their manifold wants. And this was the case in the Middle Ages. The peasant, e.g., sold to the artisan agricultural products and bought from him the products of handicraft. Into this society of individual producers, of commodity producers, the new mode of production thrust itself. In the midst of the old division of labour, grown up spontaneously and upon no *definite plan*, which had governed the whole of society, now arose division of labour upon a definite plan, as organised in the factory; side by side with individual production appeared social production. The products of both were sold in the same market, and, therefore, at prices at least approximately equal. But organisation upon a definite plan was stronger than spontaneous division of labour. The factories working with the combined social forces of a collectivity of individuals produced their commodities far more cheaply than the individual

small producers. Individual producers succumbed in one department after another. Socialised production revolutionised all the
old methods of production. But its revolutionary character was, at
the same time, so little recognised that it was, on the contrary,
introduced as a means of increasing and developing the production of commodities. When it arose, it found ready-made, and
made liberal use of, certain machinery for the production and
exchange of commodities: merchants' capital, handicraft, wage-
labour. Socialised production thus introducing itself as a new form
of the production of commodities, it was a matter of course that
under it the old forms of appropriation remained in full swing, and
were applied to its products as well.

In the medieval stage of evolution of the production of commodities, the question as to the owner of the product of labour
could not arise. The individual producer, as a rule, had, from raw
material belonging to himself, and generally his own handiwork,
produced it with his own tools, by the labour of his own hands or
of his family. There was no need for him to appropriate the new
product. It belonged wholly to him, as a matter of course. His
property in the product was, therefore, based upon his own
labour. Even where external help was used, this was, as a rule, of
little importance, and very generally was compensated by something other than wages. The apprentices and journeymen of the
guilds worked less for board and wages than for education, in
order that they might become master craftsmen themselves.

Then came the concentration of the means of production and of
the producers in large workshops and manufactories, their transformation into actual socialised means of production and socialised
producers. But the socialised producers and means of production
and their products were still treated, after this change, just as they
had been before – i.e. as the means of production and the products
of individuals. Hitherto, the owner of the instruments of labour had
himself appropriated the product, because, as a rule, it was his own
product and the assistance of others was the exception. Now, the
owner of the instruments of labour always appropriated to himself
the product, although it was no longer *his* product but exclusively
the product of the *labour of others*. Thus, the products now produced socially were not appropriated by those who had actually set
in motion the means of production and actually produced the

commodities, but by the capitalists. The means of production, and production itself, had become in essence socialised. But they were subjected to a form of appropriation which presupposes the private production of individuals, under which, therefore, every one owns his own product and brings it to market. The mode of production is subjected to this form of appropriation, although it abolishes the conditions upon which the latter rests.*

This contradiction, which gives to the new mode of production its capitalistic character, *contains the germ of the whole of the social antagonisms of today.* The greater the mastery obtained by the new mode of production over all important fields of production and in all manufacturing countries, the more it reduced individual production to an insignificant residuum, *the more clearly was brought out the incompatibility of socialised production with capitalistic appropriation.*

The first capitalists found, as we have said, alongside of other forms of labour, wage-labour ready-made for them on the market. But it was exceptional, complementary, accessory, transitory wage-labour. The agricultural labourer, though, upon occasion, he hired himself out by the day, had a few acres of his own land on which he could at all events live at a pinch. The guilds were so organised that the journeyman to today became the master of tomorrow. But all this changed, as soon as the means of production became socialised and concentrated in the hands of capitalists. The means of production, as well as the product, of the individual producer became more and more worthless; there was nothing left for him but to turn wage-worker under the capitalist. Wage-labour, aforetime the exception and accessory, now became the rule and basis of all production; aforetime complementary, it now became the sole remaining function of the worker. The wage-worker for a time became a wage-worker for life. The number of these permanent wage-workers was further enormously increased by the breaking-up of the feudal system that occurred at the same

---

* It is hardly necessary in this connection to point out that, even if the form of appropriation remains the same, the character of the appropriation is just as much revolutionised as production is by the changes described above. It is, of course, a very different matter whether I appropriate to myself my own product or that of another. Note in passing that wage-labour, which contains the whole capitalist mode of production in embryo, is very ancient; in a sporadic, scattered form, it existed for centuries alongside slave-labour. But the embryo could duly develop into the capitalistic mode of production only when the necessary historical preconditions had been furnished.

time, by the disbanding of the retainers of the feudal lords, the eviction of the peasants from their homesteads, etc. The separation was made complete between the means of production concentrated in the hands of the capitalists, on the one side, and the producers, possessing nothing but their labour-power, on the other. *The contradiction between socialised production and capitalistic appropriation manifested itself as the antagonism of proletariat and bourgeoisie.*

We have seen that the capitalistic mode of production thrust its way into a society of commodity-producers, of individual producers, whose social bond was the exchange of their products. But every society based upon the production of commodities has this peculiarity: that the producers have lost control over their own social interrelations. Each man produces for himself with such means of production as he may happen to have, and for such exchange as he may require to satisfy his remaining wants. No one knows how much of his particular article is coming on the market, nor how much of it will be wanted. No one knows whether his individual product will meet an actual demand, whether he will be able to make good his costs of production or even to sell his commodity at all. Anarchy reigns in socialised production.

But the production of commodities, like every other form of production, has it peculiar, inherent laws inseparable from it; and these laws work, despite anarchy, in and through anarchy. They reveal themselves in the only persistent form of social interrelations – i.e. in exchange – and here they affect the individual producers as compulsory laws of competition. They are, at first, unknown to these producers themselves, and have to be discovered by them gradually and as the result of experience. They work themselves out, therefore, independently of the producers, and in antagonism to them, as inexorable natural laws of their particular form of production. The product governs the producers.

In medieval society, especially in the earlier centuries, production was essentially directed toward satisfying the wants of the individual. It satisfied, in the main, only the wants of the producer and his family. Where relations of personal dependence existed, as in the country, it also helped to satisfy the wants of the feudal lord. In all this there was, therefore, no exchange; the products, consequently, did not assume the character of commodities. The family of the peasant produced almost everything they wanted: clothes and furniture, as well as the means of subsistence. Only when it began to produce more than was sufficient to supply its own wants and the payments in kind to the feudal lords, only then did it also produce commodities. This surplus, thrown into socialised exchange and offered for sale, became commodities.

The artisans of the towns, it is true, had from the first to produce for exchange. But they, also, themselves supplied the greatest part of their individual wants. They had gardens and plots of land. They turned their cattle out into the communal forest, which, also, yielded them timber and firing. The women spun flax, wool, and so forth. Production for the purpose of exchange, production of commodities, was only in its infancy. Hence, exchange was restricted, the market narrow, the methods of production stable; there was local exclusiveness without, local unity within; the mark in the country; in the town, the guild.

But with the extension of the production of commodities, and especially with the introduction of the capitalist mode of production, the laws of commodity-production, hitherto latent, came into action more openly and with greater force. The old bonds were loosened, the old exclusive limits broken through, the producers were more and more turned into independent, isolated producers of commodities. It became apparent that the production of society at large was ruled by absence of plan, by accident, by anarchy; and this anarchy grew to greater and greater height. But the chief means by aid of which the capitalist mode of production intensified this anarchy of socialised production was the exact opposite of anarchy. It was the increasing organisation of production, upon a social basis, in every individual productive establishment. By this, the old, peaceful, stable condition of things was ended. Wherever this organisation of production was introduced into a branch of industry, it brooked no other method of production by its side. The field of labour became a battle-ground. The great geographical discoveries, and the colonisation following them, multiplied markets and quickened the transformation of handicraft into manufacture. The war did not simply break out between the individual producers of particular localities. The local struggles begat, in their turn, national conflicts, the commercial wars of the seventeenth and the eighteenth centuries.

Finally, modern industry and the opening of the world-market made the struggle universal, and at the same time gave it an unheard-of virulence. Advantages in natural or artificial conditions of production now decide the existence or non-existence of individual capitalists, as well as of whole industries and countries. He that falls is remorselessly cast aside. It is the Darwinian struggle of the individual for existence transferred from Nature to society with intensified violence. The conditions of existence natural to the animal appear as the final term of human development. The contradiction between socialised production and capitalistic appropriation now presents itself as *an antagonism between the organisation of production in the individual workshop and the anarchy of production in society generally.*

The capitalistic mode of production moves in these two forms of the antagonism immanent to it from its very origin. It is never able to get out of that 'vicious circle' which Fourier had already discovered. What Fourier could not, indeed, see in his time is that this circle is gradually narrowing; that the movement becomes more and more a spiral, and must come to an end, like the movement of planets, by collision with the centre. It is the compelling force of anarchy in the production of society at large that more and more completely turns the great majority of men into proletarians; and it is the masses of the proletariat again who will finally put an end to anarchy in production. It is the compelling force of anarchy in social production that turns the limitless perfectibility of machinery under modern industry into a compulsory law by which every individual industrial capitalist must perfect his machinery more and more, under penalty of ruin.

But the perfecting of machinery is making human labour superfluous. If the introduction and increase of machinery means the displacement of millions of manual by a few machine-workers, improvement in machinery means the displacement of more and more of the machine-workers themselves. It means, in the last instance, the production of a number of available wage workers in excess of the average needs of capital, the formation of a complete industrial reserve army, as I called it in 1845,* available at the times when industry is working at high pressure, to be cast out upon the

* *The Condition of the Working Class in England.*

street when the inevitable crash comes, a constant dead weight upon the limbs of the working class in its struggle for existence with capital, a regulator for keeping of wages down to the low level that suits the interests of capital. Thus it comes about, to quote Marx, that machinery becomes the most powerful weapon in the war of capital against the working class; that the instruments of labour constantly tear the means of subsistence out of the hands of the labourer; that the very product of the worker is turned into an instrument for his subjugation. Thus it comes about that the economising of the instruments of labour becomes at the same time, from the outset, the most reckless waste of labour-power, and robbery based upon the normal conditions under which labour functions; that machinery, 'the most powerful instrument for shortening labour time, becomes the most unfailing means for placing every moment of the labourer's time and that of his family at the disposal of the capitalist for the purpose of expanding the value of his capital.' * Thus it comes about that the overwork of some becomes the preliminary condition for the idleness of others, and that modern industry, which hunts after new consumers over the whole world, forces the consumption of the masses at home down to a starvation minimum, and in doing thus destroys its own home market.

> The law that always equilibrates the relative surplus-population, or industrial reserve army, to the extent and energy of accumulation, this law rivets the labourer to capital more firmly than the wedges of Vulcan did Prometheus to the rock. It establishes an accumulation of misery, corresponding with the accumulation of capital. Accumulation of wealth at one pole is, therefore, at the same time accumulation of misery, agony of toil, slavery, ignorance, brutality, mental degradation, at the opposite pole, i.e. on the side of the class that produces *its own product in the form of capital.*†

And to expect any other division of the products from the capitalist mode of production is the same as expecting the electrodes of a battery not to decompose acidulated water, not to liberate oxygen at the positive, hydrogen at the negative pole, so long as they are connected with the battery.

---

* *Capital*, English edition, p.406.
† *Capital*, p.661

We have seen that the ever-increasing perfectibility of modern machinery is, by the anarchy of social production, turned into a compulsory law that forces the individual industrial capitalist always to improve his machinery, always to increase its productive force. The bare possibility of extending the field of production is transformed for him into a similarly compulsory law. The enormous expansive force of modern industry, compared with which that of gases is mere child's play, appears to us now as a necessity for expansion, both qualitative and quantative, that laughs at all resistance. Such resistance is offered by consumption, by sales, by the markets for the products of modern industry. But the capacity for extension, extensive and intensive, of the markets is primarily governed by quite different laws that work much less energetically. The extension of the markets cannot keep pace with the extension of production. The collision becomes inevitable, and as this cannot produce any real solution so long as it does not break in pieces the capitalist mode of production, the collisions become periodic. Capitalist production has begotten another 'vicious circle'.

As a matter of fact, since 1825, when the first general crisis broke out, the whole industrial and commercial world, production and exchange among all civilised peoples and their more or less barbaric hangers-on, are thrown out of joint about once every ten years. Commerce is at a standstill, the markets are glutted, products accumulate, as multitudinous as they are unsaleable, hard cash disappears, credit vanishes, factories are closed, the mass of the workers are in want of the means of subsistence, because they have produced too much of the means of subsistence; bankruptcy follows upon bankruptcy, execution upon execution. The stagnation lasts for years; productive forces and products are wasted and destroyed wholesale, until the accumulated mass of commodities finally filters off, more or less depreciated in value, until production and exchange gradually begin to move again. Little by little, the pace quickens. It becomes a trot. The industrial trot breaks into a canter, the canter in turn grows into the headlong gallop of a perfect steeplechase of industry, commercial credit, and speculation, which finally, after breakneck leaps, ends where it began – in the ditch of a crisis. And so over and over again. We have now, since the year 1825, gone through this five times, and at the present moment (1877), we are going through it for the sixth time. And the character of these crises is so clearly defined that Fourier hit all of them off when he described the first as *'crise pléthorique'*, a crisis from plethora.

In these crises, the contradiction between socialised production and capitalist appropriation ends in a violent explosion. The circulation of commodities is, for the time being, stopped. Money, the means of circulation, becomes a hindrance to circulation. All the laws of production and circulation of commodities are turned upside down. The economic collision has reached its apogee. *The mode of production is in rebellion against the mode of exchange.*

The fact that the socialised organisation of production within the factory has developed so far that it has become incompatible with the anarchy of production in society, which exists side by side with and dominates it, is brought home to the capitalists themselves by the violent concentration of capital that occurs during crises, through the ruin of many large, and a still greater number of small, capitalists. The whole mechanism of the capitalist mode of production breaks down under the pressure of the productive forces, its own creations. It is no longer able to turn all this mass of means of production into capital. They lie fallow, and for that very reason the industrial reserve army must also lie fallow. Means of production, means of subsistence, available labourers, all the elements of production and of general wealth, are present in abundance. But 'abundance becomes the source of distress and want' (Fourier), because it is the very thing that prevents the transformation of the means of production and subsistence into capital. For in capitalistic society, the means of production can only function when they have undergone a preliminary transformation into capital, into the means of exploiting human labour-power. The necessity of this transformation into capital of the means of production and subsistence stands like a ghost between these and the workers. It alone prevents the coming together of the material and personal levers of production; it alone forbids the means of production to function, the workers to work and live. On the one hand, therefore, the capitalistic mode of production stands convicted of its own incapacity to further direct these productive forces. On the other, these productive forces themselves, with increasing energy, press forward to the removal of the existing contradiction, to the abolition of their quality as capital, to the *practical recognition of their character as social productive forces.*

This rebellion of the productive forces, as they grow more and more powerful, against their quality as capital, this stronger and stronger command that their social character shall be recognised, forces the capital class itself to treat them more and more as social productive forces, so far as this is possible under capitalist conditions. The period of industrial high pressure, with its unbounded inflation of credit, not less than the crash itself, by the collapse of great capitalist establishments, tends to bring about that form of the socialisation of great masses of the means of production which we meet with in the different kinds of joint-stock companies. Many of these means of production and of distribution are, from the outset, so colossal that, like the railways, they exclude all other forms of capitalistic expansion. At a further stage of evolution, this form also becomes insufficient. The producers on a large scale in a particular branch of an industry in a particular country unite in a Trust, a union for the purpose of regulating production. They determine the total amount to be produced, parcel it out among themselves, and thus enforce the selling price fixed beforehand. But trusts of this kind, as soon as business becomes bad, are generally liable to break up, and on this very account compel a yet greater concentration of association. The whole of a particular industry is turned into one gigantic joint-stock company; internal competition gives place to the internal monopoly of this one company. This has happened in 1890 with the English alkali production, which is now, after the fusion of 48 large works, in the hands of one company, conducted upon a single plan, and with a capital of 6,000,000 pounds.

In the trusts, freedom of competition changes into its very opposite – into monopoly; and the production without any definite plan of capitalistic society capitulates to the production upon a definite plan of the invading socialistic society. Certainly, this is so far still to the benefit and advantage of the capitalists. But, in this case, the exploitation is so palpable, that it must break down. No nation will put up with production conducted by trusts, with so barefaced an exploitation of the community by a small band of dividend-mongers.

In any case, with trusts or without, the official representative of capitalist society – the state – will ultimately have to undertake the direction of production.* This necessity for conversion into State property is felt first in the great institutions for intercourse and communication – the post office, the telegraphs, the railways.

If the crises demonstrate the incapacity of the bourgeoisie for managing modern productive forces any longer, the transformation of the great establishments for production and distribution into joint-stock companies, trusts, and State property, show how unnecessary the bourgeoisie are for that purpose. All the social functions of the capitalist are now performed by salaried employees. The capitalist has no further social function than that of pocketing dividends, tearing off coupons, and gambling on the Stock Exchange, where the different capitalists despoil one another of their capital. At first, the capitalistic mode of production forces out the workers. Now, it forces out the capitalists, and reduces them, just as it reduced the workers, to the ranks of the surplus-population, although not immediately into those of the industrial reserve army.

But, the transformation – either into joint-stock companies and trusts, or into State-ownership – does not do away with the capitalistic nature of the productive forces. In the joint-stock companies

* I say 'have to'. For only when the means of production and distribution have *actually* outgrown the form of management by joint-stock companies, and when, therefore, the taking them over by the State has become *economically* inevitable, only then – even if it is the State of today that effects this – is there an economic advance, the attainment of another step preliminary to the taking over of all productive forces by society itself. But of late, since Bismarck went in for State-ownership of industrial establishments, a kind of spurious Socialism has arisen, degenerating, now and again, into something of flunkeyism, that without more ado declares all State-ownership, even of the Bismarkian sort, to be socialistic. Certainly, if the taking over by the State of the tobacco industry is socialistic, then Napoleon and Metternich must be numbered among the founders of Socialism. If the Belgian State, for quite ordinary political and financial reasons, itself constructed its chief railway lines; if Bismarck, not under any economic compulsion, took over for the State the chief Prussian lines, simply to be the better able to have them in hand in case of war, to bring up the railway employees as voting cattle for the Government, and especially to create for himself a new source of income independent of parliamentary votes – this was, in no sense, a socialistic measure, directly or indirectly, consciously or unconsciously. Otherwise, the Royal Maritime Company, the Royal porcelain manufacture, and even the regimental tailor-shops of the Army would also be socialistic institutions, or even, as was seriously proposed by a sly dog in Frederick William III's reign, the taking over by the State of the brothels.

and trusts, this is obvious. And the modern State, again, is only the organisation that bourgeois society takes on in order to support the external conditions of the capitalist mode of production against the encroachments as well of the workers as of individual capitalists. The modern state, no matter what its form, is essentially a capitalist machine – the state of the capitalists, the ideal personification of the total national capital. The more it proceeds to the taking over of productive forces, the more does it actually become the national capitalist, the more citizens does it exploit. The workers remain wage-workers – proletarians. The capitalist relation is not done away with. It is, rather, brought to a head. But, brought to a head, it topples over. State-ownership of the productive forces is not the solution of the conflict, but concealed within it are the technical conditions that form the elements of that solution.

This solution can only consist in the practical recognition of the social nature of the modern forces of production, and therefore in the harmonising with the socialised character of the means of production. And this can only come about by society openly and directly taking possession of the productive forces which have outgrown all control, except that of society as a whole. The social character of the means of production and of the products today reacts against the producers, periodically disrupts all production and exchange, acts only like a law of Nature working blindly, forcibly, destructively. But with the taking over by society of the productive forces, the social character of the means of production and of the products will be utilised by the producers with a perfect understanding of its nature, and instead of being a source of disturbance and periodical collapse, will become the most powerful lever of production itself.

Active social forces work exactly like natural forces: blindly, forcibly, destructively, so long as we do not understand, and reckon with, them. But, when once we understand them, when once we grasp their action, their direction, their effects, it depends only upon ourselves to subject them more and more to our own will, and, by means of them, to reach our own ends. And this holds quite especially of the mighty productive forces of today. As long as we obstinately refuse to understand the nature and the character of these social means of action – and this understanding goes against the grain of the capitalist mode of production, and its defenders – so long these forces are at work in spite of us, in opposition to us, so long they master us, as we have shown above in detail.

But when once their nature is understood, they can, in the hands of the producers working together, be transformed from master demons into willing servants. The difference is as that between the destructive force of electricity in the lightning in the storm, and electricity under command in the telegraph and the voltaic arc; the difference between a conflagration, and fire working in the service of man. With this recognition, at last, of the real nature of the productive forces of today, the social anarchy of production gives place to a social regulation of production upon a definite plan, according to the needs of the community and of each individual. Then the capitalist mode of appropriation, in which the product enslaves first the producer, and then the appropriator, is replaced by the mode of appropriation of the products that is based upon the nature of the modern means of production; upon the one hand, direct social appropriation, as means to the maintenance and extension of production – on the other, direct individual appropriation, as means of subsistence and of enjoyment.

Whilst the capitalist mode of production more and more completely transforms the great majority of the population into proletarians, it creates the power which, under penalty of its own destruction, is forced to accomplish this revolution. Whilst it forces on more and more of the transformation of the vast means of production, already socialised, into State property, it shows itself the way to accomplishing this revolution. *The proletariat seizes political power and turns the means of production into State property*.

But, in doing this, it abolishes itself as proletariat, abolishes all class distinction and class antagonisms, abolishes also the State as State. Society, thus far, based upon class antagonisms, had need of the State. That is, of an organisation of the particular class which was, *pro tempore*, the exploiting class, an organisation for the purpose of preventing any interference from without with the existing conditions of production, and, therefore, especially, for the purpose of forcibly keeping the exploited classes in the condition of oppression corresponding with the given mode of production (slavery, serfdom, wage-labour). The State was the official representative of society as a whole; the gathering of it together into a visible embodiment. But it was this only in so far as it was the State of that class which itself represented, for the time being, society as a whole: in ancient times, the State of slave-owning citizens; in the Middle Ages, the feudal lords; in our own times, the bourgeoisie.

When, at last, it becomes the real representative of the whole of society, it renders itself unnecessary. As soon as there is no longer any social class to be held in subjection; as soon as class rule, and the individual struggle for existence based upon our present anarchy in production, with the collisions and excesses arising from these, are removed, nothing more remains to be repressed, and a special repressive force, a State, is no longer necessary. The first act by virtue of which the State really constitutes itself the representative of the whole of society – the taking possession of the means of production in the name of society – this is, at the same time, its last independent act as a State. State interference in social relations becomes, in one domain after another, super-fluous, and then dies out of itself; the government of persons is replaced by the administration of things, and by the conduct of processes of production. The State is not 'abolished'. It *dies out*. This gives the measure of the value of the phrase: '*a free State*', both as to its justifiable use at times by agitators, and as to its ultimate scientific inefficiency; and also of the demands of the so-called anarchists for the abolition of the State out of hand.

Since the historical appearance of the capitalist mode of produc-tion, the appropriation by society of all the means of production has often been dreamed of, more or less vaguely, by individuals, as well as by sects, as the ideal of the future. But it could become possible, could become a historical necessity, only when the actual conditions for its realisation were there. Like every other social advance, it becomes practicable, not by men understanding that the existence of classes is in contradiction to justice, equality, etc., not by the mere willingness to abolish these classes, but by virtue of certain new economic conditions. The separation of society into an exploiting and an exploited class, a ruling and an oppressed class, was the necessary consequences of the deficient and restricted development of production in former times. So long as the total social labour only yields a produce which but slightly exceeds that barely necessary for the existence of all;

so long, therefore, as labour engages all or almost all the time of the great majority of the members of society – so long, of necessity, this society is divided into classes. Side by side with the great majority, exclusively bond slaves to labour, arises a class freed from directly productive labour, which looks after the general affairs of society: the direction of labour, State business, law, science, art, etc. It is, therefore, the law of division of labour that lies at the basis of the division into classes. But this does not prevent this division into classes from being carried out by means of violence and robbery, trickery and fraud. It does not prevent the ruling class, once having the upper hand, from consolidating its power at the expense of the working class, from turning its social leadership into an intensified exploitation of the masses.

But if, upon this showing, division into classes has a certain historical justification, it has this only for a given period, only under given social conditions. It was based upon the insufficiency of production. It will be swept away by the complete development of modern productive forces. And, in fact, the abolition of classes in society presupposes a degree of historical evolution at which the existence, not simply of this or that particular ruling class, but of any ruling class at all, and, therefore, the existence of class distinction itself, has become an obsolete anachronism. It presupposes, therefore, the development of production carried out to a degree at which appropriation of the means of production and of the products, and, with this, of political domination, of the monopoly of culture, and of intellectual leadership by a particular class of society, has become not only superfluous but economically, politically, intellectually, a hindrance to development.

This point is now reached. Their political and intellectual bankruptcy is scarcely any longer a secret to the bourgeoisie themselves. Their economic bankruptcy recurs regularly every ten years. In every crisis, society is suffocated beneath the weight of its own productive forces and products, which it cannot use, and stands helpless, face-to-face with the absurd contradiction that the producers have nothing to consume, because consumers are wanting. The expansive force of the means of production burst the bonds that the capitalist mode of production had imposed upon them. Their deliverance from these bonds is the one precondition for an unbroken, constantly-accelerated development of the productive forces, and therewith for a practically unlimited increase of production itself. Nor is this all. The socialised appropriation of the means of production does away, not only with the present artificial restrictions upon production, but also with the positive waste and devastation of productive forces and products that are at the present time the inevitable concomitants of production, and that reach their height in the crises. Further, it sets free for the community at large a mass of means of production and of products, by doing away with the senseless extravagance of the ruling classes of today, and their political representatives. The possibility of securing for every member of society, by means of socialised production, an existence not only fully sufficient materially, and becoming day by day more full, but an existence guaranteeing to all the free development and exercise of their physical and mental faculties – this possibility is now, for the first time, here, but *it is here*.*

With the seizing of the means of production by society, production of commodities is done away with, and, simultaneously, the mastery of the product over the producer. Anarchy in social production is replaced by systematic, definite organisation. The struggle for individual existence disappears. Then for the first time man, in a certain sense, is finally marked off from the rest of the animal kingdom, and emerges from mere animal conditions of existence into really human ones. The whole sphere of the conditions of life which environ man, and which have hitherto ruled man, now comes under the dominion and control of man, who for the first time becomes the real, conscious lord of

---

* A few figures may serve to give an approximate idea of the enormous expansive force of the modern means of production, even under capitalist pressure. According to Mr Giffen, the total wealth of Great Britain and Ireland amounted, in round numbers, in:

1814 to £2,200,000,000,
1865 to £6,100,000,000,
1875 to £8,500,000,000.

As an instance of the squandering of means of production and of products during a crisis, the total loss in the German iron industry alone, in the crisis of 1873–78, was given at the second German Industrial Congress (Berlin, February 21, 1878), as £22,750,000.

nature, because he has now become master of his own social organisation. The laws of his own social action, hitherto standing face-to-face with man as laws of Nature foreign to, and dominating him, will then be used with full understanding, and so mastered by him. Man's own social organisation, hitherto confronting him as a necessity imposed by Nature and history, now becomes the result of his own free action. The extraneous objective forces that have hitherto governed history pass under the control of man himself. Only from that time will man himself, more and more consciously, make his own history — only from that time will the social causes set in movement by him have, in the main and in a constantly growing measure, the results intended by him. It is the ascent of man from the kingdom of necessity to the kingdom of freedom.

Let us briefly sum up our sketch of historical evolution.

I. *Medieval Society* — Individual production on a small scale. Means of production adapted for individual use; hence primitive, ungainly, petty, dwarfed in action. Production for immediate consumption, either of the producer himself or his feudal lord. Only where an excess of production over this consumption occurs is such excess offered for sale, enters into exchange. Production of commodities, therefore, only in its infancy. But already it contains within itself, in embryo, *anarchy in the production of society at large.*

II. *Capitalist Revolution* — Transformation of industry, at first by means of simple cooperation and manufacture. Concentration of the means of production, hitherto scattered, into great workshops. As a consequence, their transformation from individual to social means of production — a transformation which does not, on the whole, affect the form of exchange. The old forms of appropriation remain in force. The capitalist appears. In his capacity as owner of the means of production, he also appropriates the products and turns them into commodities. Production has become a *social* act. Exchange and appropriation continue to be *individual* acts, the acts of individuals. *The social product is appropriated by the individual capitalist.* Fundamental contradiction, whence arise all the contradictions in which our present-day society moves, and which modern industry brings to light.

(a) Severance of the producer from the means of production. Condemnation of the worker to wage-labour for life. *Antagonism between the proletariat and the bourgeoisie.*

(b) Growing predominance and increasing effectiveness of the laws governing the production of commodities. Unbridled competition. *Contradiction between socialised organisation in the individual factory and social anarchy in production as a whole.*

(c) On the one hand, perfecting of machinery, made by competition compulsory for each individual manufacturer, and complemented by a constantly growing displacement of labourers. Industrial reserve-army. On the other hand, unlimited extension of production, also compulsory under competition, for every manufacturer. On both sides, unheard-of development of productive forces, excess of supply over demand, over-production, glutting of the markets, crises every ten years, the vicious circle: excess here, of means of production and products – excess there, of labourers, without employment and without means of existence. But these two levers of production and of social well being are unable to work together, because the capitalist form of production prevents the productive forces from working and the products from circulating, unless they are first turned into capital – which their very superabundance prevents. The contradiction has grown into an absurdity. *The mode of production rises in rebellion against the form of exchange.* The bourgeoisie are convicted of incapacity further to manage their own social productive forces.

(d) Partial recognition of the social character of the productive forces forced upon the capitalists themselves. Taking over of the great institutions for production and communication, first by joint-stock companies, later on by trusts, then by the State. The bourgeoisie demonstrated to be a superfluous class. All its social functions are now performed by salaried employees.

III. *Proletarian Revolution* – Solution of the contradictions. The proletariat seizes the public power, and by means of this transforms the socialised means of production, slipping from the hands of the bourgeoisie, into public property. By this act, the proletariat frees the means of production from the character of capital they have thus far borne, and gives their socialised character complete freedom to work itself out. Socialised production upon a predetermined plan becomes henceforth possible. The development of production makes the existence of different classes of society thenceforth an anachronism. In proportion as anarchy in social production vanishes, the political authority of the State dies out. Man, at last the master of his own form of social organisation, becomes at the same time the lord over Nature, his own master – free.

To accomplish this act of universal emancipation is the historical mission of the modern proletariat. To thoroughly comprehend the historical conditions and thus the very nature of this act, to impart to the now oppressed proletarian class a full knowledge of the conditions and of the meaning of the momentous act it is called upon to accomplish, this is the task of the theoretical expression of the proletarian movement, scientific Socialism.